# THE DELPHIAN COURSE

## A SYSTEMATIC PLAN OF EDUCATION, EMBRACING THE WORLD'S PROGRESS AND DEVELOPMENT OF THE LIBERAL ARTS

ART

DRAMA

LITERATURE

MUSIC

ARCHITECTURE

PHILOSOPHY

HISTORY

EDUCATION

### COUNCIL OF REVIEW

VERY REV. J. K. BRENNAN · · · · · · · Missouri
GISLE BOTHNE, M.A. · · · · University of Minnesota
CHAS. H. CAFFIN · · · · · · · · · New York
JAMES A. CRAIG, M.A., B.D., PH.D., University of Michigan
MRS. SARAH PLATT DECKER · · · · · Colorado
ALCÉE FORTIER, D.LT. · · · · · Tulane University
ROSWELL FIELD · · · · · · · · · Chicago
BRUCE C. KINGSLEY · Royal College of Organists, England
D. D. LUCKENBILL, A.B., PH.D. · University of Chicago
KENNETH MCKENZIE, PH.D. · · · Yale University
FRANK B. MARSH, PH.D. · · · University of Texas
DR. HAMILTON WRIGHT MABIE · · · New York
W. A. MERRILL, PH.D., L.H.D. · University of California
T. M. PARROTT, PH.D. · · · Princeton University
GRANT SHOWERMAN, Ph.D · University of Wisconsin
H. C. TOLMAN, PH.D., D.D. · Vanderbilt University
I. E. WING, M.A. · · · · · · · Michigan

VOL. III

# THE DELPHIAN SOCIETY

Greek Drama, Philosophy, and Literature
The Story of Rome
Delphian Reading Course
Part Three
Plus Study Guide

Compiled from:
The Delphian Course, by the Delphian Society, Chicago:The Delphian Society, (1912).

Study Guide, by the Delphian Society, Chicago:The Delphian Society, (1911).

Cover Image: Proclaiming Claudius Emperor by Lawrence Alma-Tadema (1867), from Wikimedia Commons

Libraries of Hope, Inc. Appomattox, Virginia 24522

Website: www.librariesofhope.com
Email: support@librariesofhope.com

Printed in the United States of America

TABLE OF CONTENTS
PART III

THE STORY OF ROME.

CHAPTER I.

Italy and Italian Settlements

CHAPTER II.

CHAPTER III.

# FULL PAGE ILLUSTRATIONS

## PART III.

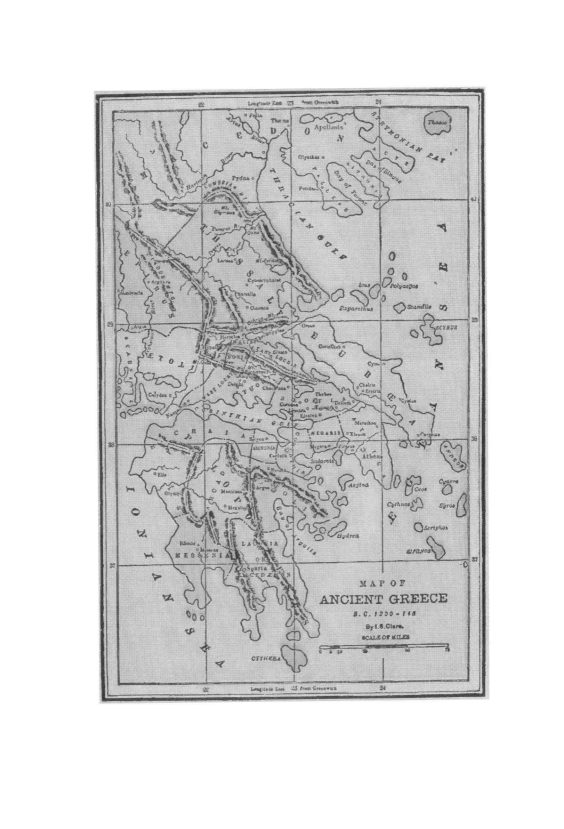

MAP OF

ANCIENT GREECE

B. C. 1200 - 146

By I.S.Clare.

SCALE OF MILES

# CHAPTER XIII.

## Beginnings of the Greek Drama.

"The first original of the drama was a religious worship, consisting only of a chorus, which was nothing else but an hymn to a deity. As luxury and voluptuousness prevailed over innocence and religion, this form of worship degenerated into tragedies; in which, however, the chorus so far remembered its first office as to brand everything that was vicious and recommend everything that was laudable, to intercede with Heaven for the innocent and to implore its vengeance on the criminal.

Homer and Hesiod intimate to us how this art should be applied, when they represent the Muses as surrounding Jupiter, and warbling their hymns about his throne."—*Addison: Spectator, 405.*

The origin of the Greek drama is to be found in the yearly celebrations observed in honor of Dionysus, god of wine. Riotous festivals were held, during which the god of wine was extolled with carousals and boisterous songs,—these having been introduced into Greece from Thrace, where they were even wilder in their nature. Dionysus had taught men how to grow the vine and how to make delicious wine from its fruit. He was conceived to be a rollicking god, jolly and restless, and was very popular in Hellas. Myths connected him with a company of satyrs—half men, half goats, who sang his praises and drank his wine, and went about leading others to join their train. That he might be appropriately worshipped, people banded together in companies at certain seasons of the year and indulged in noisy revelry, as Silenus and his satyrs were supposed to do. In fantastic dances and wild choruses they did honor to the god.

As time went on, three important festivals were observed, the greatest, known as the Greater Dionysia, occurred during the closing days of March, when spring came once more to Hellas, and life everywhere started anew. In December,

when the harvests were over, rural districts celebrated the
Lesser Dionysia, and the Lenaea was observed in January in
Athens.

For a long time it was the custom for people, masked as
satyrs, to render choruses and satyr dances on the occasion of
these festivals. This was a religious service and particularly
gave homage to the creative, productive powers of nature. The
people as a whole took part in the festivity, either as participants or spectators. The week into which a festival fell was
a prolonged holiday.

In the sixth century before Christ, Thespis inaugurated a
change in the usual method of procedure. To rest his chorus,
he himself as leader recited at intervals, followed by the usual
satyr dancing and singing. It was left for Aeschylus to introduce a second actor, and Sophocles a third. More than three
actors taking active parts in the plays were not known in
ancient Greece.

The Greek drama originated as such in Athens, and we are
able to trace it from its beginnings. Not that the earliest
plays presented have come down to us, nor that all questions
regarding their presentations have been answered, but nevertheless we are able to get a fairly clear conception of the way
in which they were given, and to follow the various changes
that came into the drama.

When the tragedy was yet an experiment, it was managed wholly as an individual enterprise. After its success
was assured, the state undertook its management, quite as it
directed other concerns of general interest. The Athenians
believed it to be the function of the state to supply amusement,
quite as it supplied public baths and gymnasiums, and in this
instance it took the form of dramas, presented during the
Greater Dionysia and the Lenaea. To attend was not only a
privilege, but far more, a religious duty. One of the first acts
of Pericles was to obtain the passage of a law entitling any
citizen who felt himself too poor to pay the entrance fee at
the theater, to receive the same at public expense. At a time
when there were no circulating papers, practically no books
available, and few able to read them in any event, the theater
took a vital part in molding public opinion, and its usefulness
was not overestimated by those who tried to make attendance
upon the plays general.

Competitions were dearly loved by the Greek, and it followed that athletic sports, games of various kinds, and soon presentation of plays, took that form. A prize was offered by the state to the poet who would bring forth the finest series of plays for the entertainment of Athenians, and this stimulated many to compete.

The Greater Dionysia was the more important occasion, and the most gifted poets seldom entered plays for the Lenaea. This was the arena for ambitious youth to win laurels. As time went on, so many desired to compete in the greater festival that many were obliged to content themselves by a chance to be heard in the winter.

Poets who wished to compete in the Greater Dionysia indicated their desire to the archon. Of the many who submitted plays, the three whose dramas were considered best were granted the opportunity and were supplied with a chorus. Each competing poet was required to present a series of three tragedies, and a fourth satyr-play. In the time of Aeschylus, at least, it was customary for a connecting vein to run through the three—the trilogy. Sophocles and Euripides did not follow this rule, but frequently made each play independent and complete in itself.

Three wealthy citizens were chosen each year by the state to defray the expenses of the chorus. This expense they took as a matter of course, quite as they provided ships for the fleet, or met their portion of the state tax. It was an honor to provide a creditable chorus, and the citizens often vied with one another in making each chorus most splendid in the matter of costume. A chorus of fifty was turned over to each competing poet, who trained them for some time before the presentation of the plays. Twelve made up the chorus for each tragedy until the time of Sophocles, who increased the number to fifteen.

In the greater Dionysia, comedy and buffoonery became subordinate, and tragedy took first place; on the other hand, comedy was of first importance in the winter festival.

Judges were carefully chosen to determine the merits of each poet and the leading actor in each play. Feeling often ran high in Athens over the decision and it was not uncommonly claimed that judges allowed themselves to be influenced

by the applause of the people.   Tradition says that in early
times a goat was the prize for the best tragedy, a basket of
figs and a jug of wine for the best comedy.   Money was paid
later by the state, but it is not definitely known today what
amount was usual.   Our word tragedy comes from the Greek
*tragos,* meaning *goat,* and has to do with those early years
when members of the chorus were dressed as satyrs.   Choruses for each play were later attired in a manner fitting the
drama, while the old burlesques were only perpetuated in
satyr plays given at the close of each trilogy, to rest the
audience.

The plays given during the Greater Dionysia attracted
strangers from all parts of Greece, and the streets were
thronged with people on the opening day, when the statue of
the god of wine was carried in procession some distance out
of the city, attended by all classes,—men, women and children.   As they passed through the forum, the procession
halted and satyr choruses were sung and dances given.   When
the end of the march was reached, the statue of Dionysus was
taken to the theater, where it remained while the plays were
presented.   Thus it was thought the god was in attendance
and any injury done in the theater was an offense against him,
and so even more blameworthy.   Any display of violence was
severely punished during these festal occasions and people were
compelled to be quiet and orderly, out of respect to him whose
kindliness to men had been demonstrated.

The first great writer of Greek plays was Aeschylus.   He
took part in the battle of Marathon and lived during stirring
days of Greek history.   He was forty years of age when his
first prize was won in the Athenian theater, and afterwards,
took many prizes.   Nevertheless, he had a checkered career
in Athens.   Born of an old noble family, he always bore the
manner of an aristocrat.   Misunderstandings frequently occurred between him and his audience, and his sympathies were
unmistakably with the upper classes.

While today people ever demand something new in a
dramatic way, the old Greek audiences enjoyed best some
story already familiar to them.   Old mythological tales supplied the theme for many of the plays.   Aeschylus called his
productions "merely crumbs that fell from Homer's banquet."

The traditions closely interwoven with their history, and stories of the deities, intimately linked with their everyday life, were brought forth again and again by the poets who vied for laurels at the Greater Dionysia, and it is beyond question that these plays were a vast source of instruction and culture to the people.

Only seven of Aeschylus' wonderful tragedies remain— three only which formed a trilogy: *Agamemnon, Choephori,* and *Eumenides.* The other four are *The Persians, The Suppliants, Seven Against Thebes* and *Prometheus Bound.*

The story of Prometheus Bound is familiar. In the story of Greek Mythology we have learned that Prometheus took part against Zeus when he strove for the kingdom, but later went over to his side, and aided him to apportion the universe. By giving fire to mortals, however, he incurred the anger of the mighty Zeus, who commanded him to be chained to a high mountain crag. Here he was to suffer until he would bend to the will of Jove, or failing that, thirteen generations later, a giant would release him. This, it will be recalled, was the task of Hercules,—for Prometheus scorned to yield. Undoubtedly many Greeks were shocked to hear the character in the play defy the will of the mighty Zeus.

The play opens with Violence and Force leading Prometheus to the rock, where he is to be bound by the unwilling Vulcan. Friendly himself toward Prometheus, he nevertheless dares not disobey the great god who rules the world. As represented in Athens, a figure was fastened to a crag, while some one from behind spoke Prometheus' lines. After Prometheus has been made fast, with bonds that none but Hercules could sunder, he is left alone on this forlorn cliff, and bursts forth in those wonderful lines:

> O holy sky! and ye, swift-winged winds!
> All fountains of all rivers!

He is interrupted by the flutter of wings, and the daughters of Oceanus come upon him. They, and their father, who shortly appears, sympathize with Prometheus, but they feel that he ought to yield to Zeus and bring his sufferings to an end. This he scorns to do. The play ends with this same demonstration on the part of the splendid Titan, and the other two plays which completed the trilogy and brought the story to some issue have been wholly lost.

Greater, probably, in its general conception, is the trilogy written by Aeschylus when an old man, Agamemnon being first of the series. The character of Clytaemnestra, Agamemnon's wife, is a marvellous conception, outstripping Lady Macbeth, and having none of the latter's redeeming qualities. This trilogy exemplifies the old belief that crime must be avenged, and that curses were transmitted from one generation to another.

There was to arise one greater than Aeschylus, but his glory was little dimmed on that account. To him belongs the honor of having given Athens a perfected drama, and the fickle Greeks, who now gave, now withheld, favor while he lived, offered a goodly sum to anyone who would attempt to again present his plays after his death.

### PROMETHEUS.

O holy sky! and ye, swift-winged winds!
All fountains of all rivers! Thou, that rollest
Laughter innumerable of ripple and wave,
O Sea, behold me! Mother of all things, Earth,
Behold me! Thou, great Sun, that seest all,
Bear record what I suffer from my peers.
    Look with what rife torment riven,
    Saw'd with agony, I am given,
        A race to run of measureless years.
    For the Lord of the Blessed new-arisen
    Binds me fast in a bitter prison,
        A bond that shames and sears.
    Throes that I have, that I apprehend,
    Both I groan for, and ask what end,
        What end to my pain appears!
Nay, my words wander : nothing can befall
But I have known it long ago. No pang
Comes unfamiliar. Wisest is to bear
The allotted burden with what ease may be,
Knowing that Fate is strong and none shall stay.
Ah! but I cannot:—neither to contain
Nor to give tongue I find the way. O wretched,

Entrammell'd in this web of agony,
For that I gave good things to men! I track
Home to its hidden spring the flowing of fire,
By stealth infringe it, drawing what doth charge
A reed; the thing, reveal'd to man, is mighty,
Teacher of every art, the main of life,
And lo, I have sinn'd!—and pay the forfeit so,
A gazing-stock beneath untemper'd heaven.
Ah!—

    What sound did smite my sense?
    Invincible redolence!
    Whence came the wafture? whence?
Was it gods, or men, or mingled fellowship,
Come to the hill, that is the limit of the world?
Wherefore? to see the pageant of my pain?
Ah! see a god then, manacled, ill-starr'd,
    To the Highest hateful, reaping hate
    From every deity, denizen
    Of the heavenly hall, because that men
He loved with a love exceeding great.
Ha, there! there again! What is it I hear
    As the whirring of birds? The shrill air sings
    To beat of nimble-driven wings.
All sound of approach is fear.

(Chorus, daughters of Oceanus, appear in the air, borne in a winged vessel).

### Chorus.

    Fear nought from us, but know
    This band is friend, not foe,
We that on swiftest pinions hither sail,—
    Nay, but with pain we bent
    Our sire to give assent,—
Borne to this hill along the streaming gale.
    To deepest caverns rang
    Of stricken iron clang,
And straight amazement cast out maiden fear:
    I flew with speed amain,
    Upon a winged wain,
I flew, my sandals left, burning to see and hear.

*Prometheus.*

Ah! is it you?
Maidens, daughters of Tethys, whose brood
Is that great and goodly multitude,
And of him that, unholden of sleep, with a girth
Of waters engirdles the body of earth,
Oceanus? ah, behold, regard
How here to the rugged gorge's head
In such imprisonmen. riveted
I keep unenvied ward.

*Chorus.*

   I see, Prometheus, thrill'd
   With awe, and sudden-fill'd
Mine eyes are troubled with a mist of tears,
   When thus, even thus, rock-hung,
   Perishing, parching, wrung
In adamantine chains thy form appears.
   For in the heavenly place
   New hands of a new race
Are on the helm, and, master uncontroll'd,
   Laws lawless maketh Zeus,
   Trampling the ancient use,
And clean blots out the great and mighty things of old.


*Prometheus.*

Truly my posture well might move my friends.

*Chorus.*

Didst thou do more beyond what thou hast said?

*Prometheus.*

Of those death-destined I askanced the eyes
From looking on their latter end.

*Chorus.*

            What cure
For such distemper did thy wisdom find?

*Prometheus.*

I caused to inhabit in the hearts of them
Blind hopes.

*Chorus.*

That truly was a mighty boon
Man had of thee!

*Prometheus.*

Also I gave them fire.

*Chorus.*

Hath mortal flesh even now the flaming thing?

*Prometheus.*

Yea, and therefore in time to come shall learn
A thousand arts.

*Chorus.*

Zeus then for this, thou sayest—

*Prometheus.*

Torments me ever, grinds and ceases not.

*Chorus.*

And to thy conflict is no term proposed?

*Prometheus.*

None save his pleasure, as he wills to end it.

*Chorus.*

His pleasure! O what hope that way? Take knowledge
Thou hast err'd: I am not fain to argue now,
To thee 'twere daggers hearing. Of all that
No more: seek now some issue from thy trial.

*Prometheus.*

'Tis a light thing for whoso hath his foot
Clear of the meshes to be large in counsel

To one unfortunate.   I am as wise as you.
I err'd: I seek not to deny it.   But
Even so to err I will'd.   I will'd it.   Succour
To men, to me travail: the terms were so.
Though sooth I had not thought that he would engine
Such torments on me, shrivelling me to shards
Here on the dizzy crags, or find a hill
So desolate and foot-forsook as this.
Now therefore wail not for my present ills,
But come to earth, and hearken the strange matter
That draweth on.   How all shall end be perfect.
Consent to me, consent, I pray you: suffer
With him that now hath anguish.   Quick of wing
Pain now alights on this one, now on that.

*Edwyn R. Bevan's trans.*

GREEK VASE
OF SIXTH CENTURY B. C.

## AGAMEMNON'S RETURN.

THE scene is in front of Agamemnon's palace at Argos, where the chorus of senators of the city have assembled to greet his return.

*Enter Agamemnon in his chariot, Cassandra following on another.*

*Agamemnon.* First, as first due, my Country I salute,
And all her tutelary Gods: all those
Who, having sent me forth, now bring me back,
After full retribution wrought on those
Who retribution owed us, and the Gods
In full consistory determined; each
With scarce a swerving eye to Mercy's side,
Dropping his vote into the urn of blood.
Caught and consuming in whose fiery wrath,
The stately City, from her panting ashes
Into the face of the revolted heavens
Gusts of expiring opulence puffs up.
For which, I say, the Gods alone be thank'd;
By whose connivance round about the wall
We drew the belt of Ares [Mars], and laid bare
The flank of Ilium to the Lion-horse,
Who sprang by night over the city-wall,
And foaled his iron progeny within,
About the setting of the Pleiades.
Thus much by way of prelude to the Gods.
    For you, O white-haired senators of Argos,
Your measur'd welcome I receive for just;
Aware on what a fickle base of fortune
The monument of human glory stands;
And, for humane congratulation, knowing
How, smile as may the mask, the man behind
Frets at the fortune that degrades his own.
This, having heard of from the wise, myself,
From long experience in the ways of men,
Can vouch for—what a shadow of a shade
Is human loyalty; and, as a proof,
Of all the host that filled the Grecian ship,
And pour'd at large along the field of Troy,
One only Chief—and he, too, like yourself,

At first with little stomach for the cause—
The wise Odysseus—once in harness, he
With all his might pull'd in the yoke with me,
Through envy, obloquy, and opposition:
And in Odysseus' honor, live or dead—
For yet we know not which—shall this be said.
Of which enough.   For other things of moment
To which you point, or human or divine,
We shall forthwith consider and adjudge
In seasonable council; what is well,
Or in our absence well deserving, well
Establish and requite; what not, redress
With salutary caution; or, if need,
With the sharp edge of Justice; and to health
Restore, and right, our ailing Commonwealth.
Now, first of all, by my own altar-hearth
To thank the Gods for my return, and pray
That Victory, which thus far by my side
Has flown with us, with us may still abide.

[*Enter Clytæmnestra from the Palace*

*Clytæmnestra.*  O men of Argos, count it not a shame
If a fond wife, and one whom riper years
From youth's becoming bashfulness excuse,
Dares own her love before the face of men;
Nor leaving it for others to enhance,
Simply declares the wretched widowhood
Which these ten years she has endured, since first
Her husband Agamemnon went to Troy.
'Tis no light matter, let me tell you, Sirs,
A woman left in charge of house and home—
And when that house and home a Kingdom—and
She left alone to rule it—and ten years!
Beside dissent and discontent at home,
Stormed from abroad with contrary reports,
Now fair, now foul; but still as time wore on
Growing more desperate; as dangerous
Unto the widowed kingdom as herself.
Why, had my husband there but half the wounds
Fame stabbed him with, he were before me now
Not the whole man we see him, but a body
Gash'd into network; aye, or had he died

But half as often as report gave out,
He would have needed thrice the cloak of earth
To cover him, that triple Geryon
Lies buried under in the world below.
Thus, back and forward baffled, and at last
So desperate—that, if I be here alive
To tell the tale—no thanks to me for that,
Whose hands had twisted round my neck the noose
Which others loosen'd—my Orestes too,
In whose expanding manhood day by day
My husband I perused—and, by the way,
Whom wonder not, my lord, not seeing here;
My simple mother-love and jealousy
Of civic treason—ever as you know,
Most apt to kindle when the lord away—
Having bestow'd him, out of danger's reach,
With Strophius of Phocis, wholly yours,
Bound by the generous usages of war,
That make the once-won foe so fast a friend.
Thus, widowed of my son as of his sire,
No wonder if I wept—not drops, but showers,
The ten years' night through which I watch'd in vain
The star that was to bring him back to me;
Or if I slept a sleep so thin as scared
Even at the slight incursion of the gnat;
And yet more thick with visionary terrors
Than thrice the waking-while had occupied.

    Well, I have borne all this: all this have borne,
Without a grudge against the wanderer
Whose now return makes more than rich amends
For all ungrateful absence—Agamemnon,
My Lord and Husband; Lord of Argos; Troy's
Confounder; mainstay of the realm of Greece;
And master-column of the house of Atreus;
Oh, wonder not if I accumulate
All honor and endearment on his head!
If to his country, how much more to me,
Welcome, as land to sailors long at sea,
Or water in the desert; whose return
Is fire to the forsaken winter-hearth;
Whose presence, like the rooted household tree
That, winter-dead so long, anew puts forth

To shield us from the Dogstar, what time Zeus
Wrings the tart vintage into blissful juice.
   Down from the chariot thou standest in,
Crown'd with the flaming towers of Troy, descend,
And to this palace, rich indeed with thee,
But beggar-poor without, return! And ye,
My women, carpet all the way before,
From the triumphal carriage to the door,
With all the gold and purple in the chest
Stor'd these ten years; and to what purpose stor'd,
Unless to strew the footsteps of their lord
Returning to his unexpected rest!
   *Agam.* Daughter of Leda, mistress of my house,
Beware lest loving welcome of your lord,
Measuring itself by his protracted absence,
Exceed the bound of rightful compliment,
And better left to other lips than yours.
Address me not! address me not! I say,
With dust-adoring adulation, meeter
For some barbarian despot from his slave;
Nor with invidious purple strew my way,
Fit only for the footstep of a God
Lighting from Heav'n to earth. Let whoso will
Trample their glories underfoot, not I.
Woman, I charge you, honor me no more
Than as the man I am; if honor-worth,
Needing no other trapping but the fame
Of the good deed I clothe myself withal;
And knowing that, of all their gifts to man,
No greater gift than self-sobriety
The Gods vouchsafe him in the race of life:
Which after thus far running, if I reach
The goal in peace, it shall be well for me.
   *Clyt.* Why, how think you old Priam would have walk'd
Had he returned to Troy your conqueror,
As you to Hellas his?
   *Agam.* What then? Perhaps
Voluptuary Asiatic-like,
On gold and purple.
   *Clyt.* Well, and grudging this,
When all that out before your footstep flows
Ebbs back into the treasury again;

Think how much more had, had fate the tables turn'd,
Irrevocably from those coffers gone,
For those barbarian feet to walk upon,
To buy your ransom back?
    *Agam.* Enough! enough!
I know my reason.
    *Clvt.* What! the jealous God?
Or, peradventure, yet more envious man?
    *Agam.* And that of no small moment.
    *Clyt.* No; the one
Sure proof of having won what others would.
    *Agam.* No matter. Strife but ill becomes a woman.
    *Clyt.* And frank submission to her simple wish
How well becomes the soldier in his strength?
    *Agam.* And I must then submit?
    *Clyt.* Aye, Agamemnon,
Deny me not this first desire on this
First morning of your long-desired return.
    *Agam.* But not till I have put these sandals off,
That, slave-like, too officiously would pander
Between the purple and my dainty feet.


## THE MURDER OF AGAMEMNON.

THE prophetess Cassandra, who was fated never to be believed,
declares to the Chorus the murder of Agamemnon by his wife.

    *Cassandra.* Phœbus! Phœbus!
Thorough trampled ashes, blood and fiery rain
Over water seething, and behind the breathing
War-horse in the darkness—till you rose again,
Took the helm—took the rein—
    *Chorus.* She speaks as one that half asleep at dawn recalls
A night of horror.
    *Cass.* Hither, whither, Phœbus? And with whom,
Leading me, lighting me—
    *Cho.* I can answer that—
    *Cass.* Down to what slaughter-house!
Foh! the smell of carnage through the door
Scares me from it—drags me tow'rd it—
Phœbus! Apollo! Apollo!

*Cho.* One of the dismal prophet·pack, it seems,
That hunt the trail of blood.   But here at fault—
This is no den of slaughter, but the house
Of Agamemnon.
   *Cass.* Down upon the towers
Phantoms of two mangled children hover—and a famish'd
      man,
At an empty table glaring, seizes and devours!
   *Cho.* Thyestes and his children !   Strange enough
For any maiden from abroad to know,
Or, knowing—
   *Cass.* And look! in the chamber below
The terrible woman, listening, watching,
Under a mask, preparing the blow
In the fold of her robe—
   *Cho.* Nay, but again at fault:
For in the tragic story of this House—
Unless, indeed, the fatal Helen—No woman—
   *Cass.* No woman—Tisiphone!   Daughter
Of Tartarus—love-grinning Woman above,
Dragon-tail'd under—honey-tongued, harpy-claw'd,
Into the glittering meshes of slaughter
She wheedles, entices him into the poisonous
Fold of the serpent—
   *Cho.* Peace, mad woman, peace!
Whose stony lips, once open, vomit out
Such uncouth horrors.
   *Cass.* I tell you the lioness
Slaughters the Lion asleep, and lifting
Her blood-dripping fangs buried deep in his mane,
Glaring about her insatiable, bellowing,
Bounds hither—Phœbus, Apollo, Apollo, Apollo!
Whither have you led me, under night alive with fire,
Through the trampled ashes of the city of my sire,
From my slaughtered kinsmen, fallen throne, insulted
      shrine,
Slavelike to be butcher'd, the daughter of a royal Line!

   *Cho.* Blasphemer, hush!
   *Cass.* Aye, hush the mouth you may,
But not the murder.
   *Cho.* Murder!   But the Gods—

*Cass.* The Gods!
Who now abet the bloody work within!
   *Cho.* Woman!—The Gods!—Abet with whom?—
   *Cass.* With her,
Who brandishing aloft the axe of doom,
That just has laid one victim at her feet,
Looks round her for that other, without whom
The banquet of revenge were incomplete.

Yet ere I fall, will I prelude the strain
Of triumph, that in full I shall repeat
When, looking from the twilight Underland,
I welcome her as she descends amain,
Gash'd like myself, but by a dearer hand.
For that old murder'd Lion with me slain,
Rolling an awful eyeball through the gloom
He stalks about of Hades up to Day,
Shall rouse the whelp of exile far away,
His only authentic offspring, ere the grim
Wolf crept between his Lioness and him;
Who, with one stroke of retribution, her
Who did the deed, and her adulterer,
Shall drive to hell, and then, himself pursued
By the wing'd Furies of his Mother's blood,

Shall drag about the yoke of madness, till
Releas'd when Nemesis has gorg'd her fill,
By that same God, in whose prophetic ray
Viewing to-morrow mirror'd as to-day,
And that this House of Atreus the same wine
Themselves must drink they brew'd for me and mine;
I close my lips forever with one prayer,
That the dark Warder of the World below
Would ope the portal at a single blow.

  *Cho.* . . . What unwelcome, what unholy,
Vapor of prognostic, slowly
Rising from the central soul's
Recesses, all in darkness rolls?
What! shall Age's torpid ashes
Kindle at the random spark
Of a raving maiden?—Hark!
What was that behind the wall?
A heavy blow—a groan—a fall—
Some one crying.—Listen further—
Hark again then, crying " Murder!"
Some one—who then?  Agamemnon?
Agamemnon?—Hark again!
Murder! murder! murder! murder!
Help within there!  Help without there!
Break the doors in!

  *Clytæmnestra.* (*Appearing from within, where lies Agamemnon
   dead.*) Spare your pain.
Look!  I who but just now before you all
Boasted of loyal wedlock unashamed,
Now unashamed dare boast the contrary.
Why, how else should one compass the defeat
Of him who underhand contrives one's own,
Unless by such a snare of circumstance
As, once enmeshed, he never shall break through?
The blow now struck was not the random blow
Of sudden passion, but with slow device
Prepared, and level'd with the hand of time.
I say it who devised it; I who did;
And now stand here to face the consequence.
Aye, in a deadlier web than of that loom
In whose blood-purple he divined his doom,
And fear'd to walk upon, but walk'd at last,

Entangling him inextricably fast,
I smote him, and he bellow'd, and again
I smote, and with a groan his knees gave way;
And, as he fell before me, with a third
And last libation from the deadly mace
I pledg'd the crowning draught to Hades due,
That subterranean Saviour—of the Dead!
At which he spouted up the ghost in such
A burst of purple as, bespatter'd with,
No less did I rejoice than the green year
Rejoices in the largess of the skies
That fleeting Iris follows as it flies.

   *Cho.* O woman, woman, woman!
By what accursed root or weed
Of Earth, or Sea, or Hell, inflamed,
Dar'st stand before us unashamed,
And, daring do, dare glory in the deed!

   *Clyt.* Oh, I that dream'd the fall of Troy, as you
Belike of Troy's destroyer. Dream or not,
Here lies your King—my husband—Agamemnon,
Slain by this right hand's righteous handicraft.
Like you, or like it not, alike to me;
To me alike whether or not you share
In making due libation over this
Great Sacrifice—if ever due, from him
Who, having charg'd so deep a bowl of blood,
Himself is forced to drink it to the dregs.

   *Cho.* Woman, what blood but that of Troy, which Zeus
Foredoom'd for expiation by his hand
For whom the penalty was pledg'd? And now,
Over his murder'd body, thou
Talk of libation!—Thou! Thou! Thou!
But mark! Not thine of sacred wine
Over his head, but ours on thine
Of curse and groan, and torn-up stone,
To slay or storm thee from the gate,
The City's curse, the People's hate,
Execrate, exterminate!

## PROMETHEUS BOUND.

THIS sublime tragedy was enacted about 460 B.C. All the characters in it are superhuman. The divine hero Prometheus has been doomed by Zeus to be chained to Mount Caucasus, in Scythia. This is his punishment for his benefactions to mankind, especially the gift of fire, which he had stolen from heaven. The god Hephæstus, with his attendants, Strength and Force, execute the king's decree. The chained hero is visited by the god Oceanus and his daughters, who commiserate his fate. Io, who has been sent wandering over the earth by the jealousy of Hera (Juno), also approaches. Prometheus, who has insight into futurity, foretells her further wanderings and also a secret which concerns Zeus himself. This monarch of heaven, though now supreme, is subject to Fate and liable to be hurled from power. He therefore sends his messenger, Hermes, to elicit the secret. But Prometheus refuses to disclose it, though threatened with further punishment. He persists in his defiance to the close.

The drama of "Prometheus Bound" is a terrible protest against the unrighteousness of the misery inflicted on a benefactor of the human race. There is reason to believe that Æschylus composed a sequel to this, called "Prometheus Unbound," which probably vindicated the government of Zeus as righteous.

The first scene, here given, shows Strength and Force personified, holding Prometheus against the desolate rock.

> *Strength.* We reach the utmost limit of the earth,
> The Scythian track, the desert without man,—
> And now, Hephæstus. thou must needs fulfill
> The mandate of our Father, and, with links
> Indissoluble of adamantine chains,
> Fasten against this beetling precipice,
> This guilty god! Because he filched away
> Thine own bright flower, the glory of plastic fire,
> And gifted mortals with it,—such a sin,
> It doth behoove he expiate to the gods,
> And learn free service to the rule of Zeus,
> And leave off his trick of loving man.
> *Hephæstus.* O Strength and Force,—for you, our Zeus's
> will
> Presents a deed for doing.—No more!—but *I*,
> I lack your daring, up this storm-rent chasm,
> To fix with violent hands a kindred god.
> Howbeit necessity compels me so

The Parthenon.

That I must dare it,—and our Zeus commands
With word as heavy as bolts—inevitable!
Ho!—lofty son of Themis, who is sage,
Thee loth, I loth must rivet fast in chains
Against this rocky height unclomb by man,
Where never human voice nor face shall find
Out thee, who lov'st them!—where thy beauty's flower,
Scorched in the sun's clear heat, shall fade away,
And night come up with garniture of stars
To comfort thee with shadow, and the sun
Disperse, with retricked beams, the morning frosts;

And through all changes, sense of present woe
Shall vex thee sore, because, with none of them
There comes a hand to free.   Such fruit is plucked
From love of man!—for in that thou, a god,
Didst brave the wrath of gods, and give away
Undue respect to mortals; for that crime
Thou art adjudged to guard this joyless rock,
Erect, unslumbering, bending not the knee,
And many a cry and unavailing moan
To utter on the air!   For Zeus is stern,
And new-made kings are cruel.

*Strength.* Be it so,
Why loiter in vain pity?  Why not hate
A god the gods hate?—one too who betrayed
Thy glory unto men?
    *Hephæstus.* An awful thing
Is kinship joined to friendship.
    *Strength.* Grant it be.
Is disobedience to the Father's word
A possible thing?  Dost quail not more for *that?*
    *Hephæstus. Thou*, at least, art a stern one! ever bold!
    *Strength.* Why, if I wept, it were no remedy!
And do not *thou* spend labor on the air
To bootless uses.
    *Hephæstus.* Cursed handicraft!
I curse and hate thee, O my craft!
    *Strength.* Why hate
Thy craft, most plainly innocent of all
These pending ills?
    *Hephæstus.* I would some other hand
Were here to work it!
    *Strength.* All work hath its pain,
Except to rule the gods.   There is none free
Except King Zeus.
    *Hephæstus.* I know it very well:
I argue not against it.
    *Strength.* Why not, then,
Make haste, and bind the fetters over HIM,
Lest Zeus behold thee lagging.
    *Hephæstus.* Here be chains—
Zeus may behold these.
    *Strength.* Seize him,—strike amain!
Strike with the hammer on each side his bands—
Rivet him to the rock.
    *Hephæstus.* The work is done,
And thoroughly done.
    *Strength.* Still faster grapple him,—
Wedge him in deeper,—leave no inch to stir!
He's terrible for finding a way out
Where others could not.
    *Hephæstus.* Here's an arm, at least,
Grappled past freeing.
    *Strength.* Now, then, clench along

The other strongly.   Let the sophist learn.
He's duller than our Zeus.

 *Hephæstus.* Oh, none but HE
Accuse me justly!

 *Strength.* Now, straight through the chest,
Take him and bite him with the clenching tooth
Of the adamantine wedge, and rivet him.

 *Hephæstus.* Alas, Prometheus! what thou sufferest here,
I sorrow over.

 *Strength.* Does thou shrink again,
And breathe groans for the enemies of Zeus?
Beware, lest thine own pity find thee out.

 *Hephæstus.* Thou dost behold a spectacle that turns
The sight o' the eyes to pity.

 *Strength.* I behold
A sinner suffer his sin's penalty,
But lash the thongs about his sides.

 *Hephæstus.* So much,
I must do.   Urge no further than I must.

 *Strength.* Ay, but I *will* urge!—and, with shout on shout,
Will hound thee at this quarry!   Get thee down,
And ring amain the iron round his legs!

 *Hephæstus.* That work was not long doing.

 *Strength.* Heavily now
Let fall the strokes upon the perforant gyves!
For He who rates the work has a heavy hand.

 *Hephæstus.* Thy speech is savage as thy shape,

 *Strength.* Be *thou*
Gentle and tender! but revile not me
For the firm will and the untruckling hate.

 *Hephæstus.* Let us go!   He is netted round with chains.

 *Strength.* Here, now, taunt on! and having spoiled the
  gods
Of honors, crown withal thy mortal men
Who live a whole day out!   Why how could *they*
Draw off from thee one single of thy griefs?
Methinks the Demons gave thee a wrong name,
*Prometheus*, which means Providence,—because
Thou dost thyself require a providence,
To escape the crushing of this rolling Doom.

     [*Hephæstus, Strength and Force depart.*

*Prometheus* O holy Æther, and swift-winged Winds,
And River-wells, and laughter infinite
Of yon Sea-waves!  Earth, mother of us all,
And all-viewing cyclic Sun, I cry on you!—
Behold me a god, what I endure from gods!
 Behold, with throe on throe,
 How, wasted by this woe,
I wrestle down the myriad years of Time!
 Behold, how, fast around me,
The new King of the Happy ones sublime
Has flung the chain he forged, has shamed and bound me!
Woe, woe! to-day's woe and the coming morrow's
I cover with one groan!  And where is found me
 A limit to these sorrows?
And yet what word do I say?  I have foreknown
Clearly all things that should be—nothing done
Comes sudden to my soul—and I must bear
What is ordained with patience, being aware
Necessity doth front the universe
With an invincible gesture.  Yet this curse
Which strikes me now, I find it hard to brave
In silence or in speech.  Because I gave
Honor to mortals, I have yoked my soul
To this compelling fate!  Because I stole
The secret fount of fire, whose bubbles went
Over the ferule's brim, and manward sent
Art's mighty means and perfect rudiment,
That sin I expiate in this agony;
Hung here in fetters, 'neath the blanching sky!

### PROMETHEUS DEFIES ZEUS.

THIS closing scene of the drama shows the descent of Hermes as
an ambassador from Zeus.  When Prometheus refuses to disclose his
secret, the elements rage, the sea dashes against the rocks, the thunder
rolls, but the chained hero remains unappalled.

*Hermes.*  I speak to thee, that sophist, speaker down
Of scorn by scorn,—that sinner against gods,—
That reverencer of men,—that thief of fire,—
I speak to and adjure thee!  Zeus commands
Thy declaration of what marriage-rite
Is this, to move thy vaunt, and cause his fall
From absolute rule!  And do not wrap thy speech

In riddles, but speak clearly! Do not cast
Ambiguous paths, Prometheus, for my feet—
Since Zeus, thou mayst perceive, is scarcely won
To mercy, by such means.

    *Prometheus.* A speech well-mouthed
In th' utterance, and full-minded in the sense,
As doth befit a servant of the gods!
New gods, ye newly reign, and think forsooth
Ye dwell in towers too high for any dart
To take a wound there!—Have I not stood by
While two kings fell from thence? and shall I not
Behold the third, the same who rules you now,
Fall shamed to sudden ruin?—Do I seem
To tremble and quail before your modern gods?
I cast the thought off far!—For thee, depart,
Re-tread thy steps in haste! To all, so asked,
I answer nothing.

    *Hermes.* 'Twas this wind of pride
That took thee of yore full sail upon these rocks.

    *Prometheus.* I would not barter—learn thou soothly that!—
My suffering for thy service! for I hold
It is a nobler thing to serve this rock
Than live a faithful slave to Father Zeus—
And thus on scorners I retort their scorn.

    *Hermes.* It seems that thou dost glory in thy despair.

    *Prometheus.* I, glory? would my foes did glory so,
And I stood by to see!—and naming them,
Thou art not unremembered.

    *Hermes.* Dost thou charge
Me also with the blame of any grief?

    *Prometheus.* I tell thee, I loathe the universal gods,
Who for the good I gave them rendered back
The ill of their injustice.

    *Hermes.* Thou art mad—
I hear thee raving, Titan, at the full!

    *Prometheus.* If it be madness to abhor my foes,
May I be mad!

    *Hermes.* Vain god, take righteous courage!—dare for
      once
To apprehend and front thine agonies
With a just prudence!

*Prometheus.* Vainly dost thou chafe
My soul with exhortation, as the sea
Goes beating on the rock.   Oh ! think no more
That I, fear-struck by Zeus to a woman's mind,
Will supplicate him, loathéd as he is,
With womanly upliftings of my hands,
To break these chains!   Far from me be the thought !
    *Hermes.*   I have indeed, methinks, said much in
          vain,—
For still my heart, beneath my showers of prayers,
Lies dry and hard !—nay, leaps like a young horse
Who bites against the new bit in his teeth,
And tugs and struggles against the new-tried rein,—
Still fiercest in the weakest thing of all,
Which sophism is,—for absolute will alone,
When left to its motions in perverted minds,
Is worse than null, for strength !   Behold and see,
Unless my words persuade thee, what a blast
And whirlwind of inevitable woe
Must sweep persuasion through thee !   For at first
The Father will split up this jut of rock
With the great thunder and the bolted flame,
And hide thy body where the hinge of stone
Shall catch it like an arm !—and when thou hast passed
A long black time within, thou shalt come out
To front the sun ; and Zeus's winged hound,
The strong carnivorous eagle, shall wheel down
To meet thee,—self-called to a daily feast,—
And set his fierce beak in thee, and tear off
The long rags of thy flesh, and batten deep
Upon thy dusky liver !   Do not look
For any end, moreover, to this curse,
Or ere some god appear, to bear thy pangs
On his own head vicarious, and descend
With unreluctant step the darks of hell,
And the deep glooms enringing Tartarus !—
Then ponder this !—the threat is not a growth
Of vain invention : it is spoken and meant !
For Zeus's mouth is impotent to lie,
And doth complete the utterance in the act—
So, look to it, thou !—take heed !—and nevermore
Forget good counsel, to indulge self-will !

*Chorus of Ocean-nymphs.* This Hermes suits his reasons
    to the times—
At least I think so!—since he bids thee drop
Self-will for prudent counsel. Yield to him!
When the wise err, their wisdom proves their shame.
    *Prometheus.* Unto me the foreknower, this mandate of
      power,
    He cries, to reveal it!
And scarce strange is my fate, if I suffer from hate,
    At the hour that I feel it!
Let the locks of the lightning, all bristling and whitening,
    Flash, coiling me round!
While the æther goes surging 'neath thunder and scourging,
    Of wild winds unbound!
Let the blast of the firmament whirl from its place
    The earth rooted below,—
And the brine of the ocean, in rapid emotion,
    Be it driven in the face
Of the stars up in heaven, as they walk to and fro!
Let him hurl me anon, into Tartarus—on—
    To the blackest degree,
With Necessity's vortices strangling me down!
But he cannot join death to a fate meant for *me!*
    *Hermes.* Why the words that he speaks and the thoughts
      that he thinks,
    Are maniacal—sad!
And if Fate, who hath bound him, just loosens the links,—
    Yet he's nigh to be mad.
    Then depart ye who groan with him,
    Leaving to moan with him—
Go in haste! lest the roar of the thunder, in nearing,
Should blast you to idiocy, living and hearing.
    *Chorus.* Change thy speech for another, thy thought for
      a new,
    If to move me and teach me, indeed be thy care!
For thy words swerve so far from the loyal and true,
    That the thunder of Zeus seems more easy to bear.
How! couldst teach me to venture such vileness? Behold!
I *choose,* with this victim, this anguish foretold!
For I turn from the traitor in hate and disdain,
And I know that the curse of the treason is worse
    Than the pang of the chain.

## CHAPTER XIV.

### SOPHOCLES.

Sophocles, greatest of Greek dramatists, was born in 497 B. C. and lived to the venerable age of ninety-one. He always remembered the little village where he was born and in one of his last plays mentioned it tenderly:

"Colonus, glistening bright,
Where evermore, in thickets freshly green,
　　The clear-voiced nightingale
　　Still haunts, and pours her song,
　　By purpling ivy hid,
And the thick leafage sacred to the God,
　　With all its myriad fruits,
　　By mortal's foot untouched,
　　By sun's hot ray unscathed,
　　Sheltered from every blast;
There wanders Dionysus evermore,
　　In full, wild revelry,
And waits upon the nymphs who nursed his youth.
And there, beneath the gentle dews of heaven,
The fair narcissus with its clustered bells
　　Blooms ever, day by day,
Of old the wreath of mightiest goddesses;
　　And crocus golden-eyed;
　　And still unslumbering flow
　　Cephissus' wandering streams;
They fail not from their springs, but evermore,
　　Swift-rushing into birth,
　　Over the plain they sweep,
　　The land of broad, full breast,
　　With clear and stainless wave;
Nor do the Muses in their minstrel choirs,
　　Hold it in light esteem,
　　Nor Aphrodite with her golden reins."[1]

[1] Œdipus at Colonus.

Sophocles was carefully educated in the branches deemed essential for an Athenian youth. Because of his graceful dancing, he was chosen as a boy to lead the chorus of youths who sang the hymn of thanksgiving after the defeat of the Persians.

When twenty-eight he presented his first series of plays at the Greater Dionysia, and won first place over Aeschylus. Excitement upon this occasion is said to have reached a high pitch. After this victory Sophocles entered upon sixty years of activity, producing many dramas and winning eighteen victories at the Greater Dionysia alone. Since four plays were each time presented, and as he is recorded to have taken prizes at the Lenaea as well, we may easily accept the statement that he wrote 123 plays in all.

Although he lived in stirring times, Sophocles cared little for political life, nor do we find special references to passing events in his tragedies.

Regarding his contributions to the Greek drama, instead of making marked innovations, this poet appears to have improved upon the drama as he found it. He introduced a third actor, thus giving prominence to the dialogues and relegating the chorus to a subordinate position. Again, he broke away from the trilogy, so carefully adhered to by Aeschylus, making each play complete in itself.

In treatment of characters, we again find a change. While Aeschylus portrayed the gods as sublime, majestic beings, Sophocles humanized them and brought the drama down from the heights of the classic calm into the realm of men. In place of religious problems, those having to do with the activities and concerns of humanity were substituted. Sophocles even went so far as to introduce characters from the humble walks of life.

For mastery of language, none excelled him. He was nicknamed the "Bee," and his lips were said to be touched with honey. The ancient Greeks regarded him as greatest of their dramatists and compared him favorably to Homer in his moderation and restraint in depicting human passions.

Seven complete dramas of Sophocles remain; *Œdipus the King, Œdipus at Colonus, Electra, Ajax,* and *Antigone* are probably the most famous.

To understand Sophocles' immortal tragedy Antigone. one must hold in mind the attitude of the ancient Greek regarding the care of the dead. Unless a body was sprinkled over with sacred earth, it was believed that the soul could not enter the realm of the departed, but wandered about, restlessly, aimlessly, until finally, dust covering the body, it joined those who had gone before.

Antigone and her sister Ismene were last of a noble house whose members, one after another, had been destroyed because of a curse which was transmitted from father to children. Two brothers had fallen, slain by each other's hand. Poly-nices led an attack against Thebes, and his brother Eteocles withstood it. The aggressors were put to flight, and Creon chosen king. He immediately decreed that all honour should be shown the slain Eteocles, while Polynices, a rebel, should be cast out—prey for fowls of the air.

When this decree became known to Antigone, she deter-mined to administer to the last needs of her dead brother, whom she loved. Hastening to Ismene, she announced her intention, and in spite of Ismene's entreaties, held firm to her resolution. When Ismene shows clearly that she lacks cour-age to oppose the king's will, Antigone replies:

> "I will not ask thee, nor though thou should'st wish
> To do it, should'st thou join with my consent.
> Do what thou wilt, I go to bury him;
> And good it were, in doing this, to die.
> Loved I shall be with him whom I have loved,
> Guilty of holiest crime. More time is mine
> In which to share the favor of the dead,
> Than that of those who live; for I shall rest
> For ever there. But thou, if thus thou please,
> Count as dishonoured what the Gods approve.

*Ismene:*

> I do them no dishonour, but I find
> Myself too weak to war against the State.

*Antigone:*

> Make what excuse thou wilt, I go to rear
> A grave above the brother whom I love.

Even while the king repeats his command that the body of
Antigone's brother be left uncared for, a guard hurries in to
say that in some way, unknown to the watch, earth has been
scattered over it. The king rages; he accuses the guard of
having received bribes from the rebel-leader's supporters.

> " They, I know,
> Have bribed these men to let the deed be done.
> No thing in use by man, for power of ill,
> Can equal money. This lays cities low,
> This drives men forth from quiet dwelling-place,
> This warps and changes minds of worthiest stamp,
> To turn to deeds of baseness, teaching men
> All shifts of cunning, and to know the guilt
> Of every impious deed. But they who, hired,
> Have wrought this crime, have laboured to their cost,
> Or soon or late to pay the penalty."

The guard is dismissed to find the one who has thus dis-
obeyed the king's behest, while the chorus sings:

> " Many the forms of life,
>   Wondrous and strange to see,
>   But nought than man appears
>   More wondrous and more strange.
>   He, with the wintry gales,
>   O'er the white foaming sea,
>   'Mid wild waves surging round,
>   Wendeth his way across:
> Earth, of all Gods, from ancient days the first,
>   Unworn and undecayed.
> He, with his ploughs that travel o'er and o'er,
>   Furrowing with horse and mule,
>   Wears ever year by year.

Presently the guard returns, leading Antigone, whom he
has discovered covering her brother's body with dust. To the
king's question as to whether or not this report is true, Antigone answers: "I own I did it, and will not deny." Asked if
she dared to disobey the laws, she speaks at length:

" Yes, for it was not Zeus who gave them forth,
  Nor Justice, dwelling with the Gods below,
  Who traced these laws for all the sons of men;
  Nor did I deem thy edicts strong enough,
  That thou, a mortal man, should'st over-pass
  The unwritten laws of God that know not change.
  They are not of today nor yesterday,
  But live forever, nor can man assign
  When first they sprang to being.   Not through fear
  Of any man's resolve was I prepared
  Before the Gods to bear the penalty
  Of sinning against thee.   That I should die
  I knew, (how should I not?) though thy decree
  Had never spoken.   And, before my time
  If I shall die, I reckon this a gain;
  For who so lives, as I in many woes,
  How can it be but he shall gain by death?
  And so for me to bear this doom of thine
  Has nothing painful.   But, if I had left
  My mother's son unburied on his death,
  In that I should have suffered; but in this
  I suffer not.   And should I seem to thee
  To do a foolish deed, 'tis simply this,—
  I bear the charge of folly from a fool."

While the guards lead her away, the chorus sings:

" Blessed are those whose life no woe doth taste!
     For unto those whose house
  The Gods have shaken, nothing fails of curse
  Or woe, that creeps to generations far.
     E'en thus a wave, (when spreads,
     With blasts from Thracian coasts,
     The darkness of the deep),
     Up from the sea's abyss
  Hither and thither rolls the black sand on,
     And every jutting peak,
     Swept by the storm-wind's strength,
     Lashed by the fierce wild waves,
  Re-echoes with the far resounding roar."

Haemon, the king's son, betrothed to Antigone, now appears. He tries to move his father on the only point where he might perhaps be approached; the indiscretion of putting Antigone to death, because popular sympathy is with her.

"The Gods, my father, have bestowed on man
His reason, noblest of all earthly gifts:
And that thou speakest wrongly these thy words
I cannot say, (God grant I ne'er know how
Such things to utter!) yet another's thoughts
May have some reason. 'Tis my lot to watch
What each man says or does, or blames in thee,
For dread thy face to one of low estate,
Who speaks what thou wilt not rejoice to hear.
But I can hear the things in darkness said,
How the whole city wails this maiden's fate,
As one 'who of all women most unjustly,
For noblest deed must die the foulest death,
Who her own brother, fallen in the fray,
Would neither leave unburied, nor expose
To carrion dogs, or any bird of prey,
May she not claim the meed of golden praise?'
Such is the whisper that in secret runs
All darkling. And for me, my father, nought
Is dearer than thy welfare. What can be
A nobler prize of honour for the son
Than a sire's glory, or for sire than son's?
I pray thee, then, wear not one mood alone,
That what thou say'st is right, and nought but that;
For he who thinks that he alone is wise,
His mind and speech above what others have,
Such men when searched are mostly empty found.
But for a man to learn, though he be wise,
Yea to learn much, and know the time to yield,
Brings no disgrace. When winter floods the streams,
Thou see'st the trees that bend before the storm,
Save their last twigs, while those that will not yield
Perish with root and branch. And when one hauls
Too tight the mainsail rope, and will not slack,
He has to end his voyage with deck o'erturned.
Do thou then yield; permit thyself to change."

III—3

He speaks in vain and Antigone is led to her doom.   Her lover takes his life, that death may not divide them, and the queen, his mother, suicides upon news of the death of her son and the king's crime.

While the disconsolate king realizes too late his terrible wrong-doing, the chorus sings:

" Man's highest blessedness,
In wisdom chiefly stands;
And in the things that touch upon the Gods,
' Tis best in word or deed,
To shun unholy pride;
Great words of boasting bring great punishments,
And so to grey-haired age
Teach wisdom at the last."

## SOPHOCLES.

Sophocles presented his first dramas in 468 B. C.   Unlike Æschylus, he seldom appeared upon the stage.   Introducing a third actor, he gave greater scope for action and plot.   No longer were the characters heroes and gods, but men and women like those who lived around him.   Sophocles did much to humanize the drama.   His tragedies show the influence of the times. Athens was now at the height of her power and intellectual activity was never more pronounced.[1]

[1]See Sophocles: Social Life in Greece.

### KING ŒDIPUS.

THE terrible story of Œdipus had a strong fascination for the Greeks, as illustrating the conflict of moral laws and the supremacy of destiny.   Laius, King of Thebes, learned from the oracle of Apollo, at Delphi, that he was destined to perish by the hand of his own son. He ordered his wife Jocasta, therefore, to destroy the infant.   She gave it to a herdsman, who left it, tied with thongs, on Mount Cithæron.   But a shepherd of Corinth found the babe and delivered it to King Polybus, who adopted it as his own child, and called it Œdipus (Swollen-foot).   When grown up, Œdipus is told by the oracle that he

would slay his father and marry his mother. On his return to Corinth
he met Laius in a narrow pass and, in a dispute about the road, slew
him. Passing to Thebes, he destroyed the Sphinx, a monster which
had been inflicting damage on the city. Œdipus was, therefore, raised
to the throne and the widowed Jocasta receives him as her husband.
A pestilence arises, and the oracle declares that it cannot be abated
until the murder of Laius is avenged. On investigation the appalling
secret is discovered, whereupon Jocasta commits suicide, and Œdipus
tears out his own eyes and goes into exile.

*Jocasta.* Princes of Thebes, we deemed it meet to seek
The temples of the gods, and in our hands
These votive wreaths, this odorous incense bear.
The soul of Œdipus on a wild sea
Of anxious care is tossed;—nor, as becomes
The prudent, weighs by former oracles
This late response, but lends a willing ear
To all who speak of terrors. Since my voice
Avails no more, Lycæan king, to thee
I fly, for thou art nearest to our need,
And come in prayer a suppliant to thy shrine,
That thou mayst grant us thine auspicious aid;
Since all now tremble, when we thus behold
Our very pilot shuddering and appalled.

*Enter Corinthian.*

*Corinthian.* Can ye inform me, strangers, where your king,
Great Œdipus, his regal state maintains;
Or, if ye know, where I may find the monarch?
*Chorus.* These are th' imperial halls—he is within—
This is his wife, the mother of his children.
*Cor.* Blest may she be, and ever with the blest
Hold glad communion; to her royal lord
A most accomplished consort.
*Joc.* Equal joy
Attend thee, stranger,—thy kind greeting claims
This due return of courtesy. But say,
Whence cam'st thou to our Thebes, and what thy tidings?
*Cor.* Joy to thy house, O lady! and thy lord.
*Joc.* What joy?—and from what region art thou come?
*Cor.* From Corinth. At my words thou wilt rejoice:
Why shouldst thou not—yet fond regrets will rise.

*Joc.* What dost thou mean, and whence this two-fold
  influence?

*Cor.* The assembled States of Isthmus, rumor tells,
Will choose thy lord to mount the vacant throne.

*Joc.* How vacant? Reigns not Polybus in Corinth?

*Cor.* No more!--His only kingdom is the tomb.

*Joc.* Haste, haste, attendant, and convey with speed
These tidings to your lord. Vain oracles!
Where are your bodings now? My Œdipus,
Fearing to slay this man, forsook his country;
Now Fate, and not his hand, hath laid him low.

*Enter Œdipus.*

*Œdipus.* Why, my beloved Jocasta, has thou sent
To bid my presence hither?

*Joc.* Hear this man—
Attend his tidings, and observe the end
Of these most true and reverend oracles.

*Œd.* Who is this stranger—with what message charged?

*Joc.* He is from Corinth, thence despatched to tell thee
That Polybus, thy father, is no more.

*Œd.* What sayest thou, stranger? Be thyself the speaker.

*Cor.* Then, in plain terms, the king is dead and gone.

*Œd.* Died he by treason, or the chance of sickness?

*Cor.* Slight ills dismiss the aged to their rest.

*Œd.* Then by disease, it seems, the monarch died.

*Cor.* And bowed beneath a withering weight of years.

*Œd.* Ha! is it thus? Then, lady, who would heed
The Pythian shrine oracular, or birds
Clanging in air, by whose vain auspices
I was fore-doomed the murderer of my father?
In the still silence of the tomb he sleeps.
While I am here—the fatal sword untouched,
Unless he languished for his absent child,
And I was thus the author of his doom.
Now in the grave he lies, and with him rest
Those vain predictions, worthy of our scorn.

*Joc.* Did I not tell thee this before?

*Œd.* Thou didst,
But terror urged me onward.

*Joc.* Banish now
This vain solicitude.

*Œd.* Should I not fear
The dark pollution of my mother's bed?

*Joc.* Oh, why should mortals fear, when fortune's sway
Rules all, and wariest foresight naught avails?
Best to live on unheeding, as thou may'st.

*Œd.* Phœbus foretold that I should wed my mother,
And shed with impious hand a father's blood.
For this I fled my own Corinthian towers
To seek a distant home—that home was blest;
Though still I languished to embrace my parents,

*Cor.* This fear then urged thee to renounce thy country?

*Œd.* Old man, I would not be a father's murderer.

*Cor.* Then wherefore, since thy welfare I regard,
Should I forbear to rid thee of this terror?

*Œd.* Do so, and rich shall be thy recompense.

*Cor.* This hope impell'd me here, that when our State
Hails thee her monarch, I might win thy favor.

*Œd.* Ne'er will I seek the authors of my birth.

*Cor.* 'Tis plain, my son, thou know'st not what thou doest!

*Œd.* How! how! old man, by heaven, unfold thy meaning.

*Cor.* If this preclude thee from returning home—

*Œd.* I fear lest Phœbus saw, alas! too clearly!

*Cor.* If thou dost dread pollution from thy parents—

*Œd.* That restless dread for ever haunts my soul.

*Cor.* Know, then, thy terrors all are causeless here.

*Œd.* How so? if of these parents I was born?

*Cor.* But Polybus is not allied to thee.

*Œd.* How say'st thou? was not Polybus my father?

*Cor.* No more than I—our claims are equal here.

*Œd.* Had he who gave me life no nearer claim
Than thou, a stranger?

*Cor.* Nor to him or me
Ow'st thou thy birth.

*Œd.* Then wherefore did he grant
A son's beloved name?

*Cor.* He from my hand
Received thee as a gift.

*Œd.* With such fond love
How could he cherish thus an alien child?

*Cor.* His former childless state to this impelled him.

*Œd.* Gav'st thou a purchased slave, or thy own child?

*Cor.* I found thee in Cithæron's shadowy glades.

*Œd.* Why didst thou traverse those remoter vales?

*Cor.* It was my charge to tend the mountain herds.

*Œd.* Wert thou a herdsman, and engaged for hire?

*Cor.* I was, my son, but thy preserver too.

*Œd.* From what affliction didst thou then preserve me?

*Cor.* This let thy scarr'd and swollen feet attest.

*Œd.* Ha! why dost thou revive a woe long passed?

*Cor.* I loosed thy bound and perforated feet.

*Œd.* Such foul reproach mine infancy endured.

*Cor.* From this event arose the name thou bear'st.

*Œd.* Thou didst receive me then from other hands,
Nor find me as by chance?

*Cor.* No; to my hand
Another herdsman gave thee.

*Œd.* Who was he?
Canst thou inform me this?

*Cor.* He was, I believe,
A slave of Laius.

*Œd.* What! of him who erst
Ruled o'er this land?

*Cor.* The same;—this man to him
Discharged an herdsman's office.

*Œd.* Lives he yet
That I may see him?

*Cor.* Ye, his countrymen,
Are best prepared this question to resolve.

*Œd.* Is there, of you who now attend our presence,
One who would know the herdsman he describes,
Familiar erst or here, or in the field?
Speak—for the time demands a prompt disclosure.

*Ch.* He is, I deem, no other than the man
Whom thou before didst summon from the fields.
This none can know more than the Queen.

*Œd.* Think'st thou, O Queen, the man whose presence late
We bade, is he of whom this stranger speaks?

*Joc.* Who—spake of whom?—Regard him not, nor dwell,
With vain remembrance, on unmeaning words!

*Œd.* Nay, Heaven forfend, when traces of my birth
Are thus unfolding, I should cease to follow.

*Joc.* Nay, by the Gods I charge thee! search no more
If life be precious still.  Be it enough
That I am most afflicted.

*Œd.* **Cheer** thee, lady,
Though my descent were proved e'en trebly servile,
No stain of infamy would light on thee.

   *Joc.* Ah yield, I do conjure thee—seek no more.

   *Œd.* I will not yield, till all be clearly known.

   *Joc.* 'Tis for thy peace I warn thee—yet be wise.

   *Œd.* That very wisdom wounds my peace most deeply.

   *Joc.* Unhappy—never may'st thou know thy birth.

   *Œd.* Will none conduct this shepherd to our presence?
Leave her to triumph in her lordly race.

   *Joc.* Woe! woe! unhappy! henceforth by that name
Alone can I address thee, and by that
Alone for ever.

   *Œd.* I will on
To trace my birth, though it be most obscure.
Pride swells her thus, for in a woman's breast
Pride reigns despotic, and she thinks foul scorn
Of my ignoble birth. I deem myself
The child of Fortune, in whose favoring smile
I shall not be dishonored. She alone
Hath been my fostering parent; from low state
My kindred mouths have raised me into greatness.
Sprung from such lineage, none I heed beside,
Nor blush reluctant to explore my birth.

### *Enter Herdsman.*

   *Œd.* Approach, old man! look on me, and reply
To my demand. Wert thou the slave of Laius?

   *Herd.* I was his slave—bred in his house—not purchased.
My better part of life was passed in tending
The monarch's flocks.

   *Œd.* What regions wert thou then
Wont to frequent?

   *Herd.* Cithæron and the meads
Adjacent.

   *Cor.* Then answer, dost thou recollect the babe
Thou gav'st me there, as mine own child to cherish?

   *Herd.* What wouldst thou? Whither do thy questions
       tend?

   *Cor.* This is that child, my friend, who stands before thee.

   *Herd.* A curse light on thee! wilt thou not be silent?

*Œd.* Reprove him not, old man, for thine own words,
Far more than his, demand a stern reprover.

*Herd.* I did:—Oh, had that moment been my last!

*Œd.* This shall be, if thou wilt not speak the truth.

*Herd.* And if I speak it, I am trebly lost.

*Œd.* This man, it seems, still struggles to elude us.

*Herd.* No, I confessed long since I gave the child.

*Œd.* And whence received? thine own, or from another?

*Herd.* No, not mine own; I from another's hand
Bare him.

*Œd.* And from what Theban, from what roof?

*Herd.* Oh, by the gods! my lord, inquire no further.

*Œd.* If I repeat th' inquiry, thou art lost.

*Herd.* The palace of King Laius gave him birth.

*Œd.* Sprung from a slave, or of the royal stock?

*Herd.* The child was called the son of Laius; here
The royal consort can inform thee better.

DEATH OF LAIUS.

*Œd.* Didst thou from her receive him?

*Herd.* Yea, O king!—

*Œd.* And for what purpose?

*Herd.* That I might destroy
him—

*Œd.* What—the unnatural
mother!

*Herd.* She was awed
By woe-denouncing oracles.

*Œd.* What woe?

*Herd.* That he should prove
the murderer of his parents.

*Œd.* Why, then, to this old man thy charge consign?

*Herd.* From pity, O my lord, I deemed that he
To his own land would bear the child afar.
He saved him to despair. If thou art he
Of whom he spake, how dark a doom is thine.

*Œd.* Woe! woe! 'tis all too fatally unveiled.
Thou Light! Oh, may I now behold thy beams
For the last time! Unhallowed was my birth;
In closest ties united, where such ties
Were most unnatural;—with that blood defiled.
From whose pollution most the heart recoils.

THESEUS AND THE MINOTAUR.
(From a vase-painting in the Vatican Museum.)

## CHAPTER XV.

### EURIPIDES.

#### *Ion.*

(It is morning at the Delphian temple of Apollo; the Temple service opens; Ion chants as he performs his duties of sweeping the Temple, sprinkling the holy water from Castalia, and driving away the birds).

> With his bright steeds now the sun
> Hath his daily course begun,
> And the stars before his light
> Hide them in the womb of night.
> Thy soaring peaks, Parnassus, now
> The fiery chariot's glory show;
> Fragrant clouds of incense sweet,
> Phoebus, fill thy holy seat;
> The priestess, on her mission high,
> Mounts the chair of prophecy,
> There to Hellas to make known
> Whate'er Apollo has foreshown.
> Ye that dwell in Delphian home,
> Liegeman of Apollo, come
> To the fount of Castaly,
> From its wake draw purity,
> Then unto the temple hie.
> See that no ill-omened word

41

From unguarded lips be heard,
When ye to the pilgrims speak
Who the shrine prophetic seek.
Mine the task once more shall be,
As ever from my infancy,
With laurel bough to sweep the ground,
Sprinkle the holy water round,
And with my bow the birds to chase,
That would defile the sacred place.
Father or mother have I none,
Ion is the temple's son.
Come then, my fair laurel bough,
That in flowery dale doth grow,
Fed by springs that ever flow—
And with myrtle there doth twine
For service of Apollo's shrine.—
Come with thee the fane I sweep,
And from all defilement keep.
So, with each returning sun,
Ion's task is duly done.
Praise and glory be to thee,
Fair Latona's progeny.
Phoebus, happy lot is mine
To wait in thy prophetic shrine.
No mortal master do I own,
The servant I of heaven alone.
Of labor that is piety
Weary can I never be.
Phoebus is my father true,
To him my grateful love is due;
From him to me all blossoms come,
Phoebus, whose temple is my home.
Praise and glory be to thee,
Fair Latona's progeny.
Now, my first task fully plied,
My laurel bough I lay aside,
And from the golden urn I fling
Water from Castalian spring,
On myself, on all around
To purify the temple's bound.

But lo! the birds are leaving now
Their nests on high Parnassus' brow;
I rede them all to keep aloof
From golden shrine and corniced roof.
Thou that heaven's messages dost bear,
Whose talons make thee lord of air,
Beware my arrows.   Here again
A swan comes sailing to the fane.
Turn, ruddy-foot, elsewhere thy flight;
Go, upon Eelian waters light;
Though sweet as Phoebus' lyre thy strain
To save thee from my bow were vain.
Birds that interpret heaven's high will
To mortals, I am loath to kill.
Yet Ion must his duty do,
And prove him Phoebus' liegeman true,
Beneath whose roof his childhood grew."

*Euripides:   Goldwin Smith's trans.*

Euripides, last of the great Athenian tragic poets, was born in 485 B. C.   As a youth and mature man he was fond of philosophy, and Socrates and Protagoras were his particular friends and congenial companions.

In 455 B. C. Euripides presented his first plays in the great theater of Athens, winning only third place.   During the following thirty years but little was accomplished; then came the productive period.   Ninety-two plays are attributed to him, while he won only five victories at the Greater Dionysia.   Some critics have held that his failure frequently came in consequence of indifference to the details of stage management; again, he not infrequently competed with Sophocles, whose popularity was particularly strong during these years in Athens.   All three dramatists lived to a ripe old age, Euripides producing the Bacchae, one of his finest works, when over seventy.

Whereas Sophocles was a genial spirit and desirable companion, Euripides was a quiet, studious, retiring man.   He cared not at all for politics and preferred to spend his time with his books.   It was said that he possessed the most complete library of his time.

Of all Greek dramatists, Euripides was most modern. Introducing no new elements into the drama, he nevertheless changed it materially. Aeschylus had invested his characters with sublimity; Sophocles prolonged his ideal, but Euripides depicted humanity as he saw it. He was a realist. When he brought the gods of Olympus upon the stage, he represented them as men, possessed of human ambitions and desires. When men and women were introduced, they were such men and women as Euripides knew—typical of the age, with all its faults and virtues. No idealistic glamour was thrown over the whole, but it was modernized, humanized and made realistic. Conditions had changed in Greece since Aeschylus created his characters, sublime as statues wrought of marble. The real rather than the ideal interested men, and this Euripides clearly saw. The fact that he did see it gives testimony to his greatness. No longer was it possible for the enlightened Hellene to hold to those conceptions of deity which had satisfied his forefathers. Man's conception of deity must always be man idealized, and the ideals of Greeks had risen above those of bygone ages. Much of Euripides' genius lay in his ability to grasp the situation and to meet it fairly.

The dramas of this last of three great poets had faults which were sufficiently exploited by the comedy-writers of the age. Because he himself was interested in speculative philosophy, Euripides sometimes allowed his characters to give discourses upon the subject, which added nothing to the force of the play, but rather distracted from it. Where one would naturally expect a passionate outburst, he finds instead a hair-splitting argument between the two actors, or one of them having reached the height of passion's heat, suddenly lapses into a reflective dissertation upon some abstract subject. The Greeks loved argument and debate and this which seems to be such a fault from our standpoint, when inserted in a play, was regarded in quite a different light by them. Aristophanes liked to point out the fact that all Euripides' characters, nurses, maidens, slaves, and ladies, were well prepared to take part in such discussions.

Although not fortunate in winning many laurels, and in spite of the wit of the comic poets, Euripides enjoyed a very fair degree of popularity while he lived. Since that time he has sometimes been very much in favor, and again severely criticized. Certain it is that he has greatly influenced modern literature. Several of his dramas are wholly free from the faults just mentioned. Among his most famous plays we may include *Medea, Hippolytus, The Suppliants, Andromache, Electra, Ion,* and the *Bacchae.* The Bacchae is given special note here, not only because of its strength and dramatic force, but because it voices in a measure the conflicting religious views of the poet's age.

The Bacchae is based upon a myth of the god of wine. The wild orgies of the Thracian women, celebrating the festival of their leader, Dionysus, easily lent spirit to a play. The Theban king Pentheus has attempted to stamp out the worship of the wine-god, and Dionysus himself, disguised, visits Thebes to establish his cult:

" Far now behind me lies the golden ground
    Of Lydian and of Phrygian; far away
    The wide hot plains where Persian sunbeams play,
    The Bactrian war-holds, and the storm-oppressed
    Clime of the Mede, and Araby the Blest,
    And Asia all, that by the salt sea lies
    In proud embattled cities, motely-wise
    Of Hellene and Barbarian interwrought;
    And now I come to Hellas—having taught
    All the world else my dances and my rite
    Of mysteries, to show me in men's sight
    Manifest God.

                    And first of Hellene lands
    I cry this Thebes to waken; set her hands
    To clasp my wand, mine ivied javelin,
    And round her shoulders hang my wild fawn-skin.
    For they have scorned me whom it least beseemed,
    Semele's sister; mocked my birth, nor deemed
    That Dionysus sprang from Dian seed.

    Now Cadmus yieldeth up his throne and use
    Of royal honour to his daughter's son
    Pentheus; who on my body hath begun

A war with God.   He thrusteth me away
From due drink-offering, and, when men pray,
My name entreats not.   Therefore on his own
Head and his people's shall my power be shown,
Then to another land, when all things here
Are well, must I fare onward, making clear
My godhead's might.   But should this Theban town
Essay with wrath and battle to drag down
My maids, lo, in their path myself shall be,
And maniac armies battled after me!
For this I veil my godhead with the wan
Form of the things that die, and walk as Man.
O Brood of Tmololus o'er the wide world flown,
O Lydian band, my chosen and mine own,
Damsels uplifted o'er the orient deep
To wander where I wander, and to sleep
Where I sleep; up, and wake the old sweet sound,
The clang that I and mystic Rhea found,
The Timbrel of the Mountain!   Gather all
Thebes to your song round Pentheus' royal hall.
I seek my new-made worshippers, to guide
Their dances up Kithaeron's pine-clad side."

Since Pentheus cannot be won over to favor the customary Bacchanal worship, the disguised god induces him to
array himself as a woman, that he may look upon the religious
ceremonies the women keep, such a thing being forbidden.
No man was permitted to attend the mysterious worship of
the Bacchae and live.   While he is making ready, and the
wine-god meditates upon the revenge he is taking, maidens
are singing, and these songs are believed to embody some of
the later reflections of the poet.   Especially the last, sung by
the leader, seems to contain sentiments that may easily have
been Euripides', in his maturer years.

*Chorus.*

Will they ever come to me, ever again,
    The long, long dances,
On through the dark till thy dim stars wane?
Shall I feel the dew on my throat, and the stream

Of wind in my hair?  Shall our white feet gleam
   In the dim expanses?
Oh, feet of a fawn to the greenwood fled,
   Alone in the grass and the loveliness;
Leap of the hunted, no more in dread,
   Beyond the snares and the deadly press:
Yet a voice still in the distance sounds,
A voice and a fear and a haste of hounds;
O wildly labouring, fiercely fleet,
   Onward yet by river and glen
Is it joy or terror, ye storm-swift feet?
   To the dear lone lands untroubled of men,
Where no voice sounds, and amid the shadowy green
The little things of the woodland live unseen.

What else is Wisdom?  What of man's endeavour
   Or God's high grace, so lovely and so great?
   To stand from fear set free, to breathe and wait;
   To hold a hand uplifted over Hate;
And shall not Loveliness be loved for ever?

### Others.

O Strength of God, slow art thou and still,
   Yet failest never!
On them that worship the Ruthless Will,
On them that dream, doth His judgment wait,
Dreams of the proud man, making great
   And greater ever,
Things which are not of God.  In wide
   And devious coverts, hunter-wise,
He coucheth Time's unhasting stride,
   Following, following, him whose eyes
Look not to Heaven.  For all is vain,
The pulse of the heart, the plot of the brain,
That striveth beyond the laws that live.
And is thy Faith so much to give,
   Is it so hard a thing to see,
   That the Spirit of God, whate'er it be,
The law that abides and changes not, ages long,
The Eternal and Nature-born—these things be strong?

What else is Wisdom?  What of man's endeavour
    Of God's high grace so lovely and so great?
    To stand from fear set free, to breathe and wait;
    To hold a hand uplifted over Hate;
And shall not Loveliness be loved for ever?

*Leader.*

    Happy he, on the weary sea
Who hath fled the tempest and won the haven.
    Happy whoso hath risen, free,
Above his striving.  For strangely graven
    Is the orb of life, that one and another
    In gold and power may outpass his brother.·
    And men in their millions float and flow
And seethe with a million hopes as leaven;
    And they win their Will, or they miss their Will,
    And the hopes are dead or are pined for still;
        But whoe'er can know,
        As the long days go,
That to live is happy, hath found his Heaven!

Pentheus is discovered by the maidens, celebrating their Dionysian mysteries, and in their rage they fall upon the unhappy king and rend him.  The messenger tells the story to those in Thebes who listen:

    A narrow glen it was, by crags o'ertowered,
Torn through by tossing waters, and there lowered
A shadow of great pines over it.  And there
The Maenad maidens sate; in toil they were,
Busily glad.  Some with an ivy chain
Tricken a worn wand to toss its locks again;
Some, wild in joyance, like young steeds set free,
Made answering songs of mystic melody.
    But my poor master saw not the great band
Before him.  'Stranger,' cried he, 'where we stand
Mine eyes can reach not these false saints of thine.
Mount we the bank, or some high-shouldered pine,
And I shall see their follies clear!'  At that
There came a marvel.  For the Stranger straight

Touched a great pine-tree's high and heavenward crown,
And lower, lower, lower, urged it down
To the herbless floor. Round like a bending bow,
Or show wheel's rim a joiner forces to,
So in those hands that tough and mountain stem
Bowed slow—oh, strength not mortal dwelt in them!—
To the very earth. And there he set the King,
And slowly, let it cast him in its spring,
Let back the young and straining trees, till high
It towered again amid the towering sky;
And Pentheus in the branches! Well, I ween,
He saw the Maenads then, and well was seen!
For scarce was he aloft, when suddenly
There was no stranger any more with me,
But out of Heaven a Voice—oh, what voice else?—
'Twas He that called! 'Behold, O damsels,
I bring ye him who turneth to despite
Both me and ye, and darkeneth my great Light.
'Tis yours to avenge.' So spake he, and there came
'Twixt earth and sky a pillar of high flame.
And silence took the air, and no leaf stirred
In all the forest dell. Thou hadst not heard
In that vast silence any wild thing's cry.
And up they sprang; but with bewildered eye,
Agaze and listening, scarce yet hearing true.
Then came the Voice again. And when they knew
Their God's clear call, old Cadmus' royal brood,
Up, like wild pigeons startled in a wood,
On flying feet they came, his mother blind,
Agave, and her sisters, and behind
All the wild crowd, more maddened then,
Through the angry rocks and torrent-tossing glen,
Until they spied him in the dark pine-tree:
Then climbed a crag hard by and furiously
Some sought to stone him, some their wands would fling
Lance-wise aloft, in cruel targeting."

Sympathy with Dionysus when the play opens, has left him before the end. The drama is full of wild touches, passion, and religious frenzy. Interest is sustained to the end. when the chorus sings:

III—4

" There be many shapes of mystery.
And many things God makes to be,
    Past hope or fear.
And the end men looked for cometh not,
And a path is there where no man thought,
    So hath it fallen here."

—*Murray's trans.*

GREEK LYRES.

## MEDEA.

MEDEA was the daughter of Æetes, king of Colchis, on the Euxine Sea. When Jason went thither in search of the golden fleece, she became enamored of the gallant stranger, and used her skill in magic to assist him in overcoming all the difficulties of his attempt. Nor did she shrink from crime to accomplish the result. After gaining the fleece Jason married his guilty preserver and fled with her to Thessaly, where he obtained for him the throne. But Jason tired of the fierce passion of the sorceress, and sought the hand of Glauce, daughter of Creon, King of Corinth. This king, justly fearing the effects of Medea's anger, banished her. Though fiercely indignant at the outrage, she pretended to submit, and sought refuge at Athens. Thence she sent back her two sons with rich presents for their father's new bride. In due time Glauce arrayed herself in the rich robes sent by Medea, only to discover that they were imbued with a deadly poison, which destroyed the wearer and her father. Jason became alarmed for the fate of his sons, who had returned to their mother. He hastened after them, but was too late. The savage mother has already slain them, and exults in her revenge. At the close of the play she is represented as flying through the air, with the bodies of her children, in a chariot drawn by winged dragons.

Medea is the greatest of the tragedies of Euripides. The opening scene shows the terrible passion which has been roused in the fierce barbarian woman by the news of the second marriage. Yet the poet makes plain that her guilty thoughts and deeds are an actual result of the selfishness of others.

## MEDEA'S WRONGS.

*Nurse of Medea.* All is variance now
And hate: for Jason, to his children false,
False to my mistress, for a royal bride
Hath left her couch, and wedded Creon's daughter,
Lord of this land. Ill doth Medea brook
This base dishonor; on his oath she calls,
Recalls their plighted hands, the firmest pledge
Of mutual faith, and calls the gods to witness
What a requital she from Jason finds.
Of food regardless, and in sorrow sunk
She lies, and melts in tears each tedious hour
Since first she knew her lord had injured her;
Nor lifts her eye, nor lifts her face from the earth,
Deaf to her friends' entreaties as a rock,
Or billow of the sea; save when she turns
Her snowy neck, and to herself bewails

Her father, and her country, and her house,
Which she betray'd to follow this base man,
Who treats her now with such indignity.
Affliction now hath taught her what it is
Not to forsake a parent and his house.
She hates her children, nor with pleasure sees them.
I fear her, lest she form some strange design;
For violent her temper, and of wrongs
Impatient: well I know her, and I fear her,
Lest, in the dead of night, when all are laid
In deep repose, she steal into the house,
And plunge into their breast the piercing sword;
Or murder ev'n the monarch of the land,
Or the new-married Jason, on herself
Drawing severer ills: for like a storm
Her passions swell, and he that dares enrage her
Will have small cause to boast his victory.
But see, her sons from the gymnastic ring
Returning, heedless of their mother's ills;
For youth holds no society with grief.

*Enter Tutor, with the Sons of Medea.*

*Tut.* Thou old domestic servant of my mistress,
Why dost thou take thy station at the gates,
And ruminate in silence on thy griefs?
How hath Medea wish'd to be alone?

*Nur.* Thou good old man, attendant on the sons
Of Jason, faithful servants with their lords
Suffer in their afflictions, and their hearts
Are touch'd with social sorrow; and my griefs
Swell, for Medea's sufferings, to such height,
That strong desire impell'd me to come forth,
And tell them to the earth and to the skies.

*Tut.* Admits she yet no respite to her groans?

*Nur.* I wonder at thee: no, these ills but now
Are rising, to their height not yet advanced.

*Tut.* I heard one say, not seeming to attend,
But passing on to where they play with dice,
Among the grave old men, who then by chance
Were sitting near Pirene's hallow'd stream.
That Creon, lord of this fair land, will drive
These children and their mother from the state

Of Corinth: whether this report be true
I know not, but I wish it otherwise.

*Nur.* Will Jason bear to see his sons thus wrong'd,
Though he regards their mother now no more?

*Tut.* To new alliances the old gives place,
And to this house he is no more a friend.

*Nur.* Ruin would follow, to the former ill
If this were added ere the first subsides.

*Tut.* Be cautious then; it were unseasonable
Our queen knew this; in silence close thy lips.

*Nur.* Go in, my children, go: all will be well;
And take thou heed, keep them aloof, nor let them
Come near their mother while her griefs are fresh:
Cruel her eye, and wild; I mark'd it late,
Expressive of some dark design on these:
Nor will she check her fury, well I know,
Till the storm bursts on some one: may its stroke
Fall on some hostile head, not on a friend.

*Medea (within.)* Wretch that I am, what anguish rends
      my heart!
Wretched Medea, how art thou undone!

*Nur.* Ay, thus it is. Your mother, my dear children,
Swells with resentment, swells with rage. Go in,
Go quickly in; but come not in her eye,
Approach her not, but keep you from the wild
And dreadful fury of her violent temper.
Go now, go quickly in; this rising cloud
Of grief forebodes a storm, which soon will fall
With greater rage: inflamed with injuries,
What will not her tempestuous spirit dare?

*Med.* Ah me! ah me! what mighty wrongs I bear,
Wrongs that demand my tears and loud laments!
Ye sons accursed of a detested mother,
Perish, together with your father perish,
And in one general ruin sink your house!

*Nur.* Ah me unhappy! in their father's fault
Why make thy sons associates? Why on them
Rises thy hatred? Oh, I fear, I fear,
My children, lest some evil threatens you.
Kings have a fiery quality of soul,
Accustom'd to command; if once they feel
Control, though small, their anger blazes out,

Not easily extinguish'd; hence I deem
An equal mediocrity of life
More to be wish'd; if not in gorgeous state,
Yet without danger glides it on to age.
There's a protection in its very name,
And happiness dwells with it: but the height
Of towering greatness long to mortal man
Remains not fix'd, and, when misfortune comes
Enraged, in deeper ruin sinks the house.

  *Chorus.* I heard the voice, I heard the loud laments
Of the unhappy Colchian: do her griefs
(Say, reverend matron), find no respite yet?
From the door's opening valve I heard her voice.
No pleasure in the sorrows of your home
I take; for deeds are done not grateful to me.

  *Nur.* This is no more a home; all here is vanish'd,
Nor leaves a trace behind.   The monarch's house
He makes his own; while my unhappy mistress
In her lone chamber melts her life away
In tears, unmoved by all the arguments
Urged by her friends to soothe her sorrowing soul.

  *Med* O that the ethereal lightning on this head
Would fall!   Why longer should I wish to live?
Unhappy me!   Death would be welcome now,
And kindly free me from this hated life.

  *Cho.* Dost thou hear this, O Jove, O Earth, O Light,
The mournful voice of this unhappy dame?
Why thus indulge this unabated force
Of nuptial love, self-rigorous, hastening death?
Let it not be thy wish: if a new bed
Now charms thy husband, be not his offence
Engraved too deep: Jove will avenge thy wrongs;
Let not thy sorrows prey upon thy heart.

  *Med.* O powerful Themis, O revered Diana,
See what I suffer, though with sacred oaths
This vile, accursed husband I had bound!
Oh, might I one day see him and his bride
Rent piecemeal in their house, who unprovoked
Have dared to wrong me thus!   Alas, my father!
Alas, my country! whom my shameful flight
Abandon'd, having first my brother slain!

  *Cho.* I hear her lamentations mixed with groans,

Which in the anguish of her heart she vents;
And on her faithless husband, who betray'd
Her bed, she calls aloud; upon the gods,
Thus basely wrong'd, she calls, attesting Themis,
Daughter of Jove, the arbitress of oaths,
Who led her to the shores of Greece, across
The rolling ocean, when the shades of night
Darken'd its waves, and steer'd her through the straits.

## MEDEA'S LAST WORDS TO HER CHILDREN.

O CHILDREN, children! you have still a city,
A home, where, lost to me and all my woe,
You will live out your lives without a mother!
But I—lo! I am for another land,
Leaving the joy of you.   To see you happy,
To deck your marriage-bed, to greet your bride,
To light your wedding torch shall not be mine!
O me, thrice wretched in my own self-will!
In vain then, dear my children! did I rear you;
In vain I travailed, and with wearing sorrow
Bore bitter anguish in the hour of childbirth!
Yea, of a sooth, I had great hope of you,
That you should cherish my old age, and deck
My corpse with loving hands, and make me blessed
'Mid women in my death.   But now, ah me!
Hath perished that sweet dream   For long without you
I shall drag out a dreary, doleful age.
And you shall never see your mother more
With your dear eyes: for all your life is changed.
Woe, woe!
Why gaze you at me with your eyes, my children?
Why smile your last sweet smile?   Ah me! ah me!
What shall I do?   My heart dissolves within me,
Friends, when I see the glad eyes of my sons!
I cannot.   No: my will that was so steady,
Farewell to it.   They too shall go with me:
Why should I wound their sire with what wounds them,
Heaping tenfold his woes on my own head?
No, no, I shall not.   Perish my proud will.
Yet whence this weakness?   Do I wish to reap
The scorn that springs from enemies unpunished?

Dare it I must.   What craven fool am I,
To let soft thoughts flow trickling from my soul!
Go, boys, into the house: and he who may not
Be present at my solemn sacrifice—
Let him see to it.   My hand shall not falter.
Ah! ah!
Nay, do not, O my heart! do not this thing!
Suffer them, O poor fool; yea, spare thy children!
There in thy exile they will gladden thee.
Not so: by all the plagues of nethermost Hell,
It shall not be that I, that I should suffer
My foes to triumph and insult my sons!
Die must they: this must be, and since it must,
I, I myself will slay them, I who bore them.
So it is fixed, and there is no escape.
Even as I speak, the crown is on her head,
The bride is dying in her robes, I know it.
But since this path most piteous I tread,
Sending them forth on paths more piteous far,
I will embrace my children.   O my sons,
Give, give your mother your dear hands to kiss!
O dearest hands, and mouths most dear to me,
And forms and noble faces of my sons!
Be happy even there: what here was yours,
Your father robs you of.   O loved embrace!
O tender touch and sweet breath of my boys!
Go, go, go, leave me!   Lo, I cannot bear
To look on you, my woes have overwhelmed me!
Now know I all the ill I have to do:
But rage is stronger than my better mind;
Rage, cause of greatest crimes and griefs to mortals.


## IPHIGENIA.

IPHIGENIA was a daughter of Agamemnon and Clytæmnestra.
Her father had killed a stag in the grove of Artemis (Diana), and the
offended goddess therefore detained the Greek fleet at Aulis, when it
assembled to sail against Troy.   The seer Calchas declared that the
sacrifice of Iphigenia was necessary to propitiate the goddess and obtain a favorable wind.   Agamemnon yielded, and his daughter was
brought to Chalcis, supposing she was to be married to Achilles.   According to the usual story which was accepted by Æschylus and
Sophocles, she was actually sacrificed by her father.   But Euripides,

probably owing to the advance of humane sentiment, modified this account as follows. When she was about to be slain at the altar, Artemis intervened and carried her off in a cloud to be priestess of her temple in Tauris (the Crimea), while a stag was substituted in the sacrifice. In Tauris it was customary to sacrifice strangers, especially Greeks, coming thither. Orestes, the brother of Iphigenia, slew his mother for her murder of his father, but was afterwards constantly pursued by the Eumenides or Furies. Pylades, who had devoted himself to watchful care of his friend, accompanied him to Tauris, whence he had been directed by the oracle to carry off the sacred image of Artemis, which was said to have fallen from heaven. These strangers were seized and were about to be sacrificed when Iphigenia recognized her brother, and fled with him, bearing away the statue. Meantime, her sister Electra heard that Orestes had been sacrificed by the priestess in Tauris, and meeting Iphigenia at Delphi, resolved to deprive her of sight. But Orestes intervened, and a general recognition and reconciliation took place. All returned to Mycenæ, but Iphigenia carried the image of Artemis to Attica, and served there as priestess. According to some traditions, she was endowed by the goddess with immortality and eternal youth.

The story has evident reference to the prevalence of human sacrifices in Greece in early times. Some critics have interpreted the name Iphigenia to mean "daughter of Jephthah," thus connecting it with the well-known story of the Hebrew Bible. This connection is increased by one form of the Greek legend, which makes Agamemnon's offence consist in having vowed in the year in which Iphigenia was born to sacrifice the most beautiful production of the year, and then neglecting to fulfill that vow. Various parts of the Greek legend were treated by the tragic poets, and Euripides used it in two dramas, "Iphigenia at Aulis," and "Iphigenia in Tauris." In modern times, also, Goethe dramatized the ancient story.

## ORESTES DISCOVERS IPHIGENIA IN TAURIS.

*Iphigenia.* I fear lest he who should convey
To Argos this epistle, when return'd
Safe to his native country, will neglect
My letter, as a thing of little worth.
*Orestes.* And wilt thou in return give him thy oath
To send him from this barbarous shore alive?
*Iph.* That's just: how should he bear my letter else?
*Ores.* Swear then; do thou propose the righteous oath.
*Iph.* This, let him say, he to my friends will give.
*Pylades.* Well, to thy friends this letter I will give.
*Iph.* Thee will I send safe through the darkening rocks.

*Pyl.* What god dost thou invoke to attest thy oath?
*Iph.* Diana, at whose shrine high charge I hold.
*Pyl.* And I heaven's potent king, the awful Jove.
*Iph.* But if thou slight thy oath, and do me wrong?
*Pyl.* Never may I return.   But if thou fail,
And save me not?
   *Iph.* Then never, while I live,
May I revisit my loved Argos more!
What in this letter is contained, what here
Is written, all I will repeat to thee,
That thou mayst bear my message to my friends.
'Gainst danger thus I guard: if thou preserve
The letter, that though silent will declare
My purport; if it perish in the sea,
Saving thyself, my words too thou wilt save.
   *Pyl.* Well hast thou said touching the gods and me.
Say then to whom at Argos shall I bear
This letter?   What relate as heard from thee?
   *Iph.* This message to Orestes, to the son
Of Agamemnon, bear:—She who was slain
At Aulis, Iphigenia, sends thee this:
She lives, but not to those who then were there.
   *Ores.* Where is she?   From the dead return'd to life?
   *Iph.* She whom thou seest: but interrupt me not.
To Argos, O my brother, ere I die,
Bear me from this barbaric land, and far
Remove me from this altar's bloody rites,
At which to slay the stranger is my charge.
   *Ores.* What shall I say?   Where are we, Pylades?
   *Iph.* Or on thy house for vengeance will I call,
Orestes.   Twice repeated, learn the name.
   *Ores.* Ye gods!
   *Iph.* In my cause why invoke the gods?
   *Ores.* Nothing: proceed: my thoughts were wandering
        wide:
Strange things of thee unask'd I soon shall learn.
   *Iph.* Tell him the goddess saved me, in exchange
A hind presenting, which my father slew
A victim, deeming that he plunged his sword
Deep in my breast: me in this land she placed.
Thou hast my charge; and this my letter speaks.
   *Pyl.* Oh, thou hast bound me with an easy oath:

What I have sworn with honest purpose, long
Defer I not, but thus discharge mine oath.
To thee a letter from thy sister, lo,
I bear, Orestes; and I give it thee.

 *Ores.* I do receive it, but forbear to unclose
Its foldings, greater pleasure first to enjoy
Than words can give. My sister, O most dear,
Astonish'd ev'n to disbelief, I throw
Mine arms around thee with a fond embrace,
In transport at the wondrous things I hear.

 *Chorus.* Stranger, thou dost not well with hands profane
Thus to pollute the priestess of the shrine,
Grasping her garments hallow'd from the touch.

 *Ores.* My sister, my dear sister, from one sire,
From Agamemnon sprung, turn not away,
Holding thy brother thus beyond all hope.

 *Iph.* My brother! Thou my brother! Wilt thou not
Unsay these words? At Argos far he dwells.

 *Ores.* Thy brother, O unhappy! is not there.

 *Iph.* Thee did the Spartan Tyndarus bring forth?

*Ores.* And from the son of Pelops' son I sprung.

*Iph.* What say'st thou? Canst thou give me proof of this?

*Ores.* I can: ask something of my father's house.

*Iph.* Nay, it is thine to speak, mine to attend.

*Ores.* First let me mention things which I have heard
Electra speak: to thee is known the strife
Which fierce 'twixt Atreus and Thyestes rose.

*Iph.* Yes, I have heard it; for the golden ram,—

*Ores.* In the rich texture didst thou not inweave it?

*Iph.* O thou most dear! Thou windest near my heart.

*Ores.* And image in the web the averted sun?

*Iph.* In the fine threads that figure did I work.

*Ores* For Aulis did thy mother bathe thy limbs?

*Iph.* I know it, to unlucky spousals led.

*Ores.* Why to thy mother didst thou send thy locks?

*Iph.* Devoted for my body to the tomb.

*Ores.* What I myself have seen I now as proofs
Will mention. In thy father's house, hung high
Within thy virgin chambers, the old spear
Of Pelops, which he brandish'd when he slew
Œnomaus, and won his beauteous bride,
The virgin Hippodamia, Pisa's boast.

*Iph.* O thou most dear (for thou art he), most dear
Acknowledged, thee, Orestes, do I hold,
From Argos, from thy country distant far?

*Ores.* And hold I thee, my sister, long deem'd dead?
Grief mix'd with joy, and tears, not taught by woe
To rise, stand melting in thy eyes and mine.

*Iph.* Thee yet an infant in thy nurse's arms
I left, a babe I left thee in the house.
Thou art more happy, O my soul, than speech
Knows to express. What shall I say? 'Tis all
Surpassing wonder and the power of words.

*Ores.* May we together from this hour be bless'd!

*Iph.* An unexpected pleasure, O my friends,
Have I received; yet fear I from my hands
Lest to the air it fly. O sacred hearths,
Raised by the Cyclops! O my country, loved
Mycenæ! Now that thou didst give me birth,
I thank thee: now I thank thee, that my youth
Thou trainedst, since my brother thou hast train'd,
A beam of light, the glory of his house.

*Ores.* We in our race are happy ; but our life,
My sister, by misfortunes is unhappy.

*Iph.* I was, I know, unhappy, when the sword
My father, frantic, pointed at my neck.

*Ores.* Ah me! methinks e'en now I see thee there.

*Iph.* When to Achilles, brother, not a bride,
I to the sacrifice by guile was led,
And tears and groans the altar compass'd round.

*Ores.* Alas, the lavers there!

*Iph.* I mourn'd the deed
My father dared; unlike a father's love;
Cruel, unlike a father's love, to me.

*Ores.* Ill deeds succeed to ill: if thou hadst slain
Thy brother, by some god impell'd, what griefs
Must have been thine at such a dreadful deed!

*Iph.* Dreadful, my brother, O how dreadful! Scarce
Has thou escaped a foul, unhallow'd death,
Slain by my hands. But how will these things end?
What Fortune will assist me? What safe means
Shall I devise to send thee from this state,
From slaughter, to thy native land, to Argos,
Ere with thy blood the cruel sword be stain'd?
This to devise, O my unhappy soul!
This to devise is thine. Ah, unhappy me!
What god, what mortal, what unlook'd-for chance
Will expedite our dangerous way, and show
Two sprung from Atreus a release from ills?

IPHIGENIA DELIVERS THE LETTER TO PYLADES.

COMEDY MASKS.

# CHAPTER XVI.

## GREEK COMEDY.

While Greek tragedy grew farther and farther away from the humor and burlesque so characteristic of the old satyr dances and songs, comedy arose to incorporate within itself much of this early spirit. The tragedies instructed the people in their past history and traditions. The comedies supplied entertainments, pure and simple, yet at the same time did much to mold public opinion. Public men were attacked, their pet theories and schemes were exploited indirectly, with subtle wit and satire. The enthusiasm and heedlessness of the masses on some particular occasion, a political crusade, a poet's peculiar treatment of a myth—almost any current happening supplied the writer of comedy with a general theme. This, however, was lightly treated, with frequent sallies, personalities, and fun often coarse and indelicate.

"The essence of the Old Comedy was a satirical censorship, unsparing in personalities, of public and of private life—of morality, of statesmanship, of education, of literature, of social usage,—in a word, of everything which had an interest for the city or which could amuse the citizens. Preserving all the freedom of banter and of riotous fun to which its origin gave it an historical right, it aimed at associating with this a strong practical purpose—the expression of a democratic public opinion in such a form that no misconduct or folly could altogether disregard it. At Athens, the poet of the Old Comedy had an influence analogous, perhaps, rather to that of a journalist than to that of the modern dramatist." [1]

In spite of many absurdities, consciously introduced, and much exaggerated criticism and satire, many a wholesome lesson came home to Athenian audiences while series of comedies were being presented at the Lenaea.

The greatest writer of comedies in ancient Greece was

[1] Jebbs: Classical Poets.

Aristophanes, born about 450 B. C. He is supposed to have
been a man of wealth, but little is definitely known of his personal life. Eleven of his comedies have been preserved. Each
satirizes some current theory, fad or undertaking. For
example, the new learning taught by the Sophists, and to some
extent by Socrates, was attacked in *The Clouds;* the inordinate
love of the Greeks for law-suits and their desire to serve on
juries was ridiculed by *The Wasps;* and *The Birds* was intended
to satirize the enthusiasm of the Athenians in attempting indis-
creet enterprises—suggested by the sending of a fleet to the
aid of Sicily when peace had just been made, although in case
of defeat, disaster was bound to overtake the city. The Athenians were ever ready to vote measures which good statesmanship would have condemned.

The chorus was retained in the Old Comedy, members
being attired in a manner fitting the play. In *The Birds,* they
came forward covered with feathers and provided with wings.
In the Wasps, they tried to impersonate those stinging insects.

The Old Comedy came to an end about 400 B. C. Then followed a transition period, known as the Middle Comedy, and
this in turn was succeeded by the New Comedy. Certain
changes came upon the general plan of the comedy during
these years. Because of the fall of Athens and strained political conditions, the providing of a chorus grew to be a burden
and it was frequently eliminated. Again, personalities had
been dwelt upon to such lengths that the state required them
to be abandoned. In place of assailing public men, writers of
comedy now confined themselves to the manners and customs
of society, or of certain social classes.

The most gifted poets of this later period were Philemon
and Menander. The two were rivals, and while victories
were often given to Philemon, later ages have awarded the
palm to his opponent. After the death of these talented men,
the comedy sank into a general decline. Comedies were sometimes given, it is true, and were still written, but the old time
vigour and originality were gone.

Aristophanes produced *The Birds* in 414 B. C., and this has
been considered his masterpiece. Two Athenians, having
grown tired of the cares and perplexities of the Greek world,

wander away to the realm of birds. They induce the king of the birds, once an Athenian king, to found a city in the air, where birds may dwell. Here, midway between heaven and earth, they are able to prevent the prayers of mortals and the smoke of incense, offered to the gods, from reaching the Mighty Ones, and compel even the gods of Olympus to mediate with them. The world, which belonged to the birds before man appropriated it, is restored to its earlier possessors.

It is quite impossible, without extended study, to appreciate the fun, the sallies and jokes in ancient Greek comedy. Ofttimes the mere mention of a public man in connection with some theory or opinion was enough to provoke laughter. Constant jests were aimed at politicians, philosophers and poets. Some of the humour lives on, in spite of translation and loss of local colour, but the little surviving for us today is but a part of the subtle wit which appealed to Athenian audiences two thousand years ago.

Peisthetairus, an Athenian citizen, and his companion Euelpides, set upon their journey to Birdland, guided thither by a jackdaw and a raven. Euelpides explains their reasons for leaving Athens in this fashion:

> "Not through disgust or hatred or disdain
> Of our illustrious birthplace, which we deem
> Glorious and free; with equal laws ordained
> For fine and forfeiture and confiscation,
> With taxes universally diffused;
> And suits and pleas abounding in the Courts.
>
> For grasshoppers sit only for a month
> Chirping upon the twigs; but our Athenians
> Sit chirping and discussing all the year,
> Perched upon points of evidence and law.
>
> Therefore we trudge upon our present travels,
> With these our sacrificial implements,
> To seek some easier unlitigious place;
> Meaning to settle there and colonize.
> Our present errand is in search of Tereus,
> (The Hoopoe that is now) to learn from him
> If in his expeditions, flights, and journeys,
> He ever chanced to light on such a spot."

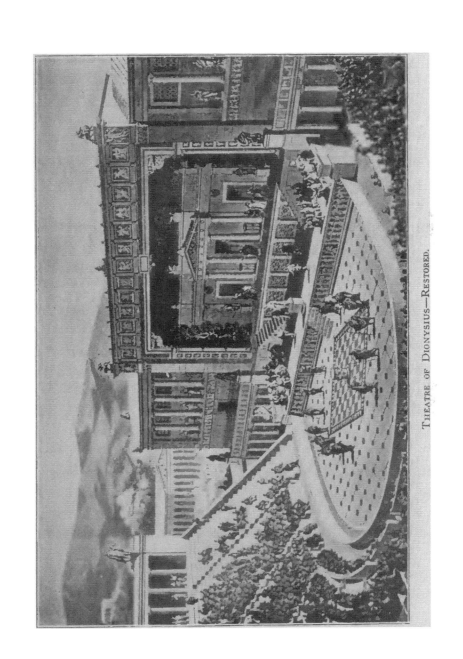

THEATRE OF DIONYSIUS—RESTORED.

The abode of Hoopoe is finally reached. As he appears in answer to their request, Euelpides cannot forbear remarking upon his curious appearance.

*Eu.* O Hercules, what a creature! What a plumage!
And a triple tier of crests; what can it be!

*Hoo.* Who called? who wanted me?

*Eu.*                     May the heavenly powers
        Confound ye, I say (*aside*).

*Hoo.*                     You mock at me perhaps,
Seeing these plumes. But, stranger, you must know—
That once I was a man.

*Eu.*             We did not laugh
At you, Sir.

*Hoo.*      What, then, were you laughing at?

*Eu.* Only that beak of yours seemed rather odd.

*Hoo.* It was your poet Sophocles that reduced me
To this condition with his tragedies.

*Eu.* What are you, Tereus? Are you a bird, or what?

*Hoo.* A bird.

*Eu.*         Then where are all your feathers?

*Hoo.*                             Gone.

*Eu.* In consequence of an illness?

*Hoo.*                     No, the birds
At this time of the year leave off their feathers,
But you! What are ye? Tell me.

*Eu.*                     Mortal men.

*Hoo.* What countrymen?

*Eu.*                 Of the country of the Triremes.

*Hoo.* Jurymen, I suppose?

*Eu.*                 Quite the reverse,
We're anti-jurymen.

*Hoo.*         Does that breed still
Continue amongst you?

*Eu.*             Some few specimens
You'll meet with, here and there, in country places.

*Hoo.* And what has brought you here? What was your
    object?

*Eu.*         We wished to advise with you.

*Hoo.*                         With me! For what?

III—5

*Eu.*   Because you were a man: the same as us;
And found yourself in debt; the same as us;
And after that, you changed into a bird;
And ever since have flown and wandered far
Over the lands and seas, and have acquired
All knowledge that a bird or man can learn.

　　Therefore we come as suppliants, to beseech
Your favor and advice to point us out
Some comfortable country, close and snug,
A country like a blanket or a rug,
Where we might fairly fold ourselves to rest.

　　*Hoo.*   Do you wish then for a greater State than Athens?
　　*Eu.*   Not greater; but more suitable for us.


　　　Peisthetairus, heretofore silent, exclaims:
　*Peis.*   Ha! What a power is here! What opportunities!
If I could only advise you.   I see it all!
The means for an infinite empire and command!
　　*Hoo.*   And what would you have us do? What's your adivce?
　　*Peis.*   Do?   What would I have ye do?   Why, first of all
Don't flutter and hurry about all open-mouthed,
In that undignified way.
　　　　　　　　　　　　　Concentrate!
Bring all your birds together.   Build a city.
　　*Hoo.*   The birds!   How could we build a city?   Where?
　　*Peis.*   Nonsense.   You can't be serious.   What a question!
Look down.
　　*Hoo.*   I do.
　　*Peis.*        Look up now.
　　*Hoo.*                   So I do.
　　*Peis.*   Now turn your neck around.
　　*Hoo.*                            I should sprain it, though.
　　*Peis.*   Come, what d'ye see?
　　*Hoo.*                     The clouds and sky; that's all.
　　*Peis.*   Well, that we call the pole, and the atmosphere;
And would it not serve you birds for a metropole?
　　*Hoo.*   Pole?   Is it called a pole?
　　*Peis.*                     Yes, that's the name.

Philosophers of late call it the pole;
Because it wheels and rolls itself about,
As it were, in a kind of roly-poly way.
Well, there then, you may build and fortify,
And call your Metropolis—your Acropolis.
From that position you'll command mankind,
And keep them in utter, thorough subjugation:
Just as you do the grasshoppers and locusts.
And if the gods offend you, you'll blockade 'em,
And starve 'em to a surrender.
  *Hoo.*      In what way?
  *Peis.* Why thus. Your atmosphere is placed, you see,
In a middle point, just betwixt earth and heaven.

   A case of the same kind occurs with us.
Our people in Athens, if they send to Delphi
With deputations, offerings, or what not,
Are forced to obtain a pass from the Boeotians:
Thus when mankind on earth are sacrificing,
If you should find the gods grown mutinous
And insubordinate, you could intercept
All their supplies of sacrificial smoke.
  *Hoo.* By the earth and all its springs! Springs and nooses!
Odds, nets and snares! This is the cleverest notion:
And I could find it in my heart to venture,
If the other birds agree to the proposal.
  *Peis.* But who must state it to them?
  *Hoo.*        You yourself,
They'll understand ye. I found them mere barbarians,
But living here a length of time amongst them,
I have taught them to converse and speak correctly.
  *Peis.* How will you summon them?
  *Hoo.*       That's easy enough;
I'll just step into the thicket here hard by,
And call my nightingale. She'll summon them.
And when they hear her voice, I promise you
You'll see them all come running here pell-mell.
  *Peis.* My dearest, best of birds! Don't lose a moment,
I beg, but go directly into the thicket;
Nay, don't stand here; go call your nightingale.

*[Exit Hoopoe. Song from behind the scene, supposed to be sung by the Hoopoe.]*

Awake! awake!
Sleep no more, my gentle mate!
With your tiny tawny bill,
Wake the tuneful echo shrill,
On vale or hill;
Or in her airy, rocky seat,
Let her listen and repeat
The tender ditty that you tell,
The sad lament,
The dire event,
To luckless Itys that befell.
Thence the strain
Shall rise again,
And soar amain,
Up to the lofty palace gate;
Where mighty Apollo sits in state;
In Jove's abode, with his ivory lyre,
Hymning aloud to the heavenly choir.
While all the gods shall join with thee
In a celestial symphony.

With much ado and lengthy argument, Peisthetairus over-comes the hostility of the birds towards mankind and puts his scheme before them. He enumerates many advantages a bird-city will give, and shows that it will prove a means of doing great good.

*Peis.* But, if men shall acknowledge your merit and worth,
As equal to Saturn, to Neptune, and Earth,
And to everything else; we shall freely bestow
All manner of blessings.
*Hoo.* Explain them and show.
*Peis.* For instance: if locusts arrive to consume
All their hopes of a crop, when the vines are in bloom,
A squadron of owls may demolish them all:
The midges, moreover, which canker and gall
The figs and the fruit, if the thrush is employed,
By a single battalion will soon be destroyed.

*Hoo.* But wealth is their object; and how can we grant it?
*Peis.* We can point them out mines; and our help will be
  wanted
To inspect and direct navigation and trade;
Their voyages all will be easily made,
With a saving of time, and a saving of cost;
And a seaman in future will never be lost.
  *Hoo.* How so?
  *Peis.*    We shall warn them: "Now hasten to sail,
Now keep within harbour; your voyage will fail."

Very independent indeed the birds become, when they are
at last well established in the skies.

CHORUS.
"Notice is hereby given,
To the deities of heaven;
 Not to trespass here,
 Upon our atmosphere;
Take notice; from the present day,
 No smoke or incense is allowed
To pass this way."

The whole comedy should be read, since it is the poet's
masterpiece, and because it is not so difficult for moderns to
understand as are some of Aristophanes' plays, which are so
wrapped up with the affairs of his day that they are not especially interesting to readers of the present time.

### THE WORSHIPPER OF THE CLOUDS.

ARISTOPHANES in his "Clouds" ridicules Socrates and attacks him
as trying to substitute the worship of the Clouds for that of Zeus and
the other recognized divinities. Strepsiades, an old Athenian, harassed
with debts on account of his spendthrift son, goes to the school of
Socrates, hoping to learn some way of cheating his creditors. There
the philosopher is found outside suspended in a basket. He is engaged
in contemplation, but is induced to descend and receive the new ap-
plicant. Strepsiades, having declared his willingness to be initiated,
is told to sit on a sacred couch and put on a chaplet. Then a basket
of stones is emptied on his head, while he crouches in fear. Socrates
invokes the Clouds in a sublime hymn, and these deities approach in
the form of lofty women.

*Socrates.* Look towards Mount Parnes as I point—There, there!
Now they descend the hill; I see them plainly,
As plain as can be.
*Strepsiades.* Where, where? I pr'ythee, show me.
*Soc.* Here! a whole troop of them, through woods and hollows,
A bye-way of their own.
*Streps.* What ails my eyes,
That I can't catch a glimpse of them?
*Soc.* Behold!
Here, at the very entrance—
*Streps.* Never trust me,
If yet I see them clearly.
*Soc.* Then you must be
Sand-blind or worse.
*Streps.* Nay, now by father Jove,
I cannot choose but see them—precious creatures!
For in good faith here's plenty and to spare.

#### Enter Chorus of Clouds.

*Soc.* And didst thou doubt if they were goddesses?
*Streps.* Not I, so help me! only I'd a notion
That they were fog, and dew, and dusty vapor.
*Soc.* For shame! Why, man, these are the nursing-mothers
Of all our famous sophists, fortune-tellers,
Quacks, medicine-mongers, bards bombastical,
Chorus projectors, star interpreters,
And wonder-making cheats—the gang of idlers,

Who pay them for their feeding with good store
Of flattery and mouth-worship.

    *Streps.* Now I see
Whom we may thank for driving them along
At such a furious dithyrambic rate,
Sun-shadowing clouds of many-color'd hues,
Air-rending tempests, hundred-headed Typhons;
Now rousing, rattling them about our ears,
Now gently wafting them adown the sky,
Moist, airy, bending, bursting into showers;
For all which fine descriptions these poor knaves
Dine daintily on scraps.

    *Soc.* And proper fare;
What better do they merit?

    *Streps.* Under favor,
If these be clouds, (d'you mark me?) very clouds,
How came they metamorphosed into women?
Clouds are not such as these.

    *Soc.* And what else are they?

    *Streps.* 'Troth, I can't rightly tell, but I should guess
Something like flakes of wool, not women, sure;
And look, these dames have noses.

    *Soc.* Hark you, friend,
I'll put a question to you.

    *Streps.* Out with it!
Be quick; let's have it.

    *Soc.* This it is in short—
Hast thou ne'er seen a cloud, which thou couldst fancy
Shaped like a centaur, leopard, wolf or bull?

    *Streps.* Yea, marry, have I, and what then?

    *Soc.* Why then,
Clouds can assume what shapes they will, believe me;
For instance: should they spy some hairy clown
Rugged and rough, and like the unlicked cub
Of Xenophantes, straight they turn to centaurs,
And kick at him for vengeance.

    *Streps.* Well done, Clouds!
But should they spy that peculating knave,
Simon—that public thief—how would they treat him?

    *Soc.* As wolves—in character most like his own.

    *Streps.* Aye, there it is now; when they saw Cleony-
mus,

That dastard runaway, they turned to hinds
In honor of his cowardice.

    *Soc.* And now,
Having seen Cleisthenes, to mock his lewdness
They changed themselves to women.

    *Streps.* Welcome, ladies!
Imperial ladies, welcome! An' it please
Your highnesses so far to grace a mortal,
Give me a touch of your celestial voices.

    *Clouds.* Hail, grandsire! who at this late hour of life
Wouldst go to school for cunning; and all hail,
Thou prince pontifical of quirks and quibbles,
Speak thy full mind, make known thy wants and wishes!
Thee and our worthy Prodicus excepted,
Not one of all your sophists have our ear:
Him for his wit and learning we esteem,
Thee for thy proud deportment and high looks,
In bare-foot beggary strutting up and down,
Content to suffer mockery for our sake,
And carry a grave face whilst others laugh.

    *Streps.* Oh! mother Earth, was ever voice like this,
So reverend, so portentous, so divine?

    *Soc.* These are your only deities, all else
I flout at.

    *Streps.* Hold! Olympian Jupiter—
Is he no god?

    *Soc.* What Jupiter? what god?
Pr'ythee no more—away with him at once!

    *Streps.* Say'st thou? Who gives us rain? answer me that:

    *Soc.* These give us rain; as I will straight demonstrate:
Come on now—When did you e'er see it rain
Without a cloud? If Jupiter gives rain,
Let him rain down his favors in the sunshine
Nor ask the clouds to help him.

    *Streps.* You have hit it.
'Tis so; heaven help me! I did think till now,
When 'twas his godship's pleasure, he made water
Into a sieve and gave the earth a shower.
But hark ye me, who thunders? tell me that:
For then it is I tremble.

    *Soc.* These—these thunder.
When they are impelled

*Streps.* How, blasphemer, how?

*Soc.* When they are charg'd with vapors full to th' burst-
 ing,
And bandied to and fro against each other,
Then with the shock they burst and crack amain.

*Streps.* And who is he that jowls them thus together
But Zeus himself?

*Soc.* Zeus! 'tis not Zeus that does it,
But the ætherial Vortex.

*Streps.* What is he?
I never heard of him; is he not Zeus?
Or is Zeus put aside and Vortex crown'd
King of Olympus in his state and place?
But let me learn some more of this same thunder.

*Soc.* Have you not learnt? I told you how the Clouds,
Being surcharged with vapor, rush together,
And, in the conflict, shake the poles with thunder.

*Streps.* Let that pass,
And tell me of the lightning, whose quick flash
Burns us to cinders; that, at least, great Zeus
Keeps in reserve to launch at perjury.

*Soc.* Dunce, dotard! were you born before the flood
To talk of perjury, whilst Simon breathes,
Theorus and Cleonymus, whilst they,
Thrice-perjured villains, brave the lightning's stroke,
And gaze the heavens unscorched? Would these escape?
Why, man, Jove's random fires strike his own fane,
Strike Sunium's guiltless top, strike the dumb oak,
Who never yet broke faith or falsely swore.

*Streps.* It may be so, good sooth! You talk this well:
But I would fain be taught the natural cause
Of these appearances.

*Soc.* Mark. When the winds,
In their free courses check'd, are pent and purs'd,
As 'twere within a bladder, stretching then
And struggling for expansion, they burst forth
With cracks so fierce as sets the air on fire.

*Streps.* The devil they do! why, now the murder's out·

*Clouds.* The envy of all Athens shalt thou be,
Happy old man, who from our lips dost suck
Into thy ears true wisdom, so thou art
But wise to learn, and studious to retain

What thou hast learnt; patient to bear the blows
And buffets of hard fortune; to persist,
Doing or suffering; firmly to abide
Hunger and cold, not craving where to dine,
To drink, to sport, and trifle time away;
But holding that for best, which best becomes
A man who means to carry all things through
Neatly, expertly, perfect at all points,
With head, hands, tongue, to force his way to fortune.

   *Streps.* Be confident; I give myself for one
Of a tough heart, watchful as care can make me,
A frugal, pinching fellow, that can sup
Upon a sprig of savory and to bed;
I am your man for this, hard as an anvil.

   *Soc.* 'Tis well, so you will ratify your faith
In these our deities—CHAOS and CLOUDS
And SPEECH—to these, and only these, adhere.

   *Streps.* If from this hour henceforth I ever waste
A single thought on any other gods,
Or give them sacrifice, libation, incense,
Nay, even common courtesy, renounce me.

   *Clouds.* Speak your wish boldly, then, so shall you prosper,
As you obey and worship us, and study
The wholesome art of thriving.

   *Streps.* Gracious ladies,
I ask no mighty favor, simply this—
Let me but distance every tongue in Greece,
And run 'em out of sight a hundred lengths.

   *Clouds.* Is that all?—then we are your friends to serve you;
We will endow thee with such powers of speech,
As henceforth not a demagogue in Athens
Shall spout such popular harangues as thou shalt.

   *Streps.* A fig for powers of spouting! give me powers
Of non-suiting my creditors.

   *Clouds.* A trifle—
Granted as soon as asked; only be bold,
And show yourself obedient to your teachers.

   *Streps.* With your help so I will, being undone,
Stript of my pelf by these high-blooded cattle,
And a fine dame, the torment of my life.
Now let them work their wicked will upon me;
They're welcome to my carcass: let 'em claw it.

Starve it with thirst and hunger, fry it, freeze it,
Nay, flay the very skin off; 'tis their own;
So that I may but fob my creditors,
Let the world talk; I care not though it call me
A bold-faced, loud-tongued, overbearing bully;
A shameless, vile, prevaricating cheat;
A tricking, quibbling, double-dealing knave;
A prating, pettifogging limb o' the law;
A sly old fox, a perjurer, a hang-dog;
A ragamuffin made of shreds and patches,
The leavings of a dunghill. Let 'em rail,
Yea, marry, let 'em turn my guts to fiddle-strings.
May my bread be my poison! if I care.

    *Clouds.* This fellow hath a prompt and daring
        spirit—
Come hither, sir; do you perceive and feel
What great and glorious fame you shall acquire
By this our schooling of you?

    *Streps.* What, I pray you?

    *Clouds.* What, but to live the envy of mankind
Under our patronage.

    *Streps.* What shall I see
Those halcyon days?

    *Clouds.* Then shall your doors be thronged
With clients waiting for your coming forth,
All eager to consult you, pressing all
To catch a word from you, with abstracts, briefs,
And cases ready drawn for your opinion.
(*To Socrates*) But come, begin and lecture this old fellow:
Sift him, that we may see what meal he's made of.

    *Soc.* Hark ye, let's hear what principles you hold,
That these being known, I may apply such tools
As tally with your stuff.

    *Streps.* Tools! by the gods;
Are you about to spring a mine upon me?

    *Soc.* Not so, but simply in the way of practice
To try your memory.

    *Streps.* Oh! as for that
My memory is of two sorts, long and short:
With them that owe me aught, it never fails:
My creditors, indeed, complain of it
As very apt to leak and lose its reck'ning,

*Soc.* But let us hear if nature hath endow'd you
With any grace of speaking.

*Streps.* None of speaking,
But a most apt propensity to cheating.

*Soc.* If this be all, how can you hope to learn?

*Streps.* Fear me not, never break your head for that.

*Soc.* Well, then be quick, and when I speak of things
Mysterious and profound, see that you make
No boggling, but— .

*Streps.* I understand your meaning;
You'd have me bolt philosophy by mouthfuls,
Just like a hungry cur.

*Soc.* Oh! brutal, gross
And barbarous ignorance! I much suspect,
Old as thou art, thou must be taught with stripes.
Tell me now, when thou art beaten, what dost feel?

*Streps.* The blows of him that beats me do I feel;
But having breathed a while, I lay my action
And cite my witnesses; anon, more cool,
I bring my cause into the court, and sue
For damages.

*Soc.* Strip off your cloak! prepare.

*Streps.* Prepare for what? What crime have I committed?

*Soc.* None; but the rule and custom is with us
That all shall enter naked.

*Streps.* And why naked?
I come with no search-warrant, fear me not:
I'll carry nought away with me.

*Soc.* No matter;
Conform yourself, and strip.

*Streps.* And if I do,
Tell me, for my encouragement, to which
Of all your scholars will you liken me.

*Soc.* You shall be call'd a second Chærephon.*

*Streps.* Ah! Chærephon is but another name
For a dead corpse,—excuse me.

*Soc.* No more words:
Pluck up your courage, answer not, but follow;
Haste and be perfected.

*Streps.* Give me my dole

* A pupil of Socrates, notoriously thin and pale.

Of honey-cake* in hand, and pass me on;
Ne'er trust me if I do not quake and tremble
As if the cavern of Trophonius yawn'd,
And I were stepping in.
    *Soc.* What ails you? enter!
Why do you halt and loiter at the door?
         [*Socrates and Strepsiades enter the house.*
*Clouds.* Go, brave adventurer, proceed!
    May fortune crown the gallant deed;
    Though far advanced in life's last stage,
    Spurning the infirmities of age,
    Thou can'st to youthful labors rise,
    And boldly struggle to be wise.

### The Chorus of Birds.

Ye children of man! whose life is a span,
Protracted with sorrow from day to day;
Naked and featherless, feeble and querulous,
Sickly, calamitous creatures of clay!
Attend to the words of the sovereign birds,
Immortal, illustrious lords of the air,
Who survey from on high, with a merciful eye,
Your struggles of misery, labor and care.
Whence you may learn and clearly discern
Such truths as attract your inquisitive turn—
Which is busied of late with a mighty debate,
A profound speculation about the creation,
And organical life and chaotical strife—
With various notions of heavenly motions,
And rivers and oceans, and valleys and mountains,
And sources of fountains, and meteors on high,
And stars in the sky. . . . We propose by-and-by
(If you'll listen and hear) to make it all clear.
    All lessons of primary daily concern
You have learned from the birds (and continue to learn),
Your best benefactors and early instructors.
We give you the warnings of seasons returning:
When the cranes are arranged, and muster afloat

*Honey-cake was used in religious ceremonies in the cave of Trophonius.

In the middle air, with a creaking note,
Steering away to the Libyan sands,
Then careful farmers sow their lands;
The craggy vessel is hauled ashore;
The sail, the ropes, the rudder, and oar
Are all unshipped and housed in store.
The shepherd is warned, by the kite re-appearing,
To muster his flock and be ready for shearing.
You quit your old cloak at the swallow's behest,
In assurance of summer, and purchase a vest.

    For Delphi, for Ammon, Dodona — in fine,
For every oracular temple and shrine—
The birds are a substitute, equal and fair;
For on us you depend, and to us you repair
For counsel and aid when a marriage is made—
A purchase, a bargain, or venture in trade:
Unlucky or lucky, whatever has struck ye—
A voice in the street, or a slave that you meet,
A name or a word by chance overheard—
If you deem it an omen you call it a *bird;*
And if birds are your omens, it clearly will follow
That birds are a proper prophetic Apollo.

### The Beggar's Suit.

In "The Acharnians" the countryman Dicæopolis, tired of the
war with Sparta, makes a private peace with the enemy. When this
is discovered, he is brought before the Athenian Assembly to be tried
for treason. As humble suitors were more likely to receive mercy, he
wishes to appear in a poor dress. The poet represents him as repairing
to the house of Euripides, who in his tragedies had brought on the
stage various heroes in distress, and begging for the dress of one of
these.

    *Servant.* Who's there?
    *Dicæopolis.* Euripides within?
    *Serv.* Within, yet not within. You comprehend me?
    *Dic.* Within and not within! why, what d'ye mean?
    *Serv.* I speak correctly, old sire! his outward man
Is in the garret writing tragedy;
While his essential being is abroad,
Pursuing whimsies in the world of fancy.
    *Dic.* O happy Euripides, with such a servant,
So clever and accomplished!—Call him out.

*Serv.* It's quite impossible.

*Dic.* But it must be done.

Positively and absolutely I must see him;
Or I must stand here rapping at the door.
Euripides! Euripides! come down,
If ever you came down in all your life!
'Tis I—'tis Dicæopolis from Chollidæ.

*Euripides.* I'm not at leisure to come down.

*Dic.* Perhaps—

But here's the scene-shifter can wheel you round.*

*Eur.* It cannot be.

*Dic.* But, however, notwithstanding——

*Eur.* Well, there then, I'm wheeled round; for I had not
time

For coming down.

*Dic.* Euripides, I say!

*Eur.* What say ye?

*Dic.* Euripides! Euripides!

Good lawk, you're there! up-stairs! you write up-stairs,
Instead of the ground floor? always up-stairs?
Well, now, that's odd!   But, dear Euripides,
If you had but a suit of rags that you could lend me!
You're he that brings out cripples in your tragedies,
A'n't ye?   You're the new poet, he that writes
Those characters of beggars and blind people?
Well, dear Euripides, if you could but lend me
A suit of tatters from a cast-off tragedy!
For mercy's sake, for I'm obliged to make
A speech in my own defence before the Chorus,
A long pathetic speech, this very day;
And if it fails, the doom of death betides me.

*Eur.* Say, what d'ye seek? is it the woful garb
In which the wretched aged Æneus acted?

*Dic.* No, 'twas a wretcheder man than Æneus, much.

*Eur.* Was it blind Phœnix?

*Dic.* No, not Phœnix, no.

A fellow a great deal wretcheder than Phœnix.

*Eur.* Whom may he mean! or whose the robe may suit
him!

Speak you of Philoctetes, friend, the beggar?

* The only change of scene on the Athenian stage was made by
wheeling round the semi-circular house which stood at the back.

*Dic.* You miss the mark a hundred miles in beggary.

*Eur.* I reach you: 'twas the robe worn by Bellerophon—

*Dic.* 'Twas one, in truth, of the same stamp: lame, beg-
garly,—

A man that had large gift of speech and tongue.

*Eur* 'Tis Telephus of Mysia.

*Dic.* Thou hast hit it.

Thou wouldst not do the thing might cross my ends:—

The loan of those same sorry rags I beg you.

*Eur.* (*to his servant*). Reach them, and crown his wishes,
boy—they lie

Above the Thyestean rags, midway

'Twixt them and Ino's.

*Serv.* (*to Dicæopolis*). Sir, you are possess'd

Of all you wish.

*Dic.* (*dressing himself*). Now Jove (and as the god

Of loop'd and window'd raggedness I pray you)

Your sacred blessing, while I try to garb me

In plight most miserable.   Thou hast done me

Most timely grace, Euripides:—wouldst win

My whole affection? add a loan (it were

Not fitting to divorce it from these rags),

And cast upon my head a Mysian bonnet.

I must put on the beggar, and dislikening

The truth, be what I am, and seem what I

Am not—possessing the spectators here

Of my true bearing, while the Chorus gape,

Unweeting who it is that speaks, and bearing

All taunts and jeers I choose to put upon them.

*Eur.* Thou show'st a teeming wit—want shall not fool it.
(*giving a bonnet*).

*Dic.* For thee, heaven prosper thee;—for Telephus

Befall what lies within my thoughts: I have

A pregnant wit, and words flow plentifully.

But softly, I must have a beggar's staff.

*Eur.* Here's one unto your hand, take it, and let

Your back cast shadow on these doors.

*Dic.* Seest, my soul,

That we must fain divorce us from this gate?

And yet my needs still ask a world of tire;

Rub oil upon thee, soul;—twist, wriggle, crouch,

Till he do crown thy wishes.   Good Euripides,

Favor me with a beggar's basket; 'tis
No matter though a torch have singed it.
   *Eur.* What's thy need on't?
   *Dic.* None—beyond the wish to have it.
   *Eur.* Away, and quit my doors: thou breedest trouble.
   *Dic.* (*aside*). A pestilence upon thee! (*Aloud*) Happy bard,
Heaven fortune thee, as erst thy lady mother!
   *Eur.* Will thou begone?
   *Dic.* Not till I have my craving:
One little cup, so please you; one whose lip
Hath lost its wholeness—
   *Eur.* Take it and begone:
Your presence breeds disturbance.
   *Dic.* But, sweet Euripides! I fain would have
A pipkin with a cleanly sponge to wipe it.
   *Eur.* The man will rob me of a tragedy complete.
Content your wish with this, and now away (*giving a pipkin*).
   *Dic.* I have an ear to your request: one thing
Remains: that one not granted me—I am
A ruin'd man;—crown it, and I am gone
For ever.  Telephus bore leaves and herbs;—
A scantling of the same within my basket.
   *Eur.* The man will be my ruin; see, 'tis granted (*giving
     him leaves*):
A whole play lost, as I'm a living man.
   *Dic.* This timely grace completes me: I retire—
It is too plain my presence breeds offence.
These eyes know not to turn their view discreet
On mighty men and pay them terms of honor—
A plague upon't, was ever such a wretch!
I have forgot the primest thing of all.
(*Addressing Euripides*) Thou dearest, best of men—I pray
     thee now
With most petitionary vehemence—
Crown but this one, one longing; if I ask
Aught more, all plagues and maladies light on me!—
Throw for the tender mercy one small potherb—
Thou canst not lack,—thy mother will supply thee.*
   *Eur.* Most frontless impudence! shut-to the door, boy.

* The enemies of Euripides said that his mother had been a seller
of potherbs.

## MENANDER.

THOUGH there are but few fragments of the comedies of Menander, he has elicited high praise both from ancient and modern critics. These fragments show, more than other Greek writings, the modern spirit. As Aristophanes was the leader of the Attic Old, or Political Comedy, so Menander was the leader of the New Comedy, or comedy of private life and manners. He wrote more than a hundred comedies, not one of which survives. Latin adaptations of them were made by Terence, who thus won greater fame than his original. The great Cæsar, who was a keen critic, pronounced the Roman writer but a "semi-Menander." These Latin plays became models for later Europe whenever the drama revived. Menander was born in 342 B.C. and died in 291. His writings show the influence of the philosopher Epicurus, whom he describes as rescuing Greece "from unreason as Themistocles had rescued her from slavery."

### MAN'S LIFE.

SUPPOSE some god should say, "Die when thou wilt,
Mortal, expect another life on earth;
And, for that life make choice of all creation,
What thou wilt be—dog, sheep, goat, man or horse;
For live again thou must, it is thy fate;
Choose only in what form—there thou art free."
So help me, Crato, I would fairly answer,—
Let me be all things, anything but man!
He only of all creatures feels affliction.
The generous horse is valued for his worth,
And dog by merit is preferred to dog;
The warrior cock is pampered for his courage,
And awes the baser brood—But what is man?
Truth, virtue, valor,—how do they avail him?
Of this world's good the first and greatest share
Is flattery's prize; the informer takes the next,
And barefaced knavery garbles what is left:
I'd rather be an ass than what I am,
And see these villains lord it o'er their betters.

## Is Life Worth Living?

THE lot of all most fortunate is his,
Who, having stayed just long enough on earth
To feast his sight with the fair face of Nature,
Sun, sea, and clouds, and heaven's bright starry fires,
Drops without pain into an early grave.
For what is life, the longest life of man,
But the same scene repeated o'er and o'er?
A few more lingering days to be consumed
In throngs and crowds, with sharpers, knaves and thieves;
From such the speediest riddance is the best.

## The Proper Use of Wealth.

WEAK is the vanity that boasts of riches,
For they are fleeting things ; were they not such,
Could they be yours to all succeeding time,
'Twere wise to let none share in the possession ;
But, if whate'er you have is held of Fortune ;
And not of right inherent, why, my father,
Why, with such niggardly jealousy engross
What the next hour may ravish from your grasp,
And cast into some worthless favorite's lap?
Snatch then the swift occasion while 'tis yours ;
Put this unstable boon to noble uses ;
Foster the wants of men, impart your wealth,
And purchase friends ; 'twill be more lasting treasure,
And when misfortune comes, your best resource.

## PHILEMON.

PHILEMON, though inferior to Menander, was a great favorite with
the Athenians, and often defeated his rival in the dramatic contests.
Though born at Soli, in Cilicia, he spent most of his life in Athens,
where he had been admitted to citizenship. He began to exhibit plays
about 330 B.C., and is said to have composed altogether ninety-seven,
yet only a few fragments of them remain. His favorite subjects were
love intrigues, as was usually the case in the New Comedy, which he
inaugurated. He is said to have died in the theatre, during the performance of one of his own compositions.

## CHAPTER XVII.

### THE DECLINE OF THE DRAMA.

Aeschylus, Sophocles, and Euripides were regarded by the
ancient Greeks as the great poets of tragedy. They were frequently called the Three Tragic Poets, it being thought
unnecessary to explain who were thus designated. They stood
unequalled, alone, and subsequent ages have produced none
greater. Their tragedies retained their popularity with the
people and, since acting was now a profession, ambitious men
frequently reproduced the old plays at the Dionysia. Realizing the danger which threatened their incomparable poets,
the Athenians decreed that authentic copies of all the tragedies written by the immortal three be placed in the archives,
and that whenever they were rendered on the stage, an officer
should attend with a copy of the text in hand, in order to see
that each was given word for word as the poet had composed it.

Lesser poets came forward with their dramas, and each
returning spring brought its ambitious writers, eager to compete for the prize. However, none of these plays have come
down to us and they were not considered remarkable by the
age which witnessed them. Athens long held her pre-eminence in the dramatic world, and poets of Asia Minor, and
other districts out of Attica, wished to have their productions represented first in the theatre where the masters of
tragedy had competed. With these new plays, some of the
older tragedies would be produced, but naturally the special
interest and excitement centered around the new production.

Although a large number of lesser writers continued to
bring forth new plays, the Greek tragedy sank into a decline.
None dared to reconstruct it on a basis which might have
given it new life and vigour. The truth was that the old
myths no longer appealed to the people as they had once done.
Times had changed entirely; new ideas, new ideals and interests absorbed the thinking man. Had one arisen with the

courage of Euripides, he might have grasped the situation and met it fairly. Once started upon different lines, the history of Greek drama might have been totally different. However, such was not destined to be the course of events. Greece was declining; her vitality was gone. That mental empire wherein she had excelled had passed its zenith, and the work of diffusion alone remained.

After the fourth century Athens lost her superiority in dramatic art. As she gradually declined, Alexandria became the intellectual center of the ancient world. Meantime, with the spread of Hellenism, the drama penetrated everywhere, aiding naturally in the diffusion of Greek civilization and culture. Each little center had its theatre and celebrated its Dionysia. After the conquests of Alexander, Greek dramas were performed in every land where Greek was spoken. However, their purely religious character was shortly lost and in the second century before Christ, plays were given upon all important state festivals. A victory might be an occasion for a series of plays, or some holiday would be celebrated thus. Sometimes tragedies were included among various amusements during a festal week.

It was the privilege of the prince or the general to provide plays, and never in ancient Greece was it left for private individuals to produce them for their own personal advantage, nor was it conducted as a money-making enterprise.

"One of the earliest of the secular performances is that which was given by Philip of Macedon in honor of his daughter's marriage and which was rendered memorable by his assassination. His son, Alexander the Great, also took the keenest delight in the theatre, and was accustomed to celebrate the close of his campaigns with theatrical exhibitions on a scale of unapproachable splendour. Pavilions of silver and gold were erected at such times, for the reception of the guests; the best actors were hired from every city of Greece; and subject kings were often compelled to fill the office of choregi. On one occasion no less than 3,000 performers were collected together to take part in the various musical and dramatic competitions. From this time forward gorgeous dramatic spectacles became a favorite amusement with the famous princes of the time. Antiochus the Great is said to have surpassed all previous monarchs in the splendour of his shows, and Antony and Cleopatra, in the winter before the final campaign against Augustus, wasted their time at Samos in a long series of similar entertainments." [1]

As has already been noted, the drama was given considerable attention in Alexandria as it declined in Athens. In this city gifted men of letters congregated and many plays were produced here. However, they seem to have testified to the extensive learning of their authors rather than to any special native genius, and they were greatly affected by the philosophy of the time. Logic and debate left their stamp upon them, and although none have come down to us from this period, we may judge from comments made upon them by contemporaries that they were not very successful.

After the decline of letters at Alexandria, the drama steadily declined. It was never popular in Rome, especially during the later periods. The Romans witnessed real tragedy in the arena and after scenes in the Coliseum. mere plays were deemed too mild by far to satisfy their audiences.

[1] Haigh: The Attic Theatre.

GREEK TRIREME.

# PHILOSOPHY

PHILOSOPHY is the systematic enquiry into the deepest and most elementary problems of existence. It tries to answer the questions, What is the world? What is God? What is man? What is the relationship between these? What is duty? Is there a life after death? Such questions are at once the deepest and the most universal. Every human being asks them at times. The child asks them and they grow in importance with our growth. Philosophy, therefore, deals with a subject about which we all want to know. But the great minds that have spoken on this subject have expressed themselves in a technical language of abstract words that carry little meaning to the every-day reader. Also these treatises are long and wearisome and often the writer does not even fully grasp his own meaning and is still less able to impart it. So the subject needs popularizing into shorter form and simpler language and books that do this deserve well of the public.

There is a general impression that philosophers have never agreed and never arrived at any conclusions—that philosophy is a barren field where the mind wanders aimlessly amid interminable discussions. Such is really not the case. Philosophy shows progress. Every great thinker has thrown some new light on his topic and it is easier for one to follow where another has gone before. But just as all our modern astronomers are busy mapping the heavens and the heavens are vast enough to keep them all busy and each can add but a little part to the total, so in the mighty circle of human thought the stars of truth are numerous enough to give all the thinkers something to do in marking out their relationships and no one mind has been great

87

enough to comprehend them all and see them as one harmonious and stupendous whole.  We need not be surprised, then, to find that as each thinker has given his answer, he has been followed by another who has said, "Your answer is defective here and here, you have not given importance enough to this fact, you have totally overlooked that, thus and so should have been your answer."  Nor need we expect that any philosopher will put truth into final and unchangeable formulas satisfactory to later generations.  The mind of man marches onward, and just as our sun with the whole planetary system, beside all their lesser movements, is traversing an unknown path through the vast distances of inter-stellar space, so the human soul in its myriad embodiments enters new fields of experience as the centuries come and go.  In the ages of the past men sought for final and unchangeable statements of truth, thought of reality as finished and immovable.  Today we perceive everything in motion, growing, expanding, developing, destined to still go on in the future as in the past.  Thus in the different fields of knowledge and human study we no longer expect a finished product but an unfinished fabric of human thought on which the weavers are still at work.  We look at all studies historically; we say, this man did so much, after him another made that addition, and so on through the lives of many workers to the present moment.  Nor is the present moment final, the men who come after us will see more clearly than we, more comprehensively.

The questions of philosophy found their first systematic expression in ancient Greece where the human intellect reached a stage of acuteness never since surpassed.  One question, debated from the time of Plato and Aristotle down through the middle ages, was this: Are the classes of objects only names or have they a real existence?  To illustrate: we see a great many individual horses of various forms.  From them we form the abstract idea, Horse.  This idea comprehends all horses.  The question is, has this idea "horse" any reality other than a name for a class?  No, said the common-sense people, it is only a *name* and is not real as the individual horse is real.  Philosophers who made this answer were called nominalists from the Latin word nomen, a *name*.  Now there were other philosophers who said, must there not exist somewhere a pattern horse after which all these individual horses are made?  Must there not be a controlling creative thought from which the individuals spring and which keeps them within the bounds of horse-hood? Must not the creative idea "horse" precede and control the actual individual horses? And if so is not the controlling idea greater, more *real* than the individual facts? Yes, said Plato, these creative ideas are the great *realities* from which any individual is only an unimportant incident. Now where do these dominating, creative, pattern ideas exist? They exist, said Plato, in the mind of God and are the supremely real and important things. Such men were called *realists* because they affirmed that universal abstract ideas had a *real* existence and were not mere *names*. There is not space in this Introduction to show that this debate between Nominalism and Realism which occupied the acutest minds from Plato to Francis Bacon is not merely academic but has a profound religious bearing.

Another great question of Philosophy discussed through all the centuries is the relationship between mind and matter. It is the fundamental question of questions. It has had no final answer. But we can think more clearly on it by knowing the history of human thought about it. The problem may be outlined thus: We are conscious through our senses of an outer world of color, form, heat and cold, hardness or softness, etc.

We are also conscious of ourselves as thinkers, having an inner life of reason, feeling, will. Now the question is, How are you, the thinker, related to the outside world? Take iron, for instance, is there any similarity between iron and thought? Iron through sight and touch produces certain ideas in our mind, weight, hardness, coldness, size, etc., produces a mental image in short. Is the mental image the same as the iron itself? If not wherein is the difference? If iron is something different from thought how can thought ever understand it? Does it exist in thought or independent of all thought? Putting it in a universal form, does the outer world exist independent of all thought or does it have an existence only in and for thought? On this question the great thinkers of the world have divided. On the one side what are known as Materialists have said: The outer world is the supreme reality, the human mind is a product of it. The brain secretes thought as the liver secretes bile, or thought comes from matter as light is generated from the friction of an electric current running through carbon.

Thought is a rather unimportant by-product of the material world. Thought burns as long as the machinery of the body runs right. Derange or stop the machinery and the light of thought goes out forever. On the other side what are known as Idealists have said, What you first know and all you ever know or ever can know is yourself as thinker and your thoughts. What you call the outer world is simply your thought about something which you recognize as not yourself. If there existed something different from thought and independent of it you could never know it, since all you can ever know are thoughts! What you call iron is simply a collection of thoughts, such as form, hardness, size, weight, color, resistance, etc. That some so-called attributes do not really exist in the object can be easily seen, color, for instance, comes from sunlight and not from the object, weight is the attraction of gravitation, etc. Start with the outer universe, cry the materialists, and how insignificant is man—a mere accidental and ephemeral atom in the total of immensity! Start with man, cry the idealists, and see him as the measure of the universe!—from a few twitches of nerves and muscles he builds within the magic of his thought, worlds, constellations, a universe of ordered beauty and sublimity!

All the grace and glory of space and time come from within. Man is the architect of his universe, since all he gets from the outside are merely vibrations of the nerves of touch and taste, sight and hearing! This outer world, says the idealist, is a thought-universe, springing from the mind of the infinite thinker, God! We are able to think it because it is His thought. We all see it alike because it is real, real with all the reality of God! But God's reality is a thought-reality! For the idealist the universe is not an immense mass of inanimate matter but is through and through alive, the living expression of a Living Thinker. Man is a smaller thinker made in the image of the Greater, therefore, able to understand Him with ever increasing ability.

Between these two extremes of materialism and idealism have been thinkers of every shade of compromise.

The history of philosophy is indeed a splendid drama of human thought. Dark and despairing, fatalistic and pessimistic, agnostic and sceptic, have been at times the visions of philosophers. But greater philosophers have risen with higher vision to confute them and raise again trust in God, duty, and immortality.

Beside the great Greek philosophers, Plato and Aristotle, there are other world-famous names, belonging to modern times, Bacon, Hobbes, Locke, Berkeley, Hume, in England; abroad, Descartes, Spinoza, Leibnitz, Kant, Fichte, Schelling, Hegel, Schopenhauer; nearer our own day, Hamilton, Compte, Herbert Spencer. Among many living philosophers none stand higher than Prof. Josiah Royce of Harvard, who ably holds aloft the banner of idealism. Prof. James of Harvard has recently advanced the doctrine of Pragmatism, simply a new dress for utilitarianism.

Among modern names Kant and Hegel are supreme, Hegel the greatest Idealist of them all. He has produced a powerful effect not only on philosophy but on modern religious views. His philosophic definition and acceptance of the doctrine of the Trinity has reconciled rationalism and orthodoxy as to the central doctrine of Christianity.

We may sum up the value of philosophy to the average man as follows:

It gives the best answers to the greatest questions.

It deepens and broadens his mental outlook.

It makes him familiar with some of the greatest names of history and literature.

It gives him an adequate basis to think for himself.

It shows him that the great thoughts and faiths of all religions—God, duty, and immortality—have a solid basis in the teaching of all the greatest philosophers, for the greatest names in philosophy taught and maintained these fundamental truths.

## CHAPTER XVIII.

### Early Greek Philosophy.

In earliest times of which we have record, the Greeks were satisfied to explain the origin of the world according to old myths. Who made the world? asked the Hellenes, in their infancy. And the answer which they gave was: The gods made it. The mighty ones of Olympus fashioned the earth, separated it from the seas, clothed it with verdure, and filled it with birds and animals. Finally they created men, or perhaps he developed from the stones of the field.

After awhile, however, such fanciful and ingenious answers no longer satisfied. If the gods made the world, from what did they make it? The first Greek who attempted to solve the problem was Thales, born in Miletus about 600 B. C. Having foretold an eclipse of the sun, he was thenceforth regarded as a wise man by his contemporaries. Might there not, he questioned, be some one element from which everything that we see about us once emanated, and to which everything would ultimately return? Thales concluded that this element was water—*water* was the *ultimate reality*.

The ancient Greeks believed that the river Oceanus encircled the earth. Water refreshed all vegetation and supported all life. Moreover, water was very important to the Ionic cities—it was their pathway to industry and wealth. All these facts may have had something to do with the solution Thales reached in his problem.

Anaximander and Anaximenes shortly followed. The former said that the world was made of the *infinite;* the latter concluded that *vapor* was the ultimate reality.

Heracleitus, born in Ephesus about 500 B. C., attempted to solve the same problem, and he said that fire was the first element from which all emanated and to which all would return. Change, according to his theory, was the law of the universe. "Nothing is constant but the law of change itself."

This conception was quickly met by Parmenides, who held that there was no such thing as change. Nothing changed; what we see as change is mere delusion.

Empedocles, a medicine-man of Sicily, advanced beyond his predecessors when he taught that one should assume nothing; every step must be proven by experiment. In place of one world-element, he substituted four,—earth, air, fire and water; to these he added two principles: love and hate. These accounted for the universe as we know it. The four elements formed the world, and the principles of love governed all and gave all a harmonious unity. Unfortunately hate came in to destroy the harmony, and brought about finally the conditions as we know them.

Anaxagoras, born about 500 B. C., was a contemporary and a friend of Pericles. He advanced the idea that the universe was made of quality atoms—atoms of heat, cold, color, etc. Everything around us has some atoms of every kind within it. It is the kind predominating which give it character. Hardness, for example, predominates in a stone; coldness in ice, etc. The sun, he said, was not a god at all, but a mass of molten fire, larger even than the Peloponnesus.

This last theory proved too much for the abused patience of the Athenians. They held too closely to the oldtime religion to consent to see their gods displaced so abruptly. During his life Anaxagoras saw Socrates put to death by the Athenians, and a charge of impiety was brought against him, whereupon he left the city. He said he had seen Athens sin once, and he could not permit her to do so a second time.

When we read the simple, childlike answers which the early Greek philosophers gave to the creation problem, we smile as we think how far in advance of them the young school boy is today. But we must not lose sight of the fact that these men had none to help them in their eager search for truth in the field of science—for science and philosophy were not separated until long after this. If every result of modern scientific inquiry were to be eliminated from the world today, together with all those persons who have studied about the planet on which we live, it might take humanity centuries to overtake the scientific knowledge thus far attained, and the

first efforts made might prove no more nearly right than those
offered so ingeniously by Thales and his materialistic successors. How far in advance of their times they were we
may judge when we find the masses furious at the suggestion
that the sun after all was not a god.

During this period—the middle of the fifth century—Zeno
appeared. He has often been misunderstood, and thought to
have been a sceptic who doubted everything. As a matter of
fact, he simply sought to show that the Pythagorians, a philosophical brotherhood then influential, had failed entirely in
their attempt to explain the nature of the world. His method
of argument was later adopted by the sceptics. For example,
he used to confront his opponents with something like this:
An arrow must either move in the place where it is or in the
place where it isn't. If it moves in the place where it is, it is
not in the place; if it moves in the place where it isn't, that is
manifestly impossible.

Lucippus and his pupil Democritus were far in advance of
their age. Democritus believed the world to be composed
of physical atoms, countless and indivisible. Again, in the
field of ethics, Democritus put things on a reasonable basis.
That is moral, he held, which is conducive to happiness,
immoral if it deters from human happiness. In making happiness the test he was anticipating the Epicurean School.

The Sophists, who came into prominence during the fifth
century, were evidently an outgrowth of their age. Greece
had passed from the rule of the oligarchs into government by
the people. He who could influence the masses to his way of
thinking might become their leader. Those who had political
ambitions needed teachers in rhetoric and dialects, or debate.
To meet the demand, the Sophists arose.

Philosophers had thus far had followers, to be sure, and
these they had instructed in their particular theories. Never,
however, had they taken compensation for such service, and
for some time the Sophists were in disrepute because they took
money for teaching. Many of their arguments were mere
hair-splitting contests, where the wrong often won out against
the right. Aristophanes presented a comedy in which a father
desired his son—a disciple of this new learning—to teach him

how he might escape paying his debts. The son proved by argument that he owed no one, then took the old man's property away from him and appropriated it for himself.

Socrates, born in 469 B. C., has often been classed as a Sophist, and he followed the system of dialectics common to them. But he had a worthy motive in his questioning: he attempted to ascertain if possible some few points upon which men were agreed. He noticed that when one man used a word, or expressed an idea, it meant one thing, and the same word, or same sentiment seemed to have a different meaning when expressed by another. To find some truths upon which they all agreed, he frequently questioned men, and almost drove them to distraction by his inquiries.

Socrates wore but one garment—the himation—summer or winter. He cared nothing for the comforts of life; even upon a northern campaign he refused to wear sandals, and in every respect lived in the greatest simplicity. This homely man might be seen constantly in the market place, on street corners,—anywhere, everywhere that men gathered, talking with them. He claimed to know nothing, to be seeking information, and the average Athenian, sure of his own political and social principles, and of a certain general store of knowledge, was generally willing, nay, eager, to enlighten the old man. "What is honesty?" Socrates would ask one. The man would explain what honesty implied. "If one be honest, must he always return what he borrows from his neighbor?" the philosopher would inquire; and the confident citizen would answer that he must do so, upon every occasion. "But," Socrates would further ask, "suppose you borrowed a man's sword and before you returned it, he lost his reason. If you return it to him he will kill himself—should one return the sword under those circumstances?" And the citizen had to admit that under such conditions it would not be necessary to return it nor would it be right. A single exception disproved a rule, and the crest-fallen man, having talked a few minutes, while the crowd gathered around to hear, felt that he had been made a laughing stock, and usually turned away indignant—sometimes perplexed.

Socrates and the later philosophers did not concern them-

selves with the question which had puzzled all the early thinkers—of what is the world made, for, as Socrates said, man's
powers were not adequate for the problem, and it mattered less
than did ethical questions.

Although ranking with philosophers, he had no special
philosophy to teach, but he possessed one of the greatest personalities the world has ever known. He refused to abide by
the old order of things; he questioned, and this the conservative Greeks resented. When nearly seventy years of age,
Socrates was brought to trial for having corrupted the youth
of Athens by leading them to doubt, to follow him about,
listening to his questions and disputations. He was accused
also of having denied the old gods and introduced new ones.
This happened to be a time of reaction. Athens had met with
losses and Socrates was the one upon whom the people vented
their indignation. He had said that only the wise were fit to
rule, and that of itself was imprudent when each man regarded
himself as a possible leader.

According to the custom of the age, Socrates was allowed
to be his own executioner, and drank the fatal hemlock.
During thirty days preceding his death he was confined in
prison, because these happened to be holy days. All this time
plenty of opportunities were given the philosopher to escape,
but this he scorned to do. As a matter of fact, his death in
this way made a profound impression upon the public; a reaction shortly followed and those who had condemned him to
death were themselves banished.

Plato, a pupil of Socrates, and later his successor, wrote
down dialogues in which Socrates had taken part. He himself committed nothing to writing and all that we know today
comes from the pens of those who knew him.

### A DIALOGUE.

When we were all seated, Protagoras began thus: "Now
that all these people are assembled, Socrates, I will beg you to
repeat what you said to me a little while ago about this youth."

"In speaking of our reason for coming, Protagoras," I
answered, "I shall begin in the same way that I did just now:
Hippocrates here has set his heart upon putting himself under

you, and he would be glad to know what will be the effect upon him if he does this. This is all the speech we have to make."

Then Protagoras took up the discourse, and said:

"Young man, this is how it will be with you if you put yourself under me. The very first day you spend under my teaching you will return home a better man, and the next day it will be the same, and each succeeding day you will grow in goodness."

On hearing this I observed:

"What you say, Protagoras, is nothing surprising, but a matter of course; for even at your age, and wise man that you are, if some one were to teach you what you happened not to know, you would be the better for it. But that was not what I meant. Suppose that the desire which Hippocrates has most at heart were on a sudden to change, and he became bent upon joining that youth who has lately come to live here,—Zeuxippus of Heracleia,—and that, going to him just as he had now come to you, he were to hear from him the very same things he had just heard from you, that each day spent under his teaching he would go on improving and growing better and better; and suppose that he were to ask, 'What do you mean by saying that I shall grow better and better, and in what shall I improve?' Zeuxippus would answer, 'In painting.' And if he put himself under Orthagoras of Thebes, and heard the same from him that he has from you, and asked in what he is to improve day by day by coming under his care, he would be told 'In flute-playing.'

"Do you then now speak in your turn and answer this youth and me who am questioning you in his name: We understand that Hippocrates here, on the very first day he puts himself under Protagoras, is to return home a better man, and on each succeeding day is to improve in like degree,—but in what way, Protagoras, and in what subject?"

When he had heard me out, Protagoras said:

"You are an excellent questioner, Socrates, and I take pleasure in answering those who ask good questions. Well, then Hippocrates in coming to me will not undergo what he would have had to undergo in joining any other of the Sophists; for they do dis-

III—7

honour to the youth who, having just escaped from the arts, are led back to the arts again, and against their will plunged into the study of calculation and astronomy and geometry and music, but he who comes to me will learn nothing but what he came to learn—judgment, which in domestic affairs will enable him to manage his household in the best way, and in affairs of state to acquire the greatest influence, both in speech and action."

"Wait," said I, "do I follow your meaning? I should say you were speaking of the art of politics, and promising to make men good citizens."

"This, Socrates," he answered, "is the very thing that I make a profession of."

"And a noble art you possess indeed," I said, "if you really do possess it; but I will tell you exactly what I think about this. I have never believed, Protagoras, that the art can be taught at all, and yet when you say it can, I know not how to disbelieve you. I am bound, however, to declare my reason for believing that it can neither be taught nor procured by one man for another.

"That the Athenians are shrewd men is well known to me, as it is to all the other Greeks. Now I notice that whenever we come together in the assembly, and action is to be taken by the state about matters which relate to building, the builders are summoned to give their advice in regard to buildings, and in case of shipbuilding, then the shipwrights are summoned; and so on of all other matters which they think may be taught and learned. And if any other man whom the people do not regard as a skilled workman undertakes to give his advice, then, be he never so well-favoured and rich and high born, they accept it none the more for that, but laugh him to scorn and hoot at him until he who is trying to speak is actually hooted down, and either stops of his own accord or is arrested by the city guard and turned out by order of the prytanes. This, then, is the action they take in regard to arts which they think may be professed; but when they come to deliberate on anything touching the management of the state, then indeed may any man arise and give his advice, carpenter as well as blacksmith, cobbler and shipmaster, rich and poor, well born and of low degree. And when these undertake to give advice no one casts in their teeth, as in the former instance, that they have never learned the art nor had any teacher in it; from which it is evident that the Athenians do not believe it can be taught.

"Nor does this hold good only where the interests of the state are concerned. In private life, also, even the best and wisest are not able to impart to others this virtue which, as citizens, they themselves possess. There is Pericles, the father of these youths. He has educated them well and carefully in all that is to be acquired from schoolmasters, but the very thing in which he most excels he neither teaches them himself nor imparts to them through another. Like sacred cattle left to range at will, they are allowed to roam about by themselves, on the mere chance that they may somewhere fall in with virtue. And perhaps you may remember how in the case of Cleinas, the younger brother of Alcibiades, the same man Pericles, who was his guardian, fearful lest he might be ruined by his brother, took him away, and sent him to Ariphon to be educated. But before six months had passed, Ariphon sent him back to his guardian, because he could do nothing with him. And I could name any number of men besides who, although good themselves, have never made anyone better, whether those of their own kin or strangers. And so, Protagoras, when I consider all these things, I come to the conclusion that virtue cannot be taught at all; but then again, when I hear you talking in this way, I am staggered, and begin to think there is something in what you say, for I hold you to be a man of varied experience, who have learned many things from others, and have found out many for yourself. If then you can bring forth any convincing proof to show us that virtue can be taught, do not, I beg of you, begrudge it to us."

"Most certainly, Socrates," said he, "I shall not begrudge it. But tell me, how would you rather have me prove my point? in a myth, as an old man does to young people, or by means of argument?"

Whereupon a number of those who were seated there called out to him to prove it in whichever way he preferred.

"It seems to me, then," he said, "that the myth would be the most pleasing way."

(Hereupon Protagoras related a myth to illustrate his point, and then by argument proved his point again.)

"As to the statement made by Socrates, that good men do not train their sons in this particular excellence, it is met by the answer that the whole life of every citizen, from beginning to end, is nothing if not an education in virtue; the fact that the sons of good fathers so often turn out badly only proving the truth that all men have an equal chance to attain it. In illustration of this, we may suppose it necessary to the existence of a state that every member of it should be a good flute-player. Were this the case, each citizen would doubtless exact a high standard in this art from all his fellow citizens; but the influences brought to bear upon each and all of them would be the same, and the son of a good flute-player would have no advantage over the son of a bad one, since the natural capacity of each, and this alone, would determine his proficiency. Even so each citizen in the state is self-constituted an educator of the young, from whose virtue he himself derives benefit.

"It were nevertheless not undesirable," continues Protagoras, "to seek some teacher who, more than other men, might be capable of promoting a yet higher standard of virtue:" (and here the great Sophist asserts his own pretensions by giving himself out to be such a teacher and as such not unworthy of his hire).

—*From Plato's Protagoras.*

## EARLY GREEK PHILOSOPHERS.

GREEK Philosophy, which reached its highest excellence at Athens in the fourth century before Christ, had its origin two hundred years earlier in the outlying settlements of the Hellenic race in Asia Minor, Thrace, Sicily and Southern Italy, rather than in Greece proper. The founding of colonies and frequent changes of government in the older states led thoughtful men to study the constitution of man and of society. Such were most of those who have become famous as "The Seven Wise Men." They were prominent in their respective cities and some were known as "tyrants," that is, persons who had seized supreme power.

### THE SEVEN WISE MEN.

THE Seven Wise Men form a remarkable group in the history of Greece. They belong to the sixth century before Christ, and mark the beginning of social philosophy. Most of them were composers in verse, but their fame is connected with certain maxims, chosen as characteristic of each. These are said to have been inscribed by order of the Amphictyonic Council in the temple of Apollo at Delphi. They mark the beginning of the use of prose instead of verse.

SOLON of Athens.........Know thyself.
CHILO of Sparta.........Consider the end.
THALES of Ephesus.......Suretyship is the forerunner of ruin.
BIAS of Priene..........Most men are bad.
CLEOBULUS of Lindus.....Nothing too much [Avoid extremes].
PITTACUS of Mitylene.....Know thy opportunity.
PERIANDER of Corinth....Nothing is impossible to labor.

### KNOWLEDGE OF GOD.

(From the poem of Empedocles " On Nature.")

BLESSED is the man who hath obtained the riches of the wisdom of God; wretched is he who hath a false opinion about things divine.

God may not be approached, nor can we reach Him with our eyes or touch Him with our hands. No human head is placed upon his limbs, nor branching arms; He has no feet to carry Him apace, nor other parts of men; but He is all pure mind, holy and infinite, darting with swift thought through the universe from end to end.

### THE GOLDEN AGE.

(From the poem of Empedocles " On Nature.")

THEN every animal was tame and familiar with men, both beasts and birds, and mutual love prevailed. Trees flourished with perpetual leaves and fruits, and ample crops adorned their boughs through all the year. Nor had these happy people any Ares (Mars) or mad Uproar for their god; nor was their monarch Zeus (Jupiter), or Cronos (Saturn), or Poseidon (Neptune), but Queen Cypris (Venus). Her favor they besought with pious symbols and images, with fragrant essences and censers of pure myrrh and frankincense, and with brown honey poured on the ground. The altars did not reek with the gore of bullocks.

### THE SYMBOLS OF PYTHAGORAS.

A FEW examples of these enigmatic sayings are given, with their probable explanations. Other interpretations, sometimes very profound, have been offered. Similar proverbs and riddles are found among the remains of early literature in many countries.

Go not beyond the balance.
  (Transgress not the laws of justice.)
Tear not the crown (or wreath) to pieces.
  (Spoil not joy. At Greek festivals it was customary to
    wear garlands.)

Having reached the border, turn not back.

(Be not dismayed at death.)

Leave not the mark of a pot in the ashes.

(Cherish no resentment after reconciliation.)

Wear not a tight ring.

(Do not oppress yourself for sake of appearances.)

Sow mallows, but do not eat them.

(Use mildness to others, but not to yourself.)

Feed the cock, but sacrifice him not.

(Cherish prophets and harm them not.)

Speak not, turned towards the sun.

(Do not tell everything to everybody.)

Abstain from beans.

(Abstain from politics. Black and white beans were
used in voting in some Greek cities.)

When the winds blow, worship echo.

(Recognize Divine Providence in human commotions.)

When you go to the temple, worship; neither do nor say anything concerning your life.

Stir not fire with a sword.

(Do not intensify quarrels.)

Help a man to take up a burden, but not to put it down.

Look not in a mirror by a torch.

(Seek not truth in human inventions.)

Decline the highways; take the footpaths.

(Seek not notoriety.)

## The Golden Verses of Pythagoras.

First, in their ranks, the Immortal Gods adore—
Thine oath keep; next great Heroes; then implore
Terrestrial Demons, with due sacrifice.
Thy parents reverence, and near allies.
Him that is first in virtue make thy friend,
And with observance his kind speech attend:
Nor, to thy power, for light faults cast him by:
Thy power is neighbor to Necessity.
These know, and with attentive care pursue;
But anger, sloth, and luxury subdue:
In sight of others or thyself, forbear
What's ill; but of thyself stand most in fear.
Let Justice all thy words and actions sway;

Nor from the even course of Wisdom stray;
For know that all men are to die ordained.
  Crosses that happen by Divine decree
(If such thy lot) bear not impatiently;
Yet seek to remedy with all thy care,
And think the just have not the greatest share.
'Mongst men discourses good and bad are spread;
Despise not those, nor be by these misled.
If any some notorious falsehood say,
Thou the report with equal judgment weigh.
Let not men's smoother promises invite,
Nor rougher threats from just resolves thee fright.
If aught thou should'st attempt, first ponder it—
Fools only inconsiderate acts commit;
Nor do what afterwards thou may'st repent:
First know the thing on which thou'rt bent.
Thus thou a life shalt lead with joy replete.
  Nor must thou care of outward health forget.
Such temperance use in exercise and diet
As may preserve thee in a settled quiet.
Meats unprohibited, not curious, choose;
Decline what any other may accuse.
The rash expense of vanity detest,
And sordidness: a mean in all is best.
  Hurt not thyself.   Before thou act, advise;
Nor suffer sleep at night to close thy eyes
Till thrice thine acts that day thou hast o'errun:
How hast thou slipped?—what duty left undone?
Thus, thine account summed up from first to last,
Grieve for the ill, joy for what good hath passed.
  These study, practice these, and these affect;
To sacred Virtue these thy steps direct:
Eternal Nature's fountain I attest,
Who the *Tetractys** on our souls impressed.

* The number *four*, as well as *one* and *seven*, was highly regarded
by the Pythagoreans.   The Tetractys or Quaternion,
meaning literally *four*, was an emblem composed of ten
dots arranged in four rows.   In the soul it represents
judgment, which is based upon the four faculties, understanding, knowledge, opinion and sense.  But in its full
mystic significance, it was a comprehensive emblem of the Deity, the
universe and reason.

Before thy mind thou to this study bend,
Invoke the Gods to grant it a good end.
These if thy labor vanquish, thou shalt then
Know the connection both of gods and men;
How everything proceeds, or by what stayed;
And know (as far as fit to be surveyed)
Nature alike throughout; that thou mayst learn
Not to hope hopeless things, but all discern;
And know those wretches whose perverser wills
Draw down upon their hearts spontaneous ills,
Unto the good that's near them deaf and blind;
Some few the cure of these misfortunes find.
This only is the Fate that harms, and rolls
Through miseries successive human souls.
Within is a continual hidden sight,
Which we to shun must study, not excite.

Great Jove! how little trouble should we know,
If thou to all men wouldst their genius show!
But fear not thou—man born of heavenly race,
Taught by diviner Nature what to embrace,
Which, if pursued, thou all I've named shall gain,
And keep thy soul clean from thy body's stain.
In time of prayer and cleansing, meats denied
Abstain from; thy mind's reins, let Reason guide;
Then stripped of flesh, up to free ether soar,
A deathless god—divine—mortal no more.

## CHAPTER XIX.

### PLATO.

Plato belonged to a noble family, and traces of his aristocratic birth and breeding are to be discovered in his teachings. As a youth he came under the influence of Socrates and always remained his devoted follower. After the death of Socrates, Plato wrote down what he could recall of his teacher's philosophy in the form of dialogues. It was inevitable that Plato should frequently attribute to his predecessor what in reality was his own later thought. Nevertheless, these conversations, recorded by Plato after the lapse of some time, give us a fair conception of Socrates' teachings.

For generations philosophers had been trying to determine what was the ultimate reality—the unchanging, in a world of change. Plato thought it was hopeless to attempt to find this in the world around us, so he conceived of a realm wholly outside this world, wherein was to be found a model, a perfect idea or concept, for everything in the world. This concept, or idea in another world, has become known as the *Platonic idea*. For Plato, ideas are the unchanging, the eternal. They always existed, but creation gave them reality. Plato believed in the immortality of the soul and taught that the soul has ideas which it acquired in the world of ideas, not born of earthly experiences. Wordsworth's Ode to Immortality bears out the same general conception.

Plato was an idealist. His philosophical treatises possess a certain touch of poetry, usually lacking in writings of such a nature.

We today are probably more interested in Plato's political and ethical views than with his notions in the realm of natural philosophy. His Republic is his greatest production. In it he attempted to explain the nature of *justice*. He maintained that ordinarily people thought of justice on too limited a plane. If they started out with the constitution of a state and endeavored to see how nearly this insured justice, then, with such an exalted conception of it, one might consider it in connection with the individual.

In his ideal state, Plato would have marriage controlled by the state. Children should be taken from their parents at an early age and brought up by those employed by the state for this purpose. Regarding these ideas, it may well be pointed out that at this time in Greece there was no romance in marriage. The position of women made it almost impossible for a woman to be a companion to her husband. His life was spent among men, while the wife managed the household and had as a rule no social interests. Plato merely gave emphasis to the general Greek conception that the individual should be subordinate to the state, and all social institutions, including marriage, should be conducted in order that the state might receive greatest strength and benefit.

On two occasions, at least, Plato took part in public affairs, and idealist that he was, his experience was of a nature to discourage him about the ultimate welfare of the state. Whatever attempts he made to introduce his individual beliefs into active affairs, proved failures. He grew discouraged about the trend of political organism, and felt that the only hope for the state was to put a philosopher at its head, yet his personal unfortunate experiences led him to doubt the probability of this being done.

So far as Plato's religious views are concerned, he objected to the immoral stories told of the Olympian gods, realizing that they tended to demoralize the people. It was impossible for him to accept the belief in these deities even yet held by the masses. Educated men in Athens had abandoned the old myths as childish, but, as was proven by the death of Socrates and the treatment of Anaxagoras, the people generally resented any innovations of a religious kind.

Greek philosophers as a rule were not appreciated by the public generally during their life time. However, it is almost possible to make an exception in the case of Plato. At least we may say that he came as near being thought great as any ancient savant. He founded the Academy, whither young men flocked to hear his discourses. After his death, the Academy was still kept up, although it gradually departed from the principles taught by its founder and sank into periods of scepticism.   After the Christian religion had gained a considerable hearing, Neo-Platonism, or new Platonism, was taught in Alexandria.   This was an attempt to give fresh life to Plato's teachings and bring them forth as an offset to Christianity.

### FROM PLATO.

"After this (oligarchy) comes Democracy.   And the change from oligarchy arises through an excess of the present advantage; I mean the accumulation of wealth in a few hands. For we have those stinged creatures, the men burdened with debts, and smarting under disgrace and political disabilities, ready to fall upon the rich class, and anxious for revolution. And the rich money-making, money-lending class increase the liabilities of their victims, stinging with their usury and filling the city with drones, *i. e.*, beggars.   There is no check on this malady, no law to prevent a man from converting his goods and his means into ready money; whilst the rulers make all they can out of the ruled, and bring up their own families in luxury.   When these two classes meet, on the road, in war, at public games, on board ship, the poor man learns that it is not an unmixed advantage after all to be rich; he sees the rich man fat and unwieldy, whilst he himself is wiry and agile; and he consequently despises him as good for nothing. And a very slight occasion will serve to bring these two opposing elements into actual war.   Then the poor conquer, and make a re-distribution of property, and a democracy is formed. How, then, will such a State fare?   First there will be free license for every man to acquire what he likes and to live as he likes; and the State will be a wonderfully variegated production, such as some people, women and children, for instance, especially admire.   It is the city of all men, for every one can suit his own taste if he come here; a man can do just what he pleases.   If you wish to go to war, your neighbor is not bound to agree with you; if you are prevented from this or that by law, you can set the law aside.   Democracy, in fact, means anarchy.

"The democratic man is the son of the oligarchic man,

whom we have already described as money-making. The son will follow his father in keeping down those desires which are not imperative. By imperative or necessary desires I mean those of which we cannot be rid, which benefit us by being satisfied, such as the desire of eating, whilst those which do us no good and can be repressed by means of training I call unnecessary, of which we may mention a fondness of delicate food for an example. The change from the oligarchic to the democratic nature is as follows: The son was brought up in a frugal manner on the money which the father accumulated, and afterwards makes the acquaintance of gay and brilliant sparks, who have carried the science of pleasure to a wonderful perfection. Then there arises in him a sedition, between the careful oligarchic temper and the pleasure-seeking prodigal; and sometimes the former is in the ascendant, sometimes the latter. And if certain desires are driven out their place is soon filled up by others, perhaps worse, because in such a man there is nothing, such as intellectual tastes, to fill the void. So the citadel of his soul is won by base pleasures and wrong opinions. These base pursuits drive away honor, and temperance, and propriety, and flaunt anarchy, incontinency, and pride, in their stead. And the man who has thus lost the right opinion treats all pleasures alike, and indulges them indiscriminately. First he spends his time in drinking and playing, then he veers round and drinks nothing but water; sometimes he practises gymnastics and next does nothing at all; again he becomes a politician and jumps up to say the first thing that comes into his head; he is

> 'Everything by starts, and nothing long.'

If he sees another engaged in making money, he will make money; if another is going to war, he will go, too. In short, his life and tastes are universal.

"The finest state of all and the finest man now remain; I mean the despotism and the despot. As excess of wealth turned oligarchy into democracy, so excess of liberty turns democracy into despotism. For men, such as we have described in a democratic city, intimidate the rulers and make them do as they wish, and not follow the law strictly: they

uphold servile rulers and decry just ones. All relations are
disturbed and reversed, sons usurp their father's prerogatives,
and fathers are afraid of their sons. Strangers usurp the
place of the citizens, masters fawn upon their pupils, and
pupils have no regard for their masters. Elders throw aside
their grave and serious bearing, and ape the flippancy of
youth, and slaves are as free as their purchasers: whilst the
very animals are imbued with this spirit of ultra-freedom and
strut about pushing people off the pathways. So free must
every one be that they disregard all law, and will call no one
master. On the principle, then, of reaction, this ultra-freedom
will result in ultra-slavery.          The change will begin
in the persons of those men whom we likened to the drones of
the hives, and some of them having stings and others stingless,
in the oligarchic State; but in the democratic this class will be
much stronger. So the strongest of these drones will do all
the speaking and working in politics, and the inferior drones
will buzz about the tribune and prevent any one from being
heard in opposition, except a very few. Then there are the
rich on which the drones subsist, and a third class, viz., the
mechanics and journeymen, who are always ready to combine
if they see an opportunity of plunder. And if the rich try
to defend themselves they are called bad citizens and oligarchi-
cal, a false accusation which makes them really become so.
And the people set up a champion in opposition to them, who
is the germ of the despot. And such a man is like to him who
once tastes human blood, as in the story of Zeus Lycaeus in
Arcadia, and must become a wolf. For if he once become
involved in prosecutions and judicial murder, he will go on
from bad to worse, banishing, killing, proclaiming abolition
of debt and redistribution of land. Then he is perhaps
expelled and reinstalled by force, and his hand is against all
who helped to drive him out. The next step is that he is
obliged to ask the people to give him a body-guard, and when
he has obtained this, the despotism stands forth complete.
And the people do not say of their champion, 'How are the
mighty fallen!' but the champion is now a full-blown despot.

"At first he is mild and gentle, and his measures are all
in the direction of lightening the people's burdens, but as he

goes on he finds it necessary to stir up war so that he may keep up his character of champion and impoverish the people by war-taxes to prevent their rising against him. And if any of his friends speak out his mind against these practices he will have to remove him, and so he will become the enemy of any magnanimous, prudent, or wealthy man. And as physicians remove all the evils of the body and encourage the development of what is good, the tyrant will remove all the good and leave the evil. He will defend himself with foreign mercenaries and with freedmen.

"And the people that has begotten the despot will have to keep him, and it will be of no use to them to say that it is not right for a child when he grows up to be a burden to his father, and that they did not help him forward as their champion that he might collect a pack of idle knaves about him, who devour the citizen's substance. Nay, he will strike his father and treat him as a son should not ; and the people trying to escape out of the frying-pan of slavery will fall into the fire of despotism, which is after all the worst kind of slavery. This, then, is the change from democracy to tyranny.' "

—*From Plato's Republic, Wells trans.*

## ARISTOTLE.

Aristotle is generally conceded to have been the greatest savant of antiquity. Born about 384 B. C., forty-three years after the birth of Plato, he grew up at the court of the Macedonian kings, his father being court-physician. When about seventeen years of age, he came under the instruction of Plato.

Socrates had belonged to the common people; Plato to the aristocracy, and Aristotle, son of a professional man, belonged to the middle class. As a natural result, he took a moderate course, intermediary between two extremes.

Aristotle is known always as the teacher of Alexander the Great, who retained his affection for his celebrated teacher throughout his life. Led by Aristotle to develop a liking for scientific study, Alexander kept up his interest in this regard throughout his later years. When away in foreign lands conducting campaigns, the young conqueror often delayed to collect rare flowers and plants, strange birds and animals, for

Aristotle's collections. These were accumulated that they might give opportunity for scientific investigation and discovery.

While we have everything that Plato is known to have written, such is not the case with Aristotle. Much of what remains was either written down in the form of notes to guide the philosopher in his lectures, or it was jotted down by his students. Neither can be very satisfactory. Nevertheless, we have sufficient material to enable us to judge very well of Aristotle's theories and teachings. He differed with Plato in the matter of a world beyond the heavens where ideas, the eternal, the unchanging, abode. Aristotle was too practical to hold the concept and the object as wholly apart and in different places; he believed that the concept of an object was in the object itself. Form and matter are not apart from each other. The form and matter are not to be distinguished from one another. The universal is to be found in the individual. This was to be a point upon which mediaeval philosophers would divide.

We today are more interested in Aristotle's theory of ethics than in his ideas regarding natural phenomena. Modern investigation has made the views of the ancients upon the natural world of interest only as we follow the gradual expansion of science. In the realm of logic, however, Aristotle developed the subject so that later ages have added very little to it.

Unlike Plato, Aristotle did not care to enter political life. Notwithstanding, he wrote to some considerable length upon the development of the Grecian states. He is known to have written treatises upon the important city-state constitutions, but only one, the constitution of Athens, has come down to us.

Aristotle founded the Lyceum after the death of Plato, and along the shady walks of the school discussed philosophical questions with his students.

### The Education of Youth.

"In the first place we have to consider (1) whether we are to establish any system of supervision for our children, next (2) whether this supervision should be public or of a private character, as in the majority of States at the present day, and lastly, (3) what the character of this supervision should be.

(1) That the education of the young has a special claim on the lawgiver's attention is beyond question. In the first place, any neglect of this by a state is injurious to its constitution. A given constitution demands an education in conformity with it; for the maintenance of any constitution, like its first establishment, is due, as a rule, to the presence of the spirit or character proper to the constitution. The establishment and maintenance of democracy is due to the presence of a democratic spirit, and that of oligarchy to the presence of an oligarchic spirit. The better the spirit, the better the constitution it gives rise to.

In the second place, in all arts and crafts we require a preliminary education and habituation to enable us to exercise them, and the same will hold of the production of activities according to goodness.

(2) Again, since the state as a whole has a single end, it is plain that the education of all must be one and the same, and that the supervision of this education must be public and not private, as it is on the present system, under which everyone looks after his own children privately and gives them any private instruction he thinks proper. Public training is wanted in all things that are of public interest. Besides, it is wrong for any citizen to think that he belongs to himself. All must be regarded as belonging to the state: for each man is a part of the state, and the treatment of the part is naturally determined by that of the whole. This is a thing for which the Lacedaemonians deserve all praise; they are thoroughly in earnest about their children, and that as a community.

(3) We now see that we will have to legislate on the subject of education, and that education must be public; but we must not overlook the question of the character and methods of this education. As it is, there is a dispute about subjects. There is no agreement as to what the young should learn, either with a view to the production of goodness or the best life, nor is it settled whether we ought to keep the intellect or the character chiefly in view. If we start from the education we see around us, the inquiry is perplexing, and there

is no certainty as to whether education should be a training in what is useful for life or in what tends to promote goodness or in more out-of-the-way subjects. Each of these views finds some supporters; but there is not even any agreement as to what tends to promote goodness. To begin with, all people do not appreciate the same kind of goodness, so it is only to be expected that they should differ about the required training.

It is, of course, obvious that we shall have to teach our children such useful knowledge as is indispensable for them; but it is equally plain that all useful knowledge is not suitable for education. There is a distinction between liberal and illiberal subjects, and it is clear that only such knowledge as does not make the learner mechanical should enter into education. By mechanical subjects we must understand all arts and studies that make the body, soul, or intellect of freemen unserviceable for the use and exercise of goodness. That is why we call such pursuits as produce an inferior condition of body mechanical, and all wage-earning occupations. They allow the mind no leisure, and they drag it down to a lower level. There are even some liberal arts, the acquisition of which up to a certain point is not unworthy of freemen, but which, if studied with excessive devotion or minuteness, are open to the charge of being injurious in the manner described. The object with which we engage in or study them also makes a great difference; if it is for our sakes or that of our friends, or to produce goodness, they are not illiberal, while a man engaging in the very same pursuits to please strangers would in many cases be regarded as following the occupation of a slave or a serf.

Now the subjects most widely disseminated at present show a double face, as was remarked above. There are, speaking broadly, four which usually enter into education: (1) Reading and writing, (2) Gymnastics, and (3) Music, to which some add (4) Drawing. Reading and writing is taught on the ground that it is of highest utility for practical life, and gymnastics as tending to promote courage; but, when we come to music, we may feel at a loss. At the present day most people take it up with the idea that its object is pleasure; but the ancient gave it a place in education because Nature herself, as we have often observed, seeks not only to be rightly busy, but

also the power of using leisure aright. That is the root of the
whole matter, if we may recur to the point once more. Both
are wanted, but leisure is more worth having and more of an
end than business, so we must find out how we are to employ
our leisure. Not, surely, in playing games; for that would
imply that amusement is the end of life. That it cannot be,
and it is rather in our busy times that we should have recourse
to games. It is the hard-worked man that needs rest, and the
object of play is rest, and we find that it is business that
involves hard work and strain. So, when we introduce games,
we should do so with a due regard to times and seasons, apply-
ing them medicinally; for motion of this character is a relax-
ation of the soul, and from its pleasantness gives it rest.
Leisure, on the other hand, we regard as containing pleasure—
nay, happiness and the blessed life—in itself. That is not a
thing that we find in busy people, but only in people at leisure.
The busy man is busy for some end,—which implies that he
has not got it,—while happiness is itself the end and by universal consent involves not pain but pleasure. To be sure,
when we come to the question, "What is pleasure?" we no longer
find a universal agreement. Each man determines it in his
own way, the best man choosing the best and that which has
the fairest source.

*—Aristotle's Politics: Burnet's trans.*

## THE VISION OF ER.

"THE Republic" is the longest and perhaps the best of the dialogues of Plato. In addition to his views about an ideal State, it
gives in conclusion this vision of the world of the dead and of the
transmigration of souls.

Well—said Socrates—I will tell you a tale; not one of
those tales which Odysseus tells to the hero Alcinous; yet
this, too, is a tale of a brave man, Er, the son of Armenius,
a Pamphylian by birth. He was slain in battle, and ten days
afterwards, when the bodies of the dead were taken up, already
in a state of corruption, his body was unaffected by decay,
and carried home to be buried. And on the twelfth day, as
he was lying on the funeral pile, he returned to life, and told
them what he had seen in the other world.

He said that when he left the body his soul went on a
journey with a great company, and that they came to a mysterious place at which there were two chasms in the earth;
they were near together, and over against them were two
other chasms in the heaven above. In the intermediate space
there were judges seated, who bade the just, after they had
judged them, ascend by the heavenly way on the right hand,
having the signs of the judgment bound on their foreheads.
And in like manner the unjust were commanded by them to
descend by the lower way on the left hand; these also had
the symbols of their deeds fastened on their backs. He drew
near, and they told him that he was to be the messenger who
would carry the report of the other world to men; and they
bade him hear and see all that was to be heard and seen in
that place.

Then he beheld and saw on one side the souls departing
at either chasm of heaven and earth when sentence had been
given them; and at the two other openings other souls, some
ascending out of the earth dusty and worn with travel, some
descending out of heaven clean and bright. And always on
their arrival they seemed as if they had come from a long
journey; and they went out into the meadow with joy, and
encamped as at a festival; and those who knew one another

embraced and conversed, the souls which came from the earth curiously inquiring about the things above, and the souls which came from heaven about the things beneath. And they told one another of what had happened by the way—those from below weeping and sorrowing at the remembrance of the things which they had endured and seen in their journey (now the journey had lasted a thousand years), while those from above were describing heavenly delights and visions of inconceivable beauty.

There is not time to tell all, but the sum is this:

He said that for every wrong which they had done to any one they suffered tenfold; that is to say, once in every hundred years—the thousand years answering to the hundred years which are reckoned as the life of man. If, for example, there were any who had been the cause of many deaths, or had betrayed or enslaved cities or armies, or been guilty of any other evil behavior, for each and all of these they received punishment ten times over; and the rewards of beneficence and justice and holiness were in the same proportion. I need hardly repeat what he said concerning young children dying almost as soon as they were born. Of piety and impiety to gods and parents, and of murders, there were retributions other and greater far, which he described.

He mentioned that he was present when one of the spirits asked another, "Where is Aridæus the Great?" (Now this Aridæus lived a thousand years before the time of Er. He had been the tyrant of some city of Pamphylia, and had murdered his aged father and his elder brother, and was said to have committed many other abominable crimes.) The answer was, "He comes not hither, and never will come. For this was one of the miserable sights witnessed by us: We were approaching the mouth of the cave, and, having seen all, were about to re-ascend, when of a sudden Aridæus appeared, and several others, most of whom were tyrants; and there were also, besides the tyrants, private individuals who had been great criminals. They were just at the mouth, being, as they fancied, about to return into the upper world; but the opening, instead of receiving them, gave forth a sound when any of these incurable or unpunished sinners tried to ascend;

and then wild men of fiery aspect, who were standing by, and
knew what that meant, seized and carried off several of them;
and Aridæus and others they bound head and hand, and threw
them down, and flayed them with scourges, and dragged them
along the road at the side, carding them on thorns like wool,
and declaring to the passers-by what were their crimes, and
that they were being taken away to be cast into hell." And
of the many terrors which they had endured, he said that
there was none like the terror which each of them felt at that
moment lest they should hear the voice; and when there was
silence, one by one they ascended with joy. "These," said
Er, "were the penalties and retributions, and there were
rewards as great."

Now when the spirits which were in the meadow had
tarried seven days, on the eighth day they were obliged to
proceed on their journey; and on the fourth day after, he said
that they came to a place where they looked down from above
upon a line of light like a column, extending right through
the whole heaven and through the earth, in coloring resembling a rainbow, only brighter and purer. Another day's
journey brought them to the place; and there, in the midst
of the light they saw reaching from heaven the ends by which
it is fastened. For this light is the belt of heaven, and holds
together the circle of the universe, like the undergirding ropes
of a trireme. From these ends is extended the spindle of
Necessity, on which all the revolutions turn. . . . The spindle
turns on the knees of Necessity; and on the upper surface
of each of the eight circles [which are described as the
orbits of the fixed stars and the planets] is a Siren who goes
round with them, hymning a single sound and note. The
eight together form one harmony. And round about at equal
intervals, there is another band, three in number, each sitting
upon her throne. These are the Fates, daughters of Necessity, who are clothed in white raiment, and have crowns of
wool upon their heads—Lachesis and Clotho and Atropos—
who accompany with their voices the harmonies of the sirens;
Lachesis singing of the Past, Clotho of the Present, and
Atropos of the Future; Clotho now and then assisting with
a touch of her right hand the motion of the outer circle or

whole of the spindle, and Atropos with her left hand touching the inner ones, and Lachesis laying hold of either in turn, first with one hand and then with the other.

When Er and the spirits arrived, their duty was to go at once to Lachesis. But first of all there came a Prophet who arranged them in order. Then he took from the knees of Lachesis lots and samples of life, and going up to a high place, spake as follows: "Hear the words of Lachesis, the daughter of Necessity. Mortal souls, behold a new cycle of mortal life. Your Genius will not choose you, but you will choose your Genius; and let him who draws the first lot first choose a life, which shall be his destiny. Virtue is free; and as a man honors or dishonors her, he will have more or less of her; the chooser is answerable—God is justified."

When the Interpreter had thus spoken, he scattered lots among them, and each one took up the lot which fell near him—all but Er himself (he was not allowed)—and each as he took his lot, perceived the number which he had obtained. Then the Interpreter placed on the ground before them the samples of lives; and there were many more lives than the souls present; and there were all sorts of lives—of every animal and of man in every condition.

And there were tyrannies among them, some continuing while the tyrant lived, others which broke off in the middle, and came to an end in poverty and exile and beggary. And there were lives of famous men; some who were famous for their form and beauty as well as for their strength and success in games; or, again, for their birth and the qualities of their ancestors; and some who were the reverse of famous for the opposite qualities; and of women likewise. There was not, however, any definite character in them, because the soul must of necessity be changed according to the life chosen. But there was every other quality; and they all mingled with one another, and also with elements of wealth and poverty, and disease and health. And there were mean estates also.

And here—said Socrates—is the supreme peril of our human state; and therefore the utmost care should be taken. Let each one of us leave every other kind of knowledge, and seek and follow one thing only, if peradventure he may find

some one who will make him able to learn and discern between good and evil, and so to choose always and everywhere
the better life as he has opportunity. . . . For we have seen
and know that this is the best choice both in life and after
death.   A man must take with him into the world below an
adamantine faith in Truth and Right, that there, too, he may
be undazzled by the desire of wealth or the other allurements
of evil, lest, coming upon tyrannies and similar villainies, he
do irremediable wrongs to others and suffer yet worse himself.
But let him know how to choose the mean, and avoid the extremes on either side, as far as possible, not only in this life,
but in all that is to come.   For this is the way to happiness.

And, according to the report of the messenger, this is
exactly what the Prophet said at the time: "Even for the
last comer, if he choose wisely, and will live diligently, there
is appointed a happy and not undesirable existence.   Let not
him who chooses first be careless, and let not the last despair."

And while the Interpreter was speaking, he who had the
first choice came forward, and in a moment chose the greatest
tyranny.   His mind having been darkened by folly and sensuality, he had not thought out the whole matter, and did not
see at first that he was fated, among other evils, to devour his
own children.   But when he had time to reflect, and saw
what was in the lot, he began to beat his breast and lament
over his choice, not abiding by the proclamation of the
Prophet; for instead of throwing the blame of his misfortune
upon himself, he accused Chance and the Gods, and everything rather than himself.

Most curious, said the messenger, was the spectacle of the
election—sad and laughable and strange; the souls generally
choosing with a reference to their experience of a previous
life.   There he saw the soul which had been Orpheus choosing the life of a swan, out of enmity to the race of women,
hating to be born of a woman, because they had been his
murderers; he saw also the soul of Thamyris choosing the
life of a nightingale; birds, on the other hand, like the swan
and other musicians, choosing to be men.

The soul which obtained the twentieth lot chose the life
of a lion; and this was Ajax, the son of Telamon, who would

not be a man—remembering the injustice which was done him in the judgment of the arms. The next was Agamemnon, who chose the life of an eagle, because, like Ajax, he hated human nature on account of his sufferings. About the middle was the lot of Atalanta; she, seeing the great fame of an athlete, was unable to resist the temptation. After her came the soul of Epeus, the son of Panopeus, passing into the nature of a woman cunning in the arts. And, far away among the last who chose, the soul of the jester Thersites was putting on the form of a monkey.

There came also the soul of Odysseus having yet to make a choice, and his lot happened to be the last of them all. Now the recollection of his former toils had disenchanted him of ambition, and he went about for considerable time in search of a private man who had no cares. He had some difficulty in finding this, which was lying about and had been neglected by everybody else; and when he saw it, he said he would have done the same had he been first instead of last, and that he was delighted at his choice.

And not only did men pass into animals, but I must also mention that there were animals, tame and wild, who changed into one another, and into corresponding human natures—the good into gentle, and the evil into savage, in all sorts of combinations.

All the souls had now chosen their lives, and they went in the order of their choice to Lachesis, who sent with them the Genius whom they had severally chosen to be the guardian of their lives and the fulfiller of the choice. This Genius led the soul first to Clotho, who drew them within the revolution of the spindle impelled by her hand, thus ratifying the choice; and then, when they were fastened to this, carried them away to Atropos, who spun the threads and made them irreversible. Then, without turning round, they passed beneath the throne of Necessity. And when they had all passed, **they marched** on in a scorching heat to the plain of Forge**tfulness, which** was a barren waste destitute of trees and verdure; **and then** towards evening they encamped by the river of Unmindfulness, the water of which no vessel can hold. Of **this they** were all obliged to drink a certain quantity, and t**hose who** were not saved by wisdom drank more than was necessary; and each one, as he drank, forgot all things. Now after they had gone to rest, about the middle of the night, there was a thunderstorm and earthquake; and then in an instant they were driven all manner of ways, like stars shooting upwards, to their birth. Er himself was hindered from drinking the water. But in what manner or by what means he returned to the body he could not say; only in the morning, awaking suddenly, he saw himself on the pyre.

And thus—says Socrates in conclusion—the tale has been saved, and has not perished, and will save us, if we are obedient to the word spoken; and we shall pass safely over the river of Forgetfulness, and our soul will not be defiled. Wherefore, my counsel is, that we hold fast to the heavenly way, and follow after Justice and Virtue always, considering that the soul is immortal, and able to endure every sort of good and every sort of evil. Thus shall we live dear to one another and to the gods, both while remaining here and when, like conquerors in the games who go round to gather gifts, we receive our reward. And it shall be well with us both in this life and in the pilgrimage of a thousand years which we have been reciting.

## PANEGYRIC OF LOVE.

THE "Symposium," or "Banquet," one of the most remarkable dialogues of Plato, illustrates the vast difference between the ancient Hellenic and the modern Christian world in regard to morality. Several prominent Athenians had met for a supper at the house of Agathon, the tragic poet, who had lately won the prize in the dramatic contest. As they were not fully recovered from the previous night's debauch, they agreed, after a few courses, to depart from the usual custom of drinking and to devote their time to the consideration of a set subject. Socrates had come in late, a little better dressed than usual, and was complimented on being the hardest-headed drinker of the company. Love was selected as the theme. Love, it must be noted, with the Greeks included chivalric devotion between men as well as mutual attraction between the opposite sexes. The ensuing discussion varies from the sublimest rhapsody to the most revolting indecency; yet there is a pervading mysticism which has attracted pious minds of other ages. After all the guests have expressed their opinions, Alcibiades bursts into the room. He is crowned with a garland, having come from another banquet. Room is made for the intoxicated intruder, who forthwith takes charge of the feast. Being informed that love has been under consideration, and asked to give his share of praise, he enters upon a long harangue, declaring his infatuation for the homely Socrates, externally like Silenus, but internally full of precious divine gifts. The self-controlled philosopher, he goes on to state, had refused to respond to his obtrusive demonstrations of affection, yet had still so mastered the speaker's will as to drive him into public affairs. The shameless profligate bears the most affectionate tribute to the virtue and power of his enchanter. Ere long the company is invaded by another band of revelers, who compel them to drink more deeply. Some slip off, others fall asleep, but at cock-crow Socrates is seen still discussing with Aristophanes about identity of tragedy and comedy. When he can get no listeners, he departs to his usual business. The following extracts are from the translation by Percy B. Shelley.

"Since then," said Eryximachus, "it is decided that no one shall be compelled to drink more than he pleases, I think that we may as well send away the flute-player to play to herself; or, if she likes, to the women within. Let us devote the present occasion to conversation between ourselves, and if you wish I will propose to you what shall be the subject of our discussion." All present desired and entreated that he would explain.

"The exordium of my speech," said Eryximachus, "will be in the style of the Menalippe of Euripides, for the story which I am about to tell belongs not to me, but to Phædrus. Phædrus has often indignantly complained to me, saying—'Is it not strange, Eryximachus, that there are innumerable hymns and pæans composed for the other gods, but that not one of the many poets who spring up in the world has ever composed a verse in honor of Love, who is such and so great a god? Nor any one of those accomplished Sophists, who, like the famous Prodicus, has celebrated the praise of Hercules and others, has ever celebrated that of Love; but what is more astonishing, I have lately met with the book of some philosopher, in which salt is extolled on account of its utility, and many other things of the same nature are in like manner celebrated with elaborate praise. That so much serious thought is expended on such trifles, and that no man has dared to this day to frame a hymn in honor of Love, who

being so great a deity, is thus neglected, may well be sufficient
to excite my indignation.'

"There seemed to me some justice in these complaints of
Phædrus; I propose, therefore, at the same time for the sake
of giving pleasure to Phædrus, and that we may on the
present occasion do something well and befitting us, that this
god should receive from those who are now present the honor
which is most due to him.  If you agree to my proposal, an
excellent discussion might arise on the subject.  Every one
ought, according to my plan, to praise Love with as much
eloquence as he can.  Let Phædrus begin first, both because
he reclines the first in order, and because he is the father of
the discussion."

"No one will vote against you, Eryximachus," said
Socrates, "for how can I oppose your proposal, who am ready
to confess that I know nothing on any subject but love?  Or
how can Agathon, or Pausanias, or even Aristophanes, whose
life is one perpetual ministration to Venus and Bacchus?  Or
how can any other whom I see here?  Though we who sit
last are scarcely on an equality with you; for if those who
speak before us shall have exhausted the subject with their
eloquence and reasonings, our discourses will be superfluous.
But in the name of Good Fortune, let Phædrus begin and
praise Love."  The whole party agreed to what Socrates said.
Phædrus began thus:

"Love is a mighty deity, and the object of admiration,
both to gods and men, for many and for various claims; but
especially on account of his origin.  For that he is to be
honored as one of the most ancient of the gods this may
serve as a testimony, that Love has no parents, nor is there
any poet or other person who has ever affirmed that there are
such.  Hesiod says, that first 'Chaos was produced; then the
broad-bosomed Earth, to be a secure foundation for all things;
then Love.'  He says that after Chaos these two were produced, the Earth and Love.  Parmenides, speaking of generation, says: 'But he created Love before any of the gods.'
Acusilaus agrees with Hesiod.  Love, therefore, is universally
acknowledged to be among the oldest of things.  And in addition to this, Love is the author of our greatest advantages; for

I cannot imagine a greater happiness and advantage to one who is in the flower of youth than an amiable lover, or to a lover, than an amiable object of his love. For neither birth, nor wealth, nor honors, can awaken in the minds of men the principles which should guide those who from their youth aspire to an honorable and excellent life, as Love awakens them. I speak of the fear of shame, which deters them from that which is disgraceful; and the love of glory, which incites to honorable deeds. For it is not possible that a state or private person should accomplish, without these incitements, anything beautiful or great. I assert, then, that should one who loves be discovered in any dishonorable action, or tamely enduring insult through cowardice, he would feel more anguish and shame if observed by the object of his passion than if he were observed by his father, or his companions, or any other person. In like manner, among warmly attached friends, a man is especially grieved to be discovered by his friend in any dishonorable act. If then, by any contrivance, a state or army could be composed of friends bound by strong attachment, it is beyond calculation how excellently they would administer their affairs, refraining from anything base, contending with each other for the acquirement of fame, and exhibiting such valor in battle as that, though few in numbers, they might subdue all mankind. For should one friend desert the ranks or cast away his arms in the presence of the other, he would suffer far acuter shame from that one person's regard, than from the regard of all other men. A thousand times would he prefer to die, rather than desert the object of his attachment, and not succor him in danger.

"There is none so worthless whom Love cannot impel, as it were by a divine inspiration, towards virtue, even so that he may through this inspiration become equal to one who might naturally be more excellent; and, in truth, as Homer says: 'The God breathes vigor into certain heroes'—so Love breathes into those who love, the spirit which is produced from himself. Not only men, but even women who love, are those alone who willingly expose themselves to die for others. Alcestis, the daughter of Pelias, affords to the Greeks a remarkable example of this opinion; she alone being willing

to die for her husband, and so surpassing his parents in the
affection with which Love inspired her, towards him, as to
make them appear, in the comparison with her, strangers to
their own child, and related to him merely in name; and so
lovely and admirable did this action appear, not only to men,
but even to the gods, that, although they conceded the pre-
rogative of bringing back the spirit from death to few among
the many who then performed excellent and honorable deeds,
yet, delighted with this action, they redeemed her soul from
the infernal regions: so highly do the gods honor zeal and
devotion in love. They sent back indeed Orpheus, the son of
Œagrus, from Hell, with his purpose unfulfilled, and, showing him only the spectre of her for whom he came, refused
to render up herself. For Orpheus seemed to them not as
Alcestis, to have dared die for the sake of her whom he loved,
and thus to secure to himself a perpetual intercourse with her
in the regions to which she had preceded him, but like a
cowardly musician, to have contrived to descend alive into
Hell; and, indeed, they appointed as a punishment for his
cowardice, that he should be put to death by women.

"Far otherwise did they reward Achilles, the son of
Thetis, whom they sent to inhabit the islands of the blessed.
For Achilles, though informed by his mother that his own
death would ensue upon his killing Hector, but that if he
refrained from it he might return home and die in old age, yet
preferred revenging and honoring his beloved Patroclus, not
to die for him merely, but to disdain and reject that life which
he had ceased to share. Therefore the Greeks honored
Achilles beyond all other men, because he thus preferred his
friend to all things else.

"On this account have the gods rewarded Achilles more
amply than Alcestis; permitting his spirit to inhabit the island
of the blessed. Hence do I assert that Love is the most ancient and venerable of deities, and most powerful to endow
mortals with the possession of happiness and virtue, both
whilst they live and after they die." . .

After others have spoken in various styles, Agathon takes up the
discourse.

"All who have already spoken seem to me not so much to

have praised Love, as to have felicitated mankind on the many advantages of which that deity is the cause; what he is, the author of these great benefits, none have yet declared. There is one mode alone of celebration which would comprehend the whole topic, namely, first to declare what are those benefits, and then what he is who is the author of those benefits, which are the subject of our discourse. Love ought first to be praised, and then his gifts declared. I assert, then, that although all the gods are immortally happy, Love, if I dare trust my voice to express so awful a truth, is the happiest, and most excellent, and the most beautiful. That he is the most beautiful is evident; first, O Phædrus, from this circumstance, that he is the youngest of the gods; and, secondly, from his fleetness, and from his repugnance to all that is old; for he escapes with the swiftness of wings from old age; a thing in itself sufficiently swift, since it overtakes us sooner than there is need; and which Love, who delights in the intercourse of the young, hates, and in no manner can be induced to enter into community with. The ancient proverb, which says that like is attracted by like, applies to the attributes of Love. I concede many things to you, O Phædrus, but this I do not concede, that Love is more ancient than Saturn and Jupiter. I assert that he is not only the youngest of the gods, but invested with everlasting youth. Those ancient deeds among the gods recorded by Hesiod and Parmenides, if their relations are to be considered as true, were produced not by Love, but by Necessity. For if Love had been then in Heaven, those violent and sanguinary crimes never would have taken place; but there would ever have subsisted that affection and peace in which the gods now live under the influence of Love.

"He is young, therefore, and being young is tender and soft. There were need of some poet like Homer to celebrate the delicacy and tenderness of Love. For Homer says, that the goddess Calamity is delicate, and that her feet are tender. 'Her feet are soft,' he says, 'for she treads not upon the ground, but makes her path upon the heads of men.' He gives as an evidence of her tenderness, that she walks not upon that which is hard, but that which is soft. The same

evidence is sufficient to make manifest the tenderness of Love.
For Love walks not upon the earth, nor over the heads of
men, which are not indeed very soft; but he dwells within,
and treads on the softest of existing things, having established
his habitation within the souls and inmost nature of gods and
men; not indeed in all souls—for wherever he chances to find
a hard and rugged disposition, there he will not inhabit, but
only where it is most soft and tender. Of needs must he be
the most delicate of all things, who touches lightly with his
feet only the softest parts of those things which are the softest
of all.

"He is then the youngest and the most delicate of all
divinities; and in addition to this, he is, as it were, the most
moist and liquid. For if he were otherwise, he could not, as
he does, fold himself around everything, and secretly flow out
and into every soul. His loveliness, that which Love possesses
far beyond all other things, is a manifestation of the liquid
and flowing symmetry of his form; for between deformity
and Love there is eternal contrast and repugnance. His life
is spent among flowers, and this accounts for the immortal
fairness of his skin; for the winged Love rests not in his
flight on any form, or within any soul, the flower of whose
loveliness is faded, but there remains most willingly where is
the odor and the radiance of blossoms, yet unwithered. Concerning the beauty of the god, let this be sufficient, though
many things must remain unsaid. Let us next consider the
virtue and power of Love.

"What is most admirable in Love is, that he neither inflicts
nor endures injury in his relations either with gods or men.
Nor if he suffers anything does he suffer it through violence,
nor in doing anything does he act with violence, for Love is
never even touched with violence. Every one willingly ad-
ministers every thing to Love; and that which every one
voluntarily concedes to another, the laws, which are the kings
of the republic, decree that is just for him to possess. In
addition to justice, Love participates in the highest temperance; for if temperance is defined to be the being superior to
and holding under dominion pleasures and desires, then Love,
than whom no pleasure is more powerful, and who is thus

more powerful than all persuasions and delights, must be excellently temperate. In power and valor Mars cannot contend with Love: the love of Venus possesses Mars; the possessor is always superior to the possessed, and he who subdues the most powerful must of necessity be the most powerful of all.

"The justice and temperance and valor of the god have been thus declared;—there remains to exhibit his wisdom. And first, that, like Eryximachus, I may honor my own profession, the god is a wise poet; so wise that he can even make a poet one who was not before: for every one, even if before he were ever so undisciplined, becomes a poet as soon as he is touched by Love;—a sufficient proof that Love is a great poet, and well skilled in that science according to the discipline of music. For what any one possesses not, or knows not, that can he neither give nor teach another. And who will deny that the divine poetry, by which all living things are produced upon the earth, is harmonized by the wisdom of Love? Is it not evident that Love was the author of all the arts of life with which we are acquainted, and that he whose teacher has been Love, becomes eminent and illustrious, whilst he who knows not Love, remains forever unregarded and obscure? Apollo invented medicine, and divination, and archery, under the guidance of desire and Love; so that Apollo was the disciple of Love. Through him the Muses discovered the arts of literature, and Vulcan that of moulding brass, and Minerva the loom, and Jupiter the mystery of the dominion which he now exercises over gods and men. So were the gods taught and disciplined by the love of that which is beautiful; for there is no love towards deformity.

"At the origin of things, as I have before said, many fearful deeds are reported to have been done among the gods, on account of the dominion of Necessity. But so soon as this deity sprang forth from the desire which forever tends in the universe towards that which is lovely, then all blessings descended upon all living things, human and divine. Love seems to me, O Phædrus, a divinity the most beautiful and the best of all, and the author to all others of the excellencies with which his own nature is endowed. Nor can I restrain the poetic enthusiasm which takes possession of my discourse and bids me declare that Love is the divinity who creates peace among men, and calm upon the sea, the windless silence of storms, repose and sleep in sadness. Love divests us of all alienation from each other, and fills our vacant hearts with overflowing sympathy; he gathers us together in such social meetings as we now delight to celebrate, our guardian and our guide in dances, and sacrifices, and feasts. Yes, Love, who showers benignity upon the world, and before whose presence all harsh passions flee and perish; the author of all soft affections; the destroyer of all ungentle thoughts; merciful, mild; the object of the admiration of the wise, and the delight of gods; possessed by the fortunate, and desired by the unhappy, therefore unhappy because they possess him not; the father of grace, and delicacy, and gentleness, and delight, and persuasion, and desire; the cherisher of all that is good, the abolisher of all evil; our most excellent pilot, defence, saviour and guardian, in labor and in fear, in desire and in reason; the ornament and governor of all things, human and divine; the best, the loveliest; in whose footsteps every one ought to follow, celebrating him excellently in song, and bearing each his part in that divinest harmony which Love sings to all things which live and are, soothing the troubled minds of gods and men. This, O Phædrus, is what I have to offer in praise of the divinity; partly composed, indeed, of thoughtless and playful fancies, and partly of such serious ones, as I could well command."

No sooner had Agathon ceased, than a loud murmur of applause arose from all present; so becomingly had the fair youth spoken, both in praise of the god, and in extenuation of himself.

### The Lawyer and the Philosopher.

(From the dialogue called "Theætetus," translated by Prof. B. Jowett.)

*Socrates.* Your remark recalls to my mind an observation which I have often made, that those who have passed their days in the pursuit of philosophy are ridiculously at fault when they have to appear and plead in court. How natural is this!

*Theodorus.* What do you mean?

*Soc.* I mean to say, that those who from their youth upwards have been knocking about in the courts and such like places, compared with those who have received a philosophical education, are slaves, and the others are freemen.

*Theod.* In what is the difference seen?

*Soc.* In the leisure of which you were speaking, and which a freeman can always command; he has his talk out in peace, and, like ourselves, wanders at will from one subject to another, and from a second to a third, if his fancy prefers a new one, caring not whether his words are many or few; his only aim is to attain the truth. But the lawyer is always in a hurry; there is the water of the clepsydra driving him on, and not allowing him to expatiate at will; and there is his adversary standing over him, enforcing his rights; the affidavit, which in their phraseology is termed the brief, is recited; and from this he must not deviate. He is a servant, and is disputing about a fellow-servant before his master, who is seated, and has the cause in his hands; the trial is never about some indifferent matter, but always concerns himself; and often he has to run for his life. The consequence has been, that he has become keen and shrewd; he has learned how to flatter his master in word and indulge him in deed; but his soul is small and unrighteous. His slavish condition has deprived him of growth and uprightness and independence; dangers and fears, which were too much for his truth and honesty, came upon him in early years, when the tenderness of youth was unequal to them, and he has been driven into crooked ways; from the first he has practiced deception and retaliation, and has become stunted and warped. And so he has passed out of youth into manhood, having no soundness in him; and is now, as he thinks, a master in wisdom. Such is the lawyer, Theodorus. Will you have the companion picture of the philosopher, who is of our brotherhood; or shall we return to the argument? Do not let us abuse the freedom of digression which we claim.

*Theod.* Nay, Socrates, let us finish what we were about; for you truly said that we belong to a brotherhood which is free, and are not the servants of the argument; but the argument is our servant, and must wait our leisure. Where is the

judge or spectator who has a right to censure or control us,
as he might the poets?

*Soc.* Then, as this is your wish, I will describe the leaders ;
for there is no use in talking about the inferior sort.   In the
first place, the lords of philosophy have never, from their youth
upwards, known their way to the Agora, or the dicastery, or
the council, or any other political assembly; they neither see
nor hear the laws or votes of the state written or spoken ; the
eagerness of political societies in the attainment of offices—
clubs, and banquets, and revels, and singing-maidens, do not
enter even into their dreams.   Whether any event has turned
out well or ill in the city, what disgrace may have descended
to any one from his ancestors, male or female, are matters of
which the philosopher no more knows than he can tell, as
they say, how many pints are contained in the ocean.   Neither
is he conscious of his ignorance.   For he does not hold aloof
in order that he may gain a reputation ; but the truth is, that
the outer form of him only is in the city; his mind, disdaining the littlenesses and nothingnesses of human things, is
"flying all abroad," as Pindar says, measuring with line and
rule the things which are under and on the earth and above
the heaven, interrogating the whole nature of each and all,
but not condescending to anything which is within reach.

*Theod.* What do you mean, Socrates?

*Soc.* I will illustrate my meaning, Theodorus, by the jest
which the clever, witty Thracian handmaid made about
Thales, when he fell into a well as he was looking up at the
stars.   She said, that he was so eager to know what was going
on in heaven, that he could not see what was before his feet.
This is a jest which is equally applicable to all philosophers.
For the philosopher is wholly unacquainted with his next-
door neighbor; he is ignorant, not only of what he is doing,
but whether he is or is not a human creature ; he is searching
into the essence of man, and is unwearied in discovering what
belongs to such a nature to do or suffer different from any
other ;—I think that you understand me, Theodorus?

*Theod.* I do, and what you say is true.

*Soc.* And thus, my friend, on every occasion, private as
well as public, as I said at first, when he appears in a law-

court, or in any place in which he has to speak of things
which are at his feet and before his eyes, he is the jest, not
only of Thracian handmaids, but of the general herd, tumbling into wells and every sort of disaster through his inex-
perience. He looks such an awkward creature, and conveys
the impression that he is stupid. When he is reviled, he has
nothing personal to say in answer to the civilities of his adversaries, for he knows no scandals of any one, and they do
not interest him; and therefore he is laughed at for his sheep-
ishness; and when others are being praised and glorified, he
cannot help laughing very sincerely in the simplicity of his
heart; and this again makes him look like a fool. When he
hears a tyrant or king eulogized, he fancies that he is listening to the praises of some keeper of cattle—a swineherd, or
shepherd, or cowherd, who is being praised for the quantity
of milk which he squeezes from them; and he remarks that
the creature whom they tend, and out of whom they squeeze
the wealth, is of a less tractable and more insidious nature.
Then, again, he observes that the great man is of necessity as
ill-mannered and uneducated as any shepherd—for he has no
leisure, and he is surrounded by a wall, which is his mountain-
pen. Hearing of enormous landed proprietors of ten thousand
acres and more, our philosopher deems this to be a trifle, because he has been accustomed to think of the whole earth;
and when they sing the praises of family, and say that some
one is a gentleman because he has had seven generations of
wealthy ancestors, he thinks that their sentiments only betray
the dulness and narrowness of vision of those who utter them,
and who are not educated enough to look at the whole, nor to
consider that every man has had thousands and thousands of
progenitors, and among them have been rich and poor, kings
and slaves, Hellenes and barbarians, many times over. And
when some one boasts of a catalogue of twenty-five ancestors,
and goes back to Heracles, the son of Amphitryon, he cannot
understand his poverty of ideas. Why is he unable to calcu-
late that Amphitryon had a twenty-fifth ancestor, who might
have been anybody, and was such as Fortune made him, and
he had a fiftieth, and so on? He is amused at the notion that
he cannot do a sum, and thinks that a little arithmetic would

have got rid of his senseless vanity. Now, in all these cases our philosopher is derided by the vulgar, partly because he is above them, and also because he is ignorant of what is before him, and always at a loss.

*Theod.* That is very true, Socrates.

*Soc.* But, O my friend, when he draws the other into upper air, and gets him out of his pleas and rejoinders into the contemplation of justice and injustice in their own nature and in their difference from one another and from all other things; or from the common places about the happiness of kings to the consideration of government, and of human happiness and misery in general—what they are, and how a man should seek after the one and avoid the other—when that narrow, keen, little legal mind is called to account about all this, he gives the philosopher his revenge; for dizzied by the height at which he is hanging, and from which he looks into space, which is a strange experience to him, he, being dismayed, and lost, and stammering out broken words, is laughed at, not by Thracian handmaidens or any other uneducated persons, for they have no eye for the situation, but by every man who has not been brought up as a slave. Such are the two characters, Theodorus: the one of the philosopher or gentleman, who may be excused for appearing simple and useless when he has to perform some menial office, such as packing up a bag, or flavoring a sauce or fawning speech; the other, of the man who is able to do every kind of service smartly and neatly, but knows not how to wear his cloak like a gentleman; still less does he acquire the music of speech, or hymn the true life which is lived by immortals or men blessed of heaven.

## The Farewell of Socrates.

(From the "Phædon," translated by Professor B. Jowett.)

SOCRATES was permitted to receive his friends in prison dur'ng the interval between his condemnation and death. He discoursed with them on the immortality of the soul, and gave his views of its future abode.

Wherefore, Simmias, seeing all these things, what ought not we to do in order to obtain virtue and wisdom in this life? Fair is the prize, and the hope great!

I do not mean to affirm that the description which I have given of the soul and her mansions is exactly true—a man of sense ought hardly to say that. But I do say that, inasmuch as the soul is shown to be immortal, he may venture to think, not improperly or unworthily, that something of the kind is true. The venture is a glorious one, and he ought to comfort himself with words like these, which is the reason why I lengthen out the tale. Wherefore, I say, let a man be of good cheer about his soul, who has cast away the pleasures and ornaments of the body as alien to him, and rather hurtful in their effects, and has followed after the pleasures of knowledge in this life ; who has adorned the soul in her own proper jewels; which are temperance, and justice, and courage, and nobility and truth—in these arrayed, she is ready to go on her journey to the world below, when her time comes. You, Simmias, and Cebes, and all other men, will depart at some time or other. Me already, as the tragic poet would say, the voice of fate calls. Soon I must drink the poison; and I think that I had better repair to the bath first, in order that the women may not have the trouble of washing my body after I am dead.

When he had done speaking, Crito said : And have you any commands for us, Socrates—anything to say about your children ; or any other matter in which we can serve you?

Nothing particular, he said : only, as I have always told you, I would have you look to yourselves ; that is a service which you may always be doing to me or mine as well as to yourselves. And you need not make professions ; for if you take no thought for yourselves, and walk not according to the precepts which I have given you, not now for the first time, the warmth of your professions will be of no avail.

We will do our best, said Crito. But in what way would you have us bury you?

In any way that you like ; only you must get hold of me, and take care that I do not walk away from you. Then he turned to us, and added, with a smile : I cannot make Crito believe that I am the same Socrates who have been talking and conducting the argument ; he fancies that I am the other Socrates whom he will soon see, a dead body—and he asks, How

shall he bury me? And though I have spoken many words
in the endeavor to show that when I have drunk the poison
I shall leave you and go to the joys of the blessed,—these
words of mine, with which I comforted you and myself, have
had, as I perceive, no effect upon Crito. And therefore I
want you to be surety for me now, as he was surety for me
at the trial: but let the promise be of another sort; for he
was my surety to the judges that I would remain, but you
must be my surety to him that I shall not remain, but go
away and depart; and then he will suffer less at my death,
and not be grieved when he sees my body being burned or
buried. I would not have him sorrow at my hard lot, or say
at the burial, Thus we lay out Socrates; or, Thus we follow him to the grave or bury him; for false words are not
only evil in themselves, but they infect the soul with evil.
Be of good cheer then, my good Crito, and say that you are
burying my body only; and do with that as is usual, and as
you think best.

When he had spoken these words he arose and went into
the bath-chamber with Crito, who bid us wait; and we
waited, talking and thinking of the subject of discourse, and
also of the greatness of our sorrow; he was like a father of
whom we were being bereaved, and we were about to pass
the rest of our lives as orphans. When he had taken the
bath, his children were brought to him (he had two young
sons and an elder one); and the women of his family also
came, and he talked to them and gave them a few directions
in the presence of Crito, and he then dismissed them and
returned to us.

Now the hour of sunset was near, for a good deal of time
had passed while he was within. When he came out he sat
down again with us after his bath, but not much was said.
Soon the jailer, who was the servant of the Eleven,* entered
and stood by him, saying: To you, Socrates, whom I know to
be the noblest and gentlest and best of all who ever came to
this place, I will not impute the angry feelings of other men,
who rage and swear at me, when in obedience to the authori-

---

* The chief magistrates of Athens at that time.

ties, I bid them drink the poison—indeed I am sure that you will not be angry with me, for others, as you are aware, and not I, are the guilty cause. And so fare you well, and try to bear lightly what must needs be; you know my errand. Then bursting into tears, he turned away and went out.

Socrates looked at him and said: I return your good wishes, and will do as you bid. Then turning to us he said, How charming the man is: since I have been in prison he has always been coming to see me, and at times he would talk to me, and was as good as could be to me, and now see how generously he sorrows for me. But we must do as he says, Crito; let the cup be brought, if the poison is prepared; if not, let the attendant prepare some.

CADMUS AND THE DRAGON.
(From a vase-painting at Naples.)

## CHAPTER XX.

### LATER PHILOSOPHERS.

After the death of Socrates several schools of philosophy grew up, each claiming to be founded upon his teachings. Some particular aspect of his philosophy would appeal to one, while another circle of thinkers would seize upon another aspect. This would be emphasized and variously interpreted, until at last it bore slight semblance to the original teaching of Socrates.

The Cyrenaic school was founded by Aristippus of Cyrene. He had grown up in this Greek colony in northern Africa, where luxury and license obtained to a greater degree than was usual in Greek towns.

Socrates had said that the good was pleasurable; Aristippus changed this and said: there is good in pleasure and pleasure is the only good. Socrates held that a good man was also a wise man—one who followed the course which in the long run would give him greatest pleasure. Aristippus thought that wisdom told men not to postpone pleasure, whatever the consequences. The licentious and luxury-loving found in this philosopher their exponent, while he himself was not at all the abandoned creature that these theories might lead one to suppose.

The substance of Cyrenaic doctrine would seem to be: seek individual pleasure; pay no regard to the happiness of others save as it contributes to your own. Individual pleasure is the one thing to be sought after. However, do not let your pleasure master you, for then you cease to enjoy it. Hegesias, of this school, felt that one could not attain pleasure, because it was always accompanied by pain. He denied that any were really happy—they merely thought they were. "Life only appears a good thing to a fool, to the wise man it is different." Since pleasure was the highest good, and this was unattainable, he recommended suicide. Many are said to have listened to him and followed his advice.

The Cynics seized upon a third aspect of Socratic teaching. Socrates had taught that many of the conveniences of life tend to make men effeminate. When reproached by Antiphon for his simple manner of living, the philosopher is reported to have said: "If it be a question of helping our friends or country, which of the two will have the larger leisure to devote to these objects? he who leads the life which I live today or he who lives in the style which you deem so fortunate? Which of the two will adopt a soldier's life more easily, the man who cannot get on without expensive living, or he to whom whatever comes to hand suffices? Which will be the readier to capitulate and cry mercy in a siege, a man of elaborate wants, or he who can get along happily with the readiest things to hand? You, Antiphon, would seem to suggest that happiness consists in luxury and extravagance; I hold a different creed. To have no wants at all is, to my mind, an attribute of godhead; to have as few wants as possible the nearest approach to godhead. And as that which is divine is mightiest, so that is next mightiest which comes closest to the divine."

Taking this phase of Socrates' philosophy, then, the Cynics founded their teachings. They cried that men should return to nature, and to natural instincts. Only those impulses, they held, natural to man are those he possesses in common with other animals. Happiness was still the chief end in life, but it was to be attained by quenching all artificial desires. Following this general plan, they abandoned the conventionalities of life, discarded all the comforts of civilization, and so far as possible receded to the condition of primitive man. Indeed, their pride in poverty became as overweening as was the pride of wealth with others. Diogenes is the best known among the devotees of this school. His eccentricities have become proverbial. Having swept away all comforts and conveniences of a house, he took up his abode in a large wooden cask, or tub. Upon seeing a child drink water from his hand, Diogenes immediately tossed away his cup, remarking that the child had proved it to be unnecessary.

The Cynics never had a large following. Their manner

of life was not attractive to many who cared little for luxury. As a matter of fact, it tended to develop the lower instincts of men and as a natural result led them away from that intellectual freedom which they thought thereby to reach. Shocking the finer sensibilities of the day, they gave nothing to compensate. In short, theirs was a destructive—not a constructive—philosophy.

Stoicism, one of the greatest philosophies developed by the Greeks, was founded by Zeno of Cypress about 306 B. C. Coming to Athens while a young man, he fell under the influence of Socrates as perpetuated by his successors. The hardihood of Socrates appealed to Zeno and his followers. At first allied with the Cynics, this school drifted away from them, however, because the latter gloried in casting aside the comforts of life, while the Stoics were willing to get along without them if circumstances rendered it necessary.

Stoicism took its name from the Stoa, or porch, where adherents of this philosophy gathered to hear lectures given by Zeno and his successors. Duty was regarded as the highest good—not pleasure. A man should cultivate calm and self-possessed demeanor and to grow indifferent to joy or sorrow, health or sickness, wealth or poverty, comfort or oppression. In short, his mind was to rise above any external state or condition of life, and was to constitute his world.

"The human soul is only a part of the divine soul, and in general the individual exists only in and through the Whole or universe. In the human soul reason is the directing power, for reason alone can comprehend general laws and make individual conduct conform to them. Happiness is attainable only by living in complete accord with the laws of nature as perceived by reason. This complete accord is called virtue, *and the wise man considers virtue the only good*. All other things are indifferent. The wise man, filled with these ideas, strives after perfect serenity, without which there can be no happiness. The Stoics therefore sought happiness in the soul, disregarding all material things." [1]

Stoicism spread from the Greeks to the Romans, and in Italy it fell indeed upon congenial soil. The conditions of life

[1] Fowler: Hist. of Greek Lit. p. 364.

under the late republic and early empire were so disheartening
for the masses, and security of person and property so uncer-
tain for even the upper classes, that this philosophy which
taught that the *mind* was the only important thing—a possession of which none might be deprived, fell on welcome ears.
Stoicism enjoined kindliness; it taught a brotherhood of men,
and in many regards was highly commendable.   Among Latin
writers, Seneca was a devout adherent of this school.

About 306 B. C. Epicurus founded the school of philosophy
which came to be known by his name.   It had much in common with the Cyrenaics.   Epicurus agreed that the wise man
will get the greatest amount of pleasure from the moment so
long as it will not be accompanied by a corresponding amount
of pain.   Life consists in a balancing of pleasure and pain.
It is folly, he taught, to seize the enjoyment of the moment
regardless of results—thereby one may bring limitless misery
upon himself for the future; weigh each pleasure—see what
will be the consequences, and if great pleasure is accompanied
by only a moderate amount of pain, it may be wise to follow
it.   The Cyrenaics emphasized the sensual; the Epicureans
the intellectual.

Men have come to be called Epicureans if they enjoy good
living inordinately; one who is devoted to delicacies, good
things to eat, rare wines to drink, and things of this order.
Such was not the significance of the word among the Greeks.
When Epicurianism was translated to Roman soil, it underwent a marked change and came to imply indulgences of
various kinds.   This, however, must not be confounded with
the philosophy as originally taught and developed in Greece.

"Be not slack to seek wisdom when thou art young, nor
weary in the search thereof when thou art grown old.   For
no age is too early or too late for the health of the soul.
And he who says that the season for philosophy has not yet
come, and that it is passed and gone, is like one who should
say that the season for happiness has not yet come or that it
has passed away.   Therefore, both old and young ought to
seek wisdom, that so a man as age comes over him may be
young in good things, because of the grace of what has been,
and while he is young may likewise be old, because he has no

fear of the things which are to come. Exercise thyself, therefore, in the things which bring happiness; for verily, while it
is with thee, thou wilt have everything, and when it is not,
thou wilt do everything if so thou mayest have it.

"          Accustom thyself in the belief that death is
nothing to us, for good and evil are only where they are felt,
and death is the absence of all feeling: therefore, a right understanding that death is nothing to us makes enjoyable the mor-
tality of life, not by adding to years an illimitable time, but by
taking away the yearning after immortality.  For in life there
can be nothing to fear to him who has thoroughly apprehended
that there is nothing to cause fear in what time we are not
alive.  Foolish, therefore, is the man who says that he fears
death, not because it will pain when it comes, but because it
pains in the prospect.

"And since pleasure is our first and native good, for that
reason we do not choose every pleasure whatsoever, but ofttimes pass over many pleasures when a greater annoyance
ensues from them.  And ofttimes we consider pains superior
to pleasures, and submit to the pain for a long time, when it
is attended for us with a greater pleasure.  All pleasure, therefore, because of its kinship with our nature, is a good, but it is
not in all cases our choice, even as every pain is an evil, though
pain is not always, and in every case, to be shunned.  It is,
however, by measuring one against another, and by looking
at the conveniences and inconveniences, that all these things
must be judged.  Sometimes we treat the good as an evil. and
the evil on the contrary, as a good; and we regard independence of outward goods as a great good, not so as in all cases
to use little, but so as to be contented with little, if we have
not much, being thoroughly persuaded that they have the
sweetest enjoyment of luxury who stand least in need of it,
and that whatever is natural is easily procured, and only the
vain and worthless hard to win.  Plain fare gives as much
pleasure as a costly diet, when once the pain due to want is
removed; and bread and water confer the highest pleasure
when they are brought to hungry lips.  To habituate self.
therefore, to plain and inexpensive diet gives all that is needed
for health, and enables a man to meet the necessary require-

ments of life without shrinking, and it places us in a better frame when we approach at intervals a costly fare, and renders us fearless of fortune.

"When we say, then, that pleasure is the end and aim, we do not mean the pleasures of the prodigal, or the pleasures of sensuality, as we are understood by some who are either ignorant and prejudiced for other views or inclined to misinterpret our statements. By pleasure we mean the absence of pain in the body and trouble in the soul. It is not an unbroken succession of drinking feasts and of revelry, not the pleasures of sexual love, not the enjoyment of the fish and other delicacies of a splendid table, which produce a pleasant life; it is sober reasoning, searching out the reasons for every choice and avoidance, and banishing those beliefs through which greater tumult takes possession of the soul. Of all this, the beginning, and the greatest good, is prudence. Wherefore, prudence is a more precious thing even than philosophy: from it grow all the other virtues, for it teaches that we cannot lead a life of pleasure which is not also a life of prudence, honour, and justice; nor lead a life of prudence, honour, and justice which is not also a life of pleasure. For the virtues have grown into one with a pleasant life, and a pleasant life is inseparable from them.

"Who, then, is superior, in thy judgment, to such a man? He holds a holy belief concerning the gods, and is altogether without fears about death; he has diligently considered the end fixed by nature, and has understood how easily the limit of good things can be satisfied and procured, and how either the length or the strength of evil is but slight. He has rejected fate, which some have introduced as universal mistress, no less than chance, in respect of what is due to human agency, for he sees that fate destroys responsibility, and that fortune is inconstant; as for our actions, there is no lord and master over them, and it is to them that blame and praise naturally ensue. Better were it, indeed, to believe the legends of the gods, than be in bondage to the destiny taught by the physical philosophers; for the theological myth gives a faint hope of deprecating divine wrath by honouring the gods, while the fate of the philosophers is deaf to all supplications.

"Exercise thyself in these and kindred precepts day and night, both by thyself and with him who is like unto thee; and never, either in waking or in dream, wilt thou be disturbed, but wilt live as a god amongst men.   For in nothing does he resemble a mortal creature, the man who lives in immortal blessedness."

—Letter of Epicurus.   Trans. Wallace.

ANCIENT GREEK SHIP.

Metope From the Parthenon.

# EARLY GREEK PROSE

## CHAPTER XXI.

Verse has invariably preceded prose in the literary development of a people. Rhythmical measures are the more easily remembered and transmitted from generation to generation; again, poetry appeals more forcefully to the minds of early men; it lends itself more readily to narration of heroic deeds, to expressions of religious adoration, and to songs of festal gayety.

We have seen that poetry among the Greeks took first the epic form. Epics were produced from an indefinite period to the seventh century, generally speaking, and were recited throughout Greek history at the national festivals. Following the epic, came the lyric, from the seventh to the fifth centuries, roughly speaking. Overlapping the period of the lyric by perhaps a century, we find the beginnings of Greek prose. Like verse, it originated in Asia Minor.

It was no mere chance which allowed literature to develop earlier in Asia Minor than in Continental Greece. Wealth and leisure are necessary to a certain degree before people can give themselves over to purely cultural pursuits. Extended commerce led to the accumulation of riches, and gradually there grew up an increasing leisure class with time for reflection and literary composition. At the same time in Greece proper, the people as a whole were too much absorbed in the mere getting of a living, in fighting out political questions and trying political experiments, to give attention to literary accomplishments.

### Aesop.

Maxims, trite sayings, and fables were probably first to find prose expression among the Greeks. Tradition says that a slave, a barbarian by the name of Aesop, made the beast-fable popular in Hellas. Living about 550 B. C., he saw the usurpations of tyrants, and is said to have drawn similitudes between the doings of men and beasts, under cover of the fable,

which insured him safety.   As a matter of fact, we know
almost nothing about Aesop.   Certain it is that he did not
invent the beast-fable, since it was known before his time.   He
may have given it fresh popularity.   Scientific investigation
has well-nigh established the fact that practically none of the
tales known to us as Aesop's were in reality his.   Nevertheless, it would appear that they were similar in spirit.   Told
many years without being committed to writing, and passing
through centuries of change, it could hardly be expected that
the fables would hold to their original versions.   However, it
is important for us to remember that tales of a nature such as
these were probably among the first to fall into prose form
among the Hellenes.   Because Aesop was a slave, and consequently a barbarian, he has been given various nationalities.
Some have argued that he was a Syrian; others have tried to
prove that he was an Egyptian, and some have believed him a
native of Arabia.   The question can hardly be settled at the
present time, and is of little moment anyway.   We are more
concerned with the kind of stories which entertained the Greeks
at this stage of their development.   Indeed, fables seem always
to have been popular in Hellas.

### The Wolf and the Lamb.

"One hot, sultry day, a Wolf and a Lamb happened to
come just at the same time to quench their thirst in the stream
of a clear silver brook, that ran tumbling down the side of a
rocky mountain.   The Wolf stood upon the higher ground,
and the Lamb at some distance from him down the current.
However, the Wolf, having a mind to pick a quarrel with
him, asked him what he meant by disturbing the water, and
making it so muddy that he could not drink it, and, at the
same time, demanded satisfaction.   The Lamb, frightened at
this threatening charge, told him, in a tone as mild as possible,
that with humble submission he could not conceive how that
could be; since the water which he drank ran down from the
Wolf to him, and therefore could not be disturbed so far up
the stream.   Be that as it will, replies the Wolf, you are a
rascal, and I have been told that you treated me with ill language behind my back, about half a year ago.   Upon my word,

says the Lamb, the time you mention was before I was born. The Wolf, finding it to no purpose to argue any longer against truth, fell into a great passion, snarling and foaming at the mouth as if he had been mad ; and, drawing nearer to the Lamb, Sirrah, says he, if it was not you, it was your father, and that is all one. So he seized the poor, innocent, helpless thing, tore it to pieces, and made a meal of it."

### The Horse and the Stag.

" The Stag, with his sharp horns, got the better of the horse, and drove him clear out of the pasture where they used to feed together. So the latter craved the assistance of man; and, in order to receive the benefit of it, suffered him to put a bridle into his mouth, and a saddle upon his back. By this way of proceeding, he entirely defeated his enemy ; but was mightily disappointed when, upon returning thanks, and desiring to be dismissed, he received this answer : No, I never knew before how useful a drudge you were; now I have found what you are good for, you may depend upon it I will keep you to it."

### Hercules and the Carter.

" As a clownish fellow was driving his cart along a deep miry lane, the wheels stuck so fast in the clay that the horses could not draw them out. Upon this he fell a-bawling and praying to Hercules to come and help him. Hercules, looking down from a cloud, bid him not lie there like an idle rascal as he was, but get up and whip his horses stoutly and clap his shoulder to the wheel, adding that this was the only way for him to obtain his assistance."

## AESOP.

He sat among the woods; he heard
　　The sylvan merriment; he saw
The pranks of butterfly and bird,
　　The humors of the ape, the daw.

And in the lion or the frog—
　　In all the life of moor and fen,
In ass and peacock, stork and dog,
　　He read similitudes of men.

" Of these, from these," he cried, " we come,
　　Our hearts, our brains descend from these."
And lo! the Beasts no more were dumb,
　　But answered out of brakes and trees;

" Not ours," they cried; " Degenerate,
　　If ours at all," they cried again,
" Ye fools who war with God and Fate,
　　Who strive and toil: strange race of men;

" For *we* are neither bond nor free,
　　For *we* have neither slaves nor kings,
But near to Nature's heart are we,
　　And conscious of her secret things.

" Content are we to fall asleep,
　　And well content to wake no more,
We do not laugh, we do not weep,
　　Nor look behind us, nor before;

" But were there cause for moan and mirth,
　　'Tis we, not you, should sigh or scorn,
Oh, latest children of the Earth,
　　Most childish children Earth has borne."

They spoke, but that misshapen slave
　　Told never of the thing he heard,
And unto men their portraits gave
　　In likenesses of beast and bird!

　　　　　　　　　　　　　　　—*A. L.*

## HERODOTUS.

Herodotus is frequently called the father of Greek prose. He lived about a century later than Aesop—that is, about 445 B. C. Born in Halicarnassus, southwestern Asia Minor, he travelled extensively through all the known world and wrote down the history of his travels and accounts of the peoples whom he visited. These he later read in part to Greek audiences, congregated at the Olympian games. His work as it has come down to us, consists of nine books, each one dedicated to one of the muses. This division of the writing, however, is comparatively modern. The first six books describe various peoples with whom Herodotus came in contact in his travels; the last three pertain to the great war with Persia.

Herodotus has often been severely censured by modern historians for not having employed recent methods in preparing his historical writings. Such criticisms avail nothing. He wrote to entertain and enlighten the people of Hellas. They liked marvellous tales above all things, and so whatever was unusual or strange was immediately incorporated into these writings by Herodotus, who not infrequently stated that he himself did not believe it to be true, or, if it were a custom, that he thought it not general. His histories, although frequently exaggerated and inaccurate, have been of great value to subsequent ages. Much light has been thrown upon the past by his observations alone, and undoubtedly the reader today finds far more pleasure in these ancient writings than he would, had Herodotus followed a strictly scientific and accurate system of investigation. While we lack an accurate narration in this way, we are the better enabled to understand the mind of the early Hellene and to know what in this remote age was accepted as history.

## THE PERSIAN INVASION.

"When the news of the battle fought at Marathon reached Darius, son of Hystaspes, who was before much exasperated with the Athenians on account of the attack upon Sardis, he then became much more incensed, and was still more eager to prosecute the war against Greece. Having therefore immediately sent messengers to the several cities, he enjoined them to prepare an army, imposing on each a much greater number than they had furnished before, and ships, horses, corn and transports. When these orders were proclaimed round about, Asia was thrown into agitation during the space of three years, the bravest men being enrolled and prepared for the purpose of invading Greece. But in the fourth year the Egyptians, who had been subdued by Cambyses, revolted from the Persians; whereupon Darius only became more eager to march against both.          However, after these things, and in the year after the revolt of Egypt, it happened that Darius himself, while he was making preparations, died, having reigned thirty-six years in all; nor was he able to avenge himself either on the Egyptians, who had revolted, or on the Athenians. When Darius was dead, the kingdom devolved on his son Xerxes.          In course of the fifth year he began his march with a vast multitude of men. For of the expeditions with which we are acquainted, this was by far the greatest.          For what nation did not Xerxes lead out of Asia against Greece? What stream, being drunk, did not fail him, except that of great rivers? Some supplied ships; others were ordered to furnish men for the infantry, from others cavalry were required, from others transports for horses, together with men to serve in the army; others had to furnish long ships for the bridges, and others provisions and vessels.

"Xerxes again summoned the most distinguished of the Persians, and when they were assembled he addressed them as follows: 'O, Persians, I have called you together to desire this of you, that you would acquit yourselves like brave men, and not disgrace the former exploits of the Persians, which are great and memorable. But let each and all of us together show our zeal; for this which we are endeavoring to accomplish is a good common to all. On this account, then, I call on you to apply yourselves earnestly to the war; for, as I am informed, we are marching against brave men; and if we conquer them, no other army in the world will dare to oppose us. Now, then, let us cross over, having first offered up prayers to the gods who protect the Persian territory.' That day they made preparations for the passage over; and on the following they waited for the sun, as they wished to see it rising, in the meantime burning all sorts of perfumes on the bridges and strewing the road with myrtle branches. When the sun rose, Xerxes pouring a libation into the sea out of a golden cup, offered up a prayer to the sun, that no such accident might befall him as would prevent him from subduing Europe, until he had reached its utmost limits. After having prayed, he threw the cup into the Hellespont, and a golden bowl, and a Persian sword, which they call acinace. But I cannot determine with certainty whether he dropped these things into the sea as an offering to the sun, or whether he repented of having scourged the Hellespont, and presented these gifts to the sea as a compensation. When these ceremonies were finished, the infantry and all the cavalry crossed over by that bridge which was towards the Pontus; and the beasts of burden and attendants by that towards the Aegean. First of all, the ten thousand Persians led the van, all wearing crowns; and after them the promiscuous host of all nations. These crossed on that day. On the following, first the horsemen and those who carried their lances downward; these also wore crowns. Next came the sacred horses and the sacred chariot; afterwards Xerxes himself and the spearmen and the thousand horsemen; after them the rest of the army closed the march; and at the same time the ships got under weigh to the opposite shore. I have also heard that Xerxes crossed over last of all."

Very different in style and manner of treatment was the historical work of a contemporary of Herodotus—the great Athenian historian, Thucydides. Although he lived in the same century as the immortal writer of Halicarnassus, Thucydides was a companion of Pericles, and in touch with the most progressive thought of his day. He was in advance of his times; Herodotus really belonged to an age before his own. Thucydides has left a monumental work—a history of the Peloponnesian war, in which he himself at first took part, and whose coming he saw before hostilities began. No historical writings could be more unlike than those of these two Greek historians. Thucydides wrote in a calm, impartial style, and never allowed his personal sympathies to influence his judgments. He tried hard to ascertain the facts in each case, and related them as they occurred, without color or modification. However, while his work remains the first scientific historical production the world had seen, it has never had the popularity of Herodotus' histories. Thucydides contributed a lasting production to the world, masterly in its dignified calm. Yet one may turn now and then from its lofty height to the simple, childlike narration of Herodotus with some sense of pleasure.

### From Thucydides.

"The feebleness of antiquity is further proved to me by the circumstance that there appears to have been no common action in Hellas before the Trojan war. And I am inclined to think that the very name was not as yet given to the whole country, and in fact did not exist at all before the time of Hellen, the son of Deucalion; the different tribes, of which the Pelasgian was the most widely spread, gave their own names to different districts.

"Minos is the first to whom tradition ascribes the possession of a navy. He made himself master of a great part of what is now termed the Hellenic sea; he conquered the Cyclades, and was the first colonizer of most of them, expelling the Carians and appointing his own sons to govern in them. Lastly, it was he who, from a natural desire to protect his growing revenues, sought, as far as he was able, to clear the sea of pirates.

"For in ancient times both Hellenes and Barbarians, as well the inhabitants of the coast as of the islands, when they began to find their way to one another by sea had recourse to piracy. They were commanded by powerful chiefs, who took this means of increasing their wealth and providing for their poorer followers. They would fall upon the unwalled and straggling towns, or rather, villages, which they plundered, and maintained themselves by the plunder of them; for, as yet, such an occupation was held to be honourable and not disgraceful.

"Even in the age which followed the Trojan war, Hellas was still in process of ferment and settlement, and had no time for peaceful growth. The return of the Hellenes from Troy after their long absence led to many changes; quarrels, too, arose in nearly every city, and those who were expelled by them went and founded other cities.

"As Hellas grew more powerful and the acquisition of wealth became more and more rapid, the revenues of her cities increased, and in most of them tyrannies were established; they had hitherto been ruled by hereditary kings, having fixed prerogatives. The Hellenes likewise began to build navies and to make the sea their element.

"Such are the results of my enquiry into the early state of Hellas. They will not readily be believed upon a bare recital of all the proofs of them. Men do not discriminate, and are too ready to receive ancient traditions about their own as well as about other countries. Yet any one who upon the grounds which I have given arrives at some such conclusions as my own about these ancient times, would not be far wrong. He must not be misled by the exaggerated fancies of the poets, or by the tales of chroniclers who seek to please the ear rather than to speak the truth. Their accounts cannot be tested by him; and most of the facts in the lapse of ages have passed into the region of romance. At such a distance of time he must make up his mind to be satisfied with conclusions resting upon the clearest evidence which can be had. And though men will always judge any war in which they are actually fighting to be the greatest at the time, but, after it is over, revert to their admiration of some other which has preceded, still the Peloponnesian, if estimated by the actual facts, will certainly prove to have been the greatest ever known." [1]

These two Greeks were by no means the only ones to use prose as their vehicle of expression, but they were the greatest to do so at this time. Some of the philosophers attempted to give utterance to their thoughts in poetry, but it soon became apparent that verse was not suited to such ideas and henceforth prose became their medium of expression.

[1] Thucydides: Peloponnesian War, Bk. I, 1-21.

### THE BATTLE OF MARATHON.

THE Persians, having brought Eretria into subjection, after waiting a few days, made sail for Attica, greatly straitening the Athenians as they approached, and thinking to deal with them as they had dealt with the people of Eretria. And, because there was no place in all Attica so convenient for their horse as Marathon, and it lay, moreover, quite close to Eretria, therefore Hippias, the son of Pisistratus, conducted them thither. When intelligence of this reached the Athenians, they likewise marched their troops to Marathon and there stood on the defensive, having at their head ten generals, of whom one was Miltiades.

Before they left the city, the generals sent off to Sparta a herald, one Pheidippides, who was by birth an Athenian, and by profession and practice a trained runner. This man, according to the account which he gave to the Athenians on his return, when he was near Mount Parthenium, above Tegea, fell in with the god Pan, who called him by his name and bade him ask the Athenians "wherefore they neglected him so entirely, when he was kindly disposed towards them, and had often helped them in times past, and would do so again in time to come?" The Athenians, entirely believing in the truth of this report, as soon as their affairs were once more in good order, set up a temple to Pan under the Acropolis, and in return for the message which I have recorded, established in his honor yearly sacrifices and a torch-race.

On the occasion of which we speak, when Pheidippides was sent by the Athenian generals, and, according to his own account, saw Pan on his journey, he reached Sparta, on the very next day after quitting the city of Athens. Upon his arrival he went before the rulers, and said to them, "Men of Lacedæmon, the Athenians beseech you to hasten to their aid, and not allow that state, which is the most ancient in all Greece, to be enslaved by the barbarians. Eretria, look you, is already carried away captive, and Greece weakened by the

loss of no mean city." Thus did Pheidippides deliver the
message committed to him. And the Spartans wished to help
the Athenians, but were unable to give them any present succor, as they did not like to break their established law. It
was then the ninth day of the first decade, and they could not
march out of Sparta on the ninth, when the moon had not
reached the full. So they waited for the full of the moon.

The barbarians were conducted to Marathon by Hippias,
the son of Pisistratus, who the night before had seen a strange
vision in his sleep. He dreamed of lying in his mother's
arms, and conjectured the dream to mean that he would be
restored to Athens, recover the power which he had lost, and
afterward live to a good old age in his native country. Such
was the sense in which he interpreted the vision. He now
proceeded to act as guide to the Persians, and in the first place
he landed the prisoners taken from Eretria upon the island
that is called Ægileia, a tract belonging to the Styreans, after
which he brought the fleet to anchor off Marathon, and mar-
shalled the bands of the barbarians as they disembarked. As
he was thus employed it chanced that he sneezed and at the
same time coughed with more violence than was his wont.
Now, as he was a man advanced in years and the greater
number of his teeth were loose, it so happened that one of
them was driven out with the force of the cough and fell
down into the sand. Hippias took all the pains he could to
find it, but the tooth was nowhere to be seen ; whereupon he
fetched a deep sigh, and said to the bystanders, "After all,
the land is not ours, and we shall never be able to bring it
under. All my share in it is the portion of which my tooth
has possession." So Hippias believed that in this way his
dream was out.

The Athenians were drawn up in order of battle in a
sacred close belonging to Hercules, when they were joined by
the Platæans, who came in full force to their aid. Some time
before, the Platæans had put themselves under the rule of the
Athenians, and these last had already undertaken many labors
on their behalf.

The Athenian generals were divided in their opinions, and
some advised not to risk a battle, because they were too few to

engage such a host as that of the Medes, while others were
for fighting at once; and among these last was Miltiades.
He, therefore, seeing that opinions were thus divided and that
the less worthy counsel appeared likely to prevail, resolved to
go to the polemarch and have a conference with him. For
the man on whom the lot fell to be polemarch at Athens was
entitled to give his vote with the ten generals, since anciently
the Athenians allowed him an equal right of voting with
them. The polemarch at this juncture was Callimachus of
Aphidnæ; to him, therefore, Miltiades went and said:

"With thee it rests, Callimachus, either to bring Athens
to slavery, or, by securing her freedom, to leave behind thee
to all future generations a memory beyond even Harmodius
and Aristogiton. For never since the time that the Athenians
became a people were they in so great a danger as now. If
they bow their necks beneath the yoke of the Medes, the woes
which they will have to suffer when given into the power of
Hippias are already determined on; if, on the other hand,
they fight and overcome, Athens may rise to be the very first
city in Greece. How it comes to pass that these things are
likely to happen, and how the determining of them in some
sort rests with thee, I will now proceed to make clear. We
generals are ten in number, and our votes are divided: half
of us wish to engage, half to avoid a combat. Now, if we do
not fight, I look to see a great disturbance at Athens which
will shake men's resolutions, and then I fear they will submit
themselves; but if we fight the battle before any unsoundness
show itself among our citizens, let the gods but give us fair
play and we are well able to overcome the enemy. On thee,
therefore, we depend in this matter, which lies wholly in thine
own power. Thou hast only to add thy vote to my side and
thy country will be free, and not free only, but the first state
in Greece. Or if thou preferrest to give thy vote to them who
would decline the combat, then the reverse will follow."

Miltiades by these words gained Callimachus, and the
addition of the polemarch's vote caused the decision to be in
favor of fighting. Hereupon all those generals who had been
desirous of hazarding a battle, when their turn came to command the army, gave up their right to Miltiades. He, how-

ever, though he accepted their offers, nevertheless waited and
would not fight until his own day of command arrived in due
course. Then at length, when his own turn was come, the
Athenian battle was set in array, and this was the order of it:
Callimachus the polemarch led the right wing; for it was at
that time a rule with the Athenians to give the right wing to
the polemarch. After this followed the tribes, according as
they were numbered, in an unbroken line; while last of all
came the Platæans, forming the left wing. And ever since
that day it has been a custom with the Athenians, in the sacrifices and assemblies held each fifth year at Athens, for the
Athenian herald to implore the blessing of the gods on the
Platæans conjointly with the Athenians. Now, as they mar-
shalled the host upon the field of Marathon, in order that the
Athenian front might be of equal length with the Median,
the ranks of the centre were diminished, and it became the
weakest part of the line, while the wings were both made
strong with a depth of many ranks.

So, when the battle was set in array and the victims
showed themselves favorable, instantly the Athenians, so soon
as they were let go, charged the barbarians at a run. Now,
the distance between the two armies was little short of eight
furlongs. The Persians, therefore, when they saw the Greeks
coming on at speed, made ready to receive them, although it
seemed to them that the Athenians were bereft of their senses,
and bent upon their own destruction; for they saw a mere
handful of men coming on at a run without either horsemen
or archers. Such was the opinion of the barbarians, but the
Athenians in close array fell upon them and fought in a manner worthy of being recorded. They were the first of the
Greeks, so far as I know, who introduced the custom of charg-
ing the enemy at a run, and they were likewise the first who
dared to look upon the Median garb and to face men clad in
that fashion. Until this time the very name of the Medes
had been a terror to the Greeks to hear.

The two armies fought together on the plain of Marathon
for a length of time, and in the mid-battle, where the Persians
themselves and the Sacæ had their place, the barbarians were
victorious, and broke and pursued the Greeks into the inner

country, but on the two wings the Athenians and the Platæans
defeated the enemy. Having so done, they suffered the routed
barbarians to fly at their ease, and, joining the two wings in
one, fell upon those who had broken their own centre, and
fought and conquered them. These likewise fled, and now
the Athenians hung upon the runaways and cut them down,
chasing them all the way to the shore; on reaching which,
they laid hold of the ships and called aloud for fire.

It was in the struggle here that Callimachus the polemarch, after greatly distinguishing himself, lost his life;
Stesilaus, too, the son of Thrasilaus, one of the generals, was
slain; and Cynægirus, the son of Euphorion, having seized
on a vessel of the enemy's by the ornament at the stern, had
his hand cut off by the blow of an axe, and so perished, as
likewise did many other Athenians of note and name.

Nevertheless, the Athenians secured in this way seven
vessels, while with the remainder the barbarians pushed off,
and, taking aboard their Eretrian prisoners from the island
where they had left them, doubled Cape Sunium, hoping to
reach Athens before the return of the Athenians. The Alc-
mæonidæ were accused by their countrymen of suggesting
this course to them, they had, it was said, an understanding
with the Persians, and made a signal to them by raising a
shield after they were embarked in their ships.

The Persians accordingly sailed round Sunium, but the
Athenians with all possible speed marched away to the defence
of their city, and succeeded in reaching Athens before the
appearance of the barbarians; and as their camp at Marathon
had been pitched in a precinct of Hercules, so now they encamped in another precinct of the same god at Cynosarges.
The barbarian fleet arrived and lay to off Phalerum, which
was at that time the haven of Athens; but after resting awhile
upon their oars, they departed and sailed away to Asia.

There fell in this battle of Marathon, on the side of the
barbarians, about 6,400 men; on that of the Athenians, 192.
Such was the number of the slain on the one side and the other.

## CHAPTER XXII.

### LATER GREEK PROSE.

Xenophon was born about 430 B. C. in Attica. He was given a good education, and while a mere boy came under the influence of Socrates. In 401 B. C. he joined a body of troops organized by Cyrus the Younger for his attack upon Artaxerxes. It will be remembered that Cyrus was killed in the battle waged by these two brothers, and the 10,000 Greek troops suddenly found themselves without a leader in a hostile land. To increase the danger, the leading generals were taken by strategy. When the outlook seemed hopeless, Xenophon came forward from the ranks and offered to lead the soldiers home. His confidence reassured the men, and under the system he organized they began their famous retreat. After five months of intermittent warfare, they reached the Black Sea, and knowing that their safety was now assured, the men were overcome with emotion. This story has been preserved to us in the Anabasis, written by Xenophon during and after the events took place.

Anabasis means *the March Up,* and refers to the progress into Asia after leaving the coast; however, only the first book deals with this part of the story. The remaining books tell of the retreat. This incident was of greater importance than at first it seems, for it showed to the Greeks for the first time the actual condition of the Persian state. In a well organized territory it would have been impossible for 10,000 soldiers to have retreated from the interior to the coast and make an escape after having taken sides against the reigning king. Persia had been the dread of Greece for many years and now it was clearly demonstrated that she was really on the verge of ruin. This information Philip of Macedon remembered later, and the experience of Xenophon's comrades gave Alexander confidence for his eastward campaign.

After 394 B. C. Xenophon went to live in retirement upon

his estate, where he spent his life writing and entertaining his friends in quiet leisure. Generally speaking, his writings have been preserved to the present day. In addition to the Anabasis, he wrote Hellenica, a history of Greece, beginning at the point where Thucydides broke off his narration. The first two books of Hellenica are supposed to have been written by aid of Thucydides' notes, and in the main they hold well to the spirit of the great Peloponnesian history. The five remaining books, however, were written later, and are plainly inferior to the rest. The impartial standpoint of Thucydides is abandoned, and the interest of the earlier historian is no longer sustained. Nevertheless, without this work we should be without sources for the period in Greece between 411-362 B. C.

From a literary point of view, Memorabilia, or the Recollections of Socrates, are perhaps as interesting to us today as any of Xenophon's writings. He retained his early affection for the philosopher and felt that he owed him a fair attempt to clear his memory of the charges which condemned him to die in Athens. Although Plato has done the same thing, and done it better, nevertheless, these recollections of Socrates are a worthy contribution to Greek literature.

Xenophon cannot be said to have been a great writer nor a genius in any particular field. We may classify him, not as a historian or a philosopher, perhaps, but better, as an essayist. In essay writing he was eminently successful.

In any discussion of Greek Literature, some mention should be made of the Attic orators, although their orations were not produced with a purely literary motive. The same might be said of the tragic poets, and the writers of comedy. Like the orators, their productions were prepared for the ancient Greeks themselves,—the poets to please, the orators to instruct and rouse the people.

When Greece shook off her oligarchal government and became a democracy, the leaders were those who could move the people to their way of thinking. Again, as the spirit of litigation developed among the argument-loving Hellenes, men on both sides of a case had to impress the juries with claims for justice. We have seen that the new conditions gave rise to the Sophists, who instructed men how to discuss questions before the people, and who wrote out pleas for the plaintiff and defendant to commit to memory. From earliest times, also, the Greeks had loved oratory. It was an art to be cultivated like music, or any other art. One who could excel in oratory always won the favor of the Hellenes. It came about naturally, then, that he who could teach men what to say, and teach them how to say it, was greatly in demand. Such was the part taken by Isocrates.

Born in 436 B. C., Isocrates was well educated, but the reverses of the Peloponnesian war left him dependent upon himself for support. Accordingly, he went to the great Gorgias, of Sicily, whose careful arrangement of words was adopted by Isocrates. Having mastered rhetoric and oratory, Isocrates returned to Athens and for ten years occupied himself in writing pleas. However, he disliked the petty cases which were frequently brought before him, and at length abandoned this work. His voice was not sufficient for public speaking and he determined to establish a school for Greek youths, where rhetoric and oratory might be studied. For fifty years he conducted this school and several noted men studied with him. He became the friend and companion of the most gifted men of Greece and was himself noted.

He regretted the degeneracy of the earlier Athenian life, and thought the navy to have been the cause of Athens' decline. In a fervent speech he urged the Athenians to return to the course of earlier years, when they were content to be first in Greece and had not yet struggled to build up an empire.

The style of this orator was particularly admired by the ancient Greeks. By arranging even the most ordinary words with care, he produced harmonizing effects, and his sentences possessed a certain musical rhythm which no translation can reproduce.

Greatest of Greek orators—perhaps greatest of all orators—was Demosthenes. He was born 384 B. C. and pursued the education usual among young Athenians. His father's property was appropriated by Demosthenes' guardians, and one of his earliest acts, upon attaining man's estate, was to bring a suit for its recovery.

Tradition says that Demosthenes was troubled by an

impediment of speech and that he struggled long to overcome it, practising beside the sea until he could make himself heard above its surges. Whatever foundation there may have been for the story, it has been repeated for hundreds of years.

Demosthenes saw with dismay the encroachments of Philip of Macedon, and in a series of Philippics attempted to rouse the Athenians to take an aggressive policy toward him. In spite of his efforts Athens was no longer able to stand against the vigour of the north. Other speeches, public and private, were delivered—the most famous being the Oration on the Crown. His style was vigorous and vivid, while he frequently arose to a point of excellence unexcelled by any, either before or since his time. The orator gives us a glimpse of impending conditions as no calm historian can do, and while these speeches were composed for immediate purposes, they remain among the monumental works of ancient Greece.

### Xenophon's Memorabilia of Socrates.

"I have often wondered by what arguments the accusers of Socrates persuaded the Athenians that he deserved death from the state; for the indictment against him was to this effect: *Socrates offends against the laws in not paying respect to those gods whom the city respects, and introducing other new deities; he also offends against the laws in corrupting the youth.*

"In the first place, *that he did not respect the gods whom the city respects,* what proof did they bring? For he was seen frequently at home, and frequently on the public altars of the city; nor was it unknown that he used divination; as it was a common subject of talk that 'Socrates used to say that the divinity instructed him'; and it was from this circumstance, indeed, that they seem chiefly to have derived the charge of introducing new deities.

"He was constantly in public, for he went in the morning to the places of walking and the gymnasia; at the time when the market was full he was to be seen there; and the rest of the day he was where he was likely to meet the greatest number of people; he was generally engaged in discourse, and all who pleased were at liberty to hear him; yet no one ever

either saw Socrates doing, or heard him saying, anything
impious or profane; for he did not dispute about the nature of
things as most other philosophers disputed, speculating how
that which is called by Sophists *the world* was produced, and
by what necessary laws everything in the heavens is effected,
but endeavored to show that those who chose such subjects
of contemplation were foolish; and used in the first place to
inquire of them whether they thought that they already knew
sufficient of human affairs, and therefore proceeded to such
subjects of meditation, or whether, when they neglected human
affairs entirely, and speculated on celestial matters, they
thought that they were doing what became them. He wondered, too, that it was not apparent to them that it is impossible
for man to satisfy himself on such points, since even those who
pride themselves most on discussing them do not hold the
same opinion one with another, but are, compared with each
other, like madmen.

"It also seems wonderful to me, that any should have been
persuaded that Socrates corrupted the youth; Socrates, who, in
addition to what has been said of him, was not only the most
rigid of all men in the government of his passions and appetites, but also the most able to withstand cold, heat, and every
kind of labor; and, besides, so inured to frugality, that though
he possessed very little, he easily made it a sufficiency. How,
then, being of such a character himself, could he have rendered
others impious, or lawless, or luxurious, or incontinent, or too
effeminate to endure labor? On the contrary, he restrained
many of them from such vices, leading them to love virtue,
and giving them hopes that if they would take care of themselves they would become honorable and worthy characters.
Not indeed that he ever professed to be an instructor in that
way, but, by showing that he was himself such a character, he
made those in his society hope that, by imitating him, they
would become such as he was.

"Of the body he was not neglectful, nor did he commend
those who were. He did not approve that a person should eat
to excess, and then use immoderate exercise, but recommended
that he should work off, by a proper degree of exercise, as
much as the appetite received with pleasure; for such a habit,

he said, was peculiarly conducive to health, and did not prevent attention to the mind. He was not, however, fine or
ostentatious in his clothes or sandals, or in any of his habits
of life; yet he did not make those about him lovers of money,
for he checked them in this as well as other passions, and
asked no remuneration from those who desired his company.
By refraining from such demand, he thought that he consulted his liberty, and called those who took money for their
discourses their own enslavers, since they must of necessity
hold discussions with those from whom they received pay.
He expressed wonder, too, that any one who professed to
teach virtue should demand money, and not think that he
gained the greatest profit in securing a good friend, but fear
that he whom he had made an honorable and worthy character would not retain the greatest gratitude toward his greatest benefactor. Socrates, indeed, never expressed so much
to any one; yet he believed that those of his associates who
imbibed what he approved, would be always good friends both
to himself and to each other. How, then, could a man of
such character corrupt the young, unless, indeed, the study of
virtue be corruption?

Not even parents themselves, when they have their sons
in their society, are blamed if their sons do anything wrong,
provided they themselves are correct in their conduct. In the
same manner it would be right to judge of Socrates; if he had
done anything immoral, he would justly be thought to be a
bad man; but if he constantly observed morality, how can he
reasonably bear the blame of vice which was not in him? . . .

"And do you think it strange," inquired Socrates, "that it
should seem better to the divinity that I should now close my
life? Do you not know that, down to the present time, I
would not admit to any man that he has lived either better or
with more pleasure than myself, for I consider that those live
best who study best to become as good as possible; and that
those live with most pleasure who feel the most assurance that
they are daily growing better and better. This assurance I
have felt, to the present day, to be the case with respect to
myself; and associating with other men, and comparing myself
with others, I have always retained this opinion respecting

myself; and not only I, but my friends also, maintain a similar feeling with regard to me, not because they love me, but because they think that while they associated with me they became greatly advanced in virtue. If I shall live a longer period, perhaps I shall be destined to sustain the evils of old age, to find my sight and hearing weakened, to feel my intellect impaired, to become less apt to learn, and more forgetful, and, in fine, to grow inferior to others in all these qualities in which I was once superior to them. And I know that I also, if I now die, shall obtain from mankind far different consideration from that which they will pay to those who take my life; for I know that they will always bear witness to me that I have never wronged any man, or rendered any man less virtuous, but that I have always endeavored to make those better who conversed with me."

*—Watson's trans.*

GREEK SCHOOL—FROM A VASE PAINTING.

PERICLES.

So long as Pericles stood at the head of Athens in time of peace, he governed it with moderation and maintained it in safety, and under him it rose to its highest power. And when the war broke out he proved that he had well calculated the resources of the State. He lived through two years and a half of it; and when he died, his foresight as to its conduct became even more generally admitted. For he always said that if they were patient and paid due attention to their navy, and did not grasp at extension of empire during the war, or expose their city to danger, they would be the victors. But they did the very contrary to all this; and in matters which seemed to have no reference to the war they followed an evil policy as to their own interests and those of their allies, and in accordance with their private jealousies and private advantage; measures which, when successful, brought honors and profits to individuals only, while, if they failed, the disadvantage was felt by the State in its results on the war.

The reason lay in this: that Pericles, powerful by his influence and ability, and manifestly incorruptible by bribes, exercised a control over the masses, combined with excellent tact, and rather led them than allowed them to lead him. For since he did not gain his ascendancy by unbecoming means, he never used language to humor them, but was able, on the strength of his high character, even to oppose their passions. That is, when he saw them overweeningly confident without just grounds, he would speak so as to inspire them with a wholesome fear; or, when they were unreasonably alarmed, he would raise their spirits again to confidence. Thus Athens was a nominal democracy, but in fact the government of the one foremost man.

## CLEON'S VICTORY AT SPHACTERIA.

At Pylos the Athenians continued to blockade the Lacedæmonians in the island of Sphacteria, and the Peloponnesian army on the mainland remained in their old position. The watch was harassing to the Athenians, for they were in want both of food and water; there was only one small well, which was inside the fort, and the soldiers were commonly in the habit of scraping away the shingle on the seashore, and drinking any water which they could get. The Athenian garrison was crowded into a narrow space, and, their ships having no regular anchorage, the crews took their meals on land by turns; one-half of the army eating while the other lay at anchor in the open sea. The unexpected length of the siege was a great discouragement to them; they had hoped to starve their enemies out in a few days, for they were on a desert island, and had only brackish water to drink. The secret of this protracted resistance was a proclamation issued by the Lacedæmonians offering large fixed prices, and freedom if he were a Helot, to any one who would convey into the island meal, wine, cheese, or any other provision suitable for a besieged place. Many braved the danger, especially the Helots; they started from all points of Peloponnesus, and before daybreak bore down upon the shore of the island looking towards the open sea. They took especial care to have a strong wind in their favor, since they were less likely to be discovered by the triremes when it blew hard from the sea. The blockade was then impracticable, and the crews of the boats were perfectly reckless in running them aground; for a value had been set upon them, and Lacedæmonian hoplites were waiting to receive them about the landing-places of the island. All, however, who ventured when the sea was calm were captured. Some, too, dived and swam by way of the harbor, drawing after them by a cord skins containing pounded linseed and poppy seeds mixed with honey. At first they were not found out, but afterwards watches were posted. The two parties had all sorts of devices, the one determined to send in food, the other to detect them.

When the Athenians heard that their own army was suffering, and that supplies were introduced into the island, they began to be anxious and were apprehensive that the blockade might extend into the winter. Cleon, knowing that he was an object of general mistrust, because he had stood in the way of peace, challenged the reports of the messengers from Pylos: who rejoined that, if their words were not believed, the Athenians should send commissioners of their own. And so Theagenes and Cleon himself were chosen commissioners. Pointedly alluding to Nicias, who was one of the generals and an enemy of his, he declared sarcastically, that, if the generals were good for anything, they might easily sail to the island and take the Lacedæmonians, and that this was what he would certainly do himself if he were general.

Nicias perceived that the multitude were murmuring at Cleon, and asking "why he did not sail—now was his time if he thought the capture of Sphacteria to be such an easy matter:" and hearing him attack the generals, he told him that, as far as they were concerned, he might take any force which he required and try. Cleon at first imagined that the offer of Nicias was only a pretence, and was willing to go; but finding that he was in earnest, he tried to back out, and said that not he but Nicias was general. He was now alarmed, for he never imagined that Nicias would go so far as to give up his place to him. Again Nicias bade him take the command of the expedition against Pylos, which he formally gave up to him in the presence of the assembly. And the more Cleon declined the proffered command and tried to retract what he had said, so much the more the multitude, as their manner is, urged Nicias to resign and shouted to Cleon that he should sail. At length, not knowing how to escape from his own words, he undertook the expedition, and, coming forward, said that he was not afraid of the Lacedæmonians, and that he would sail without drawing a single man from the city if he were allowed to have the Lemnian and Imbrian forces now at Athens, the auxiliaries from Ænus, who were targeteers, and four hundred archers from other places. With these and with the troops already at Pylos he gave his word that within twenty days he would either bring the Lacedæmonians alive or kill them on the spot. His vain words moved the Athenians to laughter; nevertheless the wiser sort of men were pleased when they reflected that of two good things they could not fail to obtain one—either there would be an end of Cleon, which they would have greatly preferred, or, if they were disappointed, he would put the Lacedæmonians into their hands.

When he had concluded the affair in the assembly, and the Athenians had passed the necessary vote, he made choice of Demosthenes, one of the commanders at Pylos, to be his colleague, and proceeded to sail with all speed. He selected Demosthenes, because he heard that he was already intending to make an attack upon the island; for the soldiers, who were suffering much from the discomfort of the place, in which they were rather besieged than besiegers, were eager to strike a decisive blow. Cleon sent and announced to Demosthenes his approach, and soon afterwards, bringing with him the army which he had requested, himself arrived at Pylos. On the meeting of the two generals they first of all sent a herald to the Lacedæmonian force on the mainland, proposing that they should avoid any further risk by ordering the men in the island to surrender with their arms; they were to be placed under surveillance, but well treated until a general peace was concluded.

Finding that their proposal was rejected, the Athenians waited for a day, and on the night of the day following put off, taking with them all their heavy-armed troops, whom they had embarked in a few ships. A little before dawn they landed on both sides of the island, towards the sea and towards the harbor, a force amounting in all to about eight hundred men. They then ran as fast as they could to the first station on the island. Now the disposition of the enemy was as follows: The first station was garrisoned by about thirty hoplites, while the main body under the command of Epitadas was posted near the spring in the centre of the island, where the ground was most level. A small force guarded the furthest extremity of the island opposite Pylos, which was precipitous towards the sea, and on the land side the strongest point of all, being protected to some extent by an ancient wall made

of rough stones, which the Spartans thought would be of use
to them if they were overpowered and compelled to retreat.

The Athenians rushed upon the first garrison and cut them
down, half asleep as they were and just snatching up their
arms. They had not seen the enemy land, and fancied that
their ships were only gone to keep the customary watch for
the night. When the dawn appeared, the rest of the army
began to disembark. They were the crews of rather more
than seventy ships, including all but the lowest rank of
rowers, variously equipped. There were also archers to the
number of eight hundred, and as many targeteers, besides the
Messenian auxiliaries and all who were on duty about Pylos,
except the guards, who could not be spared from the walls of
the fortress. Demosthenes divided them into parties of two
hundred, more or less, who seized the highest points of the
island in order that the enemy, being completely surrounded
and distracted by the number of their opponents, might not
know whom they should face first, but might be exposed to
missiles on every side. For if they attacked those who were
in front, they would be assailed by those behind; and if those
on the flank, by those posted on the other; and whichever
way they moved, the light-armed troops of the enemy were
sure to be in their rear. These were their most embarrassing
opponents, because they were armed with bows and javelins
and slings and stones, which could be used with effect at a
distance. Even to approach them was impossible, for they
conquered in their very flight, and, when an enemy retreated,
pressed close at his heels. Such was the plan of the descent
which Demosthenes had in his mind, and which he now
carried into execution.

The main body of the Lacedæmonians on the island under
Epitadas, when they saw the first garrison cut to pieces, and
an army approaching them, drew up in battle array. The
Athenian hoplites were right in front, and the Lacedæmonians
advanced against them, wanting to come to close quarters;
but, having light-armed adversaries both on their flank and
rear, they could not get at them or profit by their own military skill, for they were impeded by a shower of missiles from
both sides. Meanwhile the Athenians, instead of going to

meet them, remained in position, while the light-armed, again
and again ran up and attacked the Lacedæmonians, who drove
them back where they pressed closest. But though compelled
to retreat they still continued fighting, being lightly equipped
and easily getting the start of their enemies. The ground was
difficult and rough, the island having been uninhabited; and
the Lacedæmonians, who were encumbered by their arms,
could not pursue them in such a place.

For some little time these skirmishes continued. But soon
the Lacedæmonians became too weary to rush out upon their
assailants, who began to be sensible that their resistance grew
feebler. The sight of their own number, which was many
times that of the enemy, encouraged them more than anything; they soon found that their losses were trifling compared
with what they had expected; and familiarity made them
think their opponents much less formidable than when they
first landed, cowed by the fear of facing Lacedæmonians. They
now despised them, and with a loud cry rushed upon them in
a body, hurling at them stones, arrows, javelins, whichever
came first to hand. The shout with which they accompanied
the attack dismayed the Lacedæmonians, who were unaccus-
tomed to this kind of warfare. Clouds of dust arose from the
newly-burnt wood, and there was no possibility of a man's
seeing what was before him, owing to the showers of arrows
and stones hurled by their assailants which were flying amid
the dust. And now the Lacedæmonians began to be sorely
distressed, for their felt cuirasses did not protect them against
the arrows, and the points of the javelins broke off where
they struck them. They were at their wits' end, not being
able to see out of their eyes or to hear the word of command,
which was drowned by the cries of the enemy. Destruction
was staring them in the face, and they had no means or hope
of deliverance.

At length, finding that so long as they fought in the same
narrow spot more and more of their men were wounded, they
closed their ranks and fell back on the last fortification of the
island, which was not far off, and where their other garrison
was stationed. Instantly the light-armed troops of the Athenians pressed upon them with fresh confidence, redoubling

their cries. Those of the Lacedæmonians who were caught by them on the way were killed, but the greater number escaped to the fort and ranged themselves with the garrison, resolved to defend the heights wherever they were assailable. The Athenians followed, but the strength of the position made it impossible to surround and cut them off, and so they attacked them in face and tried to force them back. For a long time, and indeed during the greater part of the day, both armies, although suffering from the battle and thirst and the heat of the sun, held their own; the one endeavoring to thrust their opponents from the high ground, the other determined not to give way. But the Lacedæmonians now defended themselves with greater ease, because they were not liable to be taken in flank.

There was no sign of the end. At length the general of the Messenian contingent came to Cleon and Demosthenes, and told them that if they would give him some archers and light-armed troops, and let him find a path by which he might get round in the rear of the Lacedæmonians, he thought that he could force his way in. Having obtained his request, he started from a point out of sight of the enemy, and making his way wherever the broken ground afforded a footing, and where the cliff was so steep that no guards had been set, he and his men with great difficulty got round unseen and suddenly appeared on the high ground, striking panic into the astonished enemy and redoubling the courage of his own friends who were watching for his reappearance. The Lacedæmonians were now assailed on both sides, and to compare a smaller thing to a greater, were in the same case with their own countrymen at Thermopylæ. For as they perished when the Persians found a way round by the path, so now the besieged garrison were attacked on both sides, and no longer resisted. The disparity of numbers, and the failure of bodily strength arising from want of food, compelled them to fall back, and the Athenians were at length masters of the approaches.

Cleon and Demosthenes saw that if the Lacedæmonians gave way one step more they would be destroyed by the Athenians; so they stopped the engagement and proclaimed to

them that they might, if they would, surrender at discretion
to the Athenians themselves and their arms.

Upon hearing the proclamation most of them lowered their
shields and waved their hands in token of their willingness to
yield. A truce was made, and then Cleon and Demosthenes,
on the part of the Athenians, and Styphon, the son of Pharax,
on the part of the Lacedæmonians, held a parley. Epitadas,
who was the first in command, had been already slain; Hip-
pagretas, who was next in succession, lay among the slain for
dead; and Styphon had taken the place of the two others,
having been appointed, as the law prescribed, in case anything
should happen to them. He and his companions expressed
their wish to communicate with the Lacedæmonians on the
mainland as to the course which they should pursue. The
Athenians allowed none of them to stir, but themselves invited
heralds from the shore; and after two or three communica-
tions, the herald who came over last from the body of the
army brought back word, "The Lacedæmonians bid you act
as you think best, but you are not to dishonor yourselves."
Whereupon they consulted together, and then gave up themselves and their arms. During that day and the following
night the Athenians kept guard over them; on the next day
they set up a trophy on the island and made preparations to
sail, distributing the prisoners among the trierarchs. The
Lacedæmonians sent a herald and conveyed away their own
dead. Of the survivors the Spartans numbered about a hundred and twenty. But few Athenians fell.

Reckoned from the sea-fight to the final battle in the
island, the time during which the blockade lasted was ten
weeks and two days. For about three weeks the Lacedæmonians were supplied with food while the Spartan ambassadors were gone to solicit peace, but during the rest of this
time they lived on what was brought in by stealth. A store
of corn and other provisions was found in the island at the
time of the capture; for Epitadas the general had not served
out full rations. The Athenians and Peloponnesians now
withdrew their armies from Pylos and returned home. And
the mad promise of Cleon was fulfilled; for he did bring back
the prisoners within twenty days as he had said.

## XENOPHON.

### THE TEN THOUSAND REACH THE SEA.

IN four days they reached a large and prosperous well-populated city, which went by the name of Gymnias, from which the governor of the country sent them a guide to lead them through a district hostile to his own. This guide told them that within five days he would lead them to a place from which they would see the sea, "and," he added, "if I fail of my word, you are free to take my life." Accordingly he put himself at their head; but he no sooner set foot on the country hostile to himself than he fell to encouraging them to burn and harry the land; indeed his exhortations were so earnest, it was plain that it was for this he had come, and not out of the good-will he bore the Hellenes.

On the fifth day they reached the mountain, the name of which was Theches. No sooner had the men in front ascended it and caught sight of the sea than a great cry arose, and Xenophon, with the rearguard, catching the sound of it, conjectured that another set of enemies must surely be attacking in front; for they were followed by the inhabitants of the country, which was all aflame; indeed the rearguard had killed some and captured others alive by laying an ambuscade; they had taken also about twenty wicker shields, covered with the raw hides of shaggy oxen.

But as the shout became louder and nearer, and those who from time to time came up, began racing at the top of their speed towards the shouters, and the shouting continually re-commenced with yet greater volume as the numbers increased, Xenophon settled in his mind that something extraordinary must have happened, so he mounted his horse, and taking with him Lycius and the cavalry, he galloped to the rescue. Presently they could hear the soldiers shouting and passing on the joyful word, *The sea! the sea!*

Thereupon they began running, rearguard and all, and the baggage animals and horses came galloping up. But when they had treached the summit, then indeed they fell to embracing one another—generals and officers and all—and the tears trickled down their cheeks. And on a sudden, some

one, whoever it was, having passed down the order, the sol·
diers began bringing stones and erecting a great cairn, whereon they dedicated a host of untanned skins, and staves, and captured wicker shields, and with his own hand the guide hacked
the shields to pieces, inviting the rest to follow his example.
After this the Hellenes dismissed the guide with a present
raised from the common store, to wit, a horse, a silver bowl,
a Persian dress, and ten darics ; but what he most begged to
have were their rings, and of these he got several from the
soldiers. So, after pointing out to them a village where they
would find quarters, and the road by which they would proceed towards the land of the Macrones, as evening fell, he
turned his back upon them in the night and was gone.

From this point the Hellenes marched through the
country of the Macrones three stages of ten parasangs, and
on the first day they reached the river, which formed the
boundary between the land of the Macrones and the land
of the Scythenians. Above them, on their right, they had a
country of the sternest and ruggedest character, and on their
left another river, into which the frontier river discharges
itself, and which they must cross. This was thickly fringed
with trees which, though not of any great bulk, were closely
packed. As soon as they came up to them, the Hellenes proceeded to cut them down in their haste to get out of the place
as soon as possible. But the Macrones, armed with wicker
shields and lances and hair tunics, were already drawn up to
receive them immediately opposite the crossing. They were
cheering one another on, and kept up a steady pelt of stones
into the river, though they failed to reach the other side or
do any harm.

At this juncture one of the light infantry came up to Xenophon; he had been, he said, a slave in Athens, and he
wished to tell him that he recognized the speech of these people. "I think," said he, "this must be my native country,
and if there is no objection I will have a talk with them."
"No objection at all," replied Xenophon, "pray talk to them,
and ask them first who they are." In answer to this question
they said, "they were Macrones." "Well, then," said he,
"ask them why they are drawn up in battle and want to fight

with us." They answered, "Because you are invading our country." The generals bade him say: "If so, it is with no intention, certainly, of doing it or you any harm : but we have been at war with the king, and are now returning to Hellas, and all we want is to reach the sea." The others asked, "Were they willing to give them pledges to that effect?" They replied: "Yes, they were ready to give and receive pledges to that effect." Then the Macrones gave a barbaric lance to the Hellenes, and the Hellenes a Hellenic lance to them: "for these," they said, "would serve as pledges," and both sides called upon the gods to witness.

After the pledges were exchanged, the Macrones fell to vigorously, hewing down trees and constructing a road to help them across, mingling freely with the Hellenes and fraternizing in their midst, and they afforded them as good a market as they could, and for three days conducted them on their march, until they had brought them safely to the confines of the Colchians. At this point they were confronted by a great mountain chain, which, however, was accessible, and on it the Colchians were drawn up for battle. In the first instance, the Hellenes drew up opposite in line of battle, as though they were minded to assault the hill in that order; but afterwards the generals determined to hold a council of war, and consider how to make the fairest fight.

Accordingly Xenophon said: "I am not for advancing in line, but advise to form companies by columns. To begin with, the line," he urged, "would be scattered and thrown into disorder at once; for we shall find the mountain full of inequalities, it will be pathless here and easy to traverse there. The mere fact of first having formed in line, and then seeing the line thrown into disorder, must exercise a disheartening effect. Again, if we advance several deep, the enemy will none the less overlap us, and turn their superfluous numbers to account as best they like; while, if we march in shallow order, we may fully expect our line to be cut through and through by the thick rain of missiles and rush of men, and if this happen anywhere along the line, the whole line will equally suffer. No; my notion is to form columns by companies, covering ground sufficient with spaces between the companies to allow the last companies of each flank to be outside the enemy's flanks. Thus we shall with our extreme companies be outside the enemy's line, and the best men at the head of their columns will lead the attack, and every company will pick its way where the ground is easy; also it will be difficult for the enemy to force his way into the intervening spaces, when there are companies on both sides; nor will it be easy for him to cut in twain any individual company marching in column. If, too, any particular company should be pressed, the neighboring company will come to the rescue, or if at any point any single company succeed in reaching the height, from that moment not one man of the enemy will stand his ground."

This proposal was carried, and they formed into columns by companies. Then Xenophon, returning from the right wing to the left, addressed the soldiers. "Men," he said, "these men whom you see in front of you are the sole obstacles still interposed between us and the haven of our hopes so long deferred. We shall swallow them up raw, if we can."

The several divisions fell into position, the companies were formed into columns, and the result was a total of something like eighty companies of heavy infantry, each company consisting, on an average, of a hundred men. The light infantry and bowmen were arranged in three divisions—two outside to support the left and the right respectively, and the third in the centre—each division consisting of about six hundred men. Before starting, the generals passed the order to offer prayer; and with the prayer and battle-hymn rising from their lips they commenced their advance. Cheirisophus and Xenophon, and the light infantry with them, advanced outside the enemy's line to right and left, and the enemy, seeing their advance, made an effort to keep parallel and confront them; but in order to do so, as he extended partly to right and partly to left, he was pulled to pieces, and there was a large space or hollow left in the centre of his line. Seeing them separate thus, the light infantry attached to the Arcadian battalion, under command of Æschines, an Acarnanian, mistook the movement for flight, and with a loud shout rushed on, and these were the first to scale the moun-

III—12

tain summit ; but they were closely followed by the Arcadian heavy infantry, under command of Cleanor of Orchomenus. When they began running in that way, the enemy stood their ground no longer, but betook themselves to flight, one in one direction, one in another, and the Hellenes scaled the hill and found quarters in numerous villages which contained supplies in abundance.

From this place they marched on two stages—seven parasangs—and reached the sea at Trapezus, a populous Hellenic city on the Euxine Sea, a colony of the Sinopeans, in the territory of the Colchians. Here they halted about thirty days in the villages of the Colchians, which they used as a base of operations to ravage the whole territory of Colchis. The men of Trapezus supplied the army with a market, entertained them, and gave them, as gifts of hospitality, oxen and wheat and wine. Further, they negotiated with them in behalf of their neighbors the Colchians, who dwelt in the plain for the most part, and from this folk also came gifts of hospitality in the shape of cattle. And now the Hellenes made preparation for the sacrifice which they had vowed, and a sufficient number of cattle came in for them to offer thank-offerings for safe guidance to Zeus the Saviour, and to Heracles, and to the other gods, according to their vows.

### GOBRYAS THE ASSYRIAN.
#### (From the "Cyropædia.")

GOBRYAS, an Assyrian, and a man in years, arrived on horseback, attended by some cavalry, consisting of his own dependents ; and they were all provided with arms proper for cavalry. They that had been appointed to receive the arms bade them deliver their lances that they might burn them, as they had done others before; but Gobryas said that he desired first to see Cyrus. Then they that attended this service left the other horsemen behind, and conducted Gobryas to Cyrus; and as soon as he saw Cyrus, he spoke thus:

"My sovereign lord, I am by birth an Assyrian ; I have a strong fortress in my possession, and have the command of a large territory: I furnished the Assyrian king with a thou-

sand horse, and was very much his friend: but since he, who
was an excellent man, has lost his life in the war against you,
and since his son, who is my greatest enemy, now possesses
the government, I come and throw myself at your feet as a
suppliant, and give myself to you as a servant and assistant
in the war. I beg you to be my revenger: I make you my
son as far as it is possible. With respect to male issue, I am
childless; for he, O sovereign! that was my only one, an
excellent youth, who loved and honored me to as great a
degree as son could do to make a father happy; him did the
present king (the late king, the father of the present, having
sent for my son, as intending to give him his daughter, and
I sent him away, proud that I should see my son married to
the daughter of the king) invite to hunt with him, as with a
friend; and, on a bear appearing in view, they both pursued.
The present king, having thrown his javelin, missed his aim.
Oh that it had not happened so! and my son making his
throw—unhappy thing!—brought the bear to the ground
He was then enraged, but kept his envy concealed; but
then, again, a lion falling in their way, he again missed; and
that it should happen so to him I do not think at all wonderful; but my son, again hitting his mark, killed the lion, and
said, 'I have twice thrown single javelins, and brought the
beasts both times to the ground.' On this the impious wretch
restrained his malice no longer, but, snatching a lance from
one of his followers, struck it into his breast, and took away
the life of my dear and only son! Then I, miserable man!
brought him away a corpse instead of a bridegroom; and I
who am of these years, buried him, my excellent and beloved
son, a youth but just bearded. His murderer, as if he had
destroyed an enemy, has never yet appeared to have had any
remorse; nor has he, in amends for the vile action, ever
vouchsafed to pay any honor to him who is now under the
ground. His father, indeed, had compassion, and plainly
appeared to join in affliction with me at this misfortune;
therefore, had he lived, I had never applied to you to his
injury; for I had received a great many instances of
friendship from him, and I served him. But since the government has fallen to the murderer of my son, I can never

possibly bear him the least good-will; nor can he, I know
very well, ever reckon me his friend; for he knows how I
stand affected towards him; how I, who lived with that joy
and satisfaction before, must now stand in this destitute condition, passing my old age in sorrow.  If you receive me,
therefore, and I can have hopes of obtaining, by your means,
a revenge for my dear son, I shall think I arise again to new
life; I shall neither be ashamed to live, nor, if I die, do I
think that I shall end my days with grief."

Thus he spoke. And Cyrus replied, "If you make it
appear, Gobryas, that you really are in that disposition
towards us that you express, I receive you as our supplicant,
and, with the help of the gods, I promise to revenge you on
the murderer.  But tell me," said he, "if we effect these
things for you, and allow you to hold your fortress, your
territory, and your arms, and the power that you had before.
what service will you do for us in return for these things?"
He then said, "My fortress I will yield you for your habitation whenever you please; the same tribute for my territory
that I used to pay to him I will pay to you; wherever you
shall make war I will attend you in the service, with the
forces of my territory: and I have, besides," said he, "a
maiden daughter. that I tenderly love, just of an age for
marriage; one that I formerly reckoned I brought up as a
wife for the person now reigning; but she herself has now
begged me, with many tears and sighs, not to give her to the
murderer of her brother; and I join with her in opinion.  I
here give you leave to deal with her as I appear to deal by
you."  Then Cyrus said, "On these terms," said he, "with
truth and sincerity do I give you my right hand, and accept
of yours.  Let the gods be witnesses between us!"  When
these things had passed, he bade Gobryas go and keep his
arms; and he asked him at what distance his habitation was,
it being his intention to go thither.  He then said, "If you
march to-morrow morning you may quarter with us the next
day."  So Gobryas went away and left a guide.

On the second day towards the evening they reached the
habitation of Gobryas.  They saw it to be an exceeding
strong fortress, and that all things were provided on the walls

proper for a vigorous defence; and they saw abundance of oxen and sheep brought under the fortifications. Gobryas then, sending to Cyrus, bade him ride round, and see where the access was most easy, and send in to him some of those that he confided in, who, having seen how things stood within, might give him an account of them. So Cyrus, desiring in reality to see if the fortress might be taken on any side, or whether Gobryas might be discovered to be false, rode round on every side, but saw every part too strong to be approached. Those that Cyrus sent in to Gobryas brought him an account that there was such plenty of all good things within as could not, as they thought, even in the age of a man, fail the people that were there. Cyrus was under concern about what all this might mean. But Gobryas himself came out to him, and brought out all his men; some carrying wine, some meal, and others driving oxen, sheep, hogs, and goats; and of every thing that was eatable they brought sufficient to furnish a handsome supper for the whole army that was with Cyrus. They that were appointed to this service made distribution of all these things, and they all supped. But Gobryas, when all his men were come out, bade Cyrus enter in the manner that he thought the most safe. Cyrus, therefore, sending before certain people to view and search into things and a force with them, then entered himself; and when he was got in, keeping the gates open, he summoned all his friends and the commanders that had attended him; and when they were come in, Gobryas, producing cups of gold, and vessels of various kinds, all manner of furniture, and apparel, darics without number, and magnificent things of all kinds; and at last bringing out his daughter (who was astonishingly beautiful and tall, but in affliction for the death of her brother), spoke thus:

"Cyrus, all these treasures I give you, and this daughter of mine I intrust you with to dispose of as you think fit: but we are both of us your supplicants: I, before, that you would be the revenger of my son: and she, now, that you would be the revenger of her brother."

Cyrus to this said, "I promised you then, that, if you were not false to us, I would revenge you to the utmost of

my power; and now that I find you true to us, I am under
the obligation of that promise. And I now promise her,
with the help of the gods, to perform it. These treasures,"
said he, "I accept, but give them to this your daughter, and
to the man that shall marry her. But I have received one
present from you with more pleasure than I should have with
the treasures of Babylon, where there is abundance; or even
with those of the whole world, were they to be exchanged for
this that you have now presented me with."

Gobryas, wondering what it should be, and suspecting
that he meant his daughter, asked him thus: "O Cyrus!"
said he, "what is it?"

Then Cyrus replied, "Gobryas," said he, "it is this. I
believe there may be abundance of men that would not be
guilty either of impiety, injustice, or falsehood; and yet,
because nobody will throw either treasures, or power, or
strong fortresses, or lovely children in their way, die before
it comes to appear what they were. But you, by having now
put into my hands both strong fortresses, and riches of all
kinds, your whole force, and your daughter, who is so valuable a possession, have made me clearly appear to all men to
be one that would neither be guilty of impiety towards
friends that receive and entertain me, nor of injustice for the
sake of treasure, nor willingly false to faith in compacts.
This, therefore, be assured, I shall not forget, while I am
a just man, and while as such I receive the applause of men,
but I shall endeavor to make you returns of honor in all
things great and noble: and do not be afraid of wanting a
husband for your daughter, and such a one as shall be worthy
of her: for I have many excellent friends, and, among them,
whoever it is that marries her, whether he will have either as
much treasure as you have given, or a great deal more, I am
not able to say; but be assured that there are some of them
who, for all the treasures you have bestowed, do not on that
account esteem you one jot the more. But they are at this
time my rivals; they supplicate all the gods that they may
have an opportunity of showing themselves that they are not
less faithful to their friends than I am: that, while alive,
they will never yield to their enemies, unless some god should

blast their endeavors; and that for virtue and good reputation, they would not accept of all the treasures of the Syrians and Assyrians added to yours. Such men, be assured, are sitting here."

Gobryas, smiling at this, "By the gods!" said he, "Cyrus, pray show me where these men are, that I may beg one of them of you to be my son." "Do not trouble yourself," said he; "it will not be at all necessary for you to inquire of me. If you will but attend us, you yourself will be able to show them to anybody else."

And having said this, he took Gobryas by the right hand, rose, went out, and brought out all that were with him; and though Gobryas repeatedly desired him to take his supper within the fortress, yet he would not do it, but supped in the camp, and took Gobryas to sup with him.

### ARASPES AND PANTHEA.
#### (From the " Cyropædia.")

THE Medes delivered to the magi such things as they had said were to be chosen for the gods. And they had chosen for Cyrus a most beautiful tent; a Susian woman, that was said to be the most beautiful woman of all Asia; and two other women that were the finest singers. And they chose the same things over again for Cyaxares. They had fully supplied themselves with all such things as they wanted, that they might be in want of nothing in the course of their service in the war; for there were all things in great abundance.

Cyrus, then calling to him Araspes the Mede (who had been his companion from a boy, to whom he gave the Median robe, that he himself put off when he left Astyages and departed for Persia), commanded him to keep the woman and tent for him. This woman was wife of Abradatas, king of the Susians. And when the camp of the Assyrians was taken her husband was not in the camp, but was gone on an embassy to the king of the Bactrians. The Assyrians had sent him to treat of an alliance between them; for he happened to have contracted a friendship with the king of the Bactrians. This woman, therefore, Cyrus ordered Araspes to keep till such time as he took her himself.

But Araspes, having received his command, asked him this question: "Cyrus," said he, "have you seen this woman that you bid me keep?" "No," said he, "I have not." "But I did," said he, "when we chose her for you. Indeed, when we first entered her tent we did not know her; for she was sitting on the ground, with all her women servants round her, and was dressed in the same manner as her servants were; but when we looked around, being desirous to know which was the mistress, she immediately appeared to excel all the others, though she was sitting with a veil over her, and looking down on the ground. When we bade her rise, she and all the servants round her rose. Here then she excelled first in stature, then in strength, and grace, and beautiful shape, though she was standing in a dejected posture, and tears appeared to have fallen from her eyes, some on her clothes, and some at her feet. As soon as the eldest among us had said to her, 'Take courage, woman; we have heard that your husband is indeed an excellent man, but we now choose you out for a man that, be it known to you, is not inferior to him, either in person, in understanding, or in power; but, as we think, if there be a man in the world that deserves admiration, Cyrus does, and to him henceforward you shall belong.' As soon as the woman heard this she tore down her robe, and set up a lamentable cry, and her servants cried out at the same time with her. On this most part of her face was disclosed, and her neck and hands appeared. And be it known to you, Cyrus," said he, "that I, and the rest that saw her, all thought that never yet was produced, or born of mortals, such a woman, throughout all Asia. And by all means," said he, "you likewise shall see her."

Then Cyrus said, "No, not I; and much the less, if she be such a one as you say." "Why so?" said the young man. "Because," said he, "if on hearing now from you that she is handsome, I am persuaded to go and see her at a time that I have not much leisure, I am afraid that she will much more easily persuade me to go and see her again; and after that perhaps I may neglect what I am to do, and sit gazing at her." The young man then laughed, and said, "And do you think, Cyrus, that the beauty of a human crea ture can necessitate one, against his will, to act contrary to what is best?" "If this were naturally so," said he, "we should be all under the same necessity. You see how fire burns all people alike; for such is the nature of it. But of beauties, some inspire people with love, and some do not; one loves one, and another another; for it is a voluntary thing, and every one loves those that he pleases. A brother does not fall in love with a sister, but somebody else does; nor is a father in love with a daughter, but some other person is. Fear and the law are a sufficient bar to love. If, indeed," said he, "the law should enjoin that they who did not eat should not be hungry, and that they who did not drink should not be thirsty; that men should not be cold in the winter, nor hot in the summer; no law in the world could make men submit to these decisions, for by nature they are subject to these things. But love is a voluntary thing, and every one loves those that suit him, just as he does his clothes or his shoes. How comes it to pass then," said Cyrus, "if to love be a voluntary thing, that we cannot give it over when we will? For I have seen people," said he, "in tears for grief, on account of love; slaves to those they were in love with, and yet thought slavery a very great evil before they were in love; giving away many things that they were never the better for parting with; wishing to be rid of love, as they would of any other distemper, and yet not able to get rid of it; but bound down by it, as by a stronger tie of necessity than if they were bound in iron chains! They give themselves up, therefore, to those they love, to serve them in many odd and unaccountable ways; yet, with all their sufferings, they never attempt making their escape, but keep continual watch on their loves, lest they should escape from them."

The young man to this said, "There are people, indeed, that do these things; but," said he, "they are miserable wretches; and this I believe is the reason why they are always wishing themselves dead, as being wretched and unhappy; and though there are ten thousand ways of parting with life, yet they do not part with it. Just such wretches as these are they that attempt thefts, and will not abstain from what belongs to others; but when they have plundered or

stolen any thing, you see," said he, "that you are the first
that accuse the thief and the plunderer, as reckoning theft to
be no such fatal, necessary thing, and you do not pardon, but
punish it. So people that are beautiful do not necessitate
others to love them, nor to covet what they ought not; but
mean, wretched men are impotent, I know, in all their passions, and then they accuse love. Men, excellent and worthy,
though they have inclinations both for gold, fine horses, and
beautiful women, can yet with ease abstain from any of them,
so as not to touch them contrary to right: I, therefore," said
he, "who have seen this woman, and think her very beautiful, yet am here attending on you, and I go abroad on horseback, and in all other respects I discharge my duty."

"But," said Cyrus, "perhaps you retired before the time
that love naturally lays hold of a man. It is not the nature
of fire immediately to burn the man that touches it, and
wood does not immediately blaze out; yet still I am not willing either to meddle with fire, or to look at beautiful persons:
nor do I advise you, Araspes, to let your eyes dwell long on
beauties; for as fire burns those that touch it, beauties catch
hold of those that look at them, though at a distance, and set
them on fire with love."

"Be easy," said he, "Cyrus; though I look at her without ceasing, I will not be so conquered as to do any thing
that I ought not." "You speak," said he, "very hand-
somely: guard her, therefore," said he, "as I bid you, and be
careful of her; for perhaps this woman may be of service to
us on some occasion or other." And having discoursed thus
they parted.

The young man, partly by seeing the woman to be ex-
tremely beautiful, and by being apprized of her worth and
goodness, partly by waiting on her and serving her, with
intention to please her, and partly by his finding her not to
be ungrateful in return, but that she took care by her servants that all things convenient should be provided for him
when he came in, and that he should want nothing when he
was ill; by all these means he was made her captive in love:
and perhaps what happened to him in this case was what
need not be wondered at. . . . .

Some time afterward, Cyrus being desirous to send a spy into Lydia, and to learn what the Assyrian was doing, thought that Araspes, the guardian of the beautiful woman, was a proper person to go on that errand; for with Araspes things had fallen out in this manner. Having fallen in love with the woman, he was forced to make proposals to her. But she denied him, and was faithful to her husband, though he was absent, for she loved him very much. Yet she did not accuse Araspes to Cyrus, being unwilling to make a quarrel between men that were friends. Then Araspes, thinking to forward the success of his inclinations, threatened the woman that if she would not yield to his wishes she should be forced to submit against her will. On this the woman, being in fear, concealed the matter no longer, but sent a messenger to Cyrus with orders to tell him the whole affair. He, when he heard it, laughed at this man, who had said he was above the power of love. He sent Artabazus with the messenger, and commanded him to tell Araspes that he should respect the conduct of such a woman. But Artabazus, coming to Araspes, reproached him, calling the woman a deposit that had been trusted in his hands; and telling him of his impiety, injustice, and impotence of his passion, so that Araspes shed many tears for grief, was overwhelmed with shame, and almost dead with fear lest he should suffer some severity at the hands of Cyrus. Cyrus, being informed of this, sent for him, and spoke to him by himself alone.

"I see, Araspes," said he, "that you are very much in fear of me, and very much ashamed. But give them both over, for I have heard that gods have been conquered by love; I know how much men that have been accounted very wise have suffered by love; and I pronounced on myself, that if I conversed with beautiful people, I was not enough master of myself to disregard them. And I am the cause that this has befallen you, for I shut you up with this irresistible creature." Araspes then said in reply, "You are in this, too, Cyrus, as you are in other things, mild and disposed to forgive the errors of men; but other men," said he, "overwhelm me with grief and concern, for the rumor of my misfortune has got abroad, my enemies are pleased with it, and my friends come to me, and advise me to get out of the way, lest I suffer some severity at your hands, as having been guilty of a very great injustice.''

Then Cyrus said, '' Be it known to you, therefore, Araspes, that by means of this very opinion that people have taken up, it is in your power to gratify me in a very high degree, and to do very great service to our allies.'' ''I wish,'' said Araspes, ''that I had an opportunity of being again of use to you.'' ''Observe,'' said he, ''if you would act as if you fled from me, and would go over to the enemy, I believe that the enemy would trust you.'' ''And I know,'' said Araspes, ''that I should give occasion to have it said by my friends that I fled from you.'' ''Then you might return to us,'' said he, ''apprized of all the enemy's affairs. I believe, that on their giving credit to you, they would make you a sharer in their debates and councils, so that nothing would be concealed from you that I desire you should know.'' ''I will go then,'' said he, ''now, out of hand; for be assured, that my being thought to have made my escape, as one that was just about to receive punishment at your hands, will be one of the things that will give me credit.''

''And can you,'' said he, ''leave the beautiful Panthea?'' ''Yes, Cyrus; for I have plainly two souls. I have now philosophized this point out by the help of that wicked sophister love: for a single soul cannot be a good one and a bad one at the same time, nor can it at the same time affect both noble actions and vile ones. It cannot incline and be averse to the same things at the same time; but it is plain there are two souls, and when the good one prevails, it does noble things; when the bad one prevails, it attempts vile things. But now that it has got you for a support the good one prevails, and that very much.'' ''If you think it proper, therefore, to be gone,'' said Cyrus, ''thus you must do in order to gain the greater credit with them. Relate to them the state of our affairs, and relate it so as that what you say may be as great a hindrance as possible to what they intend to do: and it would be some hindrance to them, if you should say that we are preparing to make an incursion into some part of their territory: for when they hear this, they will be less able to assemble their whole force together, every one being in fear for something at home. Then stay with them," said he, "as long as you can; for what they do when they are the nearest us, will be the most for our purpose to know. Advise them likewise to form themselves into such an order as may be thought the strongest; for when you come away, and are supposed to be apprized of their order, they will be under a necessity to keep to it, for they will be afraid of making a change in it; and if they do make a change, by their being so near at hand, it will create confusion among them."

Araspes, setting out in this manner, and taking with him such of his servants as he chiefly confided in, and telling certain persons such things as he thought might be of service to his undertaking, went his way.

Panthea, as soon as she perceived that Araspes was gone, sending to Cyrus, told him thus: "Do not be afflicted, Cyrus, that Araspes is gone off to the enemy; for if you will allow me to send to my husband, I engage that there will come to you one who will be a much more faithful friend to you than Araspes. I know that he will attend you with all the force that he is able; for the father of the prince that now reigns was his friend, but he who at present reigns attempted once to part us from each other; and reckoning him, therefore, an unjust man, I know that he would joyfully revolt from him to such a man as you are."

Cyrus, hearing this, ordered her to send for her husband. She sent; and when Abradatas discovered the signs from his wife, and perceived how matters stood as to the other particulars, he marched joyfully away to Cyrus, having about two thousand horse with him. When he came up with the Persian scouts he sent to Cyrus, to tell him who he was: Cyrus immediately ordered them to conduct him to his wife.

When Abradatas and his wife saw each other they mutually embraced, as was natural to do on an occasion so unexpected. On this Panthea told him of the sanctity and virtue of Cyrus, and of his pity and compassion towards her. Abradatas, having heard of it, said, "What can I do, Panthea, to pay my gratitude to Cyrus for you and for myself?" "What else," said Panthea, "but endeavor to behave towards him as he has done towards you?" On this Abradatas came to Cyrus, and as soon as he saw him, taking him by the right hand, he said, "In return for the benefits you have bestowed on us, Cyrus, I have nothing of more consequence to say, than that I give myself to you as a friend, a servant, and an ally; and whatever designs I observe you to be engaged in, I will endeavor to be the best assistant to you in them that I am able." Then Cyrus said, "I accept your offer, and dismiss you at this time, to take your supper with your wife; but at some other time you must take a meal with me in my tent, together with your friends and mine."

## The Visit of Socrates to Theodota.

### (From the "Memorabilia of Socrates.")

THERE was at Athens a very beautiful lady called Theodota, who had the character of a loose dame. Some person, speaking of her in presence of Socrates, said that she was the most beautiful woman in the whole world; that all the painters went to see her, to draw her picture, and that they were very well received at her house. "I think," said Socrates, "we ought to go see her too, for we shall be better able to judge of her beauty after we have seen her ourselves than upon the bare relation of others." The person who began the discourse encouraged the matter, and that very moment they all went to Theodota's house. They found her with a painter who was drawing her picture; and having considered her at leisure when the painter had done, Socrates began thus: "Do you think that we are more obliged to Theodota for having afforded us the sight of her beauty than she is to us for coming to see her? If all the advantage be on her side, it must be owned that she is obliged to us; if it be on ours, it must be confessed that we are so to her." Some of the company saying there was reason to think so, Socrates continued: "Has she not already had the advantage of receiving the praises we have given her? But it will be a greater benefit to her when we make known her merit in all the companies we come into; but as for ourselves, what do we carry from hence except a desire to enjoy the things we have seen? We

go hence with souls full of love and uneasiness; and from
this time forward we must obey Theodota in all she pleases
to enjoin us." "If it be so," said Theodota, "I must return
you many thanks for your coming hither." Meanwhile Socrates took notice that she was magnificently apparelled, and
that her mother appeared likewise like a woman of condition.
He saw a great number of women attendants elegantly dressed,
and that the whole house was richly furnished. He took
occasion from hence to inform himself of her circumstances in
the world, and to ask her whether she had an estate in land
or houses in the city, or slaves, whose labor supplied the
expenses of her family. "I have nothing," answered she,
"of all this; my friends are my revenue. I subsist by their
liberality."

Upon which Socrates remarked that "friendship was one
of the greatest blessings in life, for that a good friend could
stand one in stead of all possessions whatever." And he
advised Theodota to try all her art to procure to herself some
lovers and friends that might render her happy. The lady
asking Socrates whether there were any artifices to be used
for that purpose, he answered, "there were," and proceeded
to mention several: "Some for attracting the regard of the
men, some for insinuating into their hearts; others for securing their affections and managing their passions." Whereupon Theodota, whose soul then lay open to any impression,
mistaking the virtuous design of Socrates in the whole of
this discourse for an intention of another sort, cried out in
raptures, "Ah! Socrates, why will not you help me to
friends?" "I will," replied Socrates, "if you can persuade
me to do so." "And what means must I use to persuade
you?" "You must invent the means," said Socrates, "if
you want me to serve you." "Then come to see me often,"
added Theodota. Socrates laughed at the simplicity of the
woman, and in raillery said to her, "I have not leisure enough
to come and see you; I have both public and private affairs
which take up too much of my time. Besides, I have mis-
tresses who will not suffer me to be from them neither day
nor night, and who against myself make use of the very
charms and sorceries that I have taught them." "And have

you any knowledge in those things, too?" said she. "Why do Apollodorus and Antisthenes," answered Socrates, "never leave me? why do Cebes and Simmias forsake Thebes for my company? This they would not do if I were not master of some charm." "Lend it me," said Theodota, "that I may employ it against you, and charm you to come to me." "No," said Socrates, "but I will charm you, and make you come to me." "I will," said Theodota, "if you will promise to make me welcome." "I promise you I will," answered Socrates, "provided there be nobody with me whom I love better than you."

## THE CHOICE OF HERCULES.

### (From the "Memorabilia of Socrates.")

WHEN Hercules had arrived at that part of his youth in which young men commonly choose for themselves, and show, by the result of their choice, whether they will, through the succeeding stages of their lives, enter and walk in the path of virtue or that of vice, he went out into a solitary place fit for contemplation, there to consider with himself which of those two paths he should pursue.

As he was sitting there in suspense he saw two women of a larger stature than ordinary approaching towards him. One of them had a benign and amiable aspect; her beauty was natural and easy, her person and shape fine and handsome, her eyes cast towards the ground with an agreeable reserve, her motion and behavior full of modesty, and her raiment white as snow. The other wanted all the native beauty and proportion of the former; her person was swelled, by luxury and ease, to a size quite disproportioned and uncomely. She had painted her complexion, that it might seem fairer and more ruddy than it really was, and endeavored to appear more graceful than ordinary in her mien, by a mixture of affectation in all her gestures. Her eyes were full of boldness, and her dress transparent, that the conceited beauty of her person might appear through it to advantage. She cast her eyes frequently upon herself, then turned them on those that were present, to see whether any one regarded her, and now and then looked on the figure she made in her own shadow.

As they drew nearer, the former continued the same composed pace, while the latter, striving to get before her, ran up to Hercules, and addressed herself to him:

"I perceive, my dear Hercules, you are in doubt which path in life you should pursue. If, then, you will be my friend and follow me, I will lead you to a path the most easy and most delightful, wherein you shall taste all the sweets of life, and live exempt from every trouble. You shall neither be concerned in war nor in the affairs of the world, but shall only consider how to gratify all your senses—your taste with the finest dainties and most delicious drink, your sight with the most agreeable objects, your scent with the richest perfumes and fragrancy of odors, how you may enjoy the embraces of the fair, repose on the softest beds, render your slumbers sweet and easy, and by what means enjoy, without even the smallest care, all those glorious and mighty blessings.

"And, for fear you suspect that the sources whence you are to derive those invaluable blessings might at some time or other fail, and that you might, of course, be obliged to acquire them at the expense of your mind and the united labor and fatigue of your body, I beforehand assure you that you shall freely enjoy all from the industry of others, undergo neither hardship nor drudgery, but have everything at your command that can afford you any pleasure or advantage."

Hercules, hearing the lady make him such offers, desired to know her name, to which she answered, "My friends, and those who are well acquainted with me, and whom I have conducted, call me Happiness; but my enemies, and those who would injure my reputation, have given me the name of Pleasure."

In the meantime, the other lady approached, and in her turn accosted him in this manner: "I also am come to you, Hercules, to offer my assistance; I am well acquainted with your divine origin and have observed the excellence of your nature, even from your childhood, from which I have reason to hope that, if you would follow the path that leadeth to my residence, you will undertake the greatest enterprises and achieve the most glorious actions, and that I shall thereby become more honorable and illustrious among mortals. But

III—13

before I invite you into my society and friendship I will be
open and sincere with you, and must lay down this as an established truth, that nothing truly valuable can be purchased
without pains and labor.   The gods have set a price upon
every real and noble pleasure.   If you would gain the favor
of the Deity you must be at the pains of worshiping Him;
if you would be beloved by your friends you must study to
oblige them; if you would be honored by any city you must
be of service to it; and if you would be admired by all Greece,
on account of your probity and valor, you must exert yourself
to do her some eminent service.   If you would render your
fields fruitful, and fill your arms with grain, you must labor
to cultivate the soil accordingly.   Would you grow rich by
your herds, a proper care must be taken of them; would you
extend your dominions by arms, and be rendered capable of
setting at liberty your captive friends, and bringing your enemies to subjection, you must not only learn of those that are
experienced in the art of war, but exercise yourself also in
the practice of military affairs; and if you would excel in the
strength of your body you must keep your body in due subjection to your mind, and exercise it with labor and pains.''

Here Pleasure broke in upon her discourse—''Do you see,
my dear Hercules, through what long and difficult ways this
woman would lead you to her promised delights?   Follow
me, and I will show you a much shorter and more easy way
to happiness.''

''Alas!'' replied the Goddess of Virtue, whose visage
glowed with a passion made up of scorn and pity, ''what happiness can you bestow, or what pleasure can you taste, who
would never do anything to acquire it?   You who will take
your fill of all pleasures before you feel an appetite for any;
you eat before you are hungry, you drink before you are
athirst; and, that you may please your taste, must have the
finest artists to prepare your viands; the richest wines that
you may drink with pleasure, and to give your wine the finer
taste you search every place for ice and snow luxuriously to
cool it in the heat of summer.   Then, to make your slumbers
uninterrupted, you must have the softest down and the easiest
couches, and a gentle ascent of steps to save you from the

least disturbance in mounting up to them. And all little
enough, Heaven knows! for you have not prepared yourself
for sleep by anything you have done, but seek after it only
because you have nothing to do. It is the same in the enjoyments of love, in which you rather force than follow your
inclinations, and are obliged to use arts, and even to pervert
nature, to keep your passions alive. Thus is it that you instruct your followers—kept awake for the greatest part of the
night by debaucheries, and consuming in drowsiness all the
most useful part of the day. Though immortal, you are an
outcast from the gods, and despised by good men. Never
have you heard that most agreeable of all sounds, your own
praise, nor ever have you beheld the most pleasing of all
objects, any good work of your own hands. Who would ever
give any credit to anything that you say? Who would assist
you in your necessity, or what man of sense would ever venture to be of your mad parties? Such as do follow you are
robbed of their strength when they are young, void of wisdom
when they grow old. In their youth they are bred up in in-
dolence and all manner of delicacy, and pass their old age
with difficulties and distress, full of shame for what they have
done, and oppressed with the burden of what they are to do,
squanderers of pleasures in their youth, and hoarders up of
afflictions for their old age.

"On the contrary, my association is with the gods and
with good men, and there is nothing excellent performed by
either without my influence. I am respected above all things
by the gods and by the best of mortals, and it is just I should.
I am an agreeable companion to the artisan, a faithful security
to masters of families, a kind assistant to servants, a useful
associate in the arts of peace, a faithful ally in the labors of
war, and the best uniter of all friendships.

"My votaries, too, enjoy a pleasure in everything they
either eat or drink, even without having labored for it, because
they wait for the demand of their appetites. Their sleep is
sweeter than that of the indolent and inactive; and they are
neither overburdened with it when they awake, nor do they,
for the sake of it, omit the necessary duties of life. My
young men have the pleasure of being praised by those who

are in years, and those who are in years of being honored by those who are young. They look back with comfort on their past actions, and delight themselves in their present employments. By my means they are favored by the gods, beloved by their friends, and honored by their country; and when the appointed end of their lives is come they are not lost in a dishonorable oblivion, but live and flourish in the praises of mankind, even to the latest posterity.

"Thus, my dear Hercules, who are descended from divine ancestors, you may acquire, by virtuous toil and industry, this most desirable state of perfect happiness."

Such was the discourse, my friend, which the goddess had with Hercules, according to Prodicus. You may believe that he embellished the thoughts with more noble expressions than I do. I heartily wish, my dear Aristippus, that you should make such improvement of those divine instructions, that you too may make such a happy choice as may render you happy during the future course of your life.

## ISOCRATES.

ISOCRATES is called by Cicero the "father of eloquence." Cicero learned from Isocrates, and we have learned from Cicero, who considered this eloquent Athenian not only a great orator, but a perfect teacher, and the first to observe and reduce to systematic form and method the rhythm and harmony of prose compositions. It is to him that literature owes the institution of the regular period and the melodious cadence of well-constructed sentences.

Isocrates was the son of a prosperous flute-maker; he was born at Athens B.C. 436, and lived till 338. He represents the excellence of that species of oratory which gives the highest place to artistic form and finish, and regards the subject-matter as comparatively of small importance. Some idea of the esteem in which this teacher was held may be gathered from the fact that his annual income from his pupils is said to have amounted to $25,000, especially when we consider that money in those days was worth much more than it is now. His income was also augmented by his literary productions. On a certain occasion the King of Cyprus is said to have paid him as much as $20,000 for one oration.

At first Isocrates moved in that circle of which Socrates was the centre; but he relinquished philosophy and turned his attention to making speeches for delivery by others, as he was quite unfitted to deliver them himself, from natural nervousness and weakness of voice. After a brief experience he gave up speech-making and devoted himself to the teaching of oratory. At the age of forty-four he opened that school at Athens of which Cicero said that " in it was trained and perfected the eloquence of all Greece." Pupils flocked to him from the shores of the Euxine and the Mediterranean, far and near. From a political point of view Isocrates was somewhat impractical. His great dream was the unification of

Greece for the subjugation of Asia, an illusion which was
rudely dispelled by the defeat of the allied Thebans, Corinthians and Athenians by Philip of Macedon at Chæronea in
August, 338 B.C.    The "old man eloquent" did not long
survive this humiliation and shattering of his hopes.

## SPARTA AND ATHENS.

THE most noted of the orations of Isocrates is the Panathenaicus
or Panegyric of Athens, a work on which he spent ten years, and in
which he uses all the resources of his art to extol Athens and magnify
the benefits she conferred on the whole of Greece.

THOSE who would accurately and justly praise any city,
should not make that city alone their topic, which they
design to speak of; but as we examine and try purple and
gold, by showing near them articles of the same kind and
value, I judge that small cities should not be compared with
great, nor those which have been accustomed in all times to
govern, with those who were accustomed to serve, nor those
cities which are capable of preserving others, with such as
need protection : but I judge, those cities should be compared
together, which are possessed of like power, have been conversant in the same affairs, and are of equal authority ; for
thus will they most easily come at the truth.    Now, if any
one consider Athens in this light, and compare us not with any
city, but with that of Sparta, which many praise moderately,
but some speak of as if demi-gods governed that republic, we
shall be found to have left them farther behind in beneficence
towards Greece, than they have left all others.    I shall mention hereafter our ancient conflicts for the good of Greece; but
now, I shall make my discourse of them, beginning from the
time when they seized upon the Achaic cities, and divided
the country with the Argives and Messenians ; for from hence
we ought to discourse about them.    Our ancestors will be
perceived to have preserved, from the Trojan times, the con-
cord of the Grecians and enmity with the Barbarians, and to
have persevered in the same affections.    And, first of all, in
respect of the islands Cyclades, concerning which many disputes arose under the government of Minos, when they last

were possessed by the Carians; after they drove the Carians
out, they did not make them their own provinces, but they
placed in them a colony of the most indigent Grecians: afterwards they built many and great cities on both sides of the
continent, drove the Barbarians from the sea, and taught the
Grecians by what method of government, and by carrying on
war against whom in particular, they might enlarge and ag-
grandize Greece. But the Lacedæmonians were so far, at
that time, from doing anything of this nature, as our ancestors,
who commenced war against the Barbarians and benefited
the Grecians, that they would not even remain quiet; but
having a city belonging to others, and not only a sufficient
territory, but larger than any of the other Grecian cities had,
they were not content with thi ; but learning by events, that
cities and countries appear, according to laws, to be the right
of those who justly possess them, but, in fact, pass into the
power of those who most skilfully exercise military art and
can conquer their enemies. Reflecting on this, and neglecting agriculture, trade, and all other things, they never ceased
to attack and disturb, one by one, all the cities of Peloponn-
nesus, except that of Argos. Now, the consequence of what
we did was, that Greece was enlarged, and Europe became
master of Asia; besides, that the necessitous Greeks received
cities and lands, but that the Barbarians, who before commenced insults, were driven out of the country, and became
of more submissive minds than they had been. But the consequence of what the Spartans did was that their city alone
was aggrandized and made famous, and governed all the cities
in Peloponnesus, and had great respect shown to it from
them. It is certainly just to praise that city, which was the
cause of many benefits to others, and to judge that one unjust,
which only procured itself advantages; to esteem those
friends, who treat others on the same footing as themselves,
but to fear and apprehend those who are of the most friendly
mind amongst themselves, yet administer their government
with a visible hostile intention towards others. Such, therefore, was the foundation of the government in both cities.

Afterwards, upon the commencement of the Persian war,
when Xerxes, who then reigned, had got together twelve

hundred ships and five million men, seven hundred thousand
of whom were regular troops, and entered Greece with such a
vast army, the Spartans, though they governed all Peloponnesus, sent only ten ships to the naval battle, which gave a
turn to the whole war; but our fathers, though they were
forced from their country and had abandoned the city, because
it was not at that time fortified, afforded better ships, and
better provided with forces, than all of those who ran that
danger. And the Lacedæmonians sent, as their admiral,
Eurybiades, who, could he have effected what he designed,
must have ruined all Greece; but ours sent Themistocles,
who was thought indisputably to be the cause that the naval
engagement was wisely conducted, as well as author, besides,
of all that was prosperously acted at that time; for when
they, who had been allies, had wrested the sovereignty from
the Lacedæmonians, they conferred it on us. And what better
judges can any one imagine, or more worthy of credit, of the
transactions of those times, than those who were present in
the battles? or, what benefit can be supposed greater than the
preservation of all Greece from destruction?

It happened afterwards, that each city became sovereign of
the sea; which whoever holds, must have the greatest number
of cities in subjection. Not that I praise in this regard either
city; for one may blame both in many respects. But we have
not less excelled them in this administration, than in what I
have mentioned before; for our fathers persuaded their allies
to constitute such a form of government, as they themselves
had always preferred. Now, it is certainly a sign of goodwill and kindness, when persons exhort others to use those
means, which they have found profitable to themselves.
But the Lacedæmonians constituted governments which were
neither similar to their own, nor like those constituted elsewhere, but made ten men only of each city its lords; and so
tyrannical was their administration that, should a person
endeavor, for three or four successive days, to bring accusations against them, he would not be able to express the half of
their crimes and oppressions. It would be absurd to comment
particularly upon such and so numerous instances: but, perhaps, I should have called attention to a few, which would have

excited a worthy anger in the hearers, if I had been younger. But I have now no such intention; however, it is confessed by all, that they so far exceeded all who went before them, in rapacity and injustice, that they not only ruined themselves, their friends and their countries, but likewise, by exposing the Lacedæmonians to the odium of their allies, plunged them too into so many and great calamities, as no one would have ever imagined could have befallen them. From hence any one may see, with how much more mildness and clemency we managed affairs, and likewise from what follows: for the Spartans scarce governed ten years; but we held the supremacy sixty-five years. Certainly all know, that cities, subject to others, continue longest faithful to those from whom they suffer the least evils: but both, becoming odious upon account of injuries, fell into wars and tumults; yet we shall find our city was capable of making resistance ten years, though attacked by all the Greeks and Barbarians: whereas the Lacedæmonians, though they still governed, and made war by land against the Thebans only, yet, when conquered in one battle, were stripped of all they possessed, and were afflicted with the same misfortunes and calamities as we. Besides, we shall find our city to have restored itself in fewer years than it was overthrown in; but that the Spartans, since this loss, in a very long time, have not been able to recover themselves to their former footing, but are still in the same low condition.

ANCIENT ATHENS.

## ÆSCHINES.

ÆSCHINES owes the perpetuity of his fame to the fact that he was the only rival of Demosthenes. He was five years older than that great orator, being born in 389 B.C. In early life he served as a soldier, then as a public clerk, and afterwards undertook the role of an actor. Though not successful on the stage, he acquired modification and inflection of the voice, a clear enunciation, and a certain ease, as well as boldness and impetuosity of manner. At first he was wholly opposed to the policy of Philip of Macedon, and he endeavored to organize the Greek States against that monarch. When his efforts failed, however, he advocated peace, and offered such vehement opposition to the party of Demosthenes as to give rise to the suspicion that he was bribed by Philip. The general belief in his venality rests chiefly on the unsupported evidence of his rival. The increasing opposition and hatred of these orators came to a climax in the prosecution instituted by Æschines against Ctesiphon. As a member of the Council of Five Hundred, Ctesiphon had proposed a decree that Demosthenes, for his public acts, should be presented by the Athenians with a golden crown, and that the presentation should take place in the theatre at the Dionysian festival. Owing to the Macedonian success the decree was not enacted, but six or seven years later Æschines brought a charge against Ctesiphon of proposing what was unconstitutional. As prosecutor, he had the right of first speech, and presented the legal points of his case with consummate ability, and, had he relied solely on these points, the verdict might have been different. But he launched out into a slanderous attack upon the character of his rival, thus affording him an opportunity of refuting the accusations. The trial was in reality a final combat between the representative of Greek independence and the advocate of Macedonian interference. Crowds from the remotest corners of Hellas thronged the platform. Æschines enlivened the assembly by several magnificent bursts of eloquent sarcasm. Demosthenes paid him back in his own coin; but throughout his discourse maintained a more even tenor, increasing in force as he proceeded. The critic Longinus says of him: "One might as soon face with steady eyes a descending thunderbolt as oppose a calm front to the storm of passions which Demosthenes can arouse." The Athenians returned a verdict for the defendant. Æschines, having failed to receive the quota of votes necessary to save him from fine and imprisonment, went as a voluntary exile to Rhodes, where he established a school of rhetoric. Among the first of his rhetorical recitations to his pupils was his own Speech on the Crown. This was well received, but that of Demosthenes, which was next read, elicited greater applause, upon which Æschines remarked with great candor, "What then would you have said if you had heard the beast himself?"

## His Attack on Demosthenes.

It remains that I produce some instances of his abandoned flattery. For one whole year did Demosthenes enjoy the honor of a senator; and yet in all that time it never appears that he moved to grant precedency to any ministers: for the first, the only time, he conferred this distinction on the ministers of Philip: he servilely attended to accommodate them with his cushions and his carpets: at the dawn of day he conducted them to the theatre; and by his indecent and abandoned adulation raised a universal uproar of derision. When they were on their departure towards Thebes he hired three teams of mules, and conducted them in state into that city. Thus did he expose his country to ridicule. But, that I may confine myself to facts, read the decree relative to the grant of precedency. [The decree is read.]

And yet this abject, this enormous flatterer, when he had been the first that received advice of Philip's death, from the emissaries of Charidemus, pretended a divine vision, and, with a shameless lie, declared that this intelligence had been conveyed to him, not by Charidemus, but by Zeus and Athene! Thus he dared to boast that these divinities, by whom he had sworn falsely in the day, had condescended to hold communication with him in the night, and to inform him of futurity. Seven days had now scarcely elapsed since the death of his daughter, when this wretch, before he had performed the usual rites of mourning, before he had duly paid her funeral honors, crowned his head with a chaplet, put on his white robe, made a solemn sacrifice in despite of law and decency; and this when he had lost his child—the first, the only child that had ever called him by the tender name of father! I say not this to insult his misfortunes; I mean but to display his real character: for he who hates his children, he who is a bad parent, cannot possibly prove a good minister. He who is insensible to that natural affection which should engage his heart to those who are most intimate and near to him, can never feel a greater regard for your welfare than for that of strangers. He who acts wickedly in private life cannot prove excellent in his public conduct; he who is base at home can never acquit himself with honor when sent to a strange country in a public character: for it is not the man, but the scene that changes.

I am now to speak of a third offence, and this still more heinous than the others. Philip by no means despised the Greeks; was by no means ignorant (for he was not devoid of all sense) that by a general engagement he must set his whole power on the hazard of a single day; he was inclined to treat about a compromise, and was on the point of sending deputies for this purpose; while the Theban magistrates, on their parts, were alarmed at the approaching danger, with good reason: for it was not a dastardly speaker who fled from his post in battle that presented it to their thoughts, but the Phocian war, that dreadful contest of ten years, which taught them a lesson never to be forgotten. Such was the state of affairs, and Demosthenes perceived it: he suspected that the Bœotian chiefs were on the point of making a separate peace, and would receive Philip's gold without admitting him to a

share: and deeming it worse than death to be thus excluded
from any scheme of corruption, he started up in the assembly
before any man had declared his opinion that a peace should
or should not be concluded with Philip, but with an intent
of warning the Bœotian chiefs, by a kind of public proclamation, that they were to allow him his portion of their bribes:
he swore by Athene (whom it seems Phidias made for the
use of Demosthenes in his vile trade of fraud and perjury),
that if any man should utter one word of making peace with
Philip, he himself with his own hands would drag him by
the hair to prison: imitating in this the conduct of Cleophon,
who in the war with Lacedæmon, as we are informed, brought
destruction on the state. But when the magistrates of Thebes
paid no attention to him, but, on the contrary, had counter-
manded their troops when on their march, and proposed to
you to consult about a peace, then was he absolutely frantic:
he rose up in the assembly; he called the Bœotian chiefs
traitors to Greece, and declared that he himself would move
(he who never dared to meet the face of an enemy) that you
should send ambassadors to the Thebans to demand a passage
through their territory for your forces, in their march against
Philip. And thus through shame, and fearing that they
might really be thought to have betrayed Greece, were the
magistrates of Thebes diverted from all thoughts of peace,
and hurried at once to the field of battle.

And here let us recall to mind those gallant men whom
he forced out to manifest destruction, without one sacred rite
happily performed, one propitious omen to assure them of
success; and yet, when they had fallen in battle, he presumed
to ascend their monument with those coward feet that fled
from their post, and pronounced his encomium on their
merit. But O thou who, on every occasion of great and
important action, hast proved of all mankind the most worthless, in the insolence of language the most astonishing, canst
thou attempt in the face of these thy fellow-citizens to claim
the honor of a crown for the misfortunes in which thou hast
plunged thy city? Or, should he claim it, can you Athenians
restrain your indignation? Has the memory of your slaughtered
countrymen perished with them? Indulge me for a moment,

and imagine that you are now not in this tribunal, but in the
theatre; imagine that you see the herald approaching, and
the proclamation prescribed in this decree on the point of
being delivered; and then consider, whether will the friends of
the deceased shed more tears at the tragedies, at the pathetic
stories of the great characters to be presented on the stage,
or at the insensibility of their country? What inhabitant
of Greece, what human creature who has imbibed the least
share of liberal sentiments, must not feel the deepest sorrow
when he reflects on one transaction which he must have seen
in the theatre; when he remembers, if he remembers nothing
else, that on festivals like these, when the tragedies were to
be presented, in those times when the state was well governed,
and directed by faithful ministers, a herald appeared, and
introducing those orphans whose fathers had died in battle,
now arrived at maturity, and dressed in complete armor, made
a proclamation the most noble, and the most effectual to excite
the mind to glorious actions: "That these youths, whose
fathers lost their lives in fighting bravely for their country,
the people had maintained to this their age of maturity: that
now, having now furnished them with complete suits of armor,
they dismiss them (with prayers for their prosperity) to attend
to their respective affairs, and invite them to aspire to the
highest offices of the state."

Such were the proclamations in old times; but such are
not heard now. And, were the herald to introduce the person
who had made these children orphans, what could he say, or
what could he proclaim? Should he speak in the form prescribed in this decree, yet the odious truth would still force
itself on you; it would seem to strike your ears with a language different from that of the herald; it would tell you
that "the Athenian people crowned this man, who scarcely
deserves the name of man, on account of his virtue, though a
wretch the most abandoned; and on account of his magna-
nimity, though a coward and deserter of his post." Do not,
Athenians! I conjure you by all the powers of Heaven, do
not erect a trophy in your theatre to perpetuate your own disgrace: do not expose the weak conduct of your country in
the presence of the Greeks: do not recall all their grievous

and desperate misfortunes to the minds of the wretched Thebans, who, when driven from their habitations by this man, were received within these walls; whose temples, whose children, whose sepulchral monuments were destroyed by the corruption of Demosthenes and the Macedonian gold.

## CLOSE OF HIS SPEECH AGAINST DEMOSTHENES.

A POPULAR orator, the cause of all our calamities, is found guilty of desertion in the field. This man claims a crown, and asserts his right to the honor of a proclamation. And shall not this wretch, the common pest of Greece, be driven from our borders? Or shall we not seize and drag to execution this public plunderer, whose harangues enable him to steer his piratical course through our government? Think on this critical season, in which you are to give your voices. In a few days the Pythian games are to be celebrated, and the convention of Grecian States to be assembled. There shall our state be severely censured on account of the late measures of Demosthenes. Should you crown him, you must be deemed accessories to those who violated the general peace: if, on the contrary, you reject the demand, you will clear the state from all imputation. Weigh this clause maturely, as the interest, not of a foreign state, but of your own: and do not lavish your honors inconsiderately: confer them with a scrupulous delicacy; and let them be the distinctions of exalted worth and merit: nor be contented to hear, but look round you, where your own interest is so intimately concerned, and see who are the men that support Demosthenes. Are they his former companions in the chase, his associates in the manly exercises of his youth? No, by the Olympian god! he never engaged in rousing the wild boar, or in any such exercises as render the body vigorous: he was solely employed in the sordid arts of fraud and circumvention.

And let not his arrogance escape your attention, when he tells you that by his embassy he wrested Byzantium from the hands of Philip; that his eloquence prevailed on the Acarnanians to revolt; his eloquence transported the souls of the Thebans. He thinks that you are sunk to such a degree of

weakness that he may prevail on you to believe that you
harbor the very genius of persuasion in your city, and not a
vile sycophant. And when, at the conclusion of his defence,
he calls up his accomplices in corruption as his advocates,
then imagine that you see the great benefactors of your
country in this place from which I speak, arrayed against
the villainy of those men : Solon, the man who adorned our
free constitution with the noblest laws, the philosopher, the
renowned legislator, entreating you, with that decent gravity
which distinguished his character, by no means to pay a
greater regard to the speeches of Demosthenes than to your
oaths and laws ; Aristides, who was suffered to prescribe to
the Greeks their several subsidies, whose daughters received
their portions from the people at his decease, roused to indignation at this insult on public justice, and asking whether
you are not ashamed, that when your fathers banished Arth-
mius the Zelian, who brought in gold from Persia ; when they
were scarcely restrained from killing a man connected with
the people in the most sacred ties, and by public proclamation forbade him to appear in Athens, or in any part of the
Athenian territory ; yet you are going to crown Demosthenes
with a golden crown, who did not bring in gold from Persia,
but received bribes himself, and still possesses them. And
can you not imagine that Themistocles, and those who fell at
Marathon, and those who died at Platæa, and the very sepul-
chres of our ancestors, must groan if you confer a crown on
this man, who confessedly united with the Barbarians against
the Greeks ?

And now bear witness for me, thou Earth, thou Sun, O
Virtue, and Intelligence, and thou, O Education, which teachest
us the just distinction between vice and goodness, I have stood
up, I have spoken in the cause of justice. If I have supported
my prosecution with a dignity befitting its importance, I have
spoken as my wishes dictated; if too deficiently, as my abilities
admitted. Let what has now been offered, and what your
own thoughts must supply, be duly weighed, and pronounce
such a sentence as justice and the interests of the state
demand

DEMOSTHENES.

In the oratory of more than two thousand years Demosthenes stands in the front rank, and will always hold first place among the orators of the ancient world. He was born in 384 B.C. When he was only seven years of age, his father, a wealthy manufacturer of arms in Athens, died. When the youth came of age he found himself stripped of his inheritance by dishonest trustees. Aided by Isæus he commenced a lawsuit against the chief embezzler, and succeeded in recovering about a third of his father's estate. The loss of his patrimony was the means of developing a spirit of courage and self-reliance, which might otherwise have remained latent. When Demosthenes first appeared before the public assembly he was utterly derided. He was weak in voice, awkward in manner, defective in articulation, wanting in wit or pathos, and not prepossessing in appearance. But perseverance enabled him to overcome all obstacles. Dramatic manners were fashionable; therefore he copied the example of actors. He sought in a lonely cave the solitude he desired for study and practice; he recited his speeches to the raging billows; he remedied defects of articulation by rolling pebbles in his mouth, and corrected awkwardness of manner by practising gestures before a mirror. For years he gave much of his time to writing speeches for the courts. From the charge of civil cases of increasing importance he gradually rose to the management of state questions. His critics remarked that his discourses smelt of the lamp, and the orator did not repudiate the impeachment. He made no claim to extempore speaking, but prepared all his speeches with the greatest care. Thus he became master of a style which is accepted as a type of clear, direct, and effective oratory.

For thirteen years Demosthenes had to combat the intrigues of a powerful and unscrupulous monarch. Philip's attempt to seize the pass of Thermopylæ gave the orator his first opportunity of making a determined attack on Macedonian aggressiveness. When Philip captured Elatea, the Greeks were thrown into genuine consternation, which is graphically described by Demosthenes in the second Philippic. On this occasion the whole assembly, completely overcome by the unprecedented burst of eloquence, rose and shouted, "To arms!—to arms! Lead us against Philip!"

Athens was still foremost among the leading states, although shorn of her ancient prestige; and Demosthenes abhorred the idea of her relinquishing her autonomy and independence, and becoming a member of the Macedonian Empire. He was opposed by such men as Æschines, from interested motives; and such as Phocion, who honestly believed that the Greeks must yield to Philip voluntarily, or by force of arms. The battle of Chæronea proved Phocion's foresight. Some measures were taken for the defence of Athens, and Demosthenes was foremost in the work, contributing liberally from his private resources. Ctesiphon therefore proposed that Demosthenes should be crowned in the theatre by the Athenian people, at the Dionysian Festival, as a mark of esteem for the virtue and good-will he had always shown to the state. This was a common form of reward to a citizen whose services had been appreciated by the public. Six years later an attack was made by Æschines upon Ctesiphon for violation of the constitution in making this proposal. It was really an attack upon the whole political career of Demosthenes, and gave occasion for the greatest speech by the greatest orator, the "Oration on the Crown." The very life and fame of Demosthenes are intimately bound up with this oration; it is a noble vindication of his patriotic career. The Athenians, to their credit, perceived truth and honor in the view entertained by Demosthenes, and recorded a verdict in his favor. Impartial critics concede the deep-rooted patriotism which he claimed to entertain. His sincerity and directness of purpose prove the upright man.

## PHILIP OF MACEDON.

### (From the First Philippic, delivered 351 B.C.)

WHEN, O my countrymen! will you exert your vigor? When roused by some event? When forced by some necessity? What, then, are we to think of our present condition? To freemen the disgrace attending our misconduct is, in my opinion, the most urgent necessity. Or is it your sole ambition to wander through the streets and public places, each inquiring of the other, "What news?" Can anything be more new than that a man of Macedonia should conquer the Athenians and give law to Greece? "Is Philip dead?" "No, but he is sick." How are you concerned in these rumors? Suppose he should meet some fatal stroke; you would soon raise up another Philip, if your interests are thus regarded. For it is not to his own strength that he so much owes his elevation as to our supineness. And should some accident befall him—should Fortune, who has ever been more careful of the state than we ourselves, now repeat her favors (and may she thus crown them!)—be assured of this, that by being on the spot, ready to take advantage of the confusion, you will everywhere be absolute masters; but in your present disposition, even if a favorable juncture should present you with Amphipolis,* you could not take possession of it while this suspense prevails in your councils.

Some of you wander about crying, "Philip has joined with the Lacedæmonians, and they are concerting the destruction of Thebes, and the dissolution of some free states." Others assure us that he has sent an embassy to the king [of Persia]; others, that he is fortifying places in Illyria. Thus we all go about framing our several stories. I believe, indeed, Athenians, that he is intoxicated with his greatness, and does entertain his imagination with many such visionary prospects, as he sees no power rising to oppose him, and is elated with his success. But I cannot be persuaded that he has so taken

* Amphipolis, a city of Thrace founded by the Athenians, had fallen into the hands of Philip after a siege, and the Athenians desired to recover it.

his measures that the weakest among us know what **he** is next to do—for the silliest are those who spread these rumors. Let us dismiss such talk, and remember only that Philip is our enemy—that he has spoiled us of our dominions, that we have long been subject to his insolence, that whatever we expected to be done for us by others has proved against us, that all the resource left us is in ourselves, and that, if we are not inclined to carry our arms abroad, we may be forced to fight at home. Let us be persuaded of this, and then we shall come to a proper determination; then we shall be freed from idle conjectures. We need not be solicitous to know what particular events will happen; we need to be convinced that nothing good can happen unless you attend to your duty, and are willing to act as becomes you.

As for myself, never have I courted favor by speaking what I am not convinced is for your good; and now I have spoken my whole mind frankly and unreservedly. I could have wished, knowing the advantage of good counsel to you, that I were equally certain of its advantage to the counsellor; so should I have spoken with more satisfaction. Now, with an uncertainty of the consequence to myself, but with a conviction that you will benefit by following my advice, I freely proffer it. And, of all those opinions which are offered for your acceptance, may that be chosen which will best advance the general weal.

### How the Athenians could Overcome Philip.

(From the First Olynthiac Oration, delivered 350 B.C.)

I SHALL not expatiate on the formidable power of Philip as an argument to urge you to the performance of your public duty. That would be too much both of compliment to him and of disparagement to you. I should, indeed, myself have thought him truly formidable, if he had achieved his present eminence by means consistent with justice. But he has aggrandized himself, partly through your negligence and improvidence, partly by treacherous means—by taking into pay corrupt partisans at Athens, and by cheating successively Olynthians, Thessalians, and all his other allies. These allies, having now detected his treachery, are deserting him; without them, his power will crumble away. Moreover, the Macedonians themselves have no sympathy with his personal ambition; they are fatigued with the labor imposed upon them by his endless military movements, and impoverished by the closing of their ports through the war. His vaunted officers are men of worthless and dissolute habits; his personal companions are thieves, vile ministers of amusement, outcasts from our cities. His past good fortune imparts to all this real weakness a fallacious appearance of strength; and doubtless his good fortune has been very great.

But the fortune of Athens, and her title to the benevolent aid of the gods is still greater—if only you, Athenians, will do your duty. Yet here you are, sitting still, doing nothing. The sluggard cannot even command his friends to work for him—much less the gods. I do not wonder that Philip, always in the field, always in movement, doing everything for himself, never letting slip an opportunity—prevails over you who merely talk, inquire, and vote, without action. Nay— the contrary would be wonderful—if, under such circumstances, he had *not* been the conqueror. But what I do wonder at is, that you Athenians—who in former days contended for Pan-Hellenic freedom against the Lacedæmonians—who, scorning unjust aggrandizement for yourselves, fought in person, and lavished your substance to protect the rights of other Greeks—that *you* now shrink from personal service and payment of money for the defence of your own possessions. You, who have so often rescued others, can now sit still after having lost so much of your own! I wonder you do not look back to that conduct of yours which has brought your affairs into this state of ruin, and ask yourselves how they can ever mend, while such conduct remains unchanged. It was much easier at first to preserve what we once had, than to recover it now that it is lost; we have nothing now left to lose—we have everything to recover. This must be done by ourselves, and at once; we must furnish money, we must serve in person by turns; we must give our generals means to do their work well, and then exact from them a severe account afterwards—which we cannot do so long as we ourselves will neither pay nor serve. We must correct that abuse which has grown up, whereby particular groups in the state combine to exempt themselves from burdensome duties, and to cast them all unjustly upon others. We must not only come forward vigorously and heartily, in person and with money, but each man must embrace faithfully his fair share of patriotic obligation.

## Reply to Æschines' Attack.

### (From the Oration on the Crown, delivered 330 B.C.)

CONCERNING the proclamation in the theatre, I pass over the fact, that thousands of thousands have been proclaimed, and I myself have been crowned often before. But by the Gods! are you so perverse and stupid, Æschines, as not to be able to reflect, that the party crowned has the same glory from the crown wherever it be published, and that the proclamation is made in the theatre for the benefit of those who confer the crown? For the hearers are all encouraged to render service to the state, and praise the parties who show their gratitude more than the party crowned. Therefore has our commonwealth enacted this law. Take and read me the law itself.

### THE LAW.

"Whensoever any of the townships bestow crowns, proclamations thereof shall be made by them in their several townships, unless where any are crowned by the people of Athens or the council, it shall be lawful for them to be proclaimed in the theatre at the Dionysian festival."

Do you hear, Æschines, the law distinctly saying—"unless where any are voted by the people or the council; such may be proclaimed?" Why then, wretched man, do you play the pettifogger? Why manufacture arguments? Why don't you take hellebore for your malady? Are you not ashamed to bring on a trial for spite, and not for any offence?—to alter some laws, and to garble others, the whole of which should in justice be read to persons sworn to decide according to the laws? And you that act thus describe the qualities which belong to a friend of the people, as if you had ordered a statue according to contract, and received it without getting what the contract required; or as if friends of the people were known by words, and not by acts and measures! And you bawl out, regardless of decency, a sort of cart-language, applicable to yourself and your race, not to me.

Now, men of Athens—I conceive abuse to differ from accusation in this, that accusation has to do with offences for which the laws provide penalties, abuse with the scandal which enemies speak against each other according to their feelings. And I believe our ancestors built these courts, not that we should assemble you here and bring forth the secrets of private life for mutual reproach, but to give us the means of convicting persons guilty of crimes against the state. Æschines knew this as well as I, and yet he chose to rail rather than to accuse.

Even in this way he must take as much as he gives; but before I enter upon such matters, let me ask him one question—Should one call you the state's opponent, or mine, Æschines? Mine, of course. Yet, where you might, for any offence which I committed, have obtained satisfaction for the people according to the laws, you neglected it—at the audit, on the indictments and other trials; but where I in my own person am safe on every account, by the laws, by time, by prescription, by many previous judgments on every point, by my never having been convicted of a public offence—and where the country must share, more or less, in the repute of measures which were her own—here it is you have encountered me. See if you are not the people's opponent, while you pretend to be mine!

Since therefore the righteous and true verdict is made clear to all; but I must, it seems—though not naturally fond of railing, yet on account of the calumnies uttered by my opponent—in reply to so many falsehoods, just mention some leading particulars concerning him, and show who he is, and from whom descended, that so readily begins using hard words—and what language he carps at, after uttering such as any decent man would have shuddered to pronounce.— Why, if my accuser had been Æacus, or Rhadamanthus, or Minos, instead of a prater, a hack of the market, a pestilent scribbler, I do not think he would have spoken such things, or found such offensive terms, shouting. as in a tragedy, "O Earth! O Sun! O Virtue!" and the like; and again appealing to Intelligence and Education, by which the honorable is distinguished from the base:—all this you undoubtedly heard from his lips. Accursed one! What have you or yours to do with virtue? How should you discern what is honorable or otherwise? How were you ever qualified? What right have you to talk about education? Those who really possess it would never say as much of themselves, but rather blush if another did: those who are destitute like you, but make pretensions to it from stupidity, annoy the hearers by their talk, without getting the reputation which they desire.

## The Duties of the Public Orator.

### (From the Oration on the Crown.)

On what occasions ought an orator and statesman to be vehement? Where any of the commonwealth's main interests are in jeopardy, and he is opposed to the adversaries of the people. Those are the occasions for a generous and brave citizen. But for a person, who never sought to punish me for any offence either public or private, on the state's behalf or on his own, to have got up an accusation because I am crowned and honored, and to have expended such a multitude of words —this is a proof of personal enmity and spite and meanness, not of anything good. And then his leaving the controversy with me, and attacking the defendant, comprises everything that is base.

I should conclude, Æschines, that you undertook this cause to exhibit your eloquence and strength of lungs, not to obtain satisfaction for any wrong. But it is not the language of an orator, Æschines, that has any value, nor yet the tone of his voice, but his adopting the same views with the people, and his hating and loving the same persons that his country does. He that is thus minded will say everything with loyal intention; he that courts persons from whom the commonwealth apprehends danger to herself, rides not on the same anchorage with the people, and therefore has not the same expectation of safety. But—do you see?—I have: for my

objects are the same with those of my countrymen; I have
no interest separate or distinct. Is that so with you? How
can it be—when immediately after the battle you went as
ambassador to Philip, who was at that period the author of
your country's calamities, notwithstanding that you had before persisted in refusing that office, as all men know?

And who is it that deceives the state? Surely the man
who speaks not what he thinks. On whom does the crier
pronounce a curse? * Surely on such a man. What greater
crime can an orator be charged with, than that his opinions
and his language are not the same? Such is found to be
your character. And **yet** you open your mouth, and dare to
look these men in the faces! Do you think they don't know
you?—or are sunk all in such slumber and oblivion, as not to
remember the speeches which you delivered in the assembly,
cursing and swearing that you had nothing to do with Philip,
and that I brought that charge against you out of personal
enmity without foundation? No sooner came the news of
the battle, than you forgot all that; you acknowledged and
avowed that between Philip and yourself there subsisted a
relation of hospitality and friendship—new names these for
your contract of hire. For upon what plea of equality or
justice could Æschines, son of Glaucothea the timbrel-player,
be the friend or acquaintance of Philip? I cannot see. No!
You were hired to ruin the interests of your countrymen: and
yet, though you have been caught yourself in open treason,
and informed against yourself after the fact, you revile and
reproach me for things which you will find any man is charge-
able with sooner than I.

Many great and glorious enterprises has the commonwealth, Æschines, undertaken and succeeded in through me;
and she did not forget them. Here is the proof—on the election of a person to speak the funeral oration immediately after
the event, you were proposed, but the people would not have
you, notwithstanding your fine voice, nor Demades, though
he had just made the peace, nor Hegemon, nor any other of

* At the opening of every public assembly of the Athenians a
crier pronounced a solemn curse on all who should speak against the
public interest.

your party—but me. And when you and Pythocles came forward in a brutal and shameful manner (O merciful Heaven !) and urged the same accusations against me which you now do, and abused me, they elected me all the more. The reason— you are not ignorant of it—yet I will tell you. The Athenians knew as well the loyalty and zeal with which I conducted their affairs, as the dishonesty of you and your party; for what you denied upon oath in our prosperity, you confessed in the misfortunes of the republic. They considered therefore, that men who got security for their politics by the public disasters had been their enemies long before, and were then avowedly such. They thought it right also, that the person who was to speak in honor of the fallen and celebrate their valor, should not have sat under the same roof or at the same table with their antagonists; that he should not revel the. and sing a pæan over the calamities of Greece in company with their murderers, and then come here and receive distinction; that he should not with his voice act the mourner of their fate, but that he should lament over them with his heart. This they perceived in themselves and in me, but not in any of you: therefore they chose me, and not you. Nor, while the people felt thus, did the fathers and brothers of the deceased, who were chosen by the people to perform their obsequies, feel differently. For having to order the funeral banquet (according to custom) at the house of the nearest relative to the deceased, they ordered it at mine. And with reason : because, though each to his own was nearer of kin than I was, none was so near to them all collectively. He that had the deepest interest in their safety and success, had upon their mournful disaster the largest share of sorrow for them all.

## CHAPTER XXIII.

# GREEK ELEGIAC AND LYRIC POETRY.

## TYRTÆUS.

THE name of Tyrtæus has become proverbial as a composer of war-songs. According to an old tradition, the Spartans, being engaged in war with the Messenians, suffered reverses which led them to seek advice from an oracle. They were directed to ask the Athenians for a leader. The rival state sent in derision the lame schoolmaster Tyrtæus. But the spirited songs of the new commander so roused the martial spirit of the Lacedæmonians that they achieved complete victory at Ithome. This second Messenian war lasted from 685 B.C. to 668. Tyrtæus is reported not only to have incited the Spartans to deeds of valor, but on occasion to have calmed popular riots with his verses. He was highly honored by his adopted country, and long after his death his memory was cherished. His solemn yet stirring couplets were regularly taught to the boys of Sparta and were chanted by her soldiers in the field. His marching songs have perished, and the scanty remnants of his elegies seem hardly adequate to his unique fame.

### COURAGE AND PATRIOTISM.

NE'ER would I praise that man, nor deign to sing,
First in the race, or strongest at the ring,
Not though he boast a ponderous Cyclops' force,
Or rival Boreas in his rapid course;
Not tho' Aurora might his name adore,
Tho' Eastern riches swell his countless store,
Tho' power and splendor to his name belong,
And soft persuasion dwell upon his tongue,
Tho' all but god-like valor were his own:
My muse is sacred to the brave alone;
Who can look carnage in the face, and go
Against the foremost warriors of the foe.

By heaven high courage to mankind was lent,
Best attribute of youth, best ornament.
The man whom blood and danger fail to daunt,
Fearless who fights, and ever in the front,
Who bids his comrades barter useless breath
For a proud triumph, or a prouder death,
He is my theme—He only, who can brave
With single force the battle's rolling wave,
Can turn his enemies to flight, and fall
Beloved, lamented, deified by all.
His household gods, his own parental land
High in renown, by him exalted stand;
Alike the heirs and founders of his name
Share his deserts and borrow from his fame
He, pierced in front with many a gaping wound,
Lies, great and glorious, on the bloody ground,
From every eye he draws one general tear,
And a whole nation follows to his bier;
Illustrious youths sigh o'er his early doom,
And late posterity reveres his tomb.
Ne'er shall his memorable virtue die,
Tho' cold in earth, immortal as the sky;
He for his country fought, for her expired:
Oh, would all imitate whom all admired!
But if he sleep not with the mighty dead,
And, living, laurels wreathe his honor'd head,
By old, by young, adored, he gently goes
Down a smooth pathway to his long repose,
Unaltering friends still love his hairs of snow,
And rising elders in his presence bow.
Would ye, like him, the wond'ring world engage,
Draw the keen blade, and let the battle rage!

Then let us firmly stand, and scorn to fly,
Save all we love, or with our country die,
Knit in indissoluble files, a band
Of brothers fighting for our native land;
Ne'er let us see the veteran soldier's arm
Than ours more forward, or his heart more warm;
Let us not leave him in the midst of foes,
Feeble with age, to deal unequal blows;
Or in the van lie slain, with blood besmear'd

His wrinkled forehead and his snowy beard,
Stript of his spoils through many a battle worn,
And gay assumed, that inauspicious morn,
Breathing his soul out bravely at our feet—
Ne'er may our eyes a sight so shameful meet!
But, oh, be ours, while yet our pulse beats high
For gory death, or glorious victory,
Be ours, if not an honorable grave,
Smiles of the fair, and friendships of the brave.

### To Spartan Veterans.

Ye are the sons of Hercules—a race
   Unvanquished in the fight, and nobly proud;
Then stand—for Jove not yet averts his face—
   Then stand, superior to the hostile crowd.

Fear not; advancing to the bloody strife,
   Let each oppose his buckler to the foe!
And, ready to resign his load of life,
   Through fate's dark path, with warrior-spirit, go.

Yet is that path delightful to the sun,
   His radiance smiling on heroic death!
The military course ye oft have run:
   Then lightly value life's precarious breath.

For ye have seen, on many a toilsome day,
   How sad the ruthless work of war appears;
Seen anger furious in the battle's bray,
   And Mars exulting in abundant tears.

For ye have known, full well, the rage of war;
   Whether, o'erpowered, your gaping squadrons bled,
Or, scattered o'er the purple plains afar,
   Your victor-arms the foe in terror fled.

### To Spartan Youths.

Rouse, rouse, O youths! the chain of torpor break!
   Spurn idle rest, and couch the glittering lance!
What! does not shame with blushes stain your cheek
   Quick-mantling, as ye catch the warrior's glance?

Ignoble youths! say, when shall valor's flame
   Burn in each breast? Here, here, while hosts invade,
And war's wild clangors all your courage claim,
   Ye sit, as if peace still embowered the shade.

But, sure, fair honor crowns the auspicious deed,
   When patriot love impels us to the field;
When, to defend a trembling wife, we bleed,
   And when our sheltered offspring bless the shield.

What time the fates ordain, pale death appears:
   Then, with firm step and sword high drawn, depart;
And, marching through the first thick shower of spears,
   Beneath thy buckler guard the intrepid heart.

Each mortal, though he boast celestial sires,
   Slave to the sovereign destiny of death,
Amid the carnage of the plain expires,
   Or yields unwept at home his coward breath.

Yet sympathy attends the brave man's bier,
   Sees on each wound the balmy grief bestowed,
And, as in death the universal tear,
   Through life inspires the homage of a god.

For like a turret his proud glories rise,
   And stand, above the rival's reach, alone;
While millions hail, with fond, adoring eyes,
   The deeds of many a hero meet in one!

## ARCHILOCHUS.

Ancient critics pronounced Archilochus a poet of the highest rank. But the few surviving pieces of his verse seem tame beside those of many other Greeks.

### Two Captains.

Boast me not your valiant captain,
   Strutting fierce with measur'd stride,
Glorying in his well-trimmed beard, and
   Wavy ringlets' clustered pride.
Mine be he that's short of stature,
   Firm of foot. with curved knee;
Heart of oak in limb and feature;
   And of courage bold and free.

# SAPPHO.

### Hymn to Aphrodite.

(Translated by J. Addington Symonds, in the metre of the original.)

Star-throned, incorruptible Aphrodite,
Child of Zeus, wile-weaving, I supplicate thee,
Tame not me with pangs of the heart, dread mistress,
    Nay, nor with anguish.
But come thou, if erst in the days departed
Thou didst lend thine ear to my lamentation,
And from far, the house of thy sire deserting,
    Camest with golden
Car yoked: thee, thy beautiful sparrows hurried
Swift with multitudinous pinions fluttering
Round black earth, adown from the height of heaven
    Through middle ether:
Quickly journeyed they; and thou, O blest Lady,
Smiling with those brows of undying lustre,
Asked me what new grief at my heart lay, wherefore
    Now I had called thee,
What I fain would have to assuage the torment
Of my frenzied soul; and whom now, to please thee,
Must persuasion lure to thy love, and who now,
    Sappho, hath wronged thee?

Yea, for though she flies, she shall quickly chase thee;
Yea, though gifts she spurns, she shall soon bestow them
Yea, though now she loves not, she soon shall love thee,
    Yea, though she will not!
Come, come now too! Come, and from heavy heart-ache
Free my soul, and all that my longing yearns to
Have done, do thou; be thou for me thyself too
    Help in the battle.

## ODE TO ANACTORIA.

PEER of gods he seemeth to me, the blissful
Man who sits and gazes at thee before him,
Close beside thee sits, and in silence hears thee,
    Silverly speaking,
Laughing love's low laughter. Oh, this, this only
Stirs the troubled heart in my breast to tremble!
For should I but see thee a little moment,
    Straight is my voice hushed;
Yea, my tongue is broken, and through and through me
'Neath the flesh impalpable fire runs tingling;
Nothing see mine eyes, and a noise of roaring
    Waves in my ear sounds;
Sweat runs down in rivers, a tremor seizes
All my limbs, and paler than grass in autumn,
Caught by pains of menacing death, I falter,
    Lost in the love-trance.

## TO ALCÆUS.

ARISTOTLE relates that Alcæus addressed Sappho in a verse that resembles her own in descriptive epithets:—"Violet-wearing, pure, softly-smiling Sappho, I would fain tell thee something, but shame restrains me." Sappho's reply has been thus translated:

    If aught of good, if aught of fair
    Thy tongue were laboring to declare,
    Nor shame should dash thy glance, nor fear
    Forbid thy suit to reach my ear.

ALCÆUS.

BESIDES Sappho, her friend, perhaps lover, Alcæus is almost the sole representative of the Æolic school of poetry. He was a noble of Mytilene, the capital of Lesbos. With other nobles he opposed and drove into exile the tyrant of his city. His friend Pittacus had assisted the movement, but was afterwards made dictator in order to restore order. Alcæus and his brothers stiffly adhered to the aristocratic cause and were banished. The poet reproached the new tyrant in bitter verses, and afterwards led an expedition against him. Pittacus took his former friend captive and then granted him liberty, saying, "Forgiveness is better than revenge." Alcæus sought refuge in Egypt, but eventually his friendship with Pittacus was restored.

Alcæus was acknowledged by Horace as his model and master. He invented the Alcaic metre, and sang about war, wine and love. Though a valiant soldier, he tells in one song how he threw away his shield in flight.

### THE SPOILS OF WAR.

GLITTERS with brass my mansion wide;
The roof is deck'd, on every side,
  In martial pride,
With helmets rang'd in order bright,
And plumes of horse-hair nodding white,
  A gallant sight—
Fit ornament for warrior's brow—
And round the walls, in goodly row,
  Refulgent glow
Stout greaves of brass, like burnish'd gold,
And corselets there in many a fold
  Of linen roll'd;

And shields that in the battle fray,
The routed losers of the day
  Have cast away.
Eubœan falchions too are seen,
With rich-embroidered belts between
  Of dazzling sheen:
And gaudy surcoats piled around,
The spoils of chiefs in war renown'd,
  May there be found—
These, and all else that here you see,
Are fruits of glorious victory,
  Achieved by me.


### DRINKING SONG.

WHY wait we for the torches' lights?
Now let us drink, while day invites.
In mighty flagons hither bring
 The deep-red blood of many a vine,
That we may largely quaff and sing
 The praises of the God of wine—
The son of Jove and Semele,
Who gave the jocund grape to be
A sweet oblivion to our woes.
 Fill, fill the goblet—one and two:
Let every brimmer, as it flows,
 In sportive chase, the last pursue.


## THEOGNIS.

THE strongly personal character of the Greek elegies is illustrated by the fact that from the 1,400 lines of Theognis still extant J. H. Frere undertook to construct his biography. The poet was a noble, born at Megara about 550 B.C. According to a practice common among the Greeks, and especially the Dorians, he had chosen as his intimate friend young Cyrnus, the leader of the aristocracy. When that party was driven from power by the democrats, Theognis was reduced to exile and poverty. The girl to whom he was betrothed was given by her parents in marriage to another less worthy than himself. To Cyrnus the distressed poet poured out the bitterness of his soul, and then had to complain of his friend's indifference. His life was prolonged to the age of eighty-eight, yet he never ceased to lament his lost youth and the triumph of the wicked in this world.

## THE POET'S GIFT OF FAME.

You soar aloft, and over land and wave
Are borne triumphant on the wings I gave
(The swift and mighty wings, Music and Verse).
Your name in easy numbers smooth and terse
Is wafted o'er the world; and heard among
The banquetings and feasts, chanted and sung,
Heard and admired: the modulated air
Of flutes, and voices of the young and fair
Recite it, and to future times shall tell;
When, closed within the dark sepulchral cell,
Your form shall moulder, and your empty ghost
Wander along the dreary Stygian coast.

Yet shall your memory flourish green and young,
Recorded and revived on every tongue,
In continents and islands, every place
That owns the language of the Grecian race.

No purchased prowess of a racing steed,
But the triumphant Muse, with airy speed,
Shall bear it wide and far, o'er land and main,
A glorious and imperishable strain;
A mighty prize gratuitously won,
Fixed as the earth, immortal as the sun.

## THE SHIP OF STATE.

Such is our state! in a tempestuous sea,
With all the crew raging in mutiny!
No duty followed, none to reef a sail,
To work the vessel, or to pump or bail:
All is abandoned, and without a check
The mighty sea comes sweeping o'er the deck.
Our steersman, hitherto so bold and steady,
Active and able, is deposed already.
No discipline, no sense of order felt,
The daily messes are unduly dealt.
The goods are plundered, those that ought to keep
Strict watch are idly skulking or asleep;
All that is left of order or command
Committed wholly to the basest hand.

In such a case, my friend, I needs must think
It were no marvel though the vessel sink.
This riddle to my worthy friends I tell,
But a shrewd knave will understand it well!

## SIMONIDES OF AMORGOS.

THERE were two noted Greek poets named Simonides, and both
were Ionians. The earlier, called from his birth-place Simonides of
Amorgos, flourished about 660 B.C. The iambic verse, which had been
invented and devoted to satire by Archilochus about 700 B.C., was his
chosen measure. But while the inventor attacked individuals with
such relentless severity that he is said to have driven one to suicide,
Simonides in more even verse assailed the better half of the human
race. In his principal poem he divides women into ten classes and,
comparing them to various animals, pronounces all bad except the busy
bee. And then the sly rogue concludes by withdrawing the exception.

### TEN CLASSES OF WOMEN.

THE prototype of every female mind
The Gods first made, of every form and kind.

Behold the slut—she in the dirt is found
All filth-polluted, rolling on the ground,
Unwashed, unkempt, untidy her attire,
In mud she wallows, fattens in the mire,
Her filthy house and filthier self avow
Her soul as taken from the bristly sow.

The scoundrel fox another soul supplies,
To good and evil—up to all—all-wise;
A prying spirit, ever on the watch,
At truth or lies, at right or wrong to catch;
The busy-bodies these, that roam and gad,
Some pretty good, but more, alas! are bad.

That barking woman, with her slanderous itch,
Proclaims the spirit of her parent bitch.
With eager eyes and ears, and poking snout,
She snuffs for scandal, and she paws it out;
Peering and peeping everywhere she goes,
Barking and biting both at friends and foes:
And rather than be still, the spiteful elf
Will snap and snarl at her own precious self.

What if her everlasting tongue should rouse
The angry spirit of her patient spouse
To seize a stone to quell each horrid note,
And pound her grinders down her yelping throat:
Ah! little would it boot, poor man—for she
*Will* bark, though angry or though kind he be,
Though friends or foes, or strangers should be near,
Her clamorous tongue, all, all are doomed to hear.

The lazy lump, the weary husband's load,
The Gods created of the sluggish sod—
Her earth-born spirit knows nor ill nor good,
Her knowledge is to cram herself with food.
When angry winter's biting frosts appear,
Close by the blazing hearth she posts her chair,
And the poor creature sits and shivers there.

Mark you a fifth: the never constant sea,
O fickle womankind, gave birth to thee;
So smiling, lovely, so serene to-day,
That he who knows thee not might justly say,
" Most elegant, domestic, perfect creature,
Thou cunning pattern of excelling nature."
But mark her well,—'tis hideous to behold
This perfect creature,—now a perfect scold;
Whom none dare look upon, and none come near,
Who fills both friends and foes, and all with fear,
Rages unceasingly—and howls and yelps,
Like an ungracious bitch that guards her whelps.
And as the sea, when summer smiles, is seen
The sailor's joy, so placid and serene,
Anon its waves with loud, terrific roar,
Lash with their curling crests the laboring shore,
So changeful, so deceitful, do we find
This " sea of troubles "—fickle womankind.

A heap of sluggish ashes, and an ass,
The all-enduring, form'd another class,
Whom neither force nor angry words will rouse
To do a single deed to please a spouse.
If they retire,—it is that they may eat:
If by the fire,—they cram themselves with meat:
Or if perchance they feel the amorous flame—
No choice have they—for every man's the same.

The weasel-soul'd, the grim, the sad-of-face,
The unloving, unbeloved, ungracious race,
Nor beautiful, nor fair, aught earthly deem;
Life has for them no charm, and love's a dream.
They hate their husbands with a perfect hate:
Their pilfering tricks continual broils create:
Their fiendish, thievish, sacrilegious eyes
Even on the sacred victims gormandize.

From the soft, waving-maned, the full-fed mare,
Jove made a tribe—the foes of toil and care.
These will not grind, nor winnow, ne'er are seen
To watch the oven, or their houses clean,
For fear of soot; the purses of their spouses,
Pretending love, they sweep, though not their houses.
No washings twice or thrice a-day they spare
On their own persons,—these their only care,
Nor oils, nor unguents, to perfume their hair,
Which o'er the neck luxuriantly spreads,
And, crown'd with flowers, a lovely fragrance sheds.
'Tis a fine show—another's eyes to feast,
But to a spouse—the devil at the least;
Except a king or prince they chance to find,
Who has a taste for toys of such a kind.

Another class form'd from the hideous ape,
Ugly in figure, fashion, face and shape—
Jove sent to earth—the greatest frights that e'er
Created laughter, or made people stare.
Hipless, and shapeless as a plank, they wend;
Necks stiff and short, and never meant to bend.
O wretched husband, thine's a piteous case,
Compell'd this prime of evils to embrace—
Who like the ape is crafty, full of guile,
But "never twists her lips by way of smile;"
Pries into all, but ne'er an action does
That is not hideous as her ugly phiz.
This is her object, this by night and day
Rouses her soul and being into play,—
How she may bring about, by wicked skill,
The greatest possible amount of ill.

Happy the man,—thrice happy surely he!
Whose wife was fashion'd from the busy bee.
*Her*, scandal dares not, with its slime, defile:
And wealth and honors on her husband smile.
The mother of a race renown'd and bold,
With him she loves, herself beloved, grows old.
The excellent of women! *her* is given
The encircling beauty of the grace of Heaven.
She with her sex ne'er spends the precious hours
In listening to their gossip and amours.
Thrice happy they whom gracious Heaven may bless
With wives so virtuous, prudent, good, as this!

This the exception: those, and such as those,
The ills,—that fill the life of man with woes,
Which, in the wisdom of his crafty mind,
Jove sends to earth in shape of womankind,—
Of whom, alas! the fairest and the best
A husband knows the blessing not so blest:
Since *a whole day* of happiness no man
Spent with a wife e'er since the world began:
Nor soon will gaunt starvation leave that house
Where dwells that foe of Gods and man—a spouse.
Nay, when his soul is open to delights,
Intent on solemn, or on festive rites,
This carping fury soon his bliss will blight,
And change his feasting into deadly fight.
For hospitality may never dare
To spread the table, if a wife be there,
Whose best intentions, in her wisest mood,
Are folly;—surely evil is her good.

Marriage makes man a simpleton—since he
Sees not—what all his neighbors gladly see—
That strange delusion which would make *his* bride
So perfect,—so imperfect *all* beside.
Loud in her praises, he can never see,
That as his neighbor's, so his fate must be,—
A thraldom, and a bondage, and a yoke
Which Jove hath made, and never can be broke:
Till Pluto free him from a weary life,
Perchance while fighting for a worthless wife.

## SIMONIDES OF CEOS.

### THERMOPYLÆ.

THESE two brief inscriptions on the altar-tomb of the Three Hundred who fell with Leonidas at Thermopylæ have taxed the ingenuity of translators to preserve the grand simplicity of the original.

> Go, stranger, and to Lacedæmon tell,
> That here, obedient to her laws, we fell.

> Greatly to die, if this be glory's height,
>     For the fair meed we own our fortune kind;
> For Greece and Liberty we plunged to night,
>     And left a never-dying name behind.

### CIMON'S VICTORY AT EURYMEDON.

CIMON, son of Miltiades, the victor at Marathon, distinguished himself in the war against Xerxes, and afterwards commanded the Athenian fleet which harassed the Persian possessions in Asia Minor. His most brilliant success was in 466 B.C., when at the mouth of the River Eurymedon he defeated the Persian fleet, and on the same day landed and routed their army.

> NE'ER since the olden time, when Asia stood
> First torn from Europe by the ocean-flood,
> Since horrid Mars thus poured on either shore
> The storm of battle and the wild uproar,
> Hath Man by land and sea such glory won,
> Nor seen such deeds, as thou, this day, hast done.
> By land, the Medes in thousands press the ground;
> By sea, a hundred Tyrian ships are drowned
> With all their martial host; while Asia stands
> Deep groaning by, and wrings her helpless hands.

### DANAE.

ACRISIUS, King of Argos, and father of Danaë, had been warned by an oracle that she would give birth to a child that would slay him. Thereupon he kept her shut up in a brazen tower. But Zeus descending in a golden shower, she became the mother of Perseus. The king then ordered Danaë and her child to be set adrift on the sea in an ark or chest. J. A. Symonds thus translates the pathetic poem of Simonides on these hapless castaways.

When in the carven chest,
The winds that blew and waves in wild unrest
Smote her with fear, Danaë, not with cheeks unwet,
    Her arms of love round Perseus set,
    And said: "O child, what grief is mine!
But thou dost slumber, and thy baby breast
        Is sunk in rest,
Here in the cheerless brass-bound bark,
Tossed amid starless night and pitchy dark.
    Nor dost thou heed the scudding brine
Of waves that wash above thy curls so deep,
Nor the shrill winds that sweep,—
Lapped in thy purple robe's embrace,
        Fair little face!
But if this dread were dreadful too to thee,
Then wouldst thou lend thy listening ear to me.
Therefore I cry,—Sleep, babe, and sea be still,
    And slumber our unmeasured ill!
Oh, may some change of fate, sire Zeus, from thee
        Descend, our woes to end!
    But if this prayer, too overbold, offend
    Thy justice, yet be merciful to me!"

## PINDAR.

For more than two thousand years Pindar has been recognized as the most sublime of lyric poets. He was born probably in 522 B.C., and belonged to an illustrious family of Thebes which claimed descent from the mythical heroes. Though carefully trained for choral composition in Athens, he was also instructed by the poetess Corinna of his own city. It is reported that when she bade him mingle myths with his panegyrics, he produced an ode overburdened with Theban legends. The wise instructress reproved this excess by saying, "One ought to sow with the hand, and not with the whole sack." Afterwards when the pupil competed with his mistress for public prizes, she is said to have beaten him five times. Yet the only fragment extant of her work is a mild reproof of another woman for contending with Pindar.

Though residing chiefly at Thebes, Pindar traveled through many parts of Greece, and visited the court of his munificent patron, King Hiero of Syracuse. Wherever Greek was spoken his odes were prized, and for his words of praise Athens voted him a handsome sum.

The forty-four poems of Pindar, which have been preserved entire, all belong to the class called Epinician Odes—that is, celebrations of victory in the national games. These famous festivals were reunions of the Greek race at the local shrine of some deity. The Olympian games were held at Olympia in Elis in honor of Zeus every fourth year during the summer at the time of full moon; their prize was a wreath of wild olive. The Pythian games were held at Crissa in honor of the Pythian Apollo every fourth year in the spring; their prizes were a wreath of laurel and a palm. The Nemean games were held in the Nemean grove in Argolis in honor of Zeus every second year; their prize was a wreath of parsley. The Isthmian games were held in honor of Poseidon (Neptune) at Corinth, every second year; their prize was a wreath of pine. The obligation of these seasons of Pan-Hellenic union was recognized to such an extent that hostilities were everywhere suspended for a sufficient time to allow travelers to journey to the appointed place and return. Many of the states sent ambassadors liberally equipped, and wealthy citizens vied with them in magnificence of display. In these games, doubly consecrated by religion and patriotism, only persons of Greek descent were allowed to contend.

These games were not confined to athletic contests, horse and chariot races; the assemblages attracted also poets and rhapsodists, who recited tales of heroes, and in later times historians and philosophers, painters and sculptors. Though the prizes offered seem slight and perishable, various means were taken to preserve the honor of the victors and of the cities to which they belonged. Their names were inscribed on marble or bronze tablets in the temples, their statues were erected on the sacred grounds. The genius of the greatest of living poets was invoked to do justice to their merits. Pindar celebrated fourteen Olympian victors, twelve Pythian, eleven Nemean, seven Isthmian. Yet he was no base hireling, but a noble-minded aristocrat, fully aware of his own pre-eminence and disdaining to use his poetic gifts except for lofty purposes. Many of the heroes whom he celebrated were of his own kin.

Honored through a long life, Pindar reached his seventy-ninth year. He is said to have died in the theatre at Argos, in the arms of his young friend Theoxenos, whose beauty he had praised in lofty strains. After his death various legends sprang up which seemed to give him place and honors among the gods. When Alexander the Great at the beginning of his reign vented his wrath upon Thebes for daring to rebel, he bade the house and the descendants of Pindar to be spared.

The sublimity of Pindar has been described by the use of various metaphors and similes. He is often called the Theban eagle, to show the strength and rapidity with which he carries the mind into the loftiest regions. Horace likens him to the swift-rushing, loud-roaring torrent. Symonds, to express the intoxicating rapture of his odes, chose a figure from the poet himself, where he likens himself to a wealthy noble offering rich wine in a golden goblet to a welcome son-in-law at a wedding feast. With all his bold grandeur and daring originality there is always combined an exquisite art. The religious spirit is also strongly manifested in his odes, but he does not hesitate to reject a mythical story as unsuited to the character of the gods. He seldom mentions in any detail the victory which has given occasion for his ode, but turns away to recite myths connected with the hero's family or city, and closes with reference to his merit or success.

### THE INFANT HERCULES.

(From the First Nemean Ode. To Chromius, victor in chariot race, 468 B.C.)

BUT when I fain would wake
   Some old heroic lay,
      Whose but Herakles' noble name
Should deck the exulting verse for thy dear sake?
True Son of Jove, when to the realms of Day
First with his earthly brother-twin forth from the womb he came.

E'en as his cradle-bed the babe did scale,
   The Queen of Heaven beheld him, and afire

With wrath, two horrid snakes bade trail.
Him to destroy, their dread and loathly spire.
Straight to the bower of infant rest
　　The mighty monsters pressed,
　　Their hungry jaws so grim
　To wind around each infant limb,
But as they came, the babe unterrified
Lifted his little head, and his first battle tried.

With either hand one horrid throat
　　he grasped
Beneath those jaws of terror, gaping
　　wide ;
　Fast in that knot the monsters
　　　gasped,
Loosed their long spires, and drooped
　　their heads and died.
　Pierced by a pang of sudden fear,
　　Hurried the matrons near,
　　Who their kind vigil kept
　Attentive where the mother slept.
And forth the mother rushed, her
　　feet all bare,
E'en as she lay, in hope those mon-
　　strous beasts to scare.

At the wild cry the Thebans thronged amain,
　　In brazen armor fain :
　　Amphitryon came in speed,
　Brandishing high his naked blade,
Pierced to the soul with keen paternal pain.
Full sore do hearts for their own sorrows bleed ;
But all too soon the pangs of grief for others' griefs do fade !

In mingled pain and joy of heart amazed
The hero stood that wondrous sight to view.
　　As on the babe's strong heart he gazed,
Naught but the favoring love of heaven, he knew.
　　Availed to turn to joyful cheer,
　　　That dismal tale of fear.
　　　Forthwith the Seer of Heaven,
　　To whom the gift of Truth was given,

He called :—the Seer outspake before them all,
And told what wondrous fate should that bright babe befall.

What monsters of the land and ocean wide
Before his stalwart arm should vanquished bow ;
    What haught oppressors' furious pride
His righteous club should lay in ruin low.
    Nay,—when on Phlegra's plain of blood
      The hideous Giant brood
      Should dare the Gods in fight,
Before the arrows' wingèd might,
Before his awful arm's resistless thrust,
Those sons of Earth should roll their boasted locks in dust.

So should his soul on earth by toils be tried,
    Then should long Peace betide.
      Then in high Heaven for aye
    Safe should he scale the blest abodes,
The ever-blooming Hebe for his bride :
Feasting in one eternal marriage-day,
Inmate of Jove's celestial bowers, and homed among the Gods.


## JASON.

(From the Fourth Pythian Ode. In honor of Arcesilaus, King of
Cyrene, victor in chariot race, 466 B.C.)

In time a noble stranger came,
A youth of glorious port ; his manly frame
The country tunic clasped ; two spears he bore.
    Above, to fence the shivering rain,
    A skin of spotted pard he threw.
    Adown his youthful neck amain
    His hair in glittering ringlets flew.
('Twas then in thronging crowds the people pressed,
    What time the busy forum filled),
    Then first he proved his manly breast,
And stood amid the throng by timorous fears unchilled.

Who might he be ? thus each in wonder cried ;
    Is he Apollo ? Is he Mars,
    So awful from the brazen cars,
So fair to win bright Venus for his bride ?

In Naxus sure men said
Otus and Ephialte were dead;
And earth-born Tityus' giant form
The winged shaft of Dian slew,
What time in dread avenging storm
From her unconquered bow it flew,
A warning dread that men should fear,
Nor aim audacious love beyond their mortal sphere.

So each to the other babbled;—but in haste
High on his mule-drawn chariot Pelias came,
Eager, and full of fear: in stealthy shame
A frightened glance upon the ground he cast,
That glance the single sandal spied,
The left foot bare! with easy grace
As bent his inward dread to hide,
"Tell, friend," he cried, "thy dwelling place;
What nameless mother sent her darling here,
The darling of her doting age?
Speak nor let glozing falsehood sear
Thy birth, whate'er it be, nor lies thy soul engage."

Then frank and brave the gentle youth replied,
"From Chiron's cave I come, his nurseling I,
Where Philyra my innocent infancy
And Chariclo, the Centaur's child, did guide.
Twice ten the years I count, yet ne'er
Hath word of falsehood stained my tongue,
Nor deed of ill, nor ribald jeer.
I come to claim mine own from wrong.
Home to mine own I come, my father's heir.
That crown usurped by lawless might,
Which erst old Æolus did wear,
He and his sons.   From Jove, I claim my father's right.

For yielding to vile greed of power, men say,
The promptings of a felon breast,
Pelias my sire hath dispossessed,
And torn his long descended crown away.
So when I first drew breath,
Lest ruffian hands should do me death,
My parents in the king's despite,

Feigning an infant's early doom,
Drest up with tears a funeral rite,
And laid a puppet in the tomb.
But me to Chiron's loving care,
All wrapt in princely robe, at dead of night, they bare.

Such is my tale ;—no more the occasion needs ;
Then deign, kind citizens, to show me plain
The dwelling whence my sires in lawful reign
Issued, all princely drawn by milk-white steeds.
For Æson's son, no stranger I
Come welcome to my home and free.
Ask ye my name?   The Centaur high
Who bred me, bade me Jason be.
He spoke : but him his father's heart had known ;
Down his cheeks rolled the happy tears,
To see his long-lost stripling grown
A prince of noble youths, the fairest of his peers.

Soon flock his brethren at the wondrous tale.
Pheres from Hypereia's neighbor spring,
Admetus eke, and brave Melampus bring,
And Amythaon from Messenia's vale,
Cousinly greeting.   He the while
Spread bounteous forth the genial feast,
And with kind word and courteous smile
Received each new arriving guest.
High was the lordly cheer, and loud and long ;
Flew swiftly by each mirthful hour ;
Echoed five days and nights the song,
Five days and nights they culled joy's holiest, brightest flower.

But when the sixth day dawned, his tale of wrong
To his assembled kinsman bold,
In manly phrase the Chieftain told ;
Approving murmurs broke from all the throng.
Forth from the council-tent
Amid his peers the hero went
Straightway the robber king to seek.
They passed within the portal high.
He heard and with a smiling cheek
Wore a deceitful courtesy.

Then, in sage words of peaceful flow
And counsel calm, the hero thus addressed his foe:


"Son of Poseidon! oft the blinded heart
    Of man in folly seeks for crafty gain,
    Nor heeds the after-reckoning of grim pain,
To choose the juster and the wiser part.
        Yet were it well that I and you,
            With peaceful words and counsel sage,
        Should weave a web both wise and true,
            And turn to peace our mutual rage.
    I speak of what thou know'st.   A single womb
            Cretheus and bold Salmoneus bore.
        From these in third descent we come;
But Fate shrinks back ashamed when kinsmen join in war.


It must not be that we with sword and steel
    Our great forefather's heritage should share.
    Freely the flocks and herds,—my father's heir,
Yea, and the fruitful lands to thee I deal.
        Long hast thou these unduly held.
            Keep them, and swell thy robber store.
        It doth not yearn my soul to yield
            All these to thee; do thou restore
The royal sceptre and the righteous throne,
            Where Cretheus' son, my sire, erewhile
        With princely justice ruled his own.
These, without sterner force or trick of fraudful guile,


Restore, lest thence worse evil should ensue."
        Briefly, as best his grief to hide,
        In accents calm the king replied:
"That which thy words invite me, will I do,
            But now mine age is old;
        Thy blood is young, thy heart is bold;
        Thou may'st the infernal wrath allay:
    For murdered Phrixus bids us come
        Where lives Æetes far away,
        And call his exiled spirit home,
    And fetch the fleece of golden sheen,
On which he soared erewhile to 'scape the vengeful Queen.

For so a wondrous vision of my sleep
  Enjoined; without delay my way I took,
  Lest aught of vain or false my soul should mock,
To seek the God of Delphi's holy steep.
    He bade me brook no slow delay,
      But man a bark with instant speed
    The sacred vision to obey.
      Do thou perform the holy deed;
  And by great Jove, our common sire, I swear,
    Sceptre and throne to yield thee free."
    Their mutual faith they promised fair.
That strong and sure to both should their high compact be.


## OLYMPIA.

Eighth Olympian Ode. To Alcimedon of Ægina, victor in wrestling,
B.C. 460.

OLYMPIA! mother of the old-crowned games!
    Great spring of Truth divine!
    Where seers around the holy shrine,
    With augury of sacred flames,
Essay the mind of Jove, the Thunder-King,
    If aught of hope he bring
To heroes straining for the glorious wreath.
Which bids the aching heart in triumph breathe.

(And oft success attends on pious prayers)
    O holy Pisan grove,
    Receive our revel-pomp in love!
    For glorious is his praise who shares
The grace which thy victorious garlands shed!
    Yet many a path men tread,
And various are the roads of sweet success,
When the good Gods the toils of mortals bless.

### ELYSIUM.

PINDAR differs from nearly every other Greek poet in describing with enthusiasm the delights of the souls in Elysium.

FOR them the night all through,
    In that broad realm below,
The splendor of the sun spreads endless light;
    'Mid rosy meadows bright,
Their city of the tombs with incense-trees
      And golden chalices
    Of flowers and fruitage fair,
    Scenting the breezy air,
Is laden. There with horses and with play,
With games and lyres, they while the hours away.
    On every side around
    Pure happiness is found,
With all the blooming beauty of the world;
    There fragrant smoke, upcurled
From altars where the blazing fire is dense
    With perfumed frankincense,
    Burned unto gods in heaven,
    Through all the land is driven,
Making its pleasant places odorous
With scented gales and sweet airs amorous.

## ANACREON.

THOUGH Anacreon has been famous as the poet of wine and love, few genuine fragments of his songs have come down to us. Those which pass under his name belong to his Greek imitators in later times. Specimens are given here as a relief after the prosing of historians and philosophers.

Anacreon was born at Teos, in Ionia, about 550 B.C., but emigrated with other citizens to Abdera, in Thrace, to escape the Persian yoke. Here he cultivated the muse until the fame of his talents and courtly disposition brought him an invitation from Polycrates, the tyrant of Samos. At this centre of culture he remained for eighteen years, entertaining the tyrant and his subjects with the sweetness of amatory song. Hipparchus, son of Pisistratus, afterwards invited the poet to Athens, and a barge of fifty oars was sent for him. In his new home he found a brilliant throng of cultivated men, among whom was Simonides of Ceos. After the expulsion of the sons of Pisistratus, Anacreon returned to his native place. Here, in his eighty-fifth year, according to tradition, he was choked with a grape-stone.

The songs which from ancient times have been loosely attributed to Anacreon are marked by sweet simplicity and buoyant cheerfulness. His poems in praise of wine inculcate only moderate indulgence, and are far removed from excess. His best imitators in English have been Abraham Cowley, Richard Bourne and Thomas Moore. The last has been justly called the modern Anacreon, as having the playful spirit of the Greek, but his versions are paraphrases, rather than exact translations. The following specimens are taken chiefly from Bourne, as being more faithful to the original.

243

## ON HIS LYRE.

WHILE I sweep the sounding string,
While the Atridæ's praise I sing—
Victors on the Trojan plain—
Or to Cadmus raise the strain,
Hark, in soft and whispered sighs,
Love's sweet notes the shell* replies.
 Late I strung my harp anew,
Changed the strings—the subject too.
Loud I sung Alcides's toils;
Still the lyre my labor foils;
Still with Love's sweet silver sounds
Every martial theme confounds.
Farewell, Heroes, Chiefs, and Kings!
Naught but Love will suit my strings.

## THE WEAPON OF BEAUTY.

POINTED horns—the dread of foes—
Nature on the Bull bestows;
Horny hoofs the Horse defend;
Swift-winged feet the Hare befriend;
Lions' gaping jaws disclose
Dreadful teeth in grinning rows;
Wings to Birds her care supplied;
Finny Fishes swim the tide;
Nobler gifts to Man assigned,
Courage firm and Strength of Mind.
 From her then exhausted store
Naught for Woman has she more?
How does Nature prove her care?—
Beauty's charm is Woman's share.
Stronger far than warrior's dress
Is her helpless loveliness.
Safety smiles in Beauty's eyes;
She the hostile flame defies;
Fiercest swords submissive fall:—
Lovely Woman conquers all.

* Hermes was fabled to have made the first lyre by stretching
strings over the empty shell of a tortoise.

## CUPID AS A GUEST.

'TWAS at the solemn midnight hour,
When silence reigns with awful power,
Just when the bright and glittering Bear
   Is yielding to her Keeper's care,
When spent with toil, with care opprest,
Man's busy race has sunk to rest,
Sly Cupid, sent by cruel Fate,
Stood loudly knocking at my gate.
   "Who's there?" I cried, "at this late hour?
Who is it batters at my door?
Begone! you break my blissful dreams!"—
But **he**, on mischief bent, it seems,
With feeble voice and piteous cries,
In childish accents thus replies:
   "Be not alarmed, kind Sir; 'tis I,
**A** little, wretched, wandering boy;
Pray ope the door, I've lóst my way;
This moonless night, alone I stray;
I'm stiff with cold; I'm drenched all o'er;
For pity's sake, pray, ope the door!"
   Touched with this simple tale of woe,
And little dreaming of a foe,
I rose, lit up my lamp, and straight
Undid the fastenings of the gate;
And there, indeed, a boy I spied,
With bow and quiver by his side.
Wings too he wore—a strange attire!
My guest I seated near the fire,
And while the blazing fagots shine,
I chafed his little hands in mine;
His damp and dripping locks I wrung,
That down his shoulders loosely hung.
   Soon as his cheeks began to glow,
'Come now," he cried, "let's try this bow;
For much I fear, this rainy night,
The wet and damp have spoiled it quite."
   That instant twanged the sounding string,
Loud as the whizzing gad-fly's wing.—

Too truly aimed, the fatal dart
My bosom pierced with painful smart.—
Up sprang the boy with laughing eyes,
And, "Wish me joy, mine host!" he cries;
"My bow is sound in every part;
Thou'lt find the arrow in thy heart!"

## THE IDEAL PORTRAIT.

THOU whose soft and rosy hues,
Mimic form and soul infuse;
Best of Painters, come portray
The lovely maid that's far away.
Far away, my Soul, thou art,
But I've thy beauties all by heart—
 Paint her jetty ringlets straying,
Silky twine in tendrils playing;
And, if painting hath the skill
To make the balmy spice distill,
Let every little lock exhale
A sigh of perfume on the gale.
 Where her tresses' curly flow
Darkles o'er the brow of snow,
Let her forehead beam to light,
Burnished as the ivory bright.
Let her eyebrows sweetly rise
In jetty arches o'er her eyes,
Gently in a crescent gliding,
Just commingling, just dividing.
 But hast thou any sparkles warm
The lightning of her eyes to form?—
Let them effuse the azure ray
With which Minerva's glances play;
And give them all that liquid fire
That Venus's languid eyes respire.
 O'er her nose and cheek be shed
Flushing white and mellowed red;
Gradual tints, as when there glows
In snowy milk the bashful rose.
 Then her lips, so rich in blisses;
Sweet petitioner for kisses;
Pouting nest of bland persuasion,
Ripely suing love's invasion!

Then, beneath the velvet chin,
Whose dimple shades a Love within,
Mould her neck, with grace descending
In a heaven of beauty ending;
While airy charms, above, below,
Sport and flutter on its snow.
 Now let a floating lucid veil
Shadow her limbs, but not conceal.
A charm may peep, a hue may beam;
And leave the rest to Fancy's dream.—
Enough—'tis she! 'tis all I seek;
It glows, it lives, it soon will speak!

## IN PRAISE OF WINE.

WHEN the nectar'd bowl I drain,
Gloomy cares forego their reign;
Richer than the Lydian king
Hymns of love and joy I sing;
Ivy wreaths my temples twine
And while careless I recline,
While bright scenes my vision greet
Tread the world beneath my feet.
Fill the cup, my trusty page;
Anacreon, the blithe and sage,
As his maxim ever said,
"Those slain by wine are nobly dead."

## PLEA FOR DRINKING.

THE Earth drinks up the genial rains,
Which deluge all her thirsty plains;
The lofty Trees that pierce the sky
Drink up the earth and leave her dry;
The insatiate Sea imbibes each hour
The welcome breeze that brings the shower;
The Sun, whose fires so fiercely burn,
Absorbs the waves, and in her turn
The modest Moon enjoys each night
Large draughts of his celestial light.
Then, sapient sirs, pray tell me why,
If all things drink, why may not I?

## ANACREON'S DOVE.

(Translated by Dr. Samuel Johnson.)

"Lovely courier of the sky,
  Whence and whither dost thou fly?
  Scattering as thy pinions play,
  Liquid fragrance all the way.
  Is it business?  Is it love?
  Tell me, tell me, gentle dove."
"Soft Anacreon's vows I bear,
  Vows to Myrtale the fair;
  Graced with all that charms the heart,
  Blushing nature, smiling art,
  Venus, courted by an ode,
  On the Bard her Dove bestow'd.
  Vested with a master's right,
  Now Anacreon rules my flight:
  As the letters that you see,
  Weighty charge consigned to me:
  Think not yet my service hard,
  Joyless task without reward:
  Smiling at my master's gates,
  Freedom my return awaits:
  But the liberal grant in vain
  Tempts me to be wild again.
  Can a prudent Dove decline
  Blissful bondage such as mine?
  Over hills and fields to roam,
  Fortune's guest without a home:
  Under leaves to hide one's head,
  Slightly shelter'd, coarsely fed:
  Now my better lot bestows
  Sweet repast and soft repose;
  Now the generous bowl I sip
  As it leaves Anacreon's lip;
  Void of care, and free from dread
  From his fingers snatch his bread,
  Then with luscious plenty gay,
  Round his chambers dance and play;
  Or, from wine as courage springs,

O'er his face expand my wings;
And when feast and frolic tire,
Drop asleep upon his lyre.
This is all; be quick and go,
More than all thou canst not know;
Let me now my pinions ply,—
I have chattered like a pye."


## THE GRASSHOPPER.

### (Translated by Abraham Cowley.)

HAPPY insect: what can be
In happiness compared to thee?
Fed with nourishment divine,
The dewy morning's gentle wine!
Nature waits upon thee still,
And thy verdant cup does fill;
'Tis filled wherever thou dost tread,
Nature's self's thy Ganymede.
Thou dost drink and dance and sing;
Happier than the happiest king!
All the fields which thou dost see,
All the plants belong to thee;
All that summer hours produce;
Fertile made with early juice.
Man for thee does sow and plough;
Farmer he, and landlord thou!
Thou dost innocently joy;
Nor does thy luxury destroy;
The shepherd gladly heareth thee,
More harmonious than he.
Thee country-hinds with gladness hear,
Prophet of the ripen'd year!
Thee Phœbus loves, and does inspire;
Phœbus is himself thy sire.
To thee, of all things upon earth,
Life's no longer than thy mirth.
Happy insect, happy, thou
Dost neither age nor winter know;
But, when thou'st drunk and danced and sung
Thy fill, the flowery leaves among,

(Voluptuous and wise withal,
Epicurean animal !)—
Sated with thy summer feast,
Thou retir'st to endless rest.


### CUPID AND THE BEE.

CUPID once upon a bed
Of roses laid his weary head;
Luckless urchin, not to see
Within the leaves a slumbering bee!
The bee awaked—with anger wild
The bee awaked, and stung the child.
Loud and piteous are his cries;
To Venus quick he runs, he flies;
"O mother!—I am wounded through—
I die with pain—what shall I do?
Stung by some little angry thing,
Some serpent on a tiny wing—
A bee it was—for once, I know,
I heard a peasant call it so."
Thus he spoke, and she the while
Heard him with a soothing smile;
Then said: "My infant, if so much
Thou feel the little wild-bee's touch,
How must the heart, ah, Cupid, be,
The hapless heart that's stung by thee?"

## THEOCRITUS.

THE fame of Theocritus, the prince of bucolic poetry, depends on his faithful pictures of natural scenery and the common Sicilian people. He is generally considered the only poet of the Alexandrian epoch whose works can rank with the brilliant Grecian songs of earlier days. His lays of country life and love are genuine pastorals; his damsels, reapers, herdsmen and fishermen are true to life. His idylls breathe the air and give forth the very sounds of nature. They tell of the oak-tree's shade, the murmuring of the pines, poplars and nodding elms, the soft couch of fern or flower, birds chirping on the boughs, and beetling cliffs from which the shepherds watch the fishers in the surf below. Theocritus is free from that affectation which was generally characteristic of the Alexandrian school. He had a keen sense of the ludicrous as well as of the beautiful. Not the least notable of his qualities are a facile mode of expression and remarkable descriptive power.

Theocritus was a native of Syracuse and visited Alexandria about 280 B.C. After enjoying the patronage of Ptolemy Philadelphus, which he rewarded by poetic eulogy, he returned to his native place. Its king, Hiero II., was a less generous patron, and the poet showed his dissatisfaction in Idyll XVI. Besides the thirty idylls ascribed to Theocritus, there are twenty-two epigrams. They are written in the Sicilian Doric dialect, which may be compared to the Lowland Scotch of Burns. His idylls are not all of rural scenery and life. In some cases he adopts the epic style, as in the story of Hercules the Lion-Slayer. In Idyll XV. he gives a graphic portrayal of the bustling life of Alexandria. Virgil, imitating Theocritus, became the creator of bucolic poetry in Roman literature.

## POLYPHEMUS IN LOVE.

### (From Idyll XI.)

THE poet asserts that there is no remedy for Love but the Muses. He then gives an account of the love of the Cyclops Polyphemus for the sea-nymph Galatea.

—'Twas when advancing man-
  hood first had shed
The early pride of summer o'er
  his head,
His Galatea on these plains he
  wooed,
But not, like other swains, the
  Nymph pursued
With fragrant flowers, or fruits
  or garlands fair,
But with hot madness and abrupt
  despair.
And while his bleating flocks,
  neglected, sought
Without a shepherd's care their fold, self-taught,
He, wandering on the sea-beat shore all day,
Sang of his hopeless love and pined away.
From morning's dawn he sang till evening's close—
Fierce were the pangs that robbed him of repose;
The mighty Queen of Love had barbed the dart,
And deeply fixed it rankling in his heart:
Then song assuaged the tortures of his mind,
While, on a rock's commanding height reclined,
His eye wide stretching o'er the level main,
Thus would he cheat the lingering hours of pain.
  "Fair Galatea, why my passion slight?
O Nymph, than lambs more soft, than curds more white!
Wanton as calves before the uddered kine,
Yet harsh as unripe fruitage of the vine.
You come, when pleasing sleep has closed mine eye,
And, like a vision, with my slumbers fly,
Swift as before the wolf the lambkin bounds,
Panting and trembling o'er the furrowed grounds.
Then first I loved, and thence I date my flame,
When here to gather hyacinths you came:

My mother brought you—'twas a fatal day;
And I, alas! unwary led the way:
E'er since my tortured mind has known no rest;
Peace is become a stranger to my breast:
Yet you nor pity, nor relieve my pain—
Yes, yes, I know the cause of your disdain;
For, stretched from ear to ear with shagged grace,
My single brow adds horror to my face;
My single eye enormous lids enclose,
And o'er my blubbered lips projects my nose.
Yet, homely as I am, large flocks I keep,
And drain the udders of a thousand sheep
My pails with milk, my shelves with cheese they fill
In scorching summer and in winter chill.
The vocal pipe I tune with pleasing glee,
No other Cyclops can compare with me:
Your charms I sing, sweet apple of delight!
Myself and you I sing the live-long night.
For you ten fawns, with collars decked, I feed,
And four young bears for your diversion breed.
Come, live with me; all these you may command,
And change your azure ocean for the land:
More pleasing slumbers will my cave bestow;
There spiry cypress and green laurels grow;
There round my trees the sable ivy twines,
And grapes, as sweet as honey, load my vines:
From grove-crowned Ætna, robed in purest snow,
Cool springs roll nectar to the swains below.
Say, who would quit such peaceful scenes as these
For blustering billows and tempestuous seas?
Though my rough form's no object of desire,
My oaks supply me with abundant fire;
My hearth unceasing blazes—though I swear
By this one eye, to me forever dear,
Well might that fire to warm my breast suffice,
That kindled at the lightning of your eyes.
   Had I, like fish, with fins and gills been made,
Then might I in your element have played—
With ease have dived beneath your azure tide,
And kissed your hand, though you your lips denied!
Brought lilies fair, or poppies red that grow
In summer's solstice, or in winter's snow;

These flowers I could not both together bear
That bloom in different seasons of the year.
Well, I'm resolved, fair Nymph, I'll learn to dive,
If e'er a sailor at this port arrive;
Then shall I surely by experience know
What pleasures charm you in the deeps below.
Emerge, O Galatea! from the sea,
And here forget your native home like me.
Oh, would you feed my flock and milk my ewes,
And ere you press my cheese the rennet sharp infuse!"


"Ah, Cyclops, Cyclops, where's your reason fled?—
If with the leafy spray your lambs you fed,
Or e'en wove baskets, you would seem more wise;
*Milk the first cow, pursue not her that flies:*
You'll soon, since Galatea proves unkind,
A sweeter, fairer Galatea find."
Thus Cyclops learned Love's torments to endure,
And calmed that passion which he could not cure.
More sweetly far with song he soothed his heart,
That if his gold had bribed the doctor's art.

## THE SYRACUSAN WOMEN AT THE FESTIVAL OF ADONIS.

IDYLL XV. is a dialogue of two Syracusan women residing in
Alexandria, who attend the solemn celebration of the death of Adonis,
prepared by Arsinoë, the queen of Ptolemy Philadelphus, and intended
partly in commemoration of her mother Berenice.

*Gorgo.* Is Praxinoa at home?
*Praxinoa.*              Dear Gorgo, yes!
How late you are! I wonder, I confess,
That you are come e'en now. Quick, brazen-front!
                              [*To Eunoa.*
A chair there—stupid! lay a cushion on't.
*Gor.* Thank you, 'tis very well.
*Prax.*                      Be seated, pray.
*Gor.* My untamed soul! what dangers on the way!
I scarce could get alive here: such a crowd!
So many soldiers with their trappings proud!
A weary way it is—you live so far.
*Prax.* The man whose wits with sense are ave at **war**,
Bought at the world's end but to vex my soul

This dwelling, no! this serpent's lurking hole,
That we might not be neighbors.   Plague o' my life,
His only joy is quarreling and strife.
   *Gor.* Talk not of Dinon so before the boy;
See! how he looks at you!
   *Prax.*                          My honey-joy!
My pretty dear! 'tis not papa I mean.
   *Gor.* Handsome papa! the urchin, by the queen,
Knows every word you say.
   *Prax.*                          The other day—
For this in sooth of everything we say—
That mighty man of inches went and brought me
Salt—which for nitre and ceruse he bought me.
   *Gor.* And so my Diocleide—a brother wit,
A money-waster, lately thought it fit
To give seven goodly drachms for fleeces five—
Mere rottenness, but dog's hair, as I live,
The plucking of old scrips—a work to make.
But come, your cloak and gold-clasped kirtle take,
And let us speed to Ptolemy's rich hall,
To see the fine Adonian festival.
The queen will make the show most grand, I hear.
   *Prax.* All things most rich in rich men halls appear.
To those who have not seen it, one can tell
What one has seen.
   *Gor.*           'Tis time to go.—'Tis well
For those who all the year have holidays.
   *Prax.* Eunoa, my cloak—you wanton! quickly raise,
And place it near me—cats would softly sleep;
And haste for water—how the jade does creep!
The water first—now, did you ever see?
She brings the cloak first: well, then, give it me.
You wasteful slut, not too much—pour the water!
What! have you wet my kirtle? sorrow's daughter!
Stop, now: I'm washed—gods love me: where's the key
Of the great chest? be quick, and bring it me.
   *Gor.* The gold-clasped and full-skirted gown you wear
Becomes you vastly.   May I ask, my dear,
How much in all it cost you from the loom?
   *Prax.* Don't mention it: I'm sure I did consume
More than two minæ on it: and I held on
The work with heart and soul.

*Gor.*                    But when done, well done!

*Prax.* Truly—you're right.    My parasol and cloak—
Arrange it nicely.    Cry until you choke,
I will not take you, child; horse bites, you know—
Boo! Boo! no use to have you lame.    Let's go.
Play with the little man, my Phrygian! call
The hound in; lock the street-door of the hall.—

> *[They pass into the street.*

Gods, what a crowd: they swarm like ants, how ever
Shall we work through them with our best endeavor?
From when thy sire was numbered with the blest,
Many fine things, and this among the rest,
Hast thou done, Ptolemy!    No villain walks
The street, and picks your pocket, as he talks
On some pretence with you, in Egypt's fashion:
As once complete in every style, mood, passion,
Resembling one another, rogues in grain,
Would mock and pilfer, and then—mock again.
What will become of us, dear Gorgo? see!
The king's war-horses!    Pray, don't trample me,
Good sir! the bay horse rears! how fierce a one!
Eunoa, stand from him: dog-heart! won't you run?
He'll kill his leader! what a thought of joy,
That safe at home remains my precious boy!

*Gor.* Courage! they're as they were—and we behind them.

*Prax.* I nearly lost my senses; now I find them,
And am myself again.    Two things I hold
In mortal dread—a horse and serpent cold,
And have done from a child.    Let us keep moving;
Oh! what a crowd is on us, bustling, shoving.

*Gor. (to an old woman).* Good mother, from the palace?

*Old Woman.*                    Yes, my dear.

*Gor.* Is it an easy thing to get in there?

*Old Wom.* The Achæans got to Troy, there's no denying.
All things are done, as they did that—by trying.

*Gor.* The old dame spoke oracles.

*Prax.*                    Our sex, as you know,
Know all things—e'en how Zeus espoused his Juno.

*Gor.* Praxinoa, what a crowd about the gates!

*Prax.* Immense! your hand; and, Eunoa, hold **your**
          mate's;
**D**o you keep close, I say, to Eutychis,

And close to us, for fear the way you miss.
Let us, together all, the entrance gain:
Ah me! my summer-cloak is rent in twain.
Pray, spare my cloak, heaven bless you, gentleman!
    *Stranger*. 'Tis not with me—I will do what I can:
    *Prax*. The crowd, like pigs, are thrusting.
    *Stran*.                 Cheer thy heart,
'Tis well with us.
    *Prax*.         And for your friendly part,
This year and ever be it well with you!
A kind and tender man as e'er I knew.
See! how our Eunoa is pressed—push through—
Well done! all in—as the gay bridegroom cried,
And turned the key upon himself and bride.
                              *[They enter the temple.*
    *Gor*. What rich, rare tapestry! Look, and you'll swear,
The fingers of the goddesses were here.
    *Prax*. August Athene! who such work could do?
Who spun the tissue, who the figures drew?
How life-like are they, and they seem to move!
True living shapes they are, and not inwove!
How wise is man! And there he lies outspread
In all his beauty on his silver bed,
Thrice-loved Adonis, in his youth's fresh glow,
Loved even where the rueful stream doth flow.
    *A Stranger*. Cease ye like turtles idly thus to babble:
They'll torture all of us with brogue and gabble.
    *Gor*. Who're you? what's it to you our tongues we use?
Rule your own roost, not dames of Syracuse.
And this too know we were in times foregone
Corinthians, sir, as was Bellerophon.
We speak the good old Greek of Pelops' isle:
Dorians, I guess, may Dorian talk the while.
    *Prax*. Nymph! grant we be at none but one man's
                pleasure;
A rush for you—don't wipe my empty measure.
    *Gor*. Praxinoa, hush! behold the Argive's daughter,
The girl who sings as though the Muses taught her,
That won the prize for singing Sperchis' ditty,
Prepares to chant Adonis; something pretty
I'm sure she'll sing: with motion, voice, and eye,
She now preludes—how sweetly, gracefully!

*Singing Girl.* Of Eryx, Golgos, and Idalia, Queen!
My mistress, sporting in thy golden sheen,
Bright Aphrodite! as the month comes on
Of every year, from direful Acheron,
What an Adonis—from the gloomy shore
The tender-footed Hours to thee restore!
Hours, slowest of the blest! yet ever dear,
That wished-for come, and still some blessing bear.
Cypris! Dione's daughter! thou through portal
Of death, 'tis said, hast mortal made immortal,
Sweet Berenice, dropping, ever blest!
Ambrosial dew into her lovely breast.
Wherefore her daughter, Helen-like in beauty,
Arsinoë thy love repays with duty,
For thine Adonis fairest show ordains,
Bright queen, of many names and many fanes!
All seasonable fruits, in silver cases,
His gardens sweet, and alabaster vases
Of Syrian perfumes near his couch are laid;
Cakes which with flowers and wheat the women made,
The shapes of all that creep, or take the wing,
With oil or honey wrought, they hither bring;
Here are green shades, with anise shaded more;
And the young Loves him ever hover o'er,
As the young nightingales, from branch to branch,
Hover and try their wings before they launch
Themselves in the broad air. But, Oh! the sight
Of gold and ebony! of ivory white
Behold the pair of eagles! up they move
With his cup-bearer for Saturnian Jove.
And see yon couch with softest purple spread,
Softer than sleep, the Samian born and bred
Will own, and e'en Miletus: that pavilion
Queen Cypris has—the nearer one her minion,
The rosy-armed Adonis; whose youth bears
The bloom of eighteen or nineteen years;
Nor pricks the kiss the red lip of the boy;
Having her spouse, let Cypris now enjoy.
   Him will we, ere the dew of dawn is o'er,
Bear to the waves that foam upon the shore;
Then with bare bosoms and dishevelled hair,
Begin to chant the wild and mournful air.

In all the demigods, they say, but one
Duly revisits Earth and Acheron—
Thou, dear Adonis! Agamemnon's might,
Nor Aias, raging like one mad in fight;
Nor true Patroclus; nor his mother's boast,
Hector, of twenty famed sons honored most;
Nor Pyrrhus, victor from the Trojan siege—
Not one of them enjoyed this privilege;
Nor the Deucalions; nor Lapithæ;
Argive Pelasgi; nor Pelopidæ.
Now, dear Adonis, fill thyself with glee,
And still returning, still propitious be.
    *Gor.* Praxinoa, did ever mortal ear
A sweeter song from sweeter minstrel hear?
O happy girl! to know so many things—
Thrice happy girl, that so divinely sings!
But now 'tis time for home: let us be hasting;
My man's mere vinegar, and most when fasting:
Nor has he broken yet his fast today;
When he's a-hungered, come not in his way.
Farewell, beloved Adonis! joy to see!
When come, well come to those who welcome thee.


## BION.

Bion, the second of the three Greek bucolic poets, was
born near Smyrna, in Asia Minor. The latter part of his life
was spent in Sicily, the home of pastoral poetry. He seems
to have been contemporary with Theocritus. From the idyll
of Moschus entitled "Bion's Epitaph," it is inferred that he
died from poison administered by jealous rivals, on whom
retribution duly fell. Bion is associated with the Alexandrian
school, but there is no evidence to show whether he lived
among the Alexandrians, or simply wrote for them. His
critics find in him a certain sentimentalism and over-refine-
ment, and an absence of that truth to nature and breadth of
thought which are so prominent in Theocritus. The longest
and best of his surviving poems is the "Lament for Adonis,"
which has been imitated by Shelley. Bion writes with much
harmony and tenderness, and as to his general merits, stands
as far below Theocritus as he stands above Moschus.

### THE LAMENT FOR ADONIS.

#### Idyll I.

I AND the Loves Adonis dead deplore :
   The beautiful Adonis is indeed
Departed, parted from us.   Sleep no more
   In purple, Cypris [Venus] ! but in watchet weed,*
   All-wretched ! beat thy breast and all aread—†
"Adonis is no more."   The Loves and I
   Lament him.   Oh ! her grief to see him bleed,
Smitten by white tooth on his whiter thigh,
Out-breathing life's faint sough upon the mountain high !

   Adown his snowy flesh drops the black gore ;
   Stiffen beneath his brow his sightless eyes ;
The rose is off his lip ; with him no more
   Lives Cytherea's kiss—but with him dies.
   He knows not that her lip his cold lip tries,
But she finds pleasure still in kissing him.
   Deep is his thigh-wound ; hers yet deeper lies,
E'en in her heart.   The Oread's eyes are dim ;
His hounds whine piteously ; in most disordered trim,

   Distraught, unkempt, unsandalled, Cypris rushes
   Madly along the tangled thicket-steep ;
Her sacred blood is drawn by bramble-bushes ;
   Her skin is torn ; with wailings wild and deep
   She wanders through the valley's weary sweep,
Calling her boy-spouse, her Assyrian fere.‡
   But from his thigh the purple jet doth leap
Up to his snowy navel ; on the clear
Whiteness beneath his paps the deep-red streaks appear.

   "Alas for Cypris !" sigh the Loves, "deprived
   Of her fair spouse, she lost her beauty's pride ;
Cypris was lovely while Adonis lived,
   But with Adonis all her beauty died."
   Mountains, and oaks, and streams, that broadly glide,
Or wail or weep for her ; in tearful rills

---

* Pale-blue dress.          † Warn, tell.          ‡ Companion, lover.

For her gush fountains from the mountain side;
Redden the flowers from grief; city and hills
With ditties sadly wild, lorn Cytherea fills.

Alas for Cypris! dead is her Adonis,
  And echo "Dead Adonis" doth resound.
Who would not grieve for her whose love so lone is?
  But when she saw his cruel, cruel wound,
  The purple gore that ran his wan thigh round,
She spread her arms, and lowly murmured: "Stay thee,
  That I may find thee as before I found,
My hapless own Adonis! and embay* thee,
And mingle lips with lips, whilst in my arms I lay thee.

"Up for a little! kiss me back again
  The latest kiss—brief as itself that dies
In being breathed, until I fondly drain
  The last breath of my soul, and greedy-wise
  Drink it into my core.  I will devise
To guard it as Adonis—since from me
  To Acheron my own Adonis flies,
And to the drear dread king; but I must be
A goddess still and live, nor can I follow thee.

"But thou, Persephona!† my spouse receive,
  Mightier than I, since to thy chamber drear
All bloom of beauty falls: but I must grieve
  Unceasingly.  I have a jealous fear
  Of thee, and weep for him.  My dearest dear!
Art dead, indeed? away my love did fly,
  E'en as a dream.  At home my widowed cheer
Keeps the Loves idle; with thy latest sigh
My cestus perished too; thou rash one! why, oh why

"Didst hunt? so fair, contend with monsters grim?"
  Thus Cypris wailed; but dead Adonis lies;
For every gout of blood that fell from him,
  She drops a tear; sweet flowers each dew supplies—
  Roses his blood, her tears anemonies.
Cypris! no longer in the thickets weep:
  The couch is furnished! there in loving guise

* Enclose, embrace.　　† Proserpine, wife of Pluto.

Upon thy proper bed, that odorous heap,
The lovely body lies—how lovely! as in sleep.

 Come! in those softest vestments now array him,
  In which he slept the live-long night with thee;
 And in the golden settle gently lay him,—
  A sad, yet lovely sight; and let him be
  High heaped with flowers; though withered all when he
 Surceased.  With essences him sprinkle o'er
  And ointments; let them perish utterly,
 Since he, who was thy sweetest, is no more.
He lies in purple; him the weeping Loves deplore.

 Their curls are shorn: one breaks his bow; another
  His arrows and the quiver; this unstrings,
 And takes Adonis' sandal off; his brother
  In golden urn the fountain water brings;
  This bathes his thighs; that fans him with his wings.
 The Loves, "Alas for Cypris!" weeping say:
  Hymen hath quenched his torches; shreds and flings
 The marriage wreath away; and for the lay
Of love is only heard the doleful " Wellaway."

 Yet more than Hymen for Adonis weep
  The Graces; shriller than Dione vent
 Their shrieks; for him the Muses wail and keep
  Singing the songs he hears not, with intent
  To call him back: and would the Nymph relent,
 How willingly would he the Muses hear!
  Hush! hush! today, sad Cypris! and consent
 To spare thyself—no more thy bosom tear—
For thou must wail again, and weep another year.


## MOSCHUS.

MOSCHUS is the third and least notable of the Doric
bucolic poets of the Alexandrian school.  His title to fame
rests chiefly on his "Europa," "The Teacher Taught,"
and his "Epitaph on Bion."  An excess of elegance and
elaborate finish characterizes his writings.  Simplicity and
naturalness are wanting, and his sentimentalism is even more
marked than that of his teacher Bion.  He was a polished

verse-maker rather than an original poet. Affectation and studied ornament mar his compositions, and make them labored and unnatural. Still, some of his pieces exhibit tenderness, pathos, and poetic beauty. With the exception of "Megara, the Wife of Hercules," the poems of Moschus are written in Doric. They have been translated into every language of modern Europe.

### The Lament for Bion.

Ye mountain valleys, pitifully groan!
  Rivers and Dorian springs, for Bion weep!
Ye plants, drop tears! ye groves, lamenting moan!
  Exhale your life, wan flowers; your blushes deep
  In grief, anemonies and roses, steep!
In softest murmurs, hyacinth! prolong
  The sad, sad woe thy lettered petals keep ;*
Our minstrel sings no more his friends among—
Sicilian Muses! now begin the doleful song.

Ye nightingales, that 'mid thick leaves let loose
  The gushing gurgle of your sorrow, tell
The fountains of Sicilian Arethuse
  That Bion is no more—with Bion fell
  The song, the music of the Dorian shell.
Ye swans of Strymon, now your banks along
  Your plaintive throats with melting dirges swell
For him who sang like you the mournful song :
Discourse of Bion's death the Thracian nymphs among;

The Dorian Orpheus, tell them all, is dead.
  His herds the song and darling herdsman miss,
And oaks, beneath whose shade he propped his head:
  Oblivion's ditty now he sings for Dis [Pluto]:
  The melancholy mountain silent is ;
His pining cows no longer wish to feed,
  But mourn for him : Apollo wept, I wis,
For thee, sweet Bion, and in mourning weed
The brotherhood of Fauns, and all the satyr breed.

* The Greeks fancied they could discern on the hyacinth the letters AI, an exclamation of woe.

The tears by Naiads shed are brimful bourns;
   Afflicted Pan thy stifled music rues;
Lorn Echo 'mid her rocks thy silence mourns,
   Nor with mimic tones thy voice renews;
The flowers their bloom, the trees their fruitage lose;
No more their milk the drooping ewes supply;
   The bees to press their honey now refuse;
What need to gather it and lay it by,
When thy own honey-lip, my Bion! thine is dry?

Me with thy minstrel skill as proper heir,
   Others thou didst endow with thine estate.
Alas! alas! when in a garden fair
   Mallows, crisp dill, or parsley yields to fate,
   These with another year regerminate;
But when of mortal life the bloom and crown,
   The wise, the good, the valiant, and the great
Succumb to death, in hollow earth shut down
We sleep—forever sleep—forever lie unknown.

Thus art thou pent, while frogs may croak at will;
   I envy not their croak. Thee poison slew—
How kept it in thy mouth its nature ill?
   If thou didst speak, what cruel wretch could brew
   The draught? He did, of course, thy song eschew.
But justice all o'ertakes. My tears fast flow
   For thee, my friend! Could I, like Orpheus true,
Odyssous, or Alcides, pass below
To gloomy Tartarus, how quickly would I go.

To see and haply hear thee sing for Dis!
   But in the Nymph's ear warble evermore,
My dearest friend! thy sweetest harmonies.
   For whilom, on her own Etnæan shore,
   She sang wild snatches of the Dorian lore.
Nor will thy singing unrewarded be;
   Thee to thy mountain haunts she will restore,
As she gave Orpheus his Eurydice.
Could I charm Dis with songs, I too would sing for thee.

# CALLIMACHUS.

CALLIMACHUS may be regarded as the archetype of Greek scholars, grammarian poets, and men of letters of the Alexandrian period in the third century before Christ. A native of Cyrene in Libya, he traced his ancestry to Battus, the founder of that city. He set out in life as a schoolmaster in Eleusis, near Alexandria, but soon won consideration for himself by his writings, and became librarian under Ptolemy Philadelphus. This office he conducted for twenty years with consummate ability and benefit to future generations. He died in 240 B.C. Callimachus was distinguished by high talents, vast learning and scholarship, and great literary ambition. His diligent study of the earlier Greek classics and mythology incited him to attempt poetical composition. His productions display elegance, brilliancy of expression, and great ingenuity, but the vital spark is not in them. They are all comparatively short with the exception of the "Hecale," which he wrote for the express purpose of showing that he could compose a long poem. Otherwise, he put in practice his own saying: "A great book is a great evil." Yet altogether he is said to have published eight hundred pieces in prose and verse. His prose has perished, but some hymns, epigrams and elegies remain. The Roman Catullus, although himself a greater poetical genius, adopted Callimachus as his model for taste and style.

## THE STORY OF TIRESIAS.

(From his Hymn on "The Bath of Pallas.")

. IN times of old, Minerva loved
A fair companion with exceeding love—
The mother of Tiresias; nor apart
Lived they a moment. Whether she her steeds
Drove to the Thespians old, or musky groves
Of Coronæa, and Curalius' banks,
That smoke with fragrant altars, or approached
To Haliartus, and Bœotia's fields;
Still in the chariot by her side she placed

The nymph Chariclo; nor the prattlings sweet,
Nor dances of the nymphs, to her were sweet,
Unless Chariclo spoke, or led the dance.
Yet for the nymph Chariclo was reserved
A store of tears; for her, the favored nymph,
The pleasing partner of Minerva's hours.
For once, on Helicon, they loosed the clasps
That held their flowing robes, and bathed their limbs
In Hippocrene, that beauteous glided by;
While noonday stillness wrapped the mountain round.
Both laved together; 'twas the time of noon;
And deep the stilly silence of the mount,
When, with his dogs of chase, Tiresias trod
That sacred haunt.    The darkening down just bloomed
Upon his cheek.    With thirst unutterable
Panting, he sought that fountain's gushing stream,
Unhappy; and involuntary saw
What mortal eyes not blameless may behold.
    Minerva, though incensed, thus pitying spoke:
"Who to this luckless spot conducted thee,
O son of Everes? who sightless hence
Must needs depart!" she said, and darkness fell
On the youth's eyes, astonished where he stood:
A shooting anguish all his nerves benumbed,
And consternation chained his murmuring tongue.
Then shrieked the Nymph: "What, Goddess, hast thou done
To this my child?   Are these the tender acts
Of Goddesses?   Thou hast bereaved of eyes
My son.   O miserable child! thy gaze
Has glanced upon the bosom and the shape
Of Pallas; but the sun thou must behold
No more.   O miserable me! O shades
Of Helicon! O mountain, that my steps
Shall ne'er again ascend! for small offence
Monstrous atonement! thou art well repaid
For some few straggling goats and hunted deer
With my son's eyes!"  The Nymph then folded close,
With both her arms, her son so dearly loved;
And uttered lamentation, with shrill voice,
And plaintive, like the mother nightingale.
    The Goddess felt compassion for the Nymph,
The partner of her soul. and softly said:

"Retract, divinest woman! what thy rage
Erring, has uttered. 'Tis not I that smite
Thy son with blindness. Pallas hath no joy
To rob from youths the lustre of their eyes.
The laws of Saturn thus decree:—Whoe'er
Looks on a being of immortal race,
Unless the willing God consent, must look
Thus at his peril, and atoning pay
The dreadful penalty. This act of fate,
Divinest woman, may not be recalled.
So spun the Destinies his mortal thread
When thou didst bear him. Son of Everes!
Take then thy portion. But, what hecatombs
Shall Aristæus and Autonoë,
Hereafter, on the smoking altars lay,
So that the youth Actæon, their sad son,
Might be but blind, like thee! for know that youth
Shall join the great Diana in the chase;
Yet, not the chase, nor darts in common thrown,
Shall save him; when his undesigning glance
Discerns the goddess in her loveliness
Amidst the bath. His own unconscious dogs
Shall tear their master, and his mother cull
His scattered bones, wild-wandering through the woods.
That mother, Nymph! shall call thee blest, who now
Receivest from the mount thy sightless son.
Oh, weep no more, companion! for thy sake
I yet have ample recompense in store
For this thy son. Behold! I bid him rise
A prophet, far o'er every seer renowned
To future ages. He shall read the flights
Of birds, and know whatever on the wing
Hovers auspicious, or ill-omened flies,
Or void of auspice. Many oracles
To the Bœotians shall his tongue reveal;
To Cadmus, and the great Labdacian tribe.
I will endow him with a mighty staff,
To guide his steps aright; and I will give
A lengthened boundary to his mortal life;
And, when he dies, he only, midst the dead,
Shall dwell inspired, and, honored by that king
Who rules the shadowy people of the grave."

She spoke, and gave the nod; what Pallas wills
Is sure: in her, of all his daughters, Jove
Bade all the glories of her father shine.
Maids of the bath! no mother brought her forth;
Sprung from the head of Jove. Whate'er the head
Of Jove, inclining, ratifies, the same
Stands firm; and thus his daughter's nod is fate.

She comes! in very truth, Minerva comes!
Receive the goddess, damsels! ye, whose hearts,
With tender ties, your native Argos binds,
Receive the goddess! with exulting hails,
With vows, and shouts. Hail, Goddess! Oh, protect
Inachian Argos! hail! and, when thou turn'st
Thy courses hence, or hitherward again,
Guidest thy chariot wheels, Oh! still preserve
The fortunes of the race from Danaus sprung!

## APOLLONIUS THE RHODIAN.

APOLLONIUS (Rhodius), one of the greatest of the Alexandrian poets, flourished about B.C. 235. From his earliest years he was brought under those influences which stimulate taste and mental culture. He was the pupil of Callimachus, the literary dictator and censor of Alexandria, and studied composition and methods of criticising the earlier poets under the most favorable conditions. Like the rest of the Alexandrian school, Apollonius directed his efforts to felicitous combinations of words and elegance of expression, and became ambitious at the very outset to apply the newly-acquired learning and literary finish to an imitation of the classical writers of antiquity. When not more than seventeen years of age he composed a rough draft of an epic poem in the Homeric style, and publicly recited it at a feast of Apollo. The poem was summarily condemned, mostly through the influence of his teacher Callimachus, who, with his followers, held that epics like Homer's were not the proper function of poets in a learned age, but pieces characterized by elegance and polish. The young author felt humiliated, and retired to Rhodes to hide his mortification. After spending some years in teaching rhetoric, and at the same time revising and retouching his rejected epic, his ability was universally recognized; the poem was received with marked approbation, and established his reputation in the literary world. He then returned to Alexandria, and, on the death of Eratosthenes, was appointed librarian. Apollonius wrote also epigrams and works on grammar, but his reputation depends on his epic poem, "The Argonautica," which consists of four books containing 5800 lines. He is surnamed Rhodius, or the Rhodian, to distinguish him from other eminent men bearing the name Apollonius.

## MEDEA'S LOVE.

MEANWHILE the maid her secret thoughts enjoyed,
And one dear object all her soul employed:
Her train's gay sports no pleasure can restore,
Vain was the dance, and music charmed no more;
She hates each object, every face offends,
In every wish her soul to Jason sends;
With sharpened eyes the distant lawn explores,
To find the hero whom her soul adores;
At every whisper of the passing air
She starts, she turns, and hopes her Jason there;
Again she fondly looks, nor looks in vain,
He comes—her Jason shines along the plain.
As when, emerging from the watery way,
Refulgent Sirius lifts his golden ray,
He shines terrific! for his burning breath
Taints the red air with fevers, plagues and death.
Such to the nymph approaching Jason shows,
Bright author of unutterable woes;
Before her eyes a swimming darkness spread,
Her flushed cheeks glowed,—her very heart was dead:
No more her knees their wonted office knew,
Fixed, without motion, as to earth they grew.
Her train recedes—the meeting lovers gaze
In silent wonder and in still amaze.
As two fair cedars on the mountain's brow,
Pride of the groves! with roots adjoining grow;
Erect and motionless the stately trees
Short time remain, while sleeps each fanning breeze,

Till from the Æolian caves a blast unbound
Bends their proud tops, and bids their boughs resound:
Thus gazing they, till by the breath of love,
Strongly at last inspired, they speak, they move;
With smiles the love-sick virgin he surveyed,
And fondly thus addressed the blooming maid:
   "Dismiss, my fair, my love, thy virgin fear,—
'Tis Jason speaks, no enemy is here!
Dread not in me a haughty heart to find,
In Greece I bore no proud inhuman mind.
Whom wouldst thou fly? stay, lovely virgin, stay!
Speak every thought! far hence be fears away!
Speak! and be truth in every accent found!
Scorn to deceive! we tread on hallowed ground.
By the stern power who guards this sacred place,
By the famed authors of thy royal race;
By Jove, to whom the stranger's cause belongs,
To whom the suppliant, and who feels their wrongs;
Oh, guard me, save me, in the needful hour!
Without thy aid thy Jason is no more.
To thee a suppliant in distress I bend,
To thee a stranger, one who wants a friend!
Then, when between us seas and mountains rise,
Medea's name shall sound in distant skies;
All Greece to thee shall owe her heroes' fates,
And bless Medea through her hundred states.
The mother and the wife, who now in vain
Roll their sad eyes fast-streaming o'er the main,
Shall stay their tears: the mother and the wife
Shall bless thee for a son's or husband's life!
Fair Ariadne, sprung from Minos' bed,
Saved valiant Theseus, and with Theseus fled,
Forsook her father, and her native plain,
And stemmed the tumults of the surging main;
Yet the stern sire relented, and forgave
The maid, whose only crime it was to save;
Even the just gods forgave, and now on high
A star she shines, and beautifies the sky:
What blessings, then, shall righteous Heaven decree
For all our heroes saved,—and saved by thee?
Heaven gave thee not to kill, so soft an air;
And cruelty sure never looked so fair!"

He ceased, but left so charming on her ear
His voice, that listening still she seemed to hear;
Her eyes to earth she bends with modest grace,
And heaven in smiles is opened on her face.
A look she steals,—but rosy blushes spread
O'er her fair cheek and, then she hangs her head.
A thousand words at once to speak she tries;
In vain—but speaks a thousand with her eyes;
Trembling the shining casket she expands,
Then gives the magic virtue to his hands;
And had the power been granted to convey
Her heart—had given her very heart away.
For Jason beamed in beauty's charms so bright,
The maid admiring languished with delight.
Thus, when the rising sun appears in view,
On the fair rose dissolves the radiant dew.
Now on the ground both cast their bashful eyes,
Both viewed each other now with wild surprise.
The rosy smiles now dimpling on their cheeks,
The fair at length in faltering accents speaks:
"Observant thou to my advice attend,
And hear what succor I propose to lend:
Soon as my sire Æeta shall bestow
The dragon's teeth in Mars' field to sow,
The following night in equal shares divide;
Bathe well thy limbs in some perennial tide;
Then well concealed, thyself in black array,
Dig the round foss, and there a victim slay,
A female lamb; the carcase place entire
Above the foss, then light the sacred pyre,
And Perseus' daughter, Hecate, appease
With honey, sweetest labor of the bees.
This done, retreat,—nor, while the relics burn,
Let howling dogs provoke thee to return,
Nor human footsteps; lest thou render vain
The charm, and with dishonor join thy train.
Next morn, the whole enchantment to fulfill,
This magic unguent on thy limbs distill:
Then thou with ease wilt strong and graceful move,
Not like a mortal, but the Gods above.
Forget not with this unguent to besmear
Thy sword, thy buckler, and tremendous spear:

No giant's falchions then can harm thy frame,
Nor the fell rage of bulls expiring flame.
One day, nor longer, wilt thou keep the field;
Nor thou to perils nor to labor yield.
But mark my words,—when thou, with ceaseless toil,
Hast yoked the bulls and ploughed the stubborn soil;
And seest upspringing on the teeth-sown land
Of giant foes a formidable band,
Hurl slily 'midst their ranks a rough, hard stone,
And they, like dogs contending for a bone,
Will slay each other: thou with speed renew
The glowing fight, and conquest will ensue.
Thus shalt thou bear from Æa's realms to Greece,
If such thy fixed resolve, the Golden Fleece."

 This said, her eyes were fixed upon the ground,
And her fair cheeks with streaming sorrows drowned;
Desponding anguish seized her gentle mind,
Lest he should leave her comfortless behind.
Emboldened thus, him by the hand she pressed,
And in the language of her soul addressed:
 "If safely hence thou sail'st, Oh, think of me,
As I forever shall remember thee!
And freely tell me, to relieve my pain,
Where lies thy home beyond the boundless main?
Say, is Orchomenos that native soil?
Or dwell'st thou nearer, on the Ææan isle?
Let me that far-famed virgin's name inquire,
Who boasts the same high lineage with my sire."

 She said; her tears his soft compassion won,
And thus the chief, by love inspired, begun:
 "While on my fancy bright ideas play,
Thy image never from my soul shall stray,
If safe I sail, preserved by thee, to Greece,
Nor heavier labors interrupt my peace.
But if the distant country where I dwell
Thy will demands, my ready tongue shall tell.
A land there is which lofty hills surround,
For fertile pastures and rich herds renowned,
Where from Prometheus good Deucalion came,
His royal heir; Hæmonia is the name.
Deucalion here the first foundations laid
Of towns, built fanes, and men by empire swayed;

There my Iolcos stands, and many more
Fair ample cities, that adorn the shore.
What time, as rumored by the voice of fame,
Æolian Minyas to that country came,
He built, close bordering on the Theban ground,
Orchomenos, a city far renowned.
But why your wonder should I vainly raise,
My birth-place tell, and Ariadne's praise?
For this the virgin's name you now inquire,
A lovely maid, and Minos is her sire.
Oh! may, like hers, your sire propitious prove,
Who honored Theseus with his daughter's love!"
　　Complacent thus he soothed her sorrowing soul;
Yet anxious cares within her bosom roll.
"Perchance in Greece" (the pensive maid rejoined)
"Oaths are revered, and solemn compacts bind.
But Minos greatly differs from my sire,
Nor I to Ariadne's charms aspire.
Then mention hospitality no more; ﹀
But, safe conducted to thy native shore,
Grant this, 'tis all I ask, Oh! think of me,
As I forever shall remember thee,
In my great sire, the Colchian king's despite:
But if thy pride my ardent passion slight,
Fame, or some bird, the hateful news will bring;
Then will I chase thee on the tempest's wing,
Brand thy false heart, thy cursed familiar be,
And prove thou ow'st thy life—thy all—to me."
Medea thus, and tears abundant shed;
And mildly thus the son of Æson said:
　　"In vain, dear nymph, thy missive bird shall soar,
Through air sublime, in vain the tempest roar.
But if towards Greece thou deign'st thy course to bear,
Immortal honors shall attend thee there;
There husbands, brothers, sons, so long deplored,
Safe to their native land by thee restored,
Shall as a goddess reverence thy name,
And pay thee rites which only Gods can claim.
But wouldst thou grace my bed with bridal state,
Our love can only be dissolved by fate."
　　His words with rapture all her soul subdue;
Yet gloomy objects rise before her view,

Ordained, ere long, Thessalia's realms to see;
For such was Juno's absolute decree,
That soon to Greece the Colchian maid should go,
To Pelias, source of unremitting woe.
　　Meanwhile apart her anxious handmaids stay,
In silence waiting till the close of day:
Such pleasing transports in her bosom roll,
His form, his words, so captivate her soul,
On feathered feet the hours unheeded fled,
Which warned her home: "Hence" (cautious Jason said),
" Hence let us hasten unperceived away,
And here enraptured pass some future day."
　　Thus the blest hours in converse sweet they spent,
And both unwilling from the temple went;
He to his comrades bordering on the main,
The fair Medea to her virgin train.
Her train approached, but stood unnoticed by;
Her soul sublime expatiates in the sky.
Her rapid car she mounts; this hand sustains
The polished thong, and that the flowing reins.
Fleet o'er the plain the nimble steeds conveyed
To Æa's walls the love-transported maid.


### MEDEA'S FLIGHT.

MEANWHILE the imperial queen of heaven had shed
O'er the fair virgin's breast despondent dread.
She starts, she trembles, as, pursued by hounds,
The fawn light skipping o'er the meadow bounds.
She fears the secrets of her soul betrayed,
And her sire's vengeance for her proffered aid.
Her handmaids, conscious of her crimes, she fears;
Her eyes fierce flames emit, loud murmurs fill her ears.
Her death she meditates in wild despair,
And, sadly sighing, tears her golden hair.
Now fate imbibing from the poisoned bowl.
Soon had she freed her voluntary soul,
And Juno's projects all been rendered vain,
But kindly pitying a lover's pain,
The Goddess urged with Phrixus' sons her flight,
And eased her bosom of its sorrow's weight.
Forth from her casket every drug she pours,

And to her lap consigns the magic stores.
Then with a parting kiss her bed she pressed,
Clung round each door and even the walls caressed.
A lock she tore of loosely-flowing hair,
And safe consigned it to her mother's care,
The sacred relic of her virgin-fame;
And wailing thus invoked Idya's name:
  "This lock, O mother, at my hand receive,
Which I, far-distant roaming, with thee leave.
Farewell, Chalciope; far hence I roam!
And thou farewell, my first, my dearest home!
Oh! hadst thou, stranger, in deep ocean drowned,
Perished, and never trod on Colchian ground!"
  She spoke, and tears her heart-felt woe betrayed;
Then fled she instant.  Thus the captive maid,
When, from her friends and country banished far,
She shares the miserable fate of war,
Disused to toil beneath a tyrant's sway,
Flies from oppression's rod with speed away.
With speed like hers the weeping fair withdrew:
The doors spontaneous opened as she flew,
Shook by her magic song; barefoot she strays
Through winding paths and unfrequented ways.
Beyond the city-walls with trembling haste,
Unseen of all the sentinels she passed,
Then by accustomed paths explored the fane,
Where spectres rise and plants diffuse their bane;
(Thus practice magic maids their mystic art)
Fears ill portending flutter round her heart.
  She said: impetuous hastening to the flood,
Soon on its lofty banks Medea stood.
A fire which midnight's deadly gloom dispelled,
Signal of conquest gained she here beheld.
Involved in shade, the solitary dame
Raised her shrill voice and called on Phrontis' name.
Known was her voice to Phrixus' sons, who bear
The grateful tidings to their leader's ear.
The truth discovered, the confederate host
All silent stood, in wild amazement lost.
Loud called she thrice; and with responsive cries,
His friends requesting, Phrontis thrice replies.
Quick at her call they ply the bending oar;

Nor were their halsers fastened to the shore,
When Æson's son at once decisive bound
Leaps from the lofty deck upon the ground;
Phrontis and Argus hasten to her aid,
Whose knees embracing, thus Medea prayed:

"Oh! save me, friends, from my offended sire,
Oh! save yourselves from dread Æeta's ire.
Known are our projects: sail we hence afar,
Ere Æa's monarch mounts his rapid car.
My magic charms shall close the dragon's eyes,
And soon reward you with the golden prize.
But thou, loved guest, continue faithful still,
And swear whate'er thou'st promis'd to fulfill:
Ah! leave me not to infamy a scorn,
By all my friends abandoned and forlorn."

Plaintive she spoke: his arms around her waist
Rapturous he threw, then raised her and embraced,
And solaced thus in terms of tenderest love:

"By heaven's high king I swear, Olympian Jove,
By Juno, goddess of the nuptial rite,
Soon as my native land transports my sight,
Thou, lovely virgin, shalt be duly led,
Adorned with honors, to my bridal bed."

This said, in hers he closed his plighted hand:
To Mars's grove Medea gave command,
Spite of her sire, the vessel to convey,
And bear by night the golden fleece away.
Swift at the word they sprung; the Colchian maid
Embarked, and instant was their anchor weighed.
Their crashing oars resound: she oft to land
Reverts her eye and waves her trembling hand:
But Æson's son his ready aid affords,
And soothes her sorrows with consoling words.

## CLEANTHES.

CLEANTHES, the Stoic philosopher, was born at Assos, in Asia Minor, about B.C. 300. In early life he was a pugilist, and as such went to Athens to exhibit his skill in the manly art. But, overcome by his new environment, the boxer was attracted to study philosophy, at first under Crates and afterwards under Zeno. Having now no visible means of support, he was summoned before the high court of Areopagus. There he explained that though his days were spent in philosophical pursuits, he worked at night in gardens. The judges, impressed by this industry and love of study, voted him ten minæ, but Zeno would not permit him to accept their bounty. Cleanthes succeeded Zeno as master of the Stoic school. At the age of eighty he is said to have died of voluntary starvation. His sublime "Hymn to Zeus" is the only relic of his composition. The following version is by Professor F. W. Newman.

### HYMN TO ZEUS (JUPITER).

ALMIGHTY alway! many-named! most glorious of the deathless!
Zeus! primal spring of nature, who with Law directest all things.
Hail! for to bow salute to Thee, to every man is holy;
For we from Thee an offspring are, to whom, alone of mortals
That live and move along the Earth, the mimic voice is granted!
Therefore to Thee I hymns will sing and always chant thy greatness.
Subject to Thee is yonder sky, which 'round the earth forever
Majestic rolls at thy command, and gladly feels thy guidance.
So mighty is the weapon, clenched within thy hands unconquered.
The double-edged and fiery bolt of ever-living lightning.
For Nature through her every part beneath its impulse shudders,
Whereby the universal scheme Thou guidest
Which, through all things proceeding,
Intermingles, deep with greater light and smaller,
When Thou, so vast in essence, art a king supreme forever.

Nor upon Earth is any work done without Thee, O Spirit!
Nor at the Æther's utmost height divine, nor in the Ocean,

Save whatsoe'er the infatuate work out from hearts of evil.
But Thou by wisdom knowest well to render odd things even;
Thou orderest disorder, and th' unlovely lovely makest,
For so hast Thou in one combined the noble with the baser,
That of the whole a single scheme arises, everlasting,
Which men neglect and overlook, as many as are evil:
Unhappy! who good things to get are evermore designing,
While to the common law of God nor eyes nor ears they open;
Obedient to which they might good life enjoy with wisdom.
But they, in guise unseemly, rush this way and that, at random;
One part, in glory's chase engaged with its ill-contending passion,
Some searching every path of gain, of comeliness forgetful,
Others on soft indulgence bent and on the body's pleasure,
While things right contrary to these their proper action hastens,
But Zeus all bounteous! who, in clouds enwrapt, the lightning
    wieldest;
Mayest Thou from baneful ignorance the race of men deliver!
This, Father! scatter from the soul, and grant that we the wisdom
May reach, in confidence of which Thou justly guidest all things;
That we, by Thee in honor set, with honor may repay Thee,
Raising to all Thy works a hymn, as beseemeth
A mortal soul: since neither man nor god has higher glory,
Than rightfully to celebrate Eternal Law all-ruling.

ZEUS OF OTRICOLI.
(Marble Bust in the Vatican.)

## HERMESIANAX.

THIS elegiac poet, born at Colophon, lived in the time of Alexander the Great. His chief work bore the name of his mistress, Leontium, and from it the following fragment has been preserved.

### THE LOVES OF POETS AND SAGES.

SUCH was the nymph whom Orpheus led
From the dark mansions of the dead,
Where Charon with his lazy boat
Ferries o'er Lethe's sedgy moat;
The undaunted minstrel smites the strings,
His strain through hell's vast concave rings;
Cocytus hears the plaintive theme,
And refluent turns his pitying stream;
Three-headed Cerberus, by fate
Posted at Pluto's iron gate,
Low-crouching rolls his haggard eyes
Ecstatic, and foregoes the prize;
With ears erect, at hell's wide doors,
Lies listening as the songster soars:
Thus music charmed the realm beneath,
And beauty triumph'd over death.

The bard, whom night's pale regent bore
In secret on the Athenian shore,
Musæus, felt the sacred flame,
And burnt for the fair Theban dame,
Antiope, whom mighty Love
Made pregnant by imperial Jove;
The poet plied his amorous strain,
Press'd the fond fair, nor press'd in vain;
For Ceres, who the veil undrew,
That screen'd her mysteries from view,
Propitious this kind truth reveal'd,
That woman close-besieged will yield.

Homer, of all past bards the prime,
And wonder of all future time,
Whom Jove with wit sublimely blest,
And touched with purest fire his breast,

From gods and heroes turned away
To warble the domestic lay,
And, wandering to the desert isle,
On whose parch'd rocks no seasons smile,
In distant Ithaca was seen
Chanting the suit-repelling queen.

Old Hesiod, too, his native shade
Made vocal to the Ascræan maid:
The bard his heaven-directed lore
Forsook, and hymn'd the gods no more;
Soft, love-sick ditties now he sung,
Love touch'd his harp, love tuned his tongue,
Silenced his Heliconian lyre,
And quite put out religion's fire.

Mimnermus tuned his amorous lay,
When time had turned his temples gray;
Love revelled in his aged veins,
Soft was his lyre and sweet his strains;
Frequenter of the wanton feast,
Nanno his theme and youth his guest.

Alcæus strung his sounding lyre,
And smote it with a hand of fire,
To Sappho, fondest of the fair,
Chanting the loud and lofty air.

E'en Sophocles, whose honey'd lore
Rivals the bee's delicious store,
Chorus'd the praise of wine and love,
Choicest of all the gifts of Jove.

Pythagoras, whose boundless soul
Scaled the wide globe from pole to pole,
Earth, planets, seas, and heavens above,
Yet found no spot secure from love,
With love declines unequal war,
And, trembling, drags his conqueror's car;
Theano clasped him in her arms,
And Wisdom stooped to Beauty's charms.

E'en Socrates, whose moral mind
With truth enlighten'd all mankind,

When at Aspasia's side he sate,
Still found no end to love's debate ;
For strong indeed must be the heart
Where love finds no unguarded part.

Sage Aristippus, by right rule
Of logic, purged the sophists' school,
Check'd folly in its headlong course,
And swept it down by reason's force ;
Till Venus aimed the heartfelt blow,
And laid the mighty victor low.

## HERONDAS.

AMONG the singular relics of antiquity recovered from
the sands of Egypt, not the least remarkable are seven mimes
of Herondas. A mime was a short dramatic interlude, originally in prose, but later in a kind of iambic verse. Herondas
was an Ionian Greek, and lived probably about 250 B.C.
Though his mimes were intended for the stage, they resemble
certain idylls of Theocritus more than the works of any other
Greek author extant. They are more exact pictures of real
life than the comedies afford. The translations are by J. A.
Symonds.

### THE BAD BOY TAKEN TO SCHOOL.

*Lampriscus, the master, is seated in school. Enter Metrotima
dragging her son Kottalos.*

*Metrotima.* May the dear Muses send you something to enjoy,
and may you have pleasure in life; so you will promise to drub
this boy of mine, till the soul of him, drat it, is left nowhere in his
body but the lips. He has ruined me by playing pitch and toss.
Yes, Lampriscus, it seems that knuckle-bones are not enough for
him; but he must needs be running after worse mischief. Where
the door of the grammar-master stands, or when the cursed tax-
day comes round—let me scream like Nannakos—he cannot tell.
But the gambling-place, where street-porters and runaways take
up their quarters, is so well known to him that he will point it
out to strangers. The unhappy tablets, which I take the pains
to spread with wax each month, lie abandoned by his bed-post
next the wall, unless perchance he casts a glance on them as

though they were the devil; and then, instead of writing something nice, he rubs them bare. His dice—that litter about among the bellows and the nets—are shinier than our oil-flask which we use for everything. But as for spelling out a word, he does not even know his alpha, unless one shouts it five times in his ears. The day before yesterday, when his father was teaching him Maron, what did the pretty fellow do but go and turn Maron into Simon? so that I am driven to call myself a fool for not making him a donkey-boy, instead of putting him to study in the hope of having a support for my declining years. Then if we make him repeat some child's speech—I, or his father, an old man with bad eyes and deaf,—the words run out of his head like water from a bottle with a hole in it. "Apollo the hunter!" I cry out; "even your granny will recite what one asks, and yet she has no schooling—or the first Phrygian you meet upon the road." But it's no use scolding, for if we go on, he runs away from home, stays out three days and nights, sponging upon his grandmother, poor old blind woman; or else he squats up there upon the roof, with his legs stretched out, like a tame ape, peering down. Just fancy what his wretched mother suffers when she sees him there. I don't care so much about him indeed. But he smashes all the roofing into broken biscuits; and when winter comes, I have to pay two shillings for each tile, with tears of anger in my eyes. All the neighbors sing the same old song: "Yonder's the work of master Kottalos, that boy of Metrotima's." And true it is; and I daren't wag a tooth in answer. Look at his back too, how he's scratched it all over in the wood, till he's no better than a Delian fisher with the creel who doits his life away at sea. Yet he casts feast-days and holidays better than a professional star-gazer: not even sleep will catch him forgetting when you're off your guard. So I beseech you, Lampriscus, and may these blessed ladies* give you prosperous life, and may you light on lucky days, do not ——

*Lampriscus.* Nay, Metrotima, you need not swear at him; it will not make him get the less. (*Calls to his pupils.*) Euthies, where are you? Ho, Kokkalos! ho, Phillos! Hurry up, and hoist the urchin on your shoulders; show the full moon, I say! (*Addresses Kottalos.*) I commend your ways of going on, Kottalos—fine ways, forsooth! It's not enough for you to cast dice, like the other boys here; but you must needs be running to the

---

*The Muses, whose statues adorn the school-room.

gambling-house and tossing coppers with the common porters! I'll make you more modest than a girl. You shan't stir a straw even, if that's what you want. Where is my cutting switch, the bull's tail, with which I lamm into jail-birds and good-for-nothings. Give it me, quick, before I hawk my bile up.

*Kottalos.* Nay, prithee, Lampriscus, I pray you by the Muses, by your beard, by the soul of Kottis, do not flog me with that cutting switch.

*L.* But, Kottalos, you are so gone in wickedness that there's not a slave-dealer who'd speak well of you—no, not even in some savage country where the mice gnaw iron.

*K.* How many stripes, Lampriscus; tell me, I beg, how many are you going to lay on?

*L.* Don't ask me—ask her. [*Lampriscus begins to flog the boy.*

*K.* Oh! oh! how many are you going to give me, if I can last out alive?

*Metrotima.* As many as the cruel hide can bear, I tell you.

*K.* Stop, stop, I've had enough, Lampriscus.

*L.* Do you then stop your naughtiness!

*K.* Never, never again will I be naughty. I swear, Lampriscus, by the dear Muses.

*M.* What a tongue you've got in your head, you! I'll shut your mouth up with a gag if you go on bawling.

*K.* Nay, then, I am silent. Please don't murder me!

*L.* Let him go, Kokkalos.

*M.* Don't stop, Lampriscus, flog him till the sun goes down——

*L.* But he's more mottled than a water-snake——

*M.* And he ought to get at least twenty more——

*L.* In addition to his book?—

*M.* Even though he learned to read better than Clio herself.

*K.* Yah! yah!

*M.* Stop your jaw till you've rinsed it with honey. I shall make a careful report of this to my old man, Lampriscus, when I get home; and shall come back quickly with fetters; we'll clamp his feet together; then let him jump about for the Muses he hated to look down on.

## THE TEMPLE OF ASKLEPIOS.

*Enter Coan women—Kokkale, Kunno, and their servants, and the Guardian of the Shrine.*

*Kokkale.* Hail to thee, Monarch Paiôn, who rulest over Tricca, and hast thy habitation in delightful Cos and Epidaurus; greetings to thee and to Coronis who gave thee birth, and to Apollo; as also to her whom with right hand thou touchest, Hygieia; you too, whose are these honored altars, Panacea, Epione, Iaso, hail; and ye who laid the dwellings and the walls of Laomedon waste, Podaleirios and Machaon, healers of savage diseases, hail to you, together with all gods and goddesses that sojourn at thy hearth, Sire Paiôn; propitiously accept, I pray, this cock, whilom the chanticleer of house and home, whom here I sacrifice; and take thereof the dainty bits. It is not much or serviceable that we draw from; else had we gladly brought an ox or fatted sow, and not a barn-door cock, in recompense for kind medicaments of fleshly ills, which thou didst wipe away, O King, laying thereon thy gentle hands.

*[She begins to arrange the offerings.*

*Kunno.* Place the tablet, Kokkale, on the right hand of Hygieia.

*[Then they look round the temple.*

*Ko.* O my dear Kunno, what a sight of lovely statues! Tell me who was the sculptor who wrought this marble, and who was the man who set it up here?

*Ku.* The sons of Praxiteles. Don't you see that inscription on the pedestal? And Euthies, the son of Praxon, gave them to the temple.

*Ko.* I invoke the blessings of Paiôn upon those craftsmen, and also on Euthies for such goodly workmanship. Look, dear, at that little girl there, lifting her eyes to the apple! Wouldn't one say that if she did not get the apple she would faint? And then, Kunno, that old man! Good gracious, how the boy is strangling the fox-goose!

*Ku.* Before our very noses, and unless we knew that it is stone, you would say that he was going to speak. Certes, the time is coming when men will be able to put life into senseless stones.

*Ko.* Yes; for, Kunno, see that statue of Battale, Myttis' daughter, how it stands! If some one had never seen Battale, and were to look at this portrait of her, he need not ask for flesh and blood.

*Ku.* Follow me, dear, and I will show you something, the like of which for beauty you never saw in your whole life. (*Turning to the servant.*) Kudilla, go and call the sacristan. What, ain't I talking to you, while you gaze around there? On my soul, but she won't attend to what I say! She stands and stares at me wider than a crab. Go, I say, and call the sacristan. You glutton, there's neither holy man nor layman who will call you worth your salt. It's all the same where you are. I take this god to witness, Kudilla, how you set me on fire with fury, though I do not want to rage. I take him to witness, I repeat, the day will come, when I shall make the razor shave your poll.

*Ko.* She is a slave, and dulness weighs like lead on slavish ears.

*Ku.* But day is breaking, and the crowd is pressing on all round. (*To the servant, who is setting off to look for the sacristan.*) Ho, you, stop! The gates have been thrown back, and the shrine is open. [*The women go in, and examine the pictures on the walls.*

*Ko.* My dear Kunno, only look, what lovely things! Wouldn't one say that another Athene had come down to carve these beauties! (But may the Queen herself be blessed!) That naked boy there; if I were to pinch him, wouldn't he be wounded, Kunno? For the flesh is laid upon him, hot, hot, quivering on the panel. And the silver tongs—I swear if Mueleos, or Pataikiskos, the son of Lamprion, could see them, their eyes would jump out of the sockets, thinking them to be real silver. That ox too, and the man who is leading him, and the woman walking with them, and the hook-nosed, and the snub-faced fellow, don't they all look just the living day? If I did not think it would be doing more than woman ought, I should have shrieked out for fear the beast would hurt me! He is glaring so with one eye, Kunno.

*Ku.* Yes, dear, for the hands of the Ephesian Apelles put the soul of truth into everything he painted; nor can one say "That man could see one thing, and was denied another;" but whoever, even of the gods, it came into his mind to attempt, on he sped right forwards. If a man has seen him or his works without the due astonishment they merit, he ought to be hung up by the foot in a fuller's shop.

*The Sacristan.* (*Entering after having attended to the sacrifice of the cock.*) Ladies, your offerings have turned out fair, in all points perfect, and augur for the best. No one has afforded more gratification to Paiôn than you have done. Io, io, Paiôn! Be gracious for their fair sacrifices to these ladies, and if they are wedded, to their husbands, and their next of kindred. Io, io, Paiôn! May these things be!

*Ko.* Yea, let it be so, Mightiest! And send us to come again in health, and bring a costlier offering, in company with husbands and children.

INTERIOR OF THE PARTHENON.

## CHAPTER XXIV

### Flavius Josephus

Flavius Josephus was a strange amalgamation of Jew, Greek and Roman, admittedly not what he should have been, either as a teacher of Mosaic law, as a patriot, or as a public man; and yet he performed successfully what he could not have achieved had he been any one of these only. He was born at Jerusalem in 37 A.D. He belonged to a Jewish priestly family of high rank, and was brought up at Jerusalem with his brother Matthias. After having received an excellent education, he attended successively the instructions of the Pharisees, Sadducees and Essenes, and then proceeded to the desert to practice an ascetic life. After three years he returned to Jerusalem and joined the Pharisees. At the age of twenty-six his abilities were so well recognized that he was chosen as a delegate to Nero respecting the liberation of some captive priests. Having been introduced to Poppæa, Nero's infamous wife, by a Jewish actor, he not only succeeded in his mission, but returned to Jerusalem loaded with presents, and endeavored to induce his countrymen to adopt a peace policy towards the Romans. But hopes of peace were dissipated by the massacre of the Jews in Syria and Alexandria. Then Josephus was made governor of Galilee, and led the war party with skill and courage. He was by no means universally trusted, and had political and personal foes who threatened his life. Driven into the town of Jotapata on the advance of Vespasian's army, he directed a desperate resistance for forty-seven days; and while endeavoring to escape fell into the conqueror's hands. He artfully assumed

the role of a prophet, and predicted that Vespasian would
succeed Nero as emperor of Rome.    This led to his being
honored by Vespasian, but kept as a prisoner on parole for three
years.   He was with Titus at the capture of Jerusalem, 70 A.D.,
and obtained special favors for some friends.   Most of his after
life was spent in Rome, in the prosecution of his studies and
the society of the court.   He assumed the name of Flavius,
as a dependent of the Flavian family to which Vespasian belonged.   He died about 100 A.D.

His "History of the Jewish War" is said to have been written
at first in Hebrew, or rather Syro-Chaldean, for the use
of the Jews, but was afterwards translated into Greek for
the educated Romans.   It is divided into seven books, and
traces the history of the Jews from the capture of the city by
Antiochus Epiphanes, to the destruction of the city by Titus.
More important, however, is his work called "Antiquities of
the Jews."   It consists of twenty books, is dedicated to
Epaphroditus, and gives the history of the Hebrews from the
earliest times to the beginning of the war with the Romans.
In large measure it runs parallel with the Hebrew Scriptures.
No author has been more fiercely attacked, or more ably
defended than Josephus.   He wrote his own "Life" in answer
to charges which had been made against his conduct in Galilee.   His treatise "Against Apion" is a defence of the antiquity
of the Jewish nation against those who impugned it on the ground
that early Greek writers did not mention the Jews.

As a public man, Josephus cannot be called an ideal patriot;
the course he pursued was selfish; yet probably he was sincerely convinced that it was for the true interests of his countrymen to yield to the Romans.   He was well aware of
the repugnance of the Romans to doctrines and practices which
they could not assimilate or incorporate with their own.   He
became, therefore, an apologist for Judaism.   The true object
of the "Antiquities" was to raise the reputation of his
nation in the estimation of the Gentiles, and to shield his
countrymen from the scorn and hatred which encountered them
in every city of the empire.

ERECHTHEUM, WITH PORCH OF CARYATIDES.

## HEROD THE GREAT IN HIS LAST ILLNESS.

### (From "The Antiquities of the Jews," Book xvii., chap. 6.)

HEROD'S distemper [in A.D. 4] increased upon him after a severe manner—and this, by God's judgment for his sins. A fire glowed within him slowly, which did not so much appear to the touch outwardly as it augmented his pains inwardly. For it brought upon him a vehement appetite for eating, which he could not avoid to supply with one sort of food or other. His entrails also were ulcerated: an aqueous and transparent liquor had settled itself about his feet, and a like matter afflicted him at the bottom of his belly. And when he sat upright he had a' difficulty of breathing, which was very loathsome, on account of the stench of his breath and the quickness of its return. He had also convulsions in all parts of his body, which debilitated him to an insufferable degree. It was said by those who pretended to divine, and who were endued with wisdom to foretell such things, that God inflicted that punishment on the king on account of his great impiety.

Yet was he still in hopes of recovering, though his afflictions seemed greater than any one could bear. He also sent for physicians and did not refuse to follow what they prescribed for his assistance; and went himself beyond the river Jordan, and bathed himself in the warm baths that were at Calirrhoë, which besides their other general virtues were also fit to drink, which water runs into the lake called Asphaltites [the Dead Sea]. And when the physicians once thought fit to have him bathed in a vessel full of oil, it was supposed that he was just dying. But upon the lamentable cries of his domestics he revived; and having no longer any hopes of recovering, he gave order that every soldier should be paid fifty drachmæ; and he also gave a great deal to their commanders and to his friends, and came again to Jericho.

There, however, he grew so choleric that it brought him to do all things like a madman; and though he was near his death, he contrived the following wicked designs: He commanded that all the principal men of the Jewish nation,

III—19

wheresoever they lived, should be called to him. Accordingly
a great number came, because the whole nation were called,
and all men heard of this call; and death was the penalty
of such as should neglect the epistles that were sent to call
them. And now the king was in a wild rage against them all
—the innocent as well as those that had offered grounds of
accusations. And when they were come, he ordered them to
be all shut up in the hippodrome, and sent for his sister
Salome, and her husband Alexas, and spoke thus to them:

"I shall die in a little time, so great are my pains; which
death ought to be cheerfully borne, and to be welcomed by
all men. But what chiefly troubles me is that I shall die
without being lamented, and without such mourning as men
usually expect at a king's death. For I am not unacquainted
with the temper of the Jews, but know that my death will
be a thing very desirable, and exceedingly acceptable to
them; because during my lifetime they were ready to revolt
from me, and to abuse the donations I had dedicated to God.
It is, therefore, your business to resolve to afford me some
alleviation of my great sorrows on this occasion; for if you
do not refuse your consent in what I desire, I shall have a
great mourning at my funeral, and such as never any king
had before me; for then the whole nation will mourn from
their very soul; which otherwise will be done in sport and
mockery only. I desire, therefore, that as soon as you see
that I have expired you shall place soldiers around the hippodrome; and you shall not declare my death to the multitude till this be done; but you shall give orders to have
those that are there in custody shot with darts. And this
slaughter of them all will cause that I shall not miss to
rejoice on a double account; that as I am dying, you will
make me secure that my will shall be executed in what I
charge you to do; and that I shall have the honor of a memorable mourning at my funeral."

He then deplored his condition with tears in his eyes; and
conjured them by the kindness due from them as his kindred,
and by the faith that they owed to God; and begged of them
not to hinder him of this honorable mourning at his funeral.
So they promised him not to transgress his commands.

## THE DEATH OF HEROD AGRIPPA.

FROM the "Antiquities," Book XIX., Chapters 8 and 9. With this account may be compared the statement in Acts xii. 21-23, where this king is called Herod.

Now when Agrippa had reigned three years over all Judea, he came to the city Cæsarea, which was formerly called Strato's Tower; and there he exhibited shows in honor of Claudius Cæsar, upon his being informed that there was a certain festival celebrated to make vows for his safety; at which festival a great multitude was gotten together of the principal persons who were of dignity in his province.

On the second day of these shows Agrippa put on a garment made wholly of silver, and of a contexture truly wonderful, and came into the theatre early in the morning; at which time the silver of his garment, being illuminated by the first reflection of the sun's rays upon it, shone out after a surprising manner, and was so resplendent as to spread a sort of dread over those that looked intently upon him. And presently his flatterers cried out, one from one place and another from another, that he was a god; and they added, " Be thou merciful to us; for although we have hitherto reverenced thee only as a man, yet shall we henceforth own thee as superior to mortal nature."

Upon this the king did neither rebuke them nor reject their impious flattery. But as he presently afterward looked up, he saw an owl sitting on a certain rope over his head; and immediately understood that this bird was the messenger of ill tidings, as it had once been the messenger of good tidings to him: and fell into the deepest sorrow. A severe pain also arose in his bowels, and began in a most violent manner. He therefore looked upon his friends and said, " I whom you call a god am commanded presently to depart this life; while Providence reproves the lying words you just now said to me. And I, who was by you called immortal, am immediately bound to be hurried away by death. But I am bound to accept of what Providence allots, as it pleases God; for we have by no means lived ill, but in a splendid and happy manner."

When he said this, his pain was become violent. Accordingly he was carried to his palace; and the rumor went about everywhere that he would certainly die in a little time. But the multitude presently sat in sackcloth, with their wives and children, after the law of their country, and besought God for the king's recovery. All places were also full of mourning and lamentation. Now the king rested in a high chamber; and as he saw them below lying on the ground he could not himself forbear weeping. And when he had been quite worn out by the pains in his belly for five days, he departed this life, being in the fifty-fourth year of his age, and in the seventh of his reign; for he reigned four years under Caius Cæsar [Caligula]; three of them were over Philip's tetrarchy only, and on the fourth he had that of Herod added to it; and he reigned, besides those, three years under the reign of Claudius Cæsar. While he reigned over these countries he had also Judea added to them, as well as Samaria and Cæsarea. The revenues that he received out of them were very great—no less than twelve millions of drachmæ. Yet did he borrow great sums from others; for he was so very liberal that his expenses exceeded his income, and his generosity was boundless.

When it was known that Agrippa was departed this life, the inhabitants of Cæsarea and of Sebaste forgot the kindness he had bestowed upon them, and acted the part of the bitterest enemies; for they cast such reproaches upon the deceased as are not fit to be spoken of. And so many of them as were then soldiers, who were very numerous, went to his house and hastily carried off the statues of this king's daughters unto the brothel houses; and when they had set them on the tops of those houses they abused them to the utmost of their power. They also laid themselves down in the public places, and celebrated general feastings, with garlands on their heads, and with ointments and libations to Charon, and drinking to one another for joy that the king had expired. Nay, they were not only unmindful of Agrippa, who had extended his liberality to them in abundance, but of his grandfather Herod also, who had himself rebuilt their cities, and had raised them havens and temples at vast expenses.

## THE BURNING OF THE TEMPLE AT JERUSALEM.

### (From the "History of the Jewish Wars.")

TITUS, having retired into the tower of Antonia, resolved to storm the temple the next morning with his whole army, and to encamp round about the holy house. But as for that house, God had, for certain, long ago doomed it to fire. And now that fatal day was come according to the revolution of ages; it was the tenth day of the month Lous, or Ab; upon which it was formerly burnt by the king of Babylon: but these flames took their rise from the Jews themselves, and were occasioned by them. For upon Titus retiring, the seditious lay still for a little while, and then attacked the Romans again; when those that guarded the holy house fought with those that quenched the fire that was burning the inner court of the temple. But these Romans put the Jews to flight, and proceeded as far as the holy house itself. At which time one of the soldiers, without waiting for any orders, and without any concern or dread upon him at so great an undertaking, but being hurried on by a certain divine fury, snatched something out of the materials that were on fire, and being lifted up by another soldier, set fire to a golden window, through which there was a passage to the rooms that were round about the holy house on the north side of it. As the flames went upward, the Jews made a great clamor, such as so mighty an affliction required, and ran together to prevent it. And now they spared not their lives any longer, nor suffered anything to restrain their force, since that holy house was perishing for whose sake they kept such a guard about it.

Now a certain person came running to Titus and told him of this fire, as he was reposing in his tent after the last battle; upon which he arose in great haste and ran to the holy house, in order to have a stop put to the fire. After him went all his commanders, and after them followed the several legions, in great astonishment. So there was a great clamor and tumult raised, as was natural upon the disorderly motion of so great an army. Then did Cæsar—both by calling to the soldiers that were fighting, with a loud voice, and by giving a signal to them with his right hand—order them to quench the fire. But, they did not hear what he said, though he spoke so loud, having their ears already dinned by a greater noise another way. Nor did they attend to the signal he made them with his hand; some of them being distracted with fighting and others with passion.

But as for the legions that came running thither, neither any persuasion nor threatening could restrain their violence; but each one's own passion was his commander at this time. And as they were crowding into the temple together many of them were trampled on by one another; while a great number fell among the ruins of the cloisters, which were still hot and smoking, and were destroyed in the same miserable way with those whom they had conquered. And when they were come near the holy house, they acted as if they did not so much as hear Cæsar's orders to the contrary, but even encouraged those that were before them to set it on fire. As for the seditious, they were in too great distress already to afford their assistance towards quenching the fire. They were everywhere slain, and everywhere beaten. And as for a great part of the people, they were weak and without arms, and had their throats cut wherever they were caught. Now round about the altar lay dead bodies, heaped one upon another; and at the steps going up to it ran a great quantity of their blood, whither also the dead bodies that were slain above on the altar fell down.

Now, since Cæsar was not able to restrain the fury of the soldiers, and the fire proceeded more and more, he went into the holy place of the temple, with his commanders, and saw it, with what was in it; which he found to be far superior to what had been related by foreigners, and not inferior to what we ourselves boasted and believed about it.

But as the flame had not yet reached to its inward parts, but was still consuming the rooms that were about the holy house only, Titus, supposing that the house itself might yet be saved, came up in haste, and endeavored to persuade the soldiers to quench the fire, and gave order to Liberalius the centurion, and one of those spearmen that were about him, to beat the soldiers that were refractory with their staves, and to restrain them. Yet were their passions too strong for the regard they had for Cæsar, and the dread they had of him who forbade them ; as was their hatred of the Jews and a certain vehement inclination to fight them, too hard for them also. Moreover, the hope of plunder induced many to go on ; supposing that all the places were full of money, and seeing that all around it was made of gold. And, besides, one of those that went into the place got before Cæsar, when he ran out so hastily to restrain the soldiers ; and threw the fire upon the hinges of the gate, in the dark. The flame now burst out from within the holy house itself ; when the commanders retired, and Cæsar retired with them, and when nobody any longer forbade those that were without to set fire to it. Thus was the holy house burnt down, without Cæsar's approbation.

Now, although any one would justly lament the destruction of such an edifice as this was, since it was the most admirable of all the buildings we have seen or heard, both for its curious structure and its magnitude, and also for the vast wealth bestowed upon it, as well as for the glorious reputation it had for its holiness ; yet might such a one comfort himself with this thought, that it was fate that so decreed it to be ; which is inevitable both as to living creatures, and as to works and places also. However, one cannot but wonder at the exactness of this period thereto relating. For the same month and day were now observed, as I said before, wherein the holy house was burnt formerly by the Babylonians. Now, the number of years that elapsed from its first foundation by King Solomon till this destruction, which happened in the second year of the reign of Vespasian, are computed to be one thousand one hundred and thirty, besides seven months and fifteen days. And from the second building of it, which was performed by Haggai, in the second year of Cyrus the king, till its destruction under Vespasian, there were six hundred and thirty-nine years and forty-five days.

While the holy house was on fire everything was plundered that came to hand, and ten thousand of those that were caught were slain. Nor was there a commiseration of any

age, nor any reverence of dignity ; but children and old men,
priests and lay persons, were all slain in the same manner.
So that this war affected all sorts of men, and brought them
to destruction, as well those that made supplication for their
lives as those that defended themselves by fighting.   The
flame was also carried a long way, and made an echo, together
with the groans of those that were slain.   And because this
hill was high, and the works at the temple were very great,
one would have thought the whole city had been on fire.   No
one can imagine anything even greater or more terrible than
this noise.   For there was at once a shout of the Roman
legions, who were marching all together, and a sad clamor of
the seditious, who were now surrounded with fire and sword.
The people also that were left above were beaten back upon
the enemy, and under a great consternation, and made sad
moans at the calamity they were under.   The multitude that
was in the city joined in this outcry with those that were
upon the hill.   And besides, many of those that were worn
away by the famine, and their mouths almost closed, when
they saw the fire of the holy house, exerted their utmost
strength, and broke out into groans and outcries again.
Perea [beyond the Jordan] also did return the echo, as well as
the mountains round about the city, and augmented the force
of the general noise.

Yet was the misery itself more terrible than this disorder.
For one would have thought that the very hill on which the
temple stood was red-hot—as full of fire on every part of it ;
that the blood was larger in quantity than the fire, and those
that were slain more in numbers than those that slew them.
For the ground did nowhere appear visible for the dead
bodies that lay on it, but the soldiers went over heaps of
those dead bodies, as they ran upon such as fled from them.
And now it was that the multitude of the robbers were
thrust out of the inner court of the temple by the Romans,
and had much ado to get into the outer court, and from
thence into the city ; while the remainder of the populace
fled into the cloister of that outer court.   As for the priests,
some of them picked up from the holy houses the spikes that
were upon it, with their bases, which were made of lead, and

shot them at the Romans instead of darts. But then, as they gained nothing by so doing, and as the fire burst out upon them, they retired to the wall that was eight cubits broad, and there they tarried. Yet did two of those of eminence among them, who might have saved themselves by going over to the Romans, or have borne up with courage and taken their fortune with the others, throw themselves into the fire, and were burnt together with the holy house. Their names were Meirus, the son of Belgas, and Joseph, the son of Daleus.

Now the Romans, judging that it was in vain to spare what was round about the holy house, burnt all those places, as also the remains of the cloisters and the gates, two excepted, the one on the east side and the other on the south; both of which, however, they burnt afterward. They also burnt down the treasury chambers, in which was an immense quantity of money, and a great number of garments and other precious goods. And, in a word, there it was that the entire riches of the Jews were heaped up together, while the rich people had there built themselves chambers to contain such furniture. The soldiers also came to the rest of the cloisters that were in the outer court of the temple, whither the women and children and a mixed multitude of the people fled, in number about six thousand. But before Cæsar had determined anything about these people, or given the commanders any orders relating to them, the soldiers were in such a rage that they set the cloisters on fire. By which means some of these were destroyed by throwing themselves down headlong, and some were burnt in the cloisters themselves. Nor did any of them escape with their lives.

## MELEAGER.

THE name of Meleager is inseparably connected with the Greek Anthology, the grand monument of the minor literature of many centuries. He was born at Gadara in Syria, and flourished about the middle of the first century before Christ. Yet he was of Greek descent and became a Cynic philosopher. He possessed fine artistic taste, and had a high appreciation of the beautiful. As a writer of epigrams and delicately sententious pieces he stands next to the highest. In his day skill in graceful epigrams had displaced the grander style. Epigrams had originally been inscriptions on tombs, monuments and works of art. Meleager was the first who conceived the idea of collecting the best of these and weaving them together into what he called his "Garland." They were singularly arranged in alphabetical order according to the first letter of each piece. In this heterogeneous collection are found the effusions of many minor poets which appeal to the warm affections of the heart even more forcibly than the masterpieces of Greek literature.

As an introduction to his "Garland," he wrote a poem of sixty lines, in which he characterized the various authors who had contributed to his store by plants or flowers emblematical of their special tastes or talents.

### HELIODORA'S GARLAND.

I'LL frame, my Heliodora! a garland for thy hair,
Which thou, in all thy beauty's pride, mayst not disdain to wear;
For I, with tender myrtles, white violets will twine—
White violets, but not so pure as that pure breast of thine:
With laughing lilies I will twine narcissus; and the sweet
Crocus shall in its yellow hue with purple hyacinth meet:
And I will twine with all the rest, and all the rest above,
Queen of them all, the red, red Rose, the flower which lovers love.

### LAMENT FOR HELIODORE.

(Translated by Alma Strettell.)

TEARS even far beneath the earth I send thee,
   O Heliodore—bitter tears I pour;

Tokens of love, in Hades to attend thee.
  And on thy tomb, where I have mourned so sore,
I offer—as libations poured above—
Memories of our kindness and our love.

O thou, among the dead belovèd even,
  Meleager sorely, sorely wails for thee;
Vain homage, empty prayers to Hades given!
  Ah, where may now my mourned-for blossom be?
Hades hath ravished, ravished it away,
And dust defiles my blooming flower to-day.

O Earth, all-nourishing, to thee I make
My supplication—her I weep for take,
And gently fold her in thine arms, to rest,
Mother, against thy breast.

## HUE AND CRY AFTER CUPID.

(Translated by Walter Headlam.)

HUE and cry for Love the wild! for early from his bed,
Early in the morning hath he taken wing and fled.

Sweet in tears and sly of laughter, dauntless, prattling ever,
Swift, with wings upon his back and at his side a quiver.

But the father of the rogue I cannot tell; for Sea,
Earth and Air alike declare: No son of mine is he.

For of all he is abhorred in every place; beware
Lest he setteth for your souls even now another snare.

See, why, at his lair he lies! I have discovered thee,
Archer, lurking in the eyes of my Zenophilé.

## CLEARISTA.

(Translated by Walter Headlam.)

NOT Marriage Clearista won to wait upon her wedding,
  But Death, when she unloosed the zone of her virginity:
For late the pipes at eventide were at her portal shedding
  Their music, and her chamber doors resounded noisily;

And early on the morrow they raised a note of sorrow,
   The bridal-chorus quitted became a chant of woe;
And so the self-same torches about her bower's porches,
   Gave shine and for her perishéd lit up the path below.


### MELEAGER ON HIMSELF.

(Translated by Richard Garnett.)

TYRE brought me up, who born in thee had been,
   Assyrian Athens, city Gadarene;
My name is Meleager, Eucrates
   My sire; my skill with graceful strains to please;
My Syrian lineage do not discommend;
   One world have all, one origin, one end;
Stricken in years, I yet can touch the string,
   And this unto the tomb, my neighbor, sing;
Salute my garrulous old age, and be
   Thine own, what now thou honorest in me.


## GREEK ANTHOLOGY.

WHATEVER may be the merits of the short poems grouped
under the name of Greek Anthology, they have excited schol-
arly interest and exercised the ingenuity of translators more
than any other branch of Greek poetry. Numberless are the
quotations, imitations and editions of them. The word
"Anthology," meaning "a collection of flowers," is now
applied to a compilation of the representative poems of any
nation. Whatever is found in such a collection should be
like a flower, attractive by its beauty, elegance and delicacy.
The Greek Anthology really comprises many of other kinds,
and not only entertains, but endeavors to teach wisdom by
smiles and tears and timely jests. It includes themes of history, deeds of patriotism, love and war, and all the charms
and snares of woman's voice and glance. Cyril, one of the
minor poets, makes brevity the sole characteristic of a Greek
epigram. He thus exemplifies it:

   " Two lines complete the epigram—or three;
      Write more; you aim at epic poetry."

### Timareté Puts away Childish Things.

Timareté, her wedding-day now near,
To Artemis has laid these offerings here,—
Her tambourine, her pleasant ball, the net
As a safe guardian o'er her tresses set;
Her maiden dolls, in mimic robes arrayed,
Gifts fitting for a maid to give a maid.
Goddess, thy hand upon her kindly lay,
And keep her holy in thy holy way.

### Lais' Mirror.

The celebrated courtesan Lais, growing old, dedicated to Aphrodite (Venus) her mirror. Plato is said to have written for her this epigram.

I, Lais, who on conquered Greece looked down with haughty
    pride;
I, to whose courts, in other days, a swarm of lovers hied;
O Aphrodite, now this mirror give to thee,
For my present self I would not, and my past I cannot see.

More truly epigrammatic, in the modern sense, is this condensed imitation by Matthew Prior.

Venus, take this votive glass,
Since I am not what I was.
What I shall hereafter be,
Venus, let me never see!

### For the Tomb of Myrtis.

(The poetess Erinna wrote the following inscription.)

The virgin Myrtis' sepulchre am I;
    Creep softly to the pillared mount of woe,
    And whisper to the grave, in earth below,
"Grave thou art envious in thy cruelty!"
The very torch that laughing Hymen bore
To light the virgin to the bridegroom's door,
With that same torch the bridegroom lights the fire
That dimly glimmers on her funeral pyre.
Thou, too, O Hymen! bid'st the nuptial lay
In elegiac moanings die away.

### EPITAPH ON ANTIBIA.

This epitaph, by the poetess Anyte, is translated by William Hay.

THE maid Antibia I lament; for whom
Full many a suitor sought her father's hall.
For beauty, prudence, famed was she; but doom
Destructive overwhelmed the hopes of all.

### EPITAPH ON THEONOË AND HER CHILD.

IN this epigram, by Bianor, a husband mourns the loss of wife and child. The translation is by Prof. Goldwin Smith.

I wept Theonoë's loss; but one fair child
Its father's heart of half its woe beguiled:
And now, sole source of hope and solace left,
The one fair child the envious Fates have reft.
Hear, Proserpine, my prayer, and lay to rest
My little babe on its lost mother's breast.

### TRUE WISDOM.

ENJOY your goods as if your death were near;
Save them as if 'twere distant many a year.
Sparing or spending, be thy wisdom seen
In keeping ever to the golden mean.

### THE PARTNERSHIP.

DAMON, who plied the undertaker's trade,
With Doctor Crateas an agreement made.
What linens Damon from the dead could seize,
He to the Doctor sent for bandages;
While the good Doctor, here no promise-breaker,
Sent all his patients to the undertaker.

### THE LESSON OF THE TOPS.

An Atarnean stranger once to Pittacus applied,
That ancient sage, Hyrradius' son, and Mytilene's pride;
Grave sir, betwixt two marriages I now have power to choose,
And hope you will advise me which to take and which refuse.
One of the maidens, every way, is very near myself;
The other's far above me, both in pedigree and pelf.
Now which is best?"  The old man raised the staff which
    old men bear,
And with it pointed to some boys that then were playing there,
Whipping their tops along the street: "Their steps," he
    said, "pursue,
And look and listen carefully; they'll tell you what to do."
Following them, the stranger went to see what might befall,
And "Whip the top that's nearest you!" was still their
    constant call.
He, by this boyish lesson taught, resigned the high-born dame,
And wed the maiden "nearest him."  Go thou and do the same.

### THE FLEAS OUTWITTED.

A countryman once who was troubled with fleas,
Jumped up out of bed in a thundering breeze,
And triumphantly cried, as he blew out the light,
"Now I have you; you rogues, you can't see where to bite!"

### THE WINE-CUP.

The winecup is glad: dear Zenophilé's lip
It boasts to have touched, when she stooped down to sip.
Happy winecup!  I wish that, with lips joined to mine,
All my soul at a draught she would drink up like wine.

### THE PICTURE OF APHRODITE.

This epigram on the picture of Aphrodite by Praxiteles is ascribed
to Plato.

    The Paphian Queen to Cnidus made repair
    Across the tide, to see her image there.
    Then looking up and round the prospect wide,
    "Where did Praxiteles see me thus?" she cried.

### THE MISER AND THE MOUSE.

ASCLEPIADES, the Miser, in his house
Espied one day, with some surprise, a mouse:
"Tell me, dear mouse," he cried, "to what cause is it
I owe this pleasant but unlooked for visit?"
The mouse said, smiling, "Fear not for your hoard,
I come, my friend, to lodge, and not to board."

### GRAMMAR AND MEDICINE.

#### (By Agathias.)

A THRIVING doctor sent his son to school
To gain some knowledge, should he prove no fool;
But took him soon away with little warning,
On finding out the lesson he was learning—
How great Pelides' wrath, in Homer's rhyme,
Sent many souls to Hades ere their time.
"No need for this, my boy should hither come;
That lesson he can better learn at home—
For I myself, now, I make bold to say,
Send many souls to Hades ere their day,
Nor e'er find want of grammar stop my way."

## PLUTARCH.

PLUTARCH, as the great interpreter of Greece and Rome, exerted on generations succeeding him an influence perhaps greater than any other classical author. He was born at Chæronea, in Bœotia, about 45 or 50 A.D.; was a student of philosophy at Delphi during Nero's progress through Greece in 66 A.D. In the reign of Domitian he was for some time resident at Rome, and lectured on philosophy. He afterwards held a magistracy in his native town, and died in the reign of Hadrian, about 120 A.D.

Plutarch was a voluminous writer, and his works are mostly of a practical nature. That by which his name is universally known is his "Parallel Lives." It consists mainly of forty-six biographies of representative men of Greece and Rome, arranged so that one Greek and one Roman form a set. The first pair is made up of Theseus and Romulus, as the respective founders of Athens and Rome—both now regarded as mythical. All students recognize the charm arising from the mere grouping of such men as Pericles and Q. Fabius Maximus, Aristides and Cato Major, Alexander the Great and Julius Cæsar; and the interest is permanently maintained when he finds the political and historical importance of each briefly outlined, and their characters and peculiarities clearly portrayed by a few simple touches. Plutarch does not claim to be a historian in the ordinary sense. If the great events of a man's life are described, the description is subordinate to the writer's chief aim, which is a moral one. In many of the "Lives" historical order is not observed, and the author explains that he does not write histories, but lives, and leaves to others the description of battles and great events, preferring himself to look into the signs of a man's character, which is as often revealed by a stray word, jest, or trivial circumstance, as by conspicuous acts which do not of necessity exhibit one's virtues or vices. Although Plutarch does not possess that critical acumen which is quick to separate the true from the false, and unravel a web of confusing and conflicting statements, we are still deeply indebted to him for a multitude of facts which would otherwise have been unrecorded. He had no exact system of philosophy: he favored the opinions of Plato, and opposed those of Epicurus. His writings are not marked by originality or depth of thought, but they are pervaded by amiability and love of what is great and noble. His precepts and his philosophy are practical, and he represents the better life that still survived in the Greek world.

## Appius Claudius, the Blind.

Pyrrhus, King of Epirus and nephew of Alexander the Great, invaded Italy in 281 B.C. In the battle of Heraclea the Romans first encountered the Macedonian phalanx and were utterly defeated.

Pyrrhus immediately entered the Roman camp, which he found deserted. He gained over many cities which had been in alliance with Rome, and laid waste the territories of others; nay, he advanced to within thirty-seven miles of Rome itself. The Lucanians and the Samnites joined him after the battle, and were reproved for their delay; yet it was plain that he was greatly elated and delighted with having defeated so powerful an army of Romans with the assistance of the Tarentines only.

The Romans, on this occasion, did not take the command from Lævinus, though Caius Fabricius is reported to have said, "The Romans were not overcome by the Epirots, but Lævinus by Pyrrhus;" meaning that the defeat was owing to the inferiority of the general, not of his troops. Then raising new levies, filling up their legions, and talking in a lofty and menacing tone about the war, they struck Pyrrhus with amazement. He thought proper, therefore, to send an embassy to them; first, to try whether they were disposed to peace; being satisfied that to take the city, and make an absolute conquest, was an undertaking of too much difficulty to be effected by such an army as he had at that time; whereas,

if he could bring them to terms of accommodation, and conclude a peace with them, it would be very glorious for him
after such a victory.

Cineas, who was sent to Rome with this commission, applied to the chief men, and sent to them and their wives
presents in his master's name. But all refused them, the
women as well as the men, declaring, that when Rome had
publicly ratified a treaty with the king, they should then on
their side be ready to give him every mark of their friendship
and respect. And though Cineas made a very plausible speech
to the Senate, and used many arguments to induce them to
close with him, yet they lent not a willing ear to his proposi-
tions, notwithstanding that Pyrrhus offered to restore without
ransom the prisoners he had made in the battle, and promised
to assist them in the conquest of Italy, desiring nothing in
return but their friendship for himself and security for the
Tarentines. Some, indeed, seemed inclined to peace, urging
that they had already lost a great battle, and might fear a still
greater, since Pyrrhus had been joined by several nations in
Italy. There was then an illustrious Roman, Appius Claudius,
who, on account of his great age and the loss of his sight, had
declined all attendance on public business. But when he
heard of the embassy from Pyrrhus, and the report prevailed
that the Senate was going to vote for the peace, he could not
contain himself, but ordered his servants to take him up, and
carry him in his chair through the forum to the Senate-house.
When he was brought to the door his sons and son-in-law
received him, and led him into the Senate. A respectful
silence was observed by the whole body on his appearance.
Then he declared his sentiments.

"Hitherto I have regarded my blindness as a misfortune;
but now, Romans, I wish I had been as deaf as I am blind.
For then I should not have heard of your shameful counsels
and decrees, so ruinous to the glory of Rome. Where now
are your speeches so much echoed about the world, that if
Alexander the Great had come into Italy when we were young,
and your fathers in the vigor of their age, he would not now
be celebrated as invincible, but either by his flight or his fall
would have added to the glory of Rome? You now show the

vanity and folly of that boast, while you dread the Chaonians and Molossians, who were ever a prey to the Macedonians, and while you tremble at the name of Pyrrhus, who has all his life been paying his court to one of the generals of that Alexander. At present he wanders about Italy, not so much to succor the Greeks here, as to avoid his enemies at home; and he promises to procure us the empire of this country with those forces which could not enable him to keep a small part of Macedonia. Do not expect, then, to get rid of his presence by entering into alliance with him. That step will only open a door to many invaders. For who is there that will not despise you, and think you an easy conquest, if Pyrrhus not only escapes unpunished for his insolence, but gains the Tarentines and Samnites as a reward for insulting the Romans?"

No sooner had Appius finished this speech than the Senators voted unanimously for the war, and dismissed Cineas with this answer, that "when Pyrrhus had quitted Italy, they would enter upon a treaty of friendship and alliance with him if he desired it; but while he continued there in a hostile manner, they would prosecute the war against him with all their force, though he should have defeated a thousand Lævinuses."

### CATO'S WARNING AGAINST GREEK LEARNING.

WHEN Cato was very far advanced in years, there arrived at Rome two ambassadors from Athens, Carneades the Academic, and Diogenes the Stoic. They were sent to beg off a fine of five hundred talents, which had been imposed on the Athenians for contumacy by the Sicyonians, at the suit of the people of Oropus. Upon the arrival of these philosophers, such of the Roman youth as had a taste for learning went to wait on them, and heard them with wonder and delight. Above all, they were charmed with the graceful manners of Carneades. The report ran that his eloquence, more than human, was able to soften and disarm the fiercest passions, and had made so strong an impression upon the youth, that, forgetting all other pleasures and diversions, they were quite possessed with an enthusiastic love of philosophy.

The Romans were delighted to find it so; nor could they

without uncommon pleasure behold their sons thus fondly receive the Grecian literature, and follow these wonderful men. But Cato, from the beginning, was alarmed at it. He no sooner perceived this passion for the Grecian learning prevail than he was afraid that the youth would turn their ambition that way, and prefer the glory of eloquence to that of deeds of arms. But when he found that the reputation of these philosophers rose still higher, and their first speeches were translated into Latin by Caius Acilius, a senator of great distinction, who had earnestly begged the favor of interpreting them, he had no longer patience, but resolved to dismiss these philosophers upon some decent and specious pretence.

He went, therefore, to the Senate, and complained of the magistrates for detaining so long such ambassadors as those, who could persuade the people to whatever they pleased. "You ought," said he, "to determine their affair as speedily as possible, that returning to their schools they may hold forth to the Grecian youth, and that our young men may again give attention to the laws and the magistrates." Not that Cato was induced to this by any particular pique to Carneades, which some suppose to have been the case, but by his aversion to philosophy, and his making it a point to show his contempt for the polite studies and learning of the Greeks. Nay, he scrupled not to affirm, that Socrates himself was a prating, seditious fellow, who used his utmost endeavors to tyrannize over his country by abolishing its customs and drawing the people over to opinions contrary to the laws. And to ridicule the slow methods of Isocrates' teaching, he said, "His scholars grew old in learning their art, as if they intended to exercise it in the shades below, and to plead causes there." To dissuade his own son from those studies, he told him in a louder tone than could be expected from a man of his age, and, as it were, in an oracular and prophetic way, that when the Romans came thoroughly to imbibe the Grecian literature, they would lose the empire of the world. But time has shown the vanity of that invidious assertion; for Rome was never at a higher pitch of greatness than when she was most perfect in the Grecian erudition, and most attentive to all manner of learning.

## LUCIAN.

Lucian, the humorous satirist, was a native of Samosata, in Syria, and flourished towards the end of the second century. In early life he was a sculptor, but later applied himself to the study of literature and philosophy. He was an extensive traveler, and seems to have traversed Asia Minor, Greece, Italy and Gaul, teaching and studying human nature. After having amassed wealth as a wandering sophist, he settled down at Athens, when about forty years of age, and devoted himself to those satirical and humorous works which have made his name famous.

If Plutarch, as a moralist, may be called the last of the ancients, then Lucian, as a satirist, is the first of the moderns. Between the two there is a great contrast as to the objects they had in view and their methods of accomplishing them. Plutarch tried to promote well-doing by precepts and striking examples from early history; Lucian ridiculed the past, scorning alike its philosophy and religion. He was, in many respects, the Voltaire of his age, and used much the same weapons to effect his purpose. He was the avowed enemy of superstition, delusion, fanaticism and quackery, wherever he met them. The insolent presumption and unclean lives of the philosophical quacks of his time could not escape the lash of his satire and raillery. As a student of human character, in all its lights and shades, he had a wide field of observation; and much which he meant to be applied only to his own time and country, is applicable to every age and to every country. Sometimes, in exposing and denouncing the follies and vices of men, Lucian uses expressions revolting to modern ideas. For this reason, and for his attacks on the Christian as well as the pagan religion, Suidas and later Christian writers have set him down as an immoral blasphemer. But these sweeping attacks rather go to prove that in his time Christianity was but little understood, and almost universally despised by the learned classes of society. In some of his dramatic narratives he attacks the power and the very existence of Zeus, and ridicules the exploits and attributes of the gods. The most important of Lucian's works are framed as Dialogues; among the most popular are the "Dialogues of the Gods," the "Dialogues of the Dead," the "Fisherman," and the "Banquet." Gibbon truly says, "A writer conversant with the world would never have ventured to expose the gods of his country to ridicule, had they not already been the objects of secret contempt among the polished and enlightened orders of society."

## APOLLO AND HEPHÆSTUS.

FROM an early period the tricks of Hermes (Mercury) furnished a favorite subject to comic writers.

*Hephæstus.* Have you seen this new-born son of Maia, how pretty he is, and how archly he laughs at everybody? He is still but a baby, yet has every possible indication that something excellent must come of him.

*Apollo.* What shall I anticipate of a child, Hephæstus? or what good expect of him who in mischief is already much older than Iapetus?

*Heph.* How can a child scarcely come into the world be able to do mischief?

*Apollo.* Ask Poseidon (Neptune) whom he has robbed of his trident, or Ares (Mars) whose sword he privately stole out of the scabbard; not to mention that he filched my bow and arrows.

*Heph.* A new-born babe that can scarcely stir in his swaddling-clothes!

*Apollo.* You will soon have proof of it, whenever he comes to you.

*Heph.* He has been to me already.

*Apollo.* And are none of your implements carried off? Is everything there?

*Heph.* Everything, Apollo.

*Apollo.* Look narrowly.

*Heph.* By Zeus! I miss my tongs.

*Apollo.* You will infallibly find them in the little one's cradle.

*Heph.* He is so nimble-fingered that he must have already learned the art of stealing in his mother's womb.

*Apollo.* And have you not heard how cleverly he harangues, and how glibly his tongue runs? He has already a mind to be our page. And would you think it—no longer ago than yesterday he gave a challenge to Cupid, and in an instant, somehow or other, tripped up his heels, and laid him sprawling on the ground. And as we all applauded him for his victory, while Aphrodite (Venus) took him up in her arms and kissed him, he stole her girdle and Zeus' (Jupiter's) sceptre; and if the thunderbolt had not been too heavy and too hot, he would have run away with that also.

*Heph.* A notable youngster indeed!

*Apollo.* And what is more, he is a musician too.

*Heph.* How do you make that out?

*Apollo.* He found a dead tortoise somewhere. He immediately made an instrument of the shell, fitting pins into it, with a neck and keys and bars; and stretching on it seven strings, he played gracefully and masterly upon it, so that I myself was struck with admiration and envy, though I have so long applied myself to the cithara [lyre]. Besides, his mother informed us that she cannot keep him in heaven at night; but from his superfluous energy he privately sneaks down into Tartarus—I suppose to see whether there is anything to steal; for he has somehow got wings, and a certain wand which possesses such a surprising efficacy that he attracts souls with it, and conducts the dead down into Tartarus.

*Heph.* That he had from me. I gave it him for a plaything.

*Apollo.* And to requite your kindness he stole your tongs.

*Heph.* It is well you remind me of it. I will go directly, and fetch them back. I suppose as you say, I shall find them in his cradle.

### PLUTO AND HERMES (MERCURY).

*Pluto.* Are you acquainted with a certain excessively old and excessively rich Eucrates, who has no children, but in lieu of them fifty thousand good friends in full chase after his estates?

*Hermes.* I know him very well. You mean the wealthy Sicyonian? And what of him?

*Pluto.* I wish, Hermes, that to the ninety years he has already lived you would, if possible, deal him out ninety more, and upwards.   But as to those parasites—young Charinus, Damon, and the rest—despatch them quickly to us, one after the other.

*Hermes.*  That would carry a preposterous look with it.

*Pluto.*  Not at all.   Everybody would approve it, and think it right.   For what reason have these fellows to wish for his death, and lie in wait for his wealth, being nowise related to him?   The most preposterous part of it is, that, with such sentiments they profess to the world that they are the most zealously attached to him ; and when he is sick, put up great prayers for his recovery, though everybody knows what they wish ; in short, they are an infamous pack of hypocritical scoundrels, whose artifices ought not to succeed.   Let him, therefore, be immortal!   And as for them, let them have stretched gaping beaks in vain, by being forced to march off before him.

*Hermes.*  What faces the scoundrels will make when they see themselves led away !   But Eucrates plays his part very well ; he knows how to cajole them, and lead them about by the nose. The old fox makes as if death were sitting on his lips, though in fact he is in better health than the young men who are already sharing his inheritance among them, and anticipating the happy life they shall lead after a little while.

*Pluto.*  Let Eucrates, therefore, cast his old skin, and, like Iolaus, begin again to live ; and let them receive their due reward by being snatched away while indulging delicious dreams of riches and pleasure.

*Hermes.*  Put yourself to no trouble about it, Pluto.   I will take care to conduct them hither in proper order.   I think there are seven in all.

*Pluto.*  Do so.   The old man shall see them all despatched before him ; and from a superannuated gray-beard let him be again a youth.

## CHARON'S BOAT.

### (The following is one of the "Dialogues of the Dead.")

*Charon.*  Look ye, gentlemen, thus affairs stand : we have but a small boat, as you see, and that half rotten and leaky in many places, if you lean it on one side or other we overset, and go to the bottom ; and yet so many of you will press in, and every one carrying his baggage with him ; if you do not leave it behind I am afraid you will repent it, especially those who cannot swim.

*Dead Men.*  What must we do to get safe over?

*Char.* I will tell you; you must get in naked, and then my boat will scarce be able to carry you; you, Hermes, must take care and let none come in but those who are stark naked and have left all their trumpery behind them; stand at the head of the boat, and make them strip before they come on board.

*Hermes.* Right, Charon, so I will. Who is this first?

*Menippus.* I have thrown my pouch and my staff in before me, my coat I did right to leave behind me.

*Her.* My honest friend Menippus, come in, take you the first seat at the helm, near the pilot, and observe who comes. But who is this pretty fellow?

*Charmoleus.* I am the handsome Charmoleus of Megara; a kiss from me sold for two talents.

*Her.* Please to part with your beauty, your ponderous head of hair, your sweet kissing lips, rosy cheeks, and fine skin. It is well; you are fit to come in, and may now enter. But there comes a fine fellow, clothed in purple, with a diadem on his head. Who are you?

*Lampichus.* Lampichus, king of the Geloans.

*Her.* What is all that baggage you have brought with you?

*Lam.* Was it fitting that a king should come without anything?

*Her.* A king should not, but a dead man should: therefore down with them.

*Lam.* There; I have thrown away all my riches.

*Her.* Throw away your pride and ostentation also, for if you bring them in with you you will sink the boat.

*Lam.* At least let me keep my diadem and my cloak.

*Her.* By no means; off with them immediately.

*Lam.* Be it so. Now I have thrown away everything; what more must I part with?

*Her.* Your cruelty, your folly, your insolence and your anger.

*Lam.* Now I am stark naked.

*Her.* Come in, then. . . . You, Crates, too, must lay aside your riches, your luxury, and effeminacy; nor must you bring the epitaphs made upon you, nor your glory, nor your genealogy, nor the dignity of your ancestors. . . . Even so much as the recollection of these things is enough to weigh the boat down.

*Crates.* If I must, I must. What is to be done?

*Her.* What do you do with armor, and what are these trophies for?

*Crates.* Because, Hermes, I am a conqueror, and have done noble deeds, therefore did the city reward me with these honors.

*Her.* Leave your trophies on earth ; here below we have always peace, and arms are of no use.  But who is this, in that grave and solemn habit, so proud and haughty, wrapt in meditation, with a long beard and contracted brow ?

*Men.* Some philosopher, I warrant you, some juggler, full of portents and prodigies.  Strip him, by all means: you will find something purely ridiculous under that cloak of his.

*Her.* First, then, off with that habit, and then everything else.  Oh, Zeus, what ignorance, impudence and vainglory, what a heap of ambiguous questions, knotty disputes, and perplexed thoughts, does he carry about him ! what a deal of fruitless diligence, solemn trifles and small talk !  Away with your riches, your pleasures, your anger, your luxury, your effeminacy, for I see it all, though you endeavor to conceal it,—your falsehood, pride, and high opinion which you have of yourself: should you come with all these, a five-oared bark would not be sufficient to carry you.

*Philosopher.* Your commands are obeyed.  I have parted with them all. . . .

*Men.* He has got something monstrous heavy yet under his arm.

*Her.* What is it, Menippus ?

*Men.* Flattery,—which, whilst he lived, was of no small service to him.

*Phil.* Do you, Menippus, lay aside your insolence, your flippant tongue, your mirth, your jests and ridicule : you are the only laugher amongst us.

*Her.* On no account, Menippus, part with them ; no, no: keep them by all means, they are light and easily carried ; besides, they may be useful in the voyage: but do you, Mr. Orator, lay aside those contradictions in terms, your antitheses, your labored periods, hyperboles, barbarisms, and all that weight of verbosity.

*Rhetorician.* There ; I have put them down.

*Her.* It is well.  Now cut your cable, let us weigh anchor and hoist our sails.  Charon, mind the helm : away, let us be merry.  What do you cry for, ye fools ?  Imprimis, you, Mr. Philosopher, without the beard there ?

*Phil.* Because, Mercury, I thought the soul had been immortal.

*Men.* He lies: he grieves for another reason.

*Her.* What ?

*Men.* Because he shall have no more grand suppers.

## EPICTETUS.

EPICTETUS, of Hierapolis in Phrygia, was eminent among
the Stoics of the first century of our era. He was originally
the slave of Epaphroditus, one of Nero's body-guard, but
having obtained his freedom, he applied himself with great
ardor to the study of philosophy. In the year 89 the Emperor
Domitian issued an edict banishing all philosophers, and Epictetus had then gained sufficient reputation as a teacher
of philosophy to be thus compelled to retire to Nicopolis, in
Epirus. Here he led an exemplary life, expounding the
Stoic philosophy, and putting in practice the precepts which
he taught. His doctrines are generally in accordance with those
of Christianity, and moralists of modern times often refer to
Epictetus as an authority. His great primary precept was,
"Bear and forbear;" destroy the corrupt affections; subdue
the will and make it subservient to conscience; we cannot rule
the world without, therefore let us bear the evils of life; we
are rulers of the world within, therefore let us refrain from
evil.

Epictetus wrote nothing himself, but his pupil Arrian wrote
down his master's lectures and published them in eight books,
of which only four survive. He also published the "Enchirid-
ion," or "Manual," which contains the substance of the Stoical
doctrines taught by Epictetus.

### THE VOYAGE OF LIFE.

As in a voyage, when the ship is at anchor, if you go on shore
to get water, you may amuse yourself with picking up a pretty
shell or a mussel, in your way, but your thoughts ought to be
bent towards the ship, and perpetually attentive, lest the
captain should call; and then you must leave all these things,
that you may not be thrown into the vessel, bound neck and
heels, like a sheep: thus likewise in life, if, instead of a mussel
or shell, such a thing as a wife or child be granted you,
there is no objection; but if the captain calls, run to the
ship, leave all these things, regard none of them. And if

you are old, never go far from the ship, lest, when you are called, you should be unable to come in time.

## CONTENTMENT.

As it is better to lie straitened for room upon a little couch in health than to toss upon a wide bed in sickness, so it is better to contract yourself within the compass of a small fortune and be happy, than to have a great one and be wretched.

## SUNSHINE.

As the sun does not wait for prayers and incantations to be prevailed on to rise, but immediately shines forth, and is received with universal salutation, so neither do you wait for applause, and shouts, and praises, in order to do good, but be a voluntary benefactor, and you will be beloved like the sun.

## THE TYRANT.

WHEN a person is possessed of some either real or imaginary superiority, unless he has been well instructed he will be puffed up with it. A tyrant, for instance, says, "I am supreme over all." But what can you do for *me*? Can you exempt my desires from disappointment? How should you? For do you never incur your own aversions? Are your own pursuits infallible? Whence should *you* come by that privilege? Pray, on shipboard, do you trust to yourself, or the pilot? In a chariot, to whom but to the driver? And to whom in all other arts? Just the same. In what, then, does your power consist?

"All men pay regard to me." So do I to my desk. I wash it, and wipe it, and drive a nail for the service of my oil-flask. "What, then! are these things to be valued beyond *me*?" No: but they are of some use to me, and therefore I pay regard to them. Do not I pay regard to an ass? Do I not wash his feet? Do I not clean him? Do not you know that every one pays regard to himself, and to you, just as he does to an ass? For who pays regard to you as a man? Show that. Who would wish to be like *you*? Who would desire to imitate *you*, as he would Socrates? "But I can take off your head." You say right. I had forgot that one has to pay regard to you as to a fever, or the colic, and that there should be an altar erected to you, as there is to the goddess Fever at Rome.

What is it, then, that disturbs and strikes terror into the multitude? The tyrant and his guards? By no means. What is by nature free cannot be disturbed or restrained by anything but itself. But its own principles disturb it. Thus, when the tyrant says to any one, "I will chain your leg," he who values his leg cries out for pity, while he who sets the whole value on his will and choice says, "If you imagine it for your interest, chain it." "What! do not you care?" No: I do not care. "I will show you that I am master." *You?* How should *you?* Zeus has set me free. What! do you think he would suffer his own son to be enslaved? You are master of my carcass. Take it.

## MARCUS AURELIUS.

Marcus Aurelius Antoninus stands almost alone in the history of the world as a philosopher and philanthropist clothed in royal purple. He was born A.D. 121, adopted by Antoninus Pius in 138, became consul in 140, and succeeded his adoptive father as emperor in 161. Although Lucius Verus, his brother by adoption, was debarred from the succession on account of his irregular habits, Marcus magnanimously shared the throne with him, thus furnishing for the first time the spectacle of two Roman emperors acting together. Although Marcus Aurelius was the most pacific of men, his reign was not free from war, due to the aggressions of the restless barbarian tribes north of the Danube. For eight years the emperor was absent from his capital, and underwent all the fatigue and hardships of military life with unflinching fortitude. Scarcely had he overcome his barbarian foes, when he was called to Asia Minor by a usurping

general. Before the emperor's arrival, however, the traitor
was slain. Here again Marcus Aurelius showed his magna-
nimity in his clemency towards all implicated in that conspiracy. On his return journey he visited Athens and proved
the inherent liberality of his thought by founding a profes-
sorship for each of the four principal philosophical sects.
The death of M. Aurelius, in the fifty-ninth year of his age
and the twentieth of his reign, marks the period of Rome's
transition from the Silver to the Iron age.

Although the early studies of M. Aurelius were chiefly
confined to rhetoric, he soon showed a decided predilection
for the philosophy of the Stoics, and read extensively in
morals, metaphysics, mathematics, music and poetry. Never
was a ruler more exemplary in his conduct, more just and
generous in his thoughts, or more universally esteemed and
beloved by his subjects. It seems a strange anomaly that he
should have been a persecutor of the Christians. John Stuart
Mill pronounces it one of the most tragical facts in all history; inasmuch as the emperor's writings do not perceptibly
differ from the ethical teachings of Christ. In his reign Justin
Martyr and Polycarp paid the penalty of their rejection of the
national worship; but their death and the persecutions which
followed did not stay the progress of Christianity. The work
by which Marcus Aurelius is known to his posterity is the
"Meditations," an abstract of the principles and maxims of
the Stoic philosophy, written in the author's leisure moments,
to console and uphold him in the hour of trial. It has been
called the mirror of a soul overflowing with love for humanity.
The suggestions in the "Meditations" are undoubtedly the
principles by which the author's whole life was guided. In
the first book he names his various teachers, and tells what
he has learned from each of them. He thanks the gods that
he had a good father, mother, and other kind relatives, and
that he never caused them uneasiness. He also gives thanks
for a wife loving, kind, and true; but history, unfortunately,
proves that Faustina was the very reverse, and critics are at
a loss whether to attribute his statements to gallantry or
blindness.

### THE VANITY OF MAN'S LIFE.

ART thou in love with men's praises, get thee into the
very soul of them, and see!—see what judges they be, even in
those matters which concern themselves. Wouldst thou have
their praises after death, bethink thee, that they who shall
come hereafter, and with whom thou wouldst survive by thy
great name, will be but as these, whom here thou hast found
so hard to live with. For of a truth, his soul who is aflutter
upon renown after death, presents not this aright to itself,
that of all whose memory he would have each one will likewise very quickly depart, and thereafter, again, he also who
shall receive that from him, until memory herself be put out,
as she journeys on by means of such as are themselves on the
wing but for a while, and are extinguished in their turn.—
Making so much of those thou wilt never see! It is as if
thou wouldst have had those who were before thee discourse
fair things concerning thee.

To him, indeed, whose wit hath been whetted by true doctrine, that well-worn sentence of Homer sufficeth, to guard
him against regret and fear—

> Like the race of leaves
> The race of man is:—The wind in autumn strews
> The earth with old leaves: then the spring the woods with
> new endows—

Leaves! little leaves!—thy children, thy flatterers, thine enemies! Leaves in the wind, those who would devote thee to
darkness, who scorn or miscall thee here, even as they also
whose great fame shall outlast them. For all these, and the
like of them, are born indeed in the spring season, and
soon a wind hath scattered them, and thereafter the wood
peopleth itself again with another generation of leaves. And
what is common to all of them is but the littleness of their
lives: and yet wouldst thou love and hate, as if these things
should continue forever. In a little while thine eyes also will
be closed, and he on whom thou perchance hast leaned thyself be himself a burden upon another.

TEMPLE OF WINGLESS VICTORY.

Bethink thee often of the swiftness with which the things that are, or are even now coming to be, are swept past thee: that the very substance of them is but the perpetual motion of water; that there is almost nothing which continueth: and that bottomless depth of time, so close at thy side. It is folly to be lifted up, or sorrowful, or anxious, by reason of things like these! Think of infinite matter, and thy portion—how tiny a particle of it! of infinite time, and thine own brief point there; of destiny, and the jot thou art in it; and yield thyself readily to the wheel of Clotho, to spin thee into what web she will.

As one casting a ball from his hand, the nature of things hath had its aim with every man, not as to the ending only, but the first beginning of his course, and passage thither. And hath the ball any profit of its rising, or loss as it descendeth again, or in its fall? or the bubble, as it groweth or breaketh on the air? or the flame of the lamp, from the beginning to the ending of its brief history?

All but at this present that future is, in which nature, who disposeth all things in order, will transform whatsoever thou now seest, fashioning from its substance somewhat else, and therefrom somewhat else in its turn, lest the world should grow old. We are such stuff as dreams are made of—disturbing dreams. Awake, then! and see thy dream as it is, in comparison with what erewhile it seemed to thee.

And for me, especially, it were well to mind those many mutations of empire in time past; therein peeping also upon the future, which must needs be of like species with what hath been, continuing ever within the rhythm and number of things which really are; so that in forty years one may note of man and his ways little less than in a thousand. Ah! from this higher place, let us look down upon the shipwrecks and the calm! Consider, for example, how the world went under the Emperor Vespasian. They are married and given in marriage, they breed children; love hath its way with them; they heap up riches for others or for themselves: they are murmuring at things as then they are; they are seeking for great place; crafty, flattering, suspicious, waiting upon the death of others—festivals, business, war, sickness, dissolu-

tion: and now their whole life is no longer anywhere at all.
Pass on to the reign of Trajan : all things continue the same :
and that life also is no longer anywhere at all. Ah! but look
again, and consider one after another, as it were the sepulchral
inscriptions of all peoples and times, according to one pattern
—What multitudes, after their utmost striving—a little afterwards !—were dissolved again into their dust.

Think again of life as it was far off in the old time; as it
must be when we shall be gone ; as it is now among the barbarians. How many have never heard your names and mine,
or will soon forget them ! How soon may those who shout
my name to-day begin to revile it, because glory, and the
memory of men, and all things beside, are but vanity—a sand-
heap under the senseless wind, the barking of dogs, the quarreling of children, weeping incontinently upon their laughter.

This hasteth to be ; that other to have been : of that which
is now coming into existence, even now somewhat hath been
extinguished. And wilt thou make thy treasure of any one
of those things? It were as if one set his love upon the
swallow, as it passeth out of sight through the air !

Bethink thee often, in all contentions public and private,
of those whom men have remembered by reason of their anger
and vehement spirit—those famous rages, and the occasions
of them—the great fortunes and misfortunes of men's strife
of old. What are they all now, and the dust of their battles?
Dust and ashes indeed ; a fable, a myth, or not so much as
that. Yes! keep those before thine eyes who took this or
that, the like of which happeneth to thee so hardly ; were so
querulous, so agitated. And where again are they? Wouldst
thou have it not otherwise with thee?

· Consider how quickly all things vanish away—their bodily
structure into the general substance of things ; the very memory of them into that great gulf and abysm of past thoughts.
Ah ! 'tis on a tiny space of earth thou art creeping through
life—a pigmy soul carrying a dead body to its grave. Consider
all this with thyself, and let nothing seem great to thee.

Let death put thee upon the consideration both of thy
body and thy soul—what an atom of all matter hath been
distributed to thee ; what a little particle of the universal

mind. Turn thy body about, and consider what thing it is, and that which old age, and lust, and the languor of disease can make of it. Or come to its substantial and casual qualities, its very type: contemplate that in itself, apart from the accidents of matter, and then measure also the span of time for which the nature of things, at the longest, will maintain that special type. Nay! in the very elements and first constituents of things corruption hath its part—so much dust, humor, stench, and scraps of bone! Consider that thy marbles are but the earth's callosities, thy gold and silver its fæces; this silken robe but a worm's bedding, and thy purple an unclean fish. Ah! and thy life's breath is not otherwise; as it passeth out of matters like these, into the like of them again.

For the one soul in things, taking matter like wax into its hands, moulds and remoulds—how hastily!—beast and plant and the babe, in turn: and that which dieth hath not slipped out of the order of nature, but, remaining therein, hath also its changes there, disparting into those elements of which nature herself, and thou too, art compacted. She changes without murmuring. The oaken chest falls to pieces with no more complaining than when the carpenter fitted it together. If one told thee certainly that on the morrow thou shouldst die, or at the farthest on the day after, it would be no great matter to thee to die on the day after to-morrow, rather than to-morrow. Strive to think it a thing no greater that thou wilt die—not to-morrow, but a year, or two years, or ten years from to-day.

I find that all things are now as they were in the days of our buried ancestors—all things sordid in their elements, trite by long usage, and yet ephemeral. How ridiculous, then, how like a countryman in town, is he, who wonders at aught! Doth the sameness, the repetition of the public shows, weary thee? Even so doth that likeness of events make the spectacle of the world a vapid one. And so must it be with thee to the end. For the wheel of the world hath ever the same motion, upward and downward, from generation to generation. When, when, shall time give place to eternity?

## CHAPTER XXV.

### THE BYZANTINE PERIOD.

CONSTANTINE, the first Christian emperor, removed the capital of the world-empire from Rome to Byzantium, henceforth to be called Constantinople. Though the court, with all its splendor and power, was thus transferred to a city where Greek was the vernacular, the change did not retard, it rather hastened, the decline of literature. The old Pagan mythology had been so closely interwoven with all Greek culture, and the mutual hostility of the two religions which had for over two centuries been struggling for mastery was so intense, that Christianity could triumph only by trampling on the noblest works of the Greek genius. Plato, in his "Republic," had condemned even Homer for immorality in his stories of the gods; still more must Christian teachers, so long as those gods were accepted as popular objects of worship, oppose the literature which gave them glory. The first preachers of the Gospel were chiefly rude and unlettered men, and appealed to the toiling multitude rather than to the learned. When Christianity, in spite of the opposition of the wise and noble, became dominant, these unlearned men were raised to places of honor, and used their influence to banish the venerable poets and sages from the schools and the minds of men. Meantime rude soldiers and politicians, utterly careless of religion, but ambitious of power, were easily brought to profess the **creed of** the sovereign. The gods of Olympus had already become objects of contempt to philosophers ; they were now rejected by the mass of the people. The literature, which had been permeated by their praises, entirely lost its attractiveness. Finally the Emperor Justinian prohibited the teaching of philosophy and closed the schools of Athens.

The Greek language, spoken in Constantinople, had lost its Attic purity. The crowds which thronged the streets of the capital were of various races, and their barbarism infected the speech of the court. Oriental superstitions were mingled with the doctrines of Christ as well as with the discourses of the sophists. Heresies sprang up in the Christian Church, and much of its energy was spent in doctrinal controversy. The great library of Alexandria and the schools which had been established in connection with it were closed at the end of the fourth century by the edict of Theodosius. The Emperor Julian received the infamous surname of the Apostate from his endeavor to restore Paganism and Greek philosophy to their former position of honor. The result was still more bitter antagonism between the old faith and the new. A similar renewal of strife occurred at Alexandria, and made Hypatia (in 415 A.D.) a martyr of philosophy.

Much of the literature of the Byzantine period was theological and controversial. This, however, does not belong to the domain of literature proper, any more than the Code of Laws which gives fame to the reign of Justinian. The chief occupation of the sophists in Constantinople was the cultivation of rhetoric, and its highest achievements were fulsome eulogies of princes and generals. In Asia Minor there sprang up a new department of literature, which was probably due to Eastern influence. Iamblichus, said to be a Syrian freedman, had published about 120 A.D. a love story called "Babylonian Adventures." After a considerable interval Heliodorus, who in his old age was a Christian bishop, related the loves of Theagenes and Chariclea in his "Æthiopica," and Longus wrote the more celebrated "Daphnis and Chloe," called also "The Lesbian Tale," which has been the model of many modern romances.

The most voluminous department of the Byzantine period was that of historians of various grades, yet altogether rather plodding annalists and chroniclers than true historians deserving to be separately distinguished. One may be named as being a lady of the imperial family, Anna Comnena (1083–1148). There were in Constantinople, as formerly in Alexandria, many grammarians, who, besides compiling grammars and dictionaries, wrote commentaries on the classics, and thus preserved extracts or fragments from the noblest writings of antiquity.

A few poems belong to this closing period of Greek literature. Nonnus, said to be an Egyptian, wrote in the early part of the fifth century an epic on the conquest of India by Bacchus. It is a rehearsal of all the stories of this favorite deity in the old mythology. Much more interesting is the narrative poem of "Hero and Leander," which is attributed to Musæus, a poet of the fourth or fifth century, but bearing a name associated with the very beginning of Greek literature. This graceful pathetic poem has in the original but three hundred and forty lines. It has been expanded in the English translation by the two Elizabethan poets, Marlowe and Chapman.

# GREEK ROMANCES.

THE exact origin of Greek romance is obscure. General consent ascribes it to the East, although there is a mingling of European ideas with Eastern imaginativeness, resulting in the romances as they are presented to us. The writers of this new development of Greek literature belonged to Asia Minor and its vicinity. Clearchus is credited to Cilicia, Iamblichus and Heliodorus to Syria, and Achilles Tatius to Alexandria. Among the sophists and later Greek writers there was a prevailing tendency to ascribe their own compositions to famous writers of the remote past. Speeches were invented for Xenophon, orations for Demosthenes or Solon, and debates were invented as having been held between Alexander the Great and his generals. Stories of former periods, far removed from the actual life of the time, began to be embellished and to merge into the fantastic and impossible. Finally Greek intelligence found an outlet in fanciful love-scenes, intrigues, adventures and incidents. But the delineation of character and manners is an outgrowth of later times, and was never, except incidentally, attempted or attained by the Greek romance writers. There is no necessity for the portrayal of human character till after the reader has begun to look with equanimity upon assaults of robbers, pirates and wild beasts, knowing well that there is a loophole of escape a little way ahead.

One of the earliest writers of the so-called Greek romances was Antonius Diogenes, whose work entitled, "The Wonders beyond Thule," was epitomized by Photius, patriarch of Constantinople, in the ninth century. Next in order comes Iamblichus, whose work, "Babylonica," in sixteen books, was written in the reign of Marcus Aurelius. The exact place of Xenophon of Ephesus in the list is not well ascertained. He is the author of the story of Antheia and Habrocomas. Very similar is the tale of Apollonius of Tyre.

By far the most important of the romances ascribed to this period, is the "Æthiopica" of Heliodorus, bishop of Tricca in Thessaly. The burden of the story is that "the course of true love never did run smooth." The hero is Theagenes, a Thessalian of noble birth, and the heroine Chariclea is a priestess of Diana at Delphi, who fall in love at first sight, and in due time elope together. They pass into the hands of pirates and robber chiefs, whom Chariclea's beauty always inspires with a desperate love. No sooner are they delivered from one danger than they fall into another. At last they are carried captive by a band of Ethiopians, and are about to be sacrificed, one to the sun and the other to the moon, when a mark on Chariclea's arm reveals her as the princess of the country to which they have been carried, and all ends happily in her marriage to Theagenes. Heliodorus excels in descriptive power. His descriptions of the bull-fight, the wrestling match, the Delphic procession, and the haunts of the pirates, are especially celebrated.

Next to Heliodorus in point of time comes Achilles Tatius of Alexandria, the author of "Leucippe and Cleitophon." But far more celebrated is the pastoral love story of Daphnis and Chloe by Longus, a charmingly told, yet artificial tale, the scene of which is laid near Mitylene in the island of Lesbos. It is evidently the source of the pastoral romance which spread from Italy over Western Europe.

### THE SACRIFICE AT DELPHI.

In the "Æthiopica" of Heliodorus, otherwise known as the romance of "Theagenes and Chariclea" Calasiris, a priest, tells how the lovers first met at a sacrifice in honor of Neoptolemus (Pyrrhus), the son of Achilles. This sacrifice was offered at Delphi by an embassy of Ænianians every fourth year at the time of the Pythian games. Neoptolemus was said to have been slain by Orestes, the son of Agamemnon at the altar of Apollo at Delphi. The leader of the embassy on this occasion claimed descent from Achilles.

The young leader of the embassy entered with an air and aspect truly worthy of Achilles. His neck straight and erect, his hair thrown back off his forehead; his nose and open nostrils giving signs of an impetuous temper; his eyes of a deep blue, inclining to black, imparting an animated but amiable look to his countenance, like the sea smoothing itself from a storm into a calm.

After he had received and returned our salutations, he said it was time to proceed to the sacrifice, that there might be sufficient space for the ceremonies which were to be performed to the Manes of the hero, and for the procession which was to follow them. "I am ready," replied Charicles, and rising, said to me, "if you have not yet seen Chariclea, you will see her to-day; for, as a priestess of Diana, she will be present at these rites and the procession."

But I had often seen the young woman before; I had sacrificed and conversed with her upon sacred subjects. However, I said nothing of it; and, waiting for what might happen, we went together to the temple. The Thessalians had prepared everything ready for the sacrifice. We approached the altar; the youth began the sacred rites; the priest having uttered a prayer, and from her shrine the Pythoness pronounced this oracle:

> Delphians, regard with reverential care,
> Both him the goddess-born, and her the fair;
> "*Grace*" [charis] is the sound which ushers in her name,
> The syllable wherewith it ends is "*Fame.*" [klea.]
> They both my fane shall leave, and oceans past,
> In regions torrid shall arrive at last;
> There shall the gods reward their pious vows,
> And snowy chaplets bind their dusky brows.

When those who surrounded the shrine heard this oracle, they were perplexed, and doubted what it should signify. Each interpreted it differently, as his inclinations and understanding led him: none, however, laid hold of its true meaning. Oracles indeed, and dreams are generally to be explained only by the event. And besides, the Delphians, struck with the preparations which were making for the procession, hastened to behold it, neglecting or deferring any farther scrutiny into the oracular response.

The procession began with a hecatomb of victims, led by some of the inferior ministers of the temple, rough-looking men, in white and girt-up garments. Their right hand and breasts were naked, and they bore a two-edged axe. The oxen were black, with moderately arched and brawny necks—their horns equal, and very little bent; some were gilt, others adorned with flowers—their legs bent inwards—and their deep dewlaps flowing down to their knees—their number, in accordance with the name, exactly a hundred. A variety of other different victims came afterwards, each species separate and in order, attended with pipes and flutes, sending forth a strain prelusive of the sacrifice. These were followed by a troop of fair and long-waisted Thessalian maidens, with disheveled locks—they were distributed into two companies; the first division bore baskets full of fruits and flowers; the second, vases of conserves and spices, which filled the air with fragrance: they carried these on their heads; thus, their hands being at liberty, they joined them together, so that they could move along and lead the dance. The key-note to the melody was sounded by the next division, who were to sing the whole of the hymn appointed for this festival, which contained the praises of Thetis, of Peleus, and their son Achilles, and of his son Neoptolemus.

The dance which accompanied this song was so well adapted to it, and the cadence of their steps agreed so exactly with the melody of the strain, that for a while, in spite of the magnificence of the spectacle, the sense of seeing was overpowered and suspended by that of hearing; and all who were present, attracted by the sounds, followed the advancing dancers. At length a band of youths on horseback, with their splendidly dressed commander, coming upon them, afforded a spectacle far preferable to any sounds. Their number was exactly fifty; they divided themselves into five-and-twenty on each side guarding their leader, chief of the sacred embassy, who rode in the midst: their buskins, laced with a purple thong, were tied above their ankles; their white garments, bordered with blue, were fastened by a golden clasp over their breasts. Their horses were Thessalian, and by their spirit gave token of the open plains they came from; they seemed to champ with disdain the foaming bit, yet obeyed the regulating hand of their riders, who appeared to vie with each other in the splendor of their frontlets and other trappings, which glittered with gold and silver.

But all these, splendid as they were, were utterly overlooked, and seemed to vanish, like other objects before a flash of lightning, at the appearance of their leader, my dear Theagenes, so gallant a show did he make. He too was on horseback, and in armor, with an ashen spear in his hand; his head was uncovered; he wore a purple robe, on which was worked in gold the story of the Centaurs and the Lapithæ; the clasp of it was of electrum, and represented Pallas with the Gorgon's head on her shield. A light breath of wind added to the grace of his appearance; it played upon his hair, dispersed it on his neck, and divided it from his forehead, throwing back the extremities of his cloak in easy folds on the back and sides of his horse. You would say, too, that the horse himself was conscious both of his own beauty and of the beauty of his rider; so stately did he arch his neck and carry his head, with ears erect and fiery eyes, proudly bearing a master who was proud to be thus borne. He moved along under a loose rein, balancing himself equally on each side, and, touching the ground with the extremity of his hoofs, tempered his pace into almost an insensible motion.

Every one, astonished at the appearance of this young man, joined in confessing that beauty and strength were never before so gracefully mingled. The women in the streets, unable to disguise their feelings, flung handfuls of fruit and flowers over him, in token of their admiration and affection: in short, there was but one opinion concerning him—that it was impossible for mortal form to excel that of Theagenes. But now, when "rosy-figured morn appeared," as Homer says, and the beautiful and accomplished Chariclea proceeded from the temple of Diana, we then perceived that even Theagenes might be outshone; but only so far as female beauty is naturally more engaging and alluring than that of men. She was borne in a chariot drawn by two white oxen—she was dressed in a purple robe embroidered with gold, which flowed down to her feet—she had a girdle round her waist, on which the artist had exerted all his skill : it represented two serpents, whose tails were interlaced behind her shoulders; their necks knotted beneath her bosom; and their heads, disentangled from the knot, hung down on either side as an appendage : so well were they imitated, that you would say they really glided onward. Their aspect was not at all terrible; their eyes swam in a kind of languid lustre, as if being lulled to sleep by the charms of the maiden's breast. They were wrought in darkened gold, tinged with blue, the better to represent, by this mixture of dark and yellow, the roughness and glancing color of the scales. Such was the maiden's girdle. Her hair was not entirely tied up, nor quite disheveled, but the greater part of it flowed down her neck, and wantoned on her shoulders—a crown of laurel confined the bright and ruddy locks which adorned her forehead, and prevented the wind from disturbing them too roughly—she bore a gilded bow in her left hand; her quiver hung at her right shoulder—in her other hand she had a lighted torch; yet the lustre of her eyes paled the brightness of the torch.

After the procession had thrice compassed the sepulchre of Neoptolemus, and both men and women had raised over it their appropriate shout and cry; on a signal being given, the oxen, the sheep, the goats, were slaughtered at once, as if the sacrifice had been performed by a single hand. Heaps of wood were piled on an immense altar; and the victims being placed thereon, the priest of Apollo was desired to light the pile, and begin the libation.

"It belongs, indeed, to me," said Charicles, "to make the libation; but let the chief of the sacred embassy receive the torch from the hands of Diana's priestess, and light the pile; for such has always been our custom." Having said this, he performed his part of the ceremony, and Theagenes received the torch from Chariclea. From what now happened we may infer that there is in the soul something divine, and allied to a superior nature; for their first glance at each other was such, as if each of their souls acknowledged its partner, and hastened to mingle with one which was worthy of it.

They stood awhile, as if astonished; she slowly offering and he slowly receiving the torch; and fixing their eyes on one another, for some space, they seemed **rather to** have been formerly acquainted, than to have now met for the first time, and to be returning gradually into each other's memory. Then softly, and almost imperceptibly smiling, which the eyes, rather than the lips, betrayed, they both blushed, as if ashamed of what they had done, and again turned pale, the passion reaching their hearts. In short, a thousand shades of feeling wandered·in a few moments over their countenances; their complexion and looks betraying in various ways the movements of their souls.

These emotions escaped the observation of the crowd, whose attention was engaged on other things. They escaped Charicles too, who was employed in reciting the solemn prayers and invocations, but they did not escape me, for I had particularly observed these young people from the time that the oracle was given to Theagenes in the temple; I had formed conjectures as to the future from the allusion to their names, though I could not entirely comprehend the latter part of the prediction.

At length Theagenes slowly and unwillingly turning from the maiden, lighted the pile, and the solemn ceremony ended. The Thessalians betook themselves to an entertainment, and the rest of the people dispersed to their own habitations. Chariclea putting on a white robe, retired with a few of her companions to her apartment, which was within the precincts of the temple; for she did not live with her supposed father, but dwelt apart for the better performance of the temple services.

## DAPHNIS AND CHLOE.

THIS pastoral of Longus is the first prolonged description of the rise and growth of the passion of love in the literature of the world. Though in parts a picture of ideal innocence, it is in other parts offensive on moral grounds. Both Daphnis and Chloe were of noble birth, but had been exposed in their infancy. After being nursed by beasts, they were brought up by shepherds as their foster-parents.

It was the beginning of spring, the flowers were in bloom throughout the woods, the meadows, and the mountains; there were the buzzings of the bee, the warblings of the songsters, the frolics of the lambs. The young of the flock were skipping on the mountains, the bees flew humming through the meadows, and the songs of the birds resounded through the bushes. Seeing all things pervaded with such universal joy, Daphnis and Chloe, young and susceptible as they were, imitated whatever they saw or heard. Hearing the carol of the birds, they sang; seeing the sportive skipping of the lambs, they danced; and in imitation of the bees they gathered flowers. Some they placed in their bosoms, and others they wove into chaplets and carried them as offerings to the Nymphs.

They tended their flocks in company, and all their occupations were in common. Daphnis frequently collected the sheep which had strayed, and Chloe drove back from a precipice the goats which were too venturesome. Sometimes one would take the entire management both of goats and sheep, while the other was intent upon some amusement.

Their sports were of a pastoral and childish kind. Chloe sometimes neglected her flock and went in search of stalks of asphodel, with which she wove traps for locusts; while Daphnis devoted himself to playing till nightfall upon his pipe, which he had formed by cutting slender reeds, perforating the intervals between the joints, and compacting them together with soft wax. Sometimes they shared their milk and wine, and made a common meal upon the provision which they had brought from home; and sooner might you see one part of the flock divided from the other than Daphnis separate from Chloe.

While thus engaged in their amusements, Love contrived an interruption of a serious nature. A she-wolf from the neighborhood had often carried off lambs from other shepherds' flocks, as she required a plentiful supply of food for her whelps. Upon this the villagers assembled by night and dug pits in the earth, six feet wide and twenty-four feet deep. The greater part of the loose earth, dug out of these pits, they carried to a distance and scattered about, spreading the remainder over some long dry sticks, laid over the mouth of the pits, so as to resemble the natural surface of the ground. The sticks were weaker than straws, so that if even a hare ran over them they would break, and prove that instead of substance there was but a show of solid earth. The villagers dug many of these pits in the mountains and in the plains, but they did not succeed in capturing the wolf, which discovered the contrivance of the snare. They, however, caused the destruction of many of their own goats and sheep, and very nearly, as we shall see, that of Daphnis.

Two angry he-goats engaged in fight. The contest waxed more and more violent, until one of them, having his horn broken, ran away bellowing with pain. The victor followed in hot and close pursuit. Daphnis, vexed to see that his goat's horn was broken, and that the conqueror persevered in his vengeance, seized his club and crook, and pursued the pursuer. In consequence of the former hurrying on in wrath, and the latter flying in trepidation, neither of them observed what lay in their path, and both fell into a pit, the goat first, Daphnis afterwards. This was the means of preserving his life, the goat serving as a support in his descent. Poor Daphnis remained at the bottom lamenting his sad mishap with tears, and anxiously hoping that some one might draw near and pull him out. Chloe, who had observed the accident, hastened to the spot, and finding that he was still alive, summoned a cowherd from an adjacent field to come to his assistance. He obeyed the call, but on seeking for a rope long enough to draw Daphnis out, no rope was to be found ; upon which Chloe, undoing her head-band, gave it to the cowherd to let down ; they then placed themselves at the brink of the pit and held one end, while Daphnis grasped the other with both hands, and so got out.

They then extricated the unhappy goat, who had both his horns broken by the fall, and thus suffered a just punishment for his revenge towards his defeated fellow-combatant. They gave him to the herdsman as a reward for his assistance, and if the family at home inquired after him, were prepared to say that he had been destroyed by a wolf. After this they returned to see whether their flocks were safe, and finding both goats and sheep feeding quietly and orderly, they sat down on the trunk of a tree, and began to examine whether Daphnis had received any wound. No hurt or blood was to be seen, but his hair and all the rest of his person were covered with mud and dirt. Daphnis thought it would be best to wash himself before Lamon and Myrtale [his foster-parents] should find out what had happened to him; proceeding with Chloe to the grotto of the Nymphs, he gave her his tunic and scrip in charge.

He then approached the fountain and washed his hair and his whole person. His hair was long and black, and his body sun-burnt; one might have imagined that its hue was derived from the overshadowing of his locks. Chloe thought him beautiful, and because she had never done so before, attributed his beauty to the effects of the bath. The following day, upon returning to the accustomed pasture, Daphnis sat as usual under an oak, playing upon his pipe and surveying his goats,, lying down and apparently listening to his strains. Chloe, on her part, sitting near him, looked at her sheep, but more frequently turned her eyes upon Daphnis; again he appeared to her beautiful as he was playing upon his pipe, and she attributed his beauty to the melody; so that taking the pipe she played upon it, in order, if possible, to appear beautiful herself. As she returned home she mentally admired him, and this admiration was the beginning of love. She knew not the meaning of her feelings, young as she was, and brought up in the country, and never having heard from any one so much as the name of love. She felt an oppression at her heart, she could not restrain her eyes from gazing upon him, nor her mouth from often pronouncing his name. She took no food, she lay awake at night, she neglected her flock, she laughed and wept by turns; now she would doze, then suddenly start up; at one moment her face became pale, in another moment it burnt with blushes. Such irritation is not felt even by the breeze-stung heifer. Upon one occasion, when alone, she thus reasoned with herself: "I am no doubt ill, but what my malady is I know not; I am in pain, and yet I have no wound; I feel grief, and yet I have lost none of my flock; I burn, and yet am sitting in the shade: how often have brambles torn my skin, without my shedding a single tear! how often have the bees stung me, yet I could still enjoy my meals! Whatever it is which now wounds my heart must be sharper than either of these. Daphnis is beautiful, so are the flowers; his pipe breathes sweetly, so does the nightingale; yet I take no account either of birds or flowers. Would that I could become a pipe, that he might play upon me! or a goat, that I might pasture under his care! O cruel fountain, thou madest Daphnis alone beautiful; my bathing has been all in vain! Dear Nymphs, ye see me perishing, yet neither do ye endeavor to save the maiden brought up among you! Who will crown you with flowers when I am gone? Who will take care of my poor lambs? Who will attend to my chirping locust, which I caught with so much trouble, that its song might lull me to rest in the grotto; but now I am sleepless, because of Daphnis, and my locust chirps in vain!"

Such were the feelings, and such the words of Chloe, while as yet ignorant of the name of love.

[Dorco, the cowherd who had rescued Daphnis, then tried to win the maiden's affections and brought her gifts. At first he gave some also to Daphnis, but afterwards neglected him. However, the two youths had an argument on their respective share of beauty and made Chloe umpire, who was to bestow on the victor a kiss. This prize she gave to Daphnis—"an artless, unsophisticated kiss."]

Daphnis, as though he had been stung instead of kissed, suddenly became grave, felt a shivering all over, and could not control the beating of his heart. He wished to gaze upon Chloe, but at the first glance his face was suffused with blushes. For the first time he admired her hair, because it was auburn; and her eyes, because they were brilliant; her countenance, because it was fairer than milk. One might have supposed he had just received the faculty of sight. . . .

Such were the sensations of Daphnis. He now first felt the power, and now first uttered the language of love.

## LIBANIUS.

THE writings of Libanius of Antioch have been characterized by Gibbon as the "idle compositions of an orator who cultivated the science of words." Yet he was the chief rhetorician of the fourth century. He pursued his studies first

III—22

at Athens, and soon gathered about him a large number of pupils. On removing to Constantinople his talents excited the jealousy of rivals, and he was obliged to retire to his native city, where he spent the remainder of his life. In his "Funeral Oration upon the Emperor Julian" he states that when he was lecturing at Nicomedia, Julian, although prohibited from being a pupil, secured by bribes the daily lectures. Evidently the Pagan emperor admired Libanius, and imitated his style. Both Basil and Chrysostom were his pupils, and maintained friendly relations with their former teacher in the heat of religious conflicts. Canon Farrar has composed an imaginary conversation between Chrysostom and Libanius, which indicates the attitude of cultured heathenism towards the Christian Church.

### Eulogy of the Emperor Julian.

Thus the prince, both when present and when coming, was alike victorious: and these things he achieved just starting up from amidst his books; or rather, in marching against the adversary, he marched with his books, for he had always in his hands either books or arms, believing that war was wonderfully assisted by philosophy, and that a prince competent to give counsel threw more weight into the scale than a fighting one. For example, the two following things were assuredly of the greatest advantage to the public, and display a certain ingenuity of invention—his augmenting the zeal of the brave by the rewards that he obtained for them from him who awarded things of that sort; and his making those that plundered the possessions of the enemy masters of all that they should seize: for this very thing was clearly of a piece with the order, that whoever brought in the head of an enemy should receive a piece of gold for his bravery.

His reputation spreading at once over the world, every soldier loved the man that was a lover of action; men of letters loved him also; and of those residing at Athens, such as were conscious of their merit, flocked to him, as of old the philosophers to Lydia, to the court of Crœsus. But Crœsus exhibited to Solon his treasures of money, because he possessed nothing more precious than those—whereas Julian unlocked to the comers the treasures of his soul, wherein lay the gifts of the Muses: the prince also composed verses with which to compliment his visitors; and even now you may meet with and read the same. Thus, then, did he hold revels with the servants of Hermes and of Zeus: but when the season gave the signal, he forthwith marched out, and over-turning everything in the neighborhood of the Rhine, he so terrified the natives that they begged leave to change their residence and become a part of the Roman dominion, thinking it more desirable to live under him than in their own country: they asked for lands and they received some: and he employed barbarians against barbarians, deeming it a much finer thing to pursue with such means, than to fly in company with his own side. So much indeed was achieved without fighting: but having determined to cross the river, a second time, and in the absence of boats having obliged his horse and foot to swim the river, he advanced, laying waste and taking booty, for there was no one to hinder him: late at last did the unhappy natives sue for mercy, just before the fire touched.

But he, thinking that the day had now come which should heal all the wounds of the Gauls, at first dismissed the suppliants with contempt; but when they returned again, bringing their chiefs in person as suppliants, and they who bore the sceptre humbled themselves to the ground, then, reminding them of their long-continued insolence and their innumerable offences, he bade them purchase peace by healing the mischief they had done, by rebuilding towns, and bringing back people. They promised, and did not fail: timber and iron were brought in for the rebuilding of the houses; and every one of the captives was set at liberty, and caressed by the man that just before flogged him, in order that they should bear no malice: whilst they had to give proof of the death of all whom they, did not restore amongst those they had carried off; and the truth, in such cases, was judged of by the released captives. From the ten thousand soldiers of Xenophon, verily the first sight of the sea, after such a multitude of mountains crossed and toils endured, drew forth a shout and tears mingled with joy; and they embraced one another, the partners in so many dangers: but these men did the same, not when they saw the sea, but when they saw each other; some of them beholding relatives escaped out of slavery; the latter recovering again family and home: and all wept with them who, though not sharing in the relationship, yet beheld their embracings; and tears flowed, far sweeter than the former tears; some of which were shed for those long separated from home, some for those now once more united. Thus, on that occasion, did the war both tear asunder and bring together the natives of Gaul; the first part being brought about by the cowardice of the leaders, the second part by their bravery.

Now the town halls were filled, and population and trades, and revenues of money grew apace, and the betrothals of daughters, and marriages of young men, and journeys from home, and feasts and solemn assemblies, resumed their former order; so that were one to style this prince the founder of those cities, he would not be far wrong. For some towns he gathered together again after they were dispersed, to others that were all but emptied he restored the inhabitants; and the fact of no one's fearing his neighbor inspired fear into others. No longer therefore on the approach of winter did any of the barbarians sail out on their accustomed piratical expeditions; but they stayed at home, and fed on their own things, not so much truly out of respect for treaties as out of fear of war; since even those that had not obtained a truce, the terror hanging over them warned to keep quiet. That greatest of all islands under the sun, and which the ocean encompasses [Britain], he also inspected in his tour. He sent to Constantius the accounts of the expenditure, which by name was military, but in reality was the perquisite of the governors; and those who committed fraud he compelled to be honest.

## CHAPTER XXVI.

### GREEK ARCHITECTURE.

Altars for the worship of deities are usually among the first structures raised by early people, and the Greeks proved no exception to this general rule. We have seen that they took no particular interest in the exteriors of their homes. Ordinarily the houses were crowded closely together along narrow and irregular streets. Upon public buildings, then, all the more care was expended, and to the gods who gave victory, who watched over cities and protected them from danger, the most splendid edifices were raised.

Accustomed as we are to think of churches in connection with religious matters, and other public buildings in connection with secular matters, it is not easy at once to grasp the attitude of the Greek toward his temples. Within the temple was preserved the image which symbolized the deity—the god who was thought to have watched over the city in the beginning, to have bestowed every blessing enjoyed by its inhabitants, and to have granted prosperity. In honoring such a being, therefore, the Greek was in a measure doing honor to his city. All that was best in his native land—its progress in peace, its success in war, he recognized when he worshipped the mighty gods. With feelings akin to those aroused in people today when they behold their native flag, the symbol of all that is best in their country, the ancient Greek looked upon his temples.

The earliest Greek temple was probably an altar, raised in the open air—a huge stone, or a pile of stones. Upon this the father of the family or the chieftain of a tribe offered sacrifices. Then a tiny cell was erected to contain the image of the deity. It may have been built of wood, or stone, according to the locality. A third change was to build the cell of sun-dried brick, placed upon a stone foundation. Trunks of trees strengthened the wall, it may be, and helped to support the wooden roof.    Finally stone or marble came to be used throughout.

In building material, Greece was particularly fortunate. Good building stone was plentiful, and especially was there an abundance of the white marble so extensively used in classic Greece.   A soft brown limestone was the material from which many structures were made, and sun-dried brick, covered with a coat of stucco, sufficed for private dwellings.   Although colored marbles were easily procurable in Hellas, it was left for the Romans to show their possibilities in producing pleasing effects.

We have spoken of four general stages of temple-building in Greece, but it must not be supposed that precisely this course took place throughout the land, nor is it to be thought that one kind of temple suddenly was displaced by another. Rather, these four general forms can be traced among archaeological remains, and in certain localities may have developed as outlined.

The simplest temple consisted of two parts: the cella, and the porch, or vestibule.   In the cella, or interior room, the statue of the deity was kept.   The porch, or vestibule, was merely formed by extending the side walls of the cella, and placing two or four pillars across the front.   An outer colonnade, or row of pillars, frequently surrounded the whole. Sometimes small chambers were built at both ends of the cella, for the purpose of storing vessels used in the sacrifice and vestments worn by priests.

Greek architecture is sometimes classified as Doric, Ionic and Corinthian, according to the style of the column employed. The Doric is really the only pure Grecian style, for the Ionic grew up in Asia Minor and bears distinct traces of oriental influence.   The Corinthian was never extensively used in Greece, but gained greater favor at Rome.   To be sure, while the Ionic was introduced from Asia Minor, it became very popular, as plenty of ruined temples in Greece today testify.

Of all these styles, simplest was the Doric, which is to be recognized by its massive columns and plain capital.   It has been surmised that the fluting of the columns was done originally in imitation of the bark of trees, whose trunks were the earliest pillars. Again, it has been suggested that the plain, narrow capital stood in memory of the days when plain metallic bands were fastened around the tops of the wooden pillars to make them more secure. In course of time, the origin of the pillar was lost sight of, and has only been surmised by modern investigators.

After 600 B. C. Doric temples were built in Greece. Two splendid specimens adorned the acropolis at Athens: the Parthenon and the Theseion; after this style was the great temple built to Zeus at Olympia. Many lesser temples have been found throughout Greece.

The Parthenon deserves special mention. It replaced an earlier temple sacred to Athena, destroyed by the Persians when they invaded Attica. The new temple was larger than the old, measuring 228 feet long by 101 feet wide, and its height was 65 feet. Eight pillars extended across the ends, and seventeen ran along the sides. In the main portion stood the great statue of Athena, the masterpiece of Phidias. This temple was regarded by the Athenians as one of their most beautiful structures, and in its ruins today excites the wonder of those who journey far to see it.

In 330 A. D., Constantine converted it into a Christian church, and it remained quite complete until 1687, when the Venetians bombarded Athens. The Turks had stored their powder within it, and a bomb from a Venetian ship burst the magazine. Although shattered by the explosion, the sculptures remained in part, and in 1803 Lord Elgin removed them to England, where they are preserved in the British Museum.

The Ionic columns are always to be recognized by their capitals, which take the form of a scroll. They were lighter in appearance, and were in fact more slender, and of greater height than the Doric. Temples of this style were built after 480 B. C., perhaps earlier. Two of these, the Erechtheon and Athena Nike—Wingless Victory—were also built on the Athenian acropolis.

As has already been noted, the Corinthian style was not greatly employed in Greece. Its capital was beautiful, being carved in fruit and floral designs.

Greek architecture, which so impressed him who viewed

it in antiquity, or yet today, after nature and man have done
their worst, impresses the traveller, was especially suited to its
surroundings.

"In the construction of modern cities and of great buildings little influence of the natural features of the surrounding
landscape is to be observed. In this nature has receded and
man is predominant. The same thing is in a great degree true
of the vast palaces and temples of Babylon and Egypt, built
in great plains and making, as it were, a world independent
of them. But in Greece and Asia Minor nature is more
prominent and insistent; the whole country is made up of
rugged mountains divided by narrow valleys and little plains.
The works of man occupy but a small space in any Greek
landscape. And the Greek himself, with wonderfully keen
senses and profound appreciation of his surroundings, would
be instinctively, if not consciously, averse from introducing
into the landscape what would be out of harmony with its
lines. Among Swiss mountains today one may notice the
same clear adaptation of building to surroundings; the chalet
almost seems a natural feature of the view. Any one who has
visited a partially preserved Greek temple amid its natural
surroundings, the temple at Phigaleia, those of Paestum, that
of Segesta, will realize how fatal it would be to remove these
buildings into a landscape of a different kind. To local
influences are largely due the smallness of Greek temples, the
rigid lines of their construction, their close dependence upon
stone and marble as materials." [1]

We have dwelt upon the temple because it was the masterpiece of Greek architecture. Other buildings of merit the
Greeks certainly possessed—theatres, stadiums, baths, gymnasiums, and others, for purely administrative purposes, but
the temple represented the acme of structural genius, and
hence is most satisfying to the student.

"In the case of no other people has the bond between
religion and art been so direct and so intimate as among the
ancient Greeks; indeed, we may say that art was the language
by which the Greeks expressed their ideas of their gods, and
by reflecting upon these tangible forms of the directing forces

[1] Gardiner: Grammar of Greek Art, 29.

in human affairs, they developed a still more clear and definite type of character for each of the divinities. So integral a part of the daily life of the Hellenes was their belief in the gods and heroes that their artistic activity not only found its initial impetus in worship, but gods and cults remained throughout historic times the most considerable force in Hellenic art. The unit of Greek sculpture may fittingly be called the image of the godhead. Of all the causes that lead to the supremacy of the Greeks in the plastic art none was so potent, so far-reaching, as was religion; the gods were definite, objective creatures, and the fixed and tangible forms that attached to the Olympians were expressed in stone and bronze. The artists had a great deal to do with rendering the gods comprehensible; Pheidias should have no less credit than the poets in bringing Athena and Zeus within the range of the popular understanding. Herein lay opportunity for idealism which not only distinguished Hellenic art when dealing with the immortals, but which left its impress upon the whole history of their plastic art. At whatever point we take up the history of the Greek gods and heroes from the seventh century B. C., we are confronted by art representations that place the divinities immediately before us; the Greek gods were every-day forces among men, whether in the agora or on the battlefield.

"We have to remember that no priesthood dictated to the Greeks the forms that they should follow in their worship, or controlled the expression of their religious enthusiasm; every Hellene was free to believe as he chose, and to express his belief in whatsoever manner he wished. Such perfect freedom in religious matters was new with the Greeks; the blight that marked Egyptian and Assyrian worship had passed away, and in Greece, the free, untrammelled child of nature moved under a clear sky and read fresh messages direct from Heaven to himself." [2]

[2]Huddilston: Lesson from Greek Pottery, 19.

## CHAPTER XXVII.

### GREEK SCULPTURE.

Our sources for the study of Greek sculpture, as well as Greek architecture and painting, are to be found (1) in the remains in Greece, or preserved in public and private collections; and (2) in literary records. Of these two sources, the first is naturally more important. Comment upon their art by the ancients is not very complete or satisfactory. In his Natural History, Pliny gave some account of Greek art, and Pausanias, writing in the second century after Christ, told of monuments which existed in his day. Again, reference to Greek art may be found in several of the Latin writers—Lucian, Quintilian, and Cicero.

In general we may say that Greek sculpture was closely bound up in the religion of the people. Some one has said that it was the language for interpreting the poetry of mythology. Certain it is that the development of religion and art in Greece went hand in hand.

Before the dawn of Greek art, curiously shaped stones were frequently held as fetishes, or objects of worship, because it was thought they had fallen from heaven, or were in some way connected with the mighty ones whose presences were already felt. Then the people began to shape rude figures, and these they decked with garments and garlands. Still later, images of divinity were made, these being humanized as much as skill allowed. This spirit continued, touched by the idealism of greater sculptors, who conceived of deities as human beings perfected. Every blemish was removed, and the ideals of the artists took shape in marble.

Temples were built for the now life-size or colossal statues of gods and goddesses. These temples themselves were adorned by carvings upon pediments and friezes.

To the images of their gods, votives were offered. In early times these votives were little human figures, both male and female. Or, again, they might be tripods, sacred animals, or vases. Later, such offerings were still made to the deities, although the spirit which prompted such action had probably undergone some change. Now in gratitude for particular blessings Hellenes presented votives to the favorite god. For example, an athlete presented a statue to the god who had given him victory at the Olympian games—this votive frequently being some athletic figure.

While the great majority of Greek sculptures had some connection with the national religion, many pertained to secular subjects. Busts of public men and benefactors adorned the agora; some sculptures, although probably in later periods, may have been produced for ornamental purposes pure and simple; and tombs were carved and decorated by the sculptor.

Before taking up the various periods into which Greek sculpture easily falls, let us see what materials lay at the hand of the Hellenic sculptor.

Wood was used in primitive times, and later formed the framework for colossal figures, these being covered with layers of gold and ivory. Limestone was used for friezes, but marble, plentiful throughout Hellas, was most widely used for all purposes. Bronze, although more costly, seems to have been known in remote times, and continued in favor. Gold and ivory, because of their great value, must have been the materials from which only rare statues were made. Such statues were generally preserved in the temples. Such was the nature of Phidias' Athena, in the Parthenon, and Zeus, at Olympia. Ivory was used for the flesh, and gold for drapery and other parts.

The Greeks did not leave their statues white and cold, as we do today. They loved bright colors and used to color the capitals of their pillars and other portions of architectural structures. The bodies of their marble figures were ordinarily rubbed with oil and melted wax. The eyes, eye-brows, hair and lips were painted to make them appear natural, and often the drapery was also painted. Gilt was always in favor and might be the color of the garments worn by a deity. Of course, most of the figures of later times were nude, although certain of the divinities were always draped. The notion of painting statuary seems strange to us today, accustomed as we are to the dazzling marble, but it did not seem strange to the Greek, nor do statues still remaining in the land of Greece today seem as curious as they might if transplanted to other climes.

Mycenaean art extended from 2000-1000 B. C. Very few specimens of sculpture remain from this remote age; notably among them is the Lion Gate at Mycenae. Several tombs of similar age show carvings indicative of the same degree of progress.

1000-460 B. C. is known as the archaic period. Mycenaean art had declined and been replaced by work of the Hellenes, crude indeed in the beginning, yet showing a steady advance with advancing civilization. Sculptures of this age which survive are various in subject—human figures, images of deities, votives. They are all crude and conventional. The arms are unnatural and rigid, while the feet and limbs are frequently not distinguishable from the drapery. Before the close of the long period we find marked progress, but a severe dignity and lack of grace characterize sculpture throughout.

460-400 B. C. witnessed the great and glorious age of Hellenic art. The explanation for its wonderful flower is to be found in the history of the people. In many respects the Persian invasion was a momentous event in Greece. Without such a danger, coming at a time when the Hellenes were ready, it is not apparent that the Greeks would have come so soon into possession of their faculties. In the first place, states previously disunited and isolated were forced to unite before impending disaster. To be sure, when the war was over, they tended to fall apart again, but they had learned the great lesson that was not forgotten. Then the triumph of a young nation over one long established brought an elation that created a great literature, and gave impetus to the arts of peace. Greece fairly thrilled with hope and ambition, and a new era in art was as natural as was this unexpected progress in all other fields of human activity. Especially was Athens fortunate in that the buildings upon the acropolis had been burned by the invaders and now must be replaced, in thanksgiving to Athena, who had protected her own. The name of Phidias is closely associated with this period of Greek sculpture and with the Parthenon, the noblest monument now erected upon the citadel of Athens; yet Phidias was not popular in his own time, and died in prison.

The Parthenon was begun shortly after the Persian war, and ere long Phidias was brought by Pericles from Elis, where he was at work upon sculptures which were to beautify the grove sacred to the Olympian Zeus. It has generally been accepted that much of the carving upon the pediments of this great temple to Athena was the work of this artist's own hand.

The pediments of a temple are the triangular portions upon either end, above the columns and under the roof. It was customary to have scenes carved upon them pertaining to the deity in whose honor the temple stood; while the frieze which encircled the temple might depict scenes in the history of the town, or country. On the Parthenon, the eastern pediment represented the birth of Athena, as she sprang forth in full armor from the head of Zeus, or power. The western pediment pictured the contest between Athena and Poseidon on that memorable occasion when both wished to name the city. These figures were probably for the most part the work of Phidias, and were wonderful indeed. Wonderful they still are, such as remain, among the Elgin Marbles in the British Museum. The more important figures were destroyed in the explosion of 1687.

The genius of this great sculptor was remarkable indeed, so superior were his results to anything before produced— unmatched perhaps by anything since accomplished. "He seems to have torn the veil from Olympus and revealed to us the gods in all their grandeur. His Zeus exercised a lasting influence upon the ancient world, as did also his Athene Parthenos. The majesty, dignity, and elevated beauty of his conceptions gave to his work an ideal, poetic character, even in the few instances in which he dealt with purely athletic subjects."[1]

The frieze, also Phidias' work, or at least done under his immediate supervision, was quite as successful as the pediments. Four feet in width, and five hundred and twenty-three

---

[1] Hist. of Sculpture: Marquand & Frothingham. 100.

feet in length, it told the story of a Panathenaic procession— the occasion of much elaborate preparation in Athens.

"The Panathenaic procession here represented begins on the western end of the temple, and with its various elements— horsemen, chariots, musicians, and participants in the sacri- fices—proceeds along the northern and southern sides, until at the eastern end is represented the head of the procession, the waiting magistrates, the priest and priestess of Athene in the presence of the gods. On each side the frieze presents a com- position complete within itself, composed of minor unities and forming a part of the greater whole. Through it all there is a flow of movement, resembling the crescendo and diminuendo in music, terminating with a final chord." [2]

Other artists there certainly were during this age, but the name of Phidias towers over them all.

The fourth century, or 400-300 B. C., witnessed first the sustained ascendency of Grecian art, and latterly, its decline. Among the brilliant coterie of artists conspicuous during this age, the name of Praxiteles is perhaps first. He has been called the sculptor of rest. One of the great finds of recent times was the Hermes of Praxiteles. Pausanias had described "a Hermes of marble, carrying the child Dionysus, the work of Praxiteles," and when, a few years ago, Germans who were excavating at Olympia came upon this statue, it was quickly identified. Although not the finest work of the artist, it is the one which has been thus preserved and must form the basis of all modern study of this gifted sculptor.

After the passing of this century, art fell into a decline. With the spread of Hellenism, it spread into other lands and became one thing in Rome, another in Asia, and so on. No subsequent period in the development of the world has been so remarkable so far as sculpture is concerned. The Greek statues remain, and probably must remain, the model of all ages, the most perfect examples of human effort, and the eternal fount of inspiration for others whose gifts lead them into this form of expression.

[2]Hist. of Sculpture: Marquand & Frothingham, 101.

## Greek Painting.

When we come to Greek painting, we re approaching a subject which is very difficult to consider, for all the masterpieces of ancient Greece have perished. We have the writings of the ancients—Pliny, Pausanias, and others, but these are not always accurate and never complete in their treatment of any portion of the theme. We have also vase paintings, mural paintings as preserved in Pompeii, and a few painted coffins. However, the vase paintings were done for the most part by inferior artists—at least this was the case with most that survive; the mural paintings of Pompeii are of much later date and are about as useful for the study of ancient Greece painting as Graeco-Roman statuary would be for the study of Hellenic masterpieces in marble. In spite of all these difficulties, certain facts concerning painting have been ascertained and many surmises have been offered to problems whose satisfactory solutions we can never hope to reach.

The styles of Greek painting have been classified as (1) wall painting; (2) easel painting; (3) encaustic painting; (4) votive tablets; (5) architectural and sculpture painting. Little is definitely known of any of these various styles. Wall painting is believed to date as far back as the Mycenaean period, although nothing of a remote age survives. It is supposed that a ground work of wet stucco was prepared and colours, not unlike our water-colours, were laid on with a brush. Easel painting, on the other hand, was done on a dry surface. Wood was the favorite ground, canvas being seldom used. Here again the same colours were used. Since there was no way to make these paintings durable, they must have perished early. No varnish, or any finish for the purpose of durability, seems to have been known.

The encaustic work corresponded in a measure to our oil painting, colours being mixed with melted wax and put on with a brush or bronze pencil. The work was difficult, could be but slowly accomplished, and was confined without doubt to small pieces.

A series of votive tablets was discovered at Corinth in 1879, on the site of a temple once erected to Poseidon. Upon these were pictures, figures in black and purple upon a ground of creamy-white. Few of these tablets have been found so far.

Some large terra-cotta coffins were recovered near the Gulf of Smyrna; they are believed to belong to the sixth century before Christ. Upon them scenes of battles, funerals and chariot races are depicted. These are in fact the oldest evidences of painting yet discovered, although it is well known that the art was in progress much earlier.

For many years in Greece painting meant simply an outline drawing and filling it in with colours. No gradations of tints were used, and light and shadow effects were unthought of. Perspective was not understood, and altogether, aside from light cast upon social conditions, the paintings have no greater value for the general student. Painting developed more slowly than sculpture, and the Greeks were always so devoted to form that centuries passed before it was freed from conceptions which, to be sure, gave sculpture impetus but retarded the sister art.

Polygnotos, whose work fell in the years 470-430 B. C., did more than anyone else to place painting on a fair basis, it having previously been more a trade than an art. For his service in this respect he has sometimes been called the "inventor of painting" by the Hellenes. At a later time Apelles was famous for his productions, and it is particularly stated of him by ancient writers that he had a model in painting his picture of Aphrodite. Had the custom been usual, it would not have been mentioned.

Corinth was the center of this art, as was Athens for sculpture. Many vases have been found around this great commercial city of antiquity, and rich finds probably await the explorer.

## PHIDIAS TO PERICLES.

So the old crew are at their work again,
Spitting their venom-froth of calumny,
And Menon's is the voice that now gives cry,—
A poor weak tool for those who lurk behind,
His in the dark to prick him to their work;
For who so blind as not to recognize
The hand of Cleon, the coarse demagogue,
Who rails at all to gain a place himself;
And scurrilous Hermippus, and the rest
Of that mean pack we know so well of old?


You, Pericles, and I, do what we will,
Are guilty, both of us, of an offense
That envious natures never can forgive—
The great crime of success.  If we were low
They would not heed us; but the praise of men
Lavished on us in Athens, right or wrong,
Rouses their anger.  They must pull us down.
What can we hope for better than the fate
Of Anaxagoras, Miltiades,
Themistocles, or any, in a word,
Of those who in our Athens here have stood
In lofty places?  It was crime enough
For Aristides to be called "The Just."

And yet some consolation lies in this:
'Tis at the tallest poppies that men strike;
'Tis at fruit-bearing trees that they throw stones.


Because we will not strike our hands in theirs,
Drink with them, haunt with them the market-place,
Use their low practices to court the rich,
Hint falsehoods, that we dare not frankly say,
Flatter and fawn for favors, sneer at all—
Even those we publicly profess our friends—

We are aristocrats forsooth; we lift
Our heads too high, we are too proud; a thing
Which is a shame for one in Athens born.
We should be hand and glove with everyone.
Well! let us own we are too proud, at least,
To court low company; too proud to rise
By any step that treads a brother down;
Too proud to stoop to defamating arts;
Too proud to sneer, to crawl, to cringe, to lie!
And if in Athens we select our friends,
Is this forbidden to a freeman here?
So, not content with throwing stones at you
My noble Pericles, they cast at me
Their evil scandals.   'Twas impiety
Because I wrought your figure and mine own
Upon Athena's shield; then, worse than this,
Our fair Aspasia they aspersed, and slurred
My honor and your own as well as hers.


There stands Athena, she whom Menon says
I did not make, being helped by better men,
Whose fame I thus defraud of their just rights
By claiming it as mine.   What can one say
To such a paltry charge of petty fraud?
I scorn to answer it; nay, even they
Who make it know 'tis false as 'tis absurd.


Speak! my Athena; answer thou for me!
She will not speak, yet her silence speaks
More eloquent than any words of mine.
Look, Pericles! how calm and how unmoved
She stands and gazes at us; a half scorn
On those still lips at these poor jealousies,
These foolish bickerings and strifes of men.
"What mean you, that you make this wicked noise"
(She seems to say), "you creatures of an hour?

Why do you wrangle thus your life away
With your sharp lies and envious vanities,
Buzzing and stinging a brief moment's space
In Time's thin stretch across the Infinite,
Whose awful silences shall engulf you all?
Swift evanescent flashes through the dark
Across the untroubled patience of the night,
And the still, far, unalterable stars.
Ye boasters! what is all your vaunted work
That with such pride ye build, save that the gods
Smile on you and assist you? 'Tis not yours,
If any good be in it. Bend your hearts
Before the Powers august. Strive not to rob
Your fellow-mortals of the gift the gods
Bestow upon him. Humbly do the work
That is appointed, and in confidence
Await the end, secure of Nemesis."

—*W. W. Story.*

VICTORY OF SAMOTHRACE.

## CHAPTER XXVIII.

### THE OLYMPIAN GAMES.

In recent years there has been a great effort put forth to revive the old games of the Greeks, held in antiquity every four years at Olympia. Athletes from many countries have competed for honors and in many lands lovers of athletic sports have taken a deep interest in the contests. The student of ancient Greek history cannot fail to find a certain satisfaction in the movement.

Elis has great fascination for us because of its importance to the ancient Greek. The ravages of time and man have done their worst in eliminating traces of the life which was once the pride of the Hellenes. Until 1874 nothing of importance was recovered on the banks of the Alpheus. At that time the German government negotiated a treaty with Greece by which permission was given German scholars to open operations there. Within six years a comparatively large extent, 650 by 575 feet, was laid bare of refuse and river deposits to a depth of anywhere from 16-23 feet. This prodigious effort involved a cost of over $200,000, but it gave to the world 130 marble statues, 13,000 bronze objects, besides many inscriptions. These recoveries, while of inestimable value to students of ancient Greece, were but a fragment of the splendour that once made Olympia dear to the hearts of men. Pliny estimated 3,000 marble statues alone as adorning the place in his time. For centuries after the decline of Greece the sacred grove stood practically unhurt. An earthquake threw down the temple of Zeus, and subsequent shocks laid low other ancient monuments. The early Christians, with misdirected zeal, destroyed several of the temples, but the greatest injury of all was done by the Alpheus river.

A glance at the map will show the course of this stream. During high water one spring, the bed of the river was changed. Turning out of its channel, it covered the sacred grove with debris and earth, covering some monuments and breaking down others. After so many calamities, then, we are fortunate to possess the Hermes of Praxiteles and these other statues, even though they are in partial ruins.

No subject could be more suitable for the conclusion of our study of ancient Hellenic life than the Olympian games, to which reference has frequently been made in this and the preceding volume.

Four great national festivals tended to bind the Greeks together: the Olympia, held every four years at Olympia, in Elis, in honor of Zeus; the Pythia, held in honor of Apollo once in four years at Delphi; the Nemea, every two years at Nemea, in honor of Zeus; and the Isthmia, held at Corinth every other year in honor of Poseidon. Of first importance were the Olympian celebrations, in which every Greek state took part. A sacred truce was declared while this festival lasted and those who molested travellers journeying to and fro were severely punished.

Several months before the festival heralds went through Greece, announcing it in all the leading cities. All pure born Greek youths were eligible to enter various athletic contests. For months before the time they were practising for the running, jumping, wrestling contests,—for honor awaited the victors.

At length, when the time drew near, people started in companies from all over the country. Travelling in mountainous Greece was slow work, and since there were no inns at Olympia, it was necessary to carry along whatever was deemed essential to one's comfort. Outside the sacred grove, the country suddenly took on the aspect of a fair; merchants brought thither their goods, for this opportunity to reach large numbers of people was not to be missed. Artists displayed their work, and many attractions centered here during the festival.

We think always of the games in connection with the Olympia, but attention was given first to the sacrifices. After these came contests, particularly of an athletic nature. They lasted several days, and musical contests were sometimes held. However, music was a more essential part of the Pythian festival, since Apollo was god of music. Writers read portions of their productions before the audiences gathered here, and Gorgias, for example, delivered one of his orations. Chariot races, although not a part of the earlier celebrations, found a place as increased wealth enabled men to make a display of fine horses.

Poets were not lacking to commemorate the victories. It is to be remembered that for a series of years Pindar was a desirable attendant upon these occasions, since he had the gift of happily turning the story of a victory into a graceful poem. Wreaths of olive and bay leaves rewarded the winner in the contests, but this was not all. He who won did honor to his native town. Upon his return a general thanksgiving was made. Henceforth he was entitled to a front seat at the theatre, and in other ways he was treated as a hero. The praise of his fellowmen was very dear to the ancient Greek, and he desired most of all to excel in some particular that he might receive it.

A great stadium provided seats for witnessing the games, and we know that these were constantly filled. The stadium has been located, but has not been wholly excavated up to the present time.

After several days spent in this way, wandering through the grove when the games were over, seeing the finest art of Greece—for only the best was admitted to the grove of the gods—it is small wonder that the Hellene started homeward with new ambitions, new hope in his soul. It is not strange that he grew to think of the Greeks as the cultured people, developing what was best, and to classify all the rest as barbarians. It is indisputable that these national festivals served as a strong bond between the states and in many ways worked for the good of Hellas.

And here we must leave the Hellene of antiquity. And where could we better leave him than at his beloved Olympia?

## HELEN AT THE LOOM

Helen, in her silent room,
Weaves upon the upright loom,
Weaves a mantle rich and dark,
Purpled over deep.  But mark
How she scatters o'er the wool
Woven shapes, till it is full
Of men that struggle close, complex;
Horses clipped, with wrinkled necks
Arching high; spear, shield, and all
The panoply that doth recall
Mighty war, such war as e'en
For Helen's sake is waged, I ween.
Purple is the groundwork; good!
All the field is stained with blood,
Blood poured out for Helen's sake;
(Thread, run on; and, shuttle, shake!)
But the shapes of men that pass
Are as ghosts within a glass,
Woven with whiteness of the swan,
Pale, sad memories, gleaming wan
From the garment's purple fold
Where Troy's tale is twined and told.
Well may Helen, as with tender
Touch of rosy fingers slender
She doth knit the story in
Of Troy's sorrow and her sin,
Feel sharp filaments of pain
Reeled off with the well-spun skein,
And faint blood-stains on her hands
From the shifting sanguine strands.
Gently, sweetly she doth sorrow:
What has been must be tomorrow;
Meekly to her fate she bows.
Heavenly beauties still will rouse
Strife and savagery in men:
Shall the lucid heavens, then,
Lose their high serenity,
Sorrowing over what must be?
If she taketh to her shame,
Lo, they give her not the blame,—

Priam's wisest counsellors,
Aged men, not loving wars;
When she goes forth, clad in white,—
Day-cloud touched with first moonlight,—
With her fair hair, amber-hued
As vapor by the moon imbued
With burning brown, that round her clings,
See, she sudden silence brings
On the gloomy whisperers
Who would make the wrong all hers.

So, Helen, in thy silent room,
Labor at the storied loom;
(Thread, run on; and, shuttle, shake!)
Let thy tender sorrow make
Something strangely beautiful
Of this fabric, since the wool
Comes so tinted from the Fates,
Dyed with loves, hopes, fears, and hates.
Thou shalt work with subtle force
All thy deep shade of remorse
In the texture of the weft,
That no stain on thee be left;—
Ay, sweet queen, shalt fashion grief,
Grief and wrong, to sweet relief.

There are people on the earth
Doomed with doom of their great worth.
Look on Helen not with hate,
Therefore, but compassionate.
If she suffer not too much,
Seldom does she feel the touch
Of that fresh, auroral joy
Lesser spirits may decoy
To their slight and sunny lives.
Heavy honey 'tis she hives.
To her sweet though saddening soul
All that here she doth control—
What of bitter memories,
What of coming fate's surmise,
Paris' passion, distant din
Of the war now drifting in
To her quiet—idle seems;

Natural as lazy gleams
Of some stilly water's reach,
Seen from where broad vine-leaves pleach
A heavy arch, and, looking through,
Far away the doubtful blue
Glimmers, on a drowsy day,
Crowded with the sun's rich gray,
As she stands within her room,
Weaving, weaving at the loom.

—*G. P. Lathrop.*

A SACRIFICE.

(From a vase-painting by Polygnotus.)

# MODERN GREECE

## CHAPTER XXIX.

The majority of travelers approach Greece from Piræus, Athen's harbor; yet lovers of Homer like best to wander first among the Ionian Islands, two of which will be remembered as long as literature is read. From Italy it is possible to sail to Corfu, largest of the group, the *Corcyra* of the ancients. Few spots in the world are more beautiful than Corfu. Its mild and even climate enables flowers to blossom throughout the year; the air is always balmy, the skies blue. Great forests of olive trees, left unpruned, tower to a surprising height and contrast strikingly with the cypress.

The Ionian Islands have passed through many periods of change. Settled first in 734 B. C., Corcyra, it will be remembered, was originally a colony of Corinth. The Corcyreans took an unenviable part in the Peloponnesus War, and later, like the rest of Greece, fell to the share of Rome. During the Middle Ages Venice held these islands; after short intervals of Neapolitan rule and Turkish assault they were transferred to France, only to be given to England after the defeat of Napoleon. The benefits of English occupation from 1814 to 1863 may be seen today in the splendid roads that traverse the islands. Finally, when King George was called to the throne, the people of the seven largest Ionian Isles petitioned England so earnestly to be united with the kingdom that the English government voluntarily relinquished them.

Corfu is the Phæacia of the Odyssey. It will be remembered that upon the shores of Phæacia Odysseus was ship-wrecked. Athena, who was befriending the wearied traveler, buffeted about by fickle fortune for ten years after the fall of Troy, inspired Nausicaä, daughter of the king, to take her maidens down by the seashore to wash the royal linen. While it dried in the bright sunshine, the maidens had a game of ball.

362

Palatine probably comes from a word meaning pasture, and is clearly connected with Pales, god of pastures. This name commemorated the early occupation of the people. They were herders, who drove their cattle off to the northeastern part of the later city during the day and brought them back for safe keeping within the Palatine walls at night. Many of the oldest legends center around the Palatine. Beneath it, by the river, was the Lupercal, the cave whence issued the wolf who cared for the abandoned children. At the top of a flight of stairs leading down to the foot of the hill was the house of Romulus, the first king, according to tradition.

The history of the Roman state and its religion are inseparably interwoven. The family, not the individual, was the unit of the Roman state. Three gods were important in every household: Janus, god of the door, or the doorkeeper; Vesta, goddess of the hearth; Penates, god of the store-closet. These divinities who presided over each hut, presided as well over the collection of huts, or the village; and to the Palatine, Janus and Vesta gave their protection. We shall see that when settlements upon nearby hills united with the hamlet the Palatine, the hearth of Vesta and the temple of Janus had to be moved down into the valley, in the center of the new city.

Capitoline was another hill to be early peopled. This is smallest of the seven. Until the time of Trajan it was not wholly isolated, being connected with a spur to the Quirinal. This ridge was excavated to make room for Trajan's forum.

The Aventine is largest and highest of the Roman hills. The others, Quirinal, Viminal, Caelian and Esquiline, are but outlying spurs of a high tableland that reaches off to the east. In course of time all these heights were settled, and the various tribes occupying them found it of mutual benefit to affiliate rather than make war upon one another. Thus, all the hills were included within the city wall; paths leading from one place to another grew into highways, then into streets. The intervening valleys gradually were appropriated for meeting places, markets, sites for national festivals and games. This came about slowly, and we do not know by just what stages it was accomplished. Rome, like other ancient cities, originated in obscurity, and many stages of progress had been passed before authentic records begin.

Even Homeric maidens seem to have been unequal to this game, for soon the ball missed its course and fell into the "deep eddy," whereupon they screamed and awakened Odysseus, who wondered among what creatures fate had now thrown him. Having lost his apparel in the wreck and being covered with brine, he seemed a loathsome object and none but Nausicaä had courage to remain. She bade her maidens toss him clothing and heard his tale of suffering with sympathy, bidding him seek the king, her father.

"Near our road you will see a stately grove of poplar trees, belonging to Athens; in it a fountain flows, and round it is a meadow. That is my father's park, his fruitful vineyard, as far from the town as one can call. Easily it is known; a child, though young, could show the way; for the Phæacians do not build their houses like the dwelling of Alcinous, their prince. But when his house and court receives you, pass quickly through the hall until you find my mother. She sits in the firelight by the hearth, spinning sea-purple yarn, a marvel to behold, and resting against a pillar. Her handmaids sit behind her. Here, too, my father's seat rests on the selfsame pillar, and here he sits and sips his wine like an immortal."

Then the poet describes the locality and especially the palace of the king:

"Without the court and close beside its gate is a large garden, covering four acres; around it runs a hedge on either side. Here grow tall thrifty trees—pears, pomegranates, apples with shining fruit, sweet figs and thrifty olives. On them fruit never fails; it is not gone in winter or in summer, but lasts throughout the year; for constantly the west wind's breath brings some to bud and mellows others. Pear ripens upon pear, apple upon apple, cluster on cluster, fig on fig. Here, too, the teeming vineyard has been planted, one part of which, the drying place, lying level on the ground, is heating in the sun; elsewhere men gather grapes; and elsewhere they tread them. In front the grapes are green and shed their flowers, but a second row are now just turning dark. And here trim garden-beds, along the outer line, spring up in every kind and all the year are gay. Near by, two fountains rise, one scattering its streams throughout the garden, one bounding another course beneath the court-yard gate toward the house; from this the townfolk draw their water. Such at the palace of Alcinous were the gods' splendid gifts."

If one is traveling merely to see beautiful cities and stately mansions, Greece were better omitted from his route. The great centers of Europe and America have more to offer from this standpoint. Travel in countries of venerable age and historical association is enjoyable only to those familiar with their past, or at least people thus informed will derive the greatest pleasure, and it is unnecessary for anyone possessing leisure to wander through lands unversed in the main outlines of their historical development. The Odyssey is as fascinating as any story—more fascinating than most stories, since it has delighted people for three thousand years. Well has Lanson said: "Men do not love Homer because he is three thousand years old, but he is three thousand years old because men have loved and admired him."

King George has a garden in Corfu today which might be described somewhat as Homer described the park surrounding the ancient king's palace.

In modern times, the Empress Elizabeth built a palace on the island of Corfu, whither she might retreat as opportunity offered from pressing cares of state. Built upon a summit, it commands an imposing view of the sea. In keeping with ancient associations, the palace was surrounded by a peristyle of marble pillars, at the base of each resting an ancient statue. On the terrace were planted twenty-five thousand roses, which owing to the happy conditions of climate, bloom all the year. A park beyond was beautified with palms from Africa, tropical shrubs and native trees. A tiny temple, erected as a memorial to Heine, her favorite poet, gave added charm. The Empress is said to have expended $16,000,000 in making her retreat, but in recent years it was purchased by the German Emperor for only $200,000. Since his ownership, garages and barracks have been added, detracting from the earlier atmosphere of the charming island home.

Of the Phæacians, Homer said: "Swift are their ships as wing or thought." Swifter ships than theirs have been built since the days of Homer, but still are the men of Corfu sailors, and their boats carry wine and oil to lands far away.

Even better remembered is the second island to which some travelers repair—Ithaca, known wherever the story of Odysseus has been told.

"Now in the land of Ithaca there is a certain harbor sacred to Phorcys, the old man of the sea. Here two projecting jagged cliffs slope inward toward the harbor and break the heavy waves raised by wild winds without. Inside, without a cable ride the well-benched ships when once they reach the roadstead. Just at the harbor's head a leafy olive stands, and near it a pleasant darksome cave sacred to nymphs, called Naiada." And when Odysseus questions Athene, disguised as a shepherd: "And tell me truly this, that I may know full well, what land is this? What people? What sort of men dwell here? Is it a far-seen island, or a tongue of fertile mainland that stretched out to sea?" The goddess returns: "You are simple, stranger, or come from far away, to ask about this land. It is not quite so nameless. Many men know it well, men dwelling toward the east and rising sun, and those behind us also toward the darksome west. It is a rugged land, not fit for driving horses, yet not so very poor though lacking plains. Grain grows abundantly and wine as well; the showers are frequent and the dews refreshing; there is good pasturage for goats and cattle; trees of all kinds are here, and never-failing springs. So, stranger, the name of Ithaca has gone as far as Troy, which is, they say, a long way from Achæa."[1]

Thanks to fifty years of English occupation, there is to-day a carriage road on the island; it is rocky, with abrupt peaks and, except to the lover of Homer, has small attractions. The island is seventeen miles long and four miles at its greatest width.

In 1878 Schliemann attempted some work of excavation on this island; subsequently other attempts have been made, none of them very satisfactory. Coins have been found with the head of Ulysses stamped upon them; outlines of walls which were raised in antiquity have been revealed; the evidences of an old fortress may be seen. Ithaca was hardly the land to bring rich rewards to the modern digger; its inhabitants were sturdy sailors, brave soldiers and not lacking in

---

[1] Citations from Palmer's Translation.

valour; but the very conditions of the place. inaccessible and remote from such centers as the age afforded, were conducive to the simplicity of life which the Odyssey portrays.

"But why go to Ithaca? It has no temples, no great churches, no paintings, no monuments of architecture, no sculptures, no ruins, and no history of more than local interest. The fame of Ithaca was not made by sword, trowel, chisel, or brush; it was made wholly by the pen. Literature, as well as art and religion, has its shrines, and every country with a literature has them. So Ithaca is a shrine, a monument of literature; and it has this peculiar interest, that its fame lies wholly and absolutely in this direction. The Odyssey was built with Ithaca as one of its foundation stones; but now it is Ithaca that rests on the Odyssey, which Lowell has said is the one long story that will bear continuous reading."[2]

Although Corinth lies some distance from Ithaca, it nevertheless suggests the sea. A canal has been constructed across the Isthmus of Corinth, making a veritable island of the Peloponnesus. Corinth should ever attract Americans because of the splendid excavations which have been carried on there by the American School of Classical Studies. This was founded in 1882 by scholars of various American universities who appreciated the great opportunities Greece affords for classical students, who had seen the results of the French School in Athens and themselves desired to have a part in the laudable undertaking of uncovering the past. Such universities as desired to have access to the Greek field contributed $250 per annum to defray the expenses. In 1887 the matter of erecting a permanent home in Athens for the American School was agitated. Cities made contributions. people of substance who loved Greek antiques came forward; not alone was money subscribed, but an architect planned the structure, manufacturers of doors and sashes, windows, plumbing fixtures, lumber and other utilities offered whatever was required, a steamship lessened the freight, and as a result a fire-proof building worth thirty thousand dollars was erected in Athens.

[2] Barrows: Isles and Shrines of Greece.

Unlike the French School, the American receives no assistance from the government, but periodical appeals for funds have enabled scholars in charge of the field work to accomplish creditable results in the one locality where they have attempted anything extensive.

It will be recalled that Corinth was rich in ancient art. Her position gave commercial prestige and her citizens became famed for their wealth. In 146 B. C. Rome destroyed the city; it was refounded by Cæsar and quickly became the leading commercial center of Greece. This was the Corinth of St. Paul, and his reproaches upon its frivolous life may still be read. During the Middle Ages the town amounted to little. Nevertheless a village continued upon the site of the former metropolis, being destroyed in 1858 by an earthquake.

Modern Corinth has been built up since that date. A little to the side of the earlier settlement, it is now a town of about 5000. The completion of the canal in 1893 has given considerable shipping advantage. About four miles long, seventy-five feet wide and twenty-six feet deep, until recently the canal had been used only by Greek coasting vessels and small craft, but in 1907 a new company gained possession of it and it is purposed to have it made adequate for large vessels.

More interesting to many is the old town—the site of the recent excavations. Begun in 1896, the old theater was located and partially revealed; the Turkish war prevented a continuance of activities in 1897 but the year following the agora was uncovered; two fountains, one of them the famous Pirene, were alone worth the effort expended. Corinth was formerly mentioned as the City of Pirene. Some statuary was recovered, the lifesize head of Ariadne being particularly worthy of mention. Of no small interest was the discovery of a lintel stone bearing the Greek inscription "Synagogue of the Hebrews," probably the church of St. Paul.

The Greek government has from the start manifested the deepest interest in the labor of archæologists throughout the kingdom and, appreciating the pricelessness of the articles laid bare by the spade of the excavator, has erected a museum in Corinth for their preservation.

Olympia attracts only those travelers who are interested in ancient Greece. Neither in antiquity nor in modern times has there been a town there. The number of visitors in recent years has necessitated the building of a hotel for their accommodation and one may come thither by rail from Athens or Patras.

The Greeks regarded physical exercise and symmetrical development as necessary as mental development. The gods themselves were believed to encourage athletic sports and to delight in competitive games. In the sacred precinct set aside for the celebration of the Olympic Games, observed every four years, a beautiful temple was erected to the greatest of all deities, Zeus; within it stood Phidias' wonderful statue. For a thousand years these games were enjoyed by all free-born men and youths. Those of foreign birth were not allowed, either as participants or spectators. After the discontinuance of these feats in the fourth century after Christ, nature and man conspired to ruin this once splendid spot. Earthquakes threw down the temples and other buildings; barbarians destroyed and plundered. A Christian village was built here and the fragments of temples of incomparable beauty were used as material for huts. The river abandoned its earlier course and covered the entire district with débris to a depth of fifteen or twenty feet.

In 1874 the German Archæological Institute at Athens was founded. While an early attempt had been made by Germans to explore Olympia, the gigantic task of removing the deposit of sand caused the plan to be abandoned. However, from 1875 to 1881 the new German School, under the leadership of Dörpfeld gave itself to the task of excavation upon this site and the work was crowned with success. Although time and tide had done their worst, yet the general plan of the early buildings was revealed. The pediments of the temple of Zeus had been shattered by a fall of forty feet but still the priceless sculptures remained in fragments. The stadium was unearthed; greatest of the finds was probably the Hermes of Praxiteles, the finest specimen of manly beauty left us by the ancients.

A Greek banker by the name of Syngros, inspired by patriotism and reverence for the past, built a museum at Olympia to store the sixteen thousand bronzes and sculptures recovered by the archæologists. It was copied in part after the model of the temple of Zeus.

Through the efforts of Baron de Coubertin of France and Professor Sloane of Princeton the old Olympic games were recently revived. It was felt that the first celebration could be held only in Greece. There being no adequate facilities for the accommodation of a large number of guests at Olympia, and furthermore, the magnitude of the task of preparing a stadium suitable for the occasion caused the decision to be made in favor of Athens, where in 1896 the first modern series of contests were held. On April sixth, following Easter, the King of Greece opened the games in the presence of visitors from all countries, while nine-tenths of the 60,000 people thus assembled were themselves Greeks. Their enthusiasm knew no bounds when a Greek peasant won the Marathon. Subsequently every four years the Olympic games have been held, once in America and last in England. The prevailing spirit is to keep these contests wholly free from a professional atmosphere and to revive the Greek attitude toward physical ease and dexterity. Only the sacred olive and medals are awarded as prizes, thus removing any possibility for a commercial spirit to creep in.

One could hardly take leave of the Peloponnesus without a glance at Sparta, which, during a considerable portion of its history, was the most influential state in Greece. Probably none view the region without recalling the words of Thucydides to the effect that if Sparta should be destroyed, it would be difficult for future generations to credit its former greatness, so meager were its buildings during the period of its power. The boast of the Spartan, that the walls of Sparta were her citizens, is inadequate to the extent that no mention is thus made of her mountains, without which it is doubtful if she could have felt so secure. The present town of Sparta is entirely modern. It numbers about 5,000 people, who till the soil for the most part, although there are a few silk spinning factories of recent date.

Not many travelers go to Sparta, for there are few if any ruins of antiquity to be found there. The site of the old temple is now a cornfield; the agora, a mulberry grove. Even the so-called Tomb of Leonidas is not generally accepted as his, although to be sure his bravery is commended by it. The words of Pericles, spoken upon the occasion of the memorial service held in memory of soldiers who fell during the first year of the Peloponnesian war apply as well to him: "For the whole earth is the sepulcher of famous men; not only are they commemorated by columns and inscriptions in their own country, but in foreign lands there dwells also an unwritten memorial of them, graven not on stone but in the hearts of men."

Until chosen as capital of the new kingdom in 1834, Athens was but a poor straggling village of some three hundred homes. The city which greets the stranger today has grown up since that time and numbers about 150,000 people. Its white glittering buildings contrast strikingly with the green of the olive trees. The modern city has been laid out with regularity, the principal streets being broad and spacious. The fashionable rendezvous is the public square, Place de la Constitution, with the king's palace overlooking one side, the others surrounded by the leading hotels and cafes. The street chiefly occupied by shops is appropriately named for Hermes, god of commerce.

Winter finds the Greek capital filled with Europeans, who flock thither because of the mild climate; in summer, on the other hand, visitors congregate from Turkey, Egypt and other southern regions. Like their illustrious ancestors, the modern Greeks live much in the open air, restaurants providing tables under the trees in pleasant weather. Holidays are numerous and widely observed. Life is not strenuous and all aspire to get as much pleasure out of it as possible.

Like their forefathers, modern Greeks value education. No country can today show a larger proportion of its population in school and university. Four departments are maintained at the University of Athens; arts and science, medicine, theology and, as might be expected, law, which department is always well attended. More than two thousand students are registered there yearly.

One cannot think of the modern city apart from the past. Evidences of antiquity are everywhere; each mountain recalls immortal associations, each brook and river bears its story. Until 1886 the Acropolis was a heap of ruins, the remaining portions of temples being concealed by general débris. The Greeks were largely instrumental in clearing it up, carefully preserving in the National Museum whatever of value was recovered. These are prized by all students of Greek antiquities.

The beauty of Athens is greatly praised by all her visitors. The mountains and sea are bathed in wonderful light at sunrise and sunset. "It will pay us to keep our eyes fixed upon the slopes of Hymettus just as the sun is going down. During the few moments immediately following the disappearance of that luminary the sides of the mountain are bathed in a deep, soft, yet quite vivid violet hue. This is the most transporting, most poetic spectacle on earth—the far-famed transfiguration of Hymettus. The mountain is wrapped in the atmosphere of happy dreams; it appears unreal because it has become too beautiful for this latter-day world. It was a fitting apparition, perhaps, in that golden age when love of beauty was man's religion, but it looks lonely and strange now. No painter can paint it, no words can tell it. The man who has once lived within sight of Hymettus cherishes to his dying day the intention to return and live there again. The poet or the dreamer who has looked but once upon that violet glow is homesick for it ever after. It is the light of the soul's desire, the light of utter loveliness, of lost years, of unforgotten loves and songs unsung."[3]

A drive of thirteen miles brings one to Eleusis, once the religious head of Attica, as Athens was its civil head. The Greek Archæological Society has done extensive excavating here and the Great Hall of mysteries has been located.

Probably no complete conception of the Eleusinian Mysteries can ever be acquired, for only to the initiated were the secrets disclosed and upon them the ban of silence was laid. They were founded upon the Demeter myth. Demeter, it will be remembered, was goddess of the harvest—of whatever the earth produced in the way of food for her children. When Demeter was seeking her missing daughter, in distraction

---

[3] Horton: Modern Athens.

searching here, there and everywhere, she came to Eleusis in the guise of an old woman and was kindly received by the king. She rewarded his kindness by giving some grains of barley to his son, teaching him the art of husbandry. The memory of the gift was celebrated by the Greater and the Lesser Eleusinia, only the initiated being allowed to participate in the secret observances. Being essentially agricultural in the beginning, the rites grew more and more elaborate. If the rituals and observances of secret societies today were to become generally known, there is no question but that they would soon appear trivial and commonplace; the same may be said of the Eleusinian Mysteries, we may be sure. We know that the initiated drank of the "mixture"—barley-meal and water; and partook of the pomegranates and sacred sesame cakes and salt. The sanctity surrounding these may be compared to that which surrounds the communion table of Christians. Ears of barley were awarded the victors in the competitive sports, without which no Greek festival would have been complete. It is surmised that Egyptian influence is discernible in this solemn festival, particularly in the faith inculcated. It is easy to see how the Prosephone story carried with it an idea of immortality, this being symbolized by the yearly resurrection at the spring-tide. Cicero, who was initiated into these Mysteries said of them that they taught one "not only to live happily, but to die with a fairer hope."

Twenty-five miles from Athens lies Marathon, sanctified by the patriots who gladly offered their lives to preserve the freedom of the West and save their country from the thraldom of the East. In 1890 excavation was undertaken on this site and but a few feet below the surface were found, supposedly, the bones of soldiers who fell fighting for their country. They had been interred with much pottery of that period.

It is fitting to leave Greece at its greatest sanctuary— Delphi, loved by Pan-Hellenic citizens. Its very location was imposing, made sublime by mighty mountains which form there a kind of amphitheater. Strange caverns and caves existed and in these vapor was found rising from a fissure. This vapor was said to have had an unusual effect upon those who inhaled it, and the conclusion was quickly reached that here

Apollo revealed himself to those who listened aright.    For
centuries a priestess sat upon the tripod and inhaled the
vapor, while priests interpreted her answers to those who
sought the oracle's advice.    It is known that they maintained
a large coterie of attendants whose business it was to keep
continually informed concerning strangers coming thither; to
know the conditions in other lands and to be ready to give
counsel in matters small or mighty.    Princes and kings and
peasants alike turned to Delphi with their perplexing problems.    Peace or war was not infrequently here determined
upon.    All coming to Apollo's favorite abode brought votive
offerings, many of them very costly.    For their safe keeping,
*treasuries* were built, each city or state providing thus for
the protection of its citizens' offerings.    Because of these great
riches, Delphi was always the coveted place for invaders, and
several times it was plundered.

The French Archæological School at Athens was founded
in 1846, the French realizing the rare opportunities afforded
to those desiring to learn of the past, then but partially understood by scholars.    In 1872 the Greek government gave the
land upon which a building was erected as the home of this
school in Athens.    Among all excavations that have been attempted, none has elicited more deserved praise than that of
this school at Delphi.    Started in 1893, the excavations were
concluded in 1903.    Material was removed to the oldest
strata, and the recovery of some of the most primitive statues
of Apollo resulted.    The beautiful temple of Apollo, the
theater, stadium and many of the treasuries were located.
The city of Athens asked to have the honor of rebuilding the
Treasury of Athens, as its birth-right.    Inscriptions, monuments, sculptures and votive offerings from every part of the
ancient world were found.    A patriotic Greek donated funds
to build a museum at Delphi in which these riches might be
preserved, that all who desired might come hither to see them.

Upon the conclusion of the work of the French school in
1903, a fitting celebration was made.    Two steamers were char-
tered and sent to Greece with educators and distinguished
guests.    The region was turned over to the Greek government with all the discoveries resultant from this laborious and

expensive undertaking.   The French Minister of Education
and Fine Arts was present and speeches were made in many
languages.

Earthquakes have been most disastrous at Delphi in the
past and it is realized that these recoveries might be destroyed
at any time, but the plan proposed to move them to Athens met
with violent opposition on the part of Greeks living in Phocis,
and was abandoned.

SATYR OF PRAXITELES.

ATTIC JARS.

A. Water-jar, *Hydria*.
B. Cup, *Kantharos*.
C. A wine-jar, *Pelike*.
D. Ladle, *Kyathos*.
E. Water-jar, *Hydria*.
F. Jar for carrying wine, *Amphora*.

G. Wine-jar, *Stamnos*.
H. Oil-jar, *Lekythos*.
J. Cup, *Kylix*.
K. Mixing Bowl, *Kelebe*.
L. Wine-jug, *Oinochoe*.
M. Jar for unguents, *Aryballos*.

## To a Greek Girl.

With breath of thyme and bees that hum,
Across the years you seem to come,—
Across the years with nymph-like head,
And wind-blown brows unfilleted;
A girlish shape that slips the bud
   In lines of unspoiled symmetry;
A girlish shape that stirs the blood
   With pulse of spring, Antonoë!

Where'er you pass,—where'er you go,
I hear the pebbly rillet flow;
Where'er you go,—where'er you pass,
There comes a gladness on the grass;
You bring blithe airs where'er you tread,—
   Blithe airs that blow from down and sea;
You wake in me a Pan not dead,—
   Not wholly dead!—Antonoë!

How sweet with you on some green sod
To wreath the rustic garden-god;
How sweet beneath the chestnut's shade
With you to weave a basket-braid;
To watch across the stricken chords
   Your rosy-twinkling fingers flee;
To woo you in soft woodland words,
   With woodland pipe, Antonoë!

In vain,—in vain! The years divide:
Where Thamis rolls a murky tide,
I sit and fill my painful reams,
And see you only in my dreams;—
A vision, like Alcestes, brought
   From under lands of Memory,—
A dream of Form in days of Thought,—
   A dream,—a dream, Antonoë!
              *—Austin Dobson.*

ROMAN FORUM.

# ROME

Thou art in Rome! the City that so long
Reigned absolute, the mistress of the world;
The mighty vision that the prophet saw,
And trembled; that from nothing, from the least,
The lowliest village—what but here and there
A mud-roofed cabin by a river-side?—
Grew into everything; and year by year,
Patiently, fearlessly working out her way
O'er brook and field, o'er continent and sea,
Not like the merchant with his merchandise,
Or traveller with staff and scrip exploring,
But hand to hand, and foot to foot through hosts,
Through nations numberless in battle array,
Each behind each, each when the other fell,
Up and in arms, at length subdued them all.

—SAMUEL ROGERS.

# THE STORY OF ROME

## CHAPTER I.

### Italy and Italian Settlements.

Italy comprises the second of three peninsulas extending to the south of Europe. East of it lies Greece; west, Spain. Its position determined, then, that Italy should receive from the east, assimilate, and in turn, transmit to the west.

The Alps form a well-nigh impassable barrier on the north, and the sea washes the land on the three remaining sides. Mountains traverse the entire length of the peninsula and give general character to the country. Roughly speaking, Italy falls into three natural divisions—the valley of the Po; the peninsula proper; and southern Italy, together with Sicily. For while Sicily is separated from the mainland by a channel two or three miles in width, the island is in reality but the extremity of a mountain range which forms the backbone of the peninsula.

The valley of the Po is surrounded on three sides by mountain ranges. From north and south, streams hurry along the heights, cutting down their channels, and in times of high water, depositing a rich silt over the broad valley. As a result of such deposits, reaching over thousands of years, this is one of the most productive areas in the world. However, the ancient Romans knew this region as Cisalpine Gaul. and not until the later republic did it become vital to the Roman world.

The peninsula proper, or the leg of Italy. extends in a southeasterly direction about 500 miles. Nowhere over 100 miles in width, much of the land is broken by a mountain system that reaches along its entire length. On either side. the hills melt away into the plains, richer and more spacious on the west than on the east. Two rivers upon the western slopes became closely identified with early Roman development—the Tiber and the Arno.

Sicily and southern Italy should be considered together.

Their history has always been closely related, and although unity was lacking in antiquity, the geography of the two regions was similar and produced similar conditions.

The eastern shores of Italy have few harbors. On the west coast several ports attracted the sailor in early times. While Greece lay open to the east, Italy was accessible from the west. Few bays, gulfs and inlets break into the entire Italian shore, Tarentum on the south being largest. Few islands are scattered along the land, and altogether, physical conditions encouraged farming and herding among the earliest Romans.

The beauty of Italy has been proverbial. For hundreds of years men said that her beauty was her curse. The productive fields of Lombardy invited roving peoples, and time after time the land was devastated by barbarous hordes. Much of the charm of the land has been due to its climate.

"Strip Italy of its delightful climate, its poetic haze, its brilliant moon, its golden sun, and make the peninsula project into a grey and chill northern sea, and Scandinavia, rimmed with icicles, frozen into inhospitable cliffs and lusterless lakes, would be the result. Transplant Scandinavia to the Mediterranean and project its sharp angles into the Adriatic, the Tyrrhenian and the Messenian Seas, and there would spring forth a wonderful civilization such as actually sprang up in Sicily and Naples."

As a matter of fact, the peninsula presents a variety of climates throughout its 700 miles. The northern portion is often cold and raw in winter, the olive trees just escaping damaging effects of frost. As one journeys southward, the climate is more even and the southern portion of the country is famous for its warm sunshine and clear blue skies.

As has been said, people were early attracted to this peninsula. Vine-covered hills, olive-covered plains, with a background of the everlasting heights, snow-crowned and dazzling; the blue sky above—these sights gladdened the hearts of those who braved the passage of the Alps. Rumours of this earthly paradise reached those who dwelt far north, and thus for hundreds of years Italy was a coveted country, quickly to be appropriated if weakness manifested itself in its possessors.

Contrasting Italy with Greece, we are struck at once by the difference in the two coast-lines. Few harbors in Italy and many in Greece determined that the Hellenes would be lured to the sea, while the Romans remained a nation of land-lubbers. In the course of their provincial expansion they attempted any difficulty of land passage in preference to embarking by sea. Again, although both countries were mountainous, Italy was not a disunited land. Frequent passes through the Apennines made communication from east to west comparatively easy. Thus, while Greece remained disunited, broken into many small states, Rome was able to establish a strong central government, effective in all parts of the Italian peninsula.

Having considered the more striking characteristics of the peninsula as a whole, we shall find that only a comparatively small portion of this territory concerns us in our study of early Roman history. In the central portion of the western plain lay Latium, with Etruria to the north and the Campania to the south. Here was the arena of early Roman activities.

The earliest inhabitants of Italy had no Homeric singers to immortalize a prehistoric civilization, and inspire men three thousand years later to discover within the earth remains of a forgotten people. While evidences point to early occupancy of Italy, scanty remains survive to mark the coming or departure of primitive tribes which held successive sway in the peninsula. From occasional remains, from language tests, and from legendary lore, certain general facts concerning the early occupants of Italy have been established.

At a remote time, it would appear, tribes migrated from western Asia—the Cradle of the Human Race—and gradually took their way into Europe, and thence into Italy. One of these tribes was known to the later Romans by the name *Siculi*. Spreading out over the peninsula, these people were driven south by new comers, and made their homes at last in the large island called today from their name, Sicily. The Ligurians also pushed over the mountains and occupied the valley of the Po. They were probably crowded by the incoming Gauls into the corner of Italy known by their name. The Pelasgians, that numerous race which peopled Asia Minor and Hellas, penetrated into the Italian peninsula and held first place for several generations.

All these had passed away before the appearance of the three tribes strongest in Italy when Rome came into being—the Latins, Sabines and Etruscans. There is little to show that these later peoples were greatly influenced by earlier occupants of the land. That is to say, we find no parallelism in Italy to the condition in Greece when invading Hellenes found Hellas held by a race superior in culture, inferior in strength, and assimilated their civilization while subjecting them. Rather, the primitive tribes of Italy dwelt awhile in the valleys and were either crowded out by more vigorous men or took refuge in inaccessible parts of the country, to later unite with other tribes until their identity was lost.

The Etruscans, called Tyrrhenians by the Greeks, seem to have once overrun the greater portion of Italy. Gradually they were forced back by the Italians. Where they originally came from is not known. Indeed, they have always been baffling to the historian. From surviving monuments they are shown to have been a sturdy, thick-set race. Some of their number developed agriculture to such a degree that they were able to transmit much farming lore to the Romans. Others took to the sea. The Etruscans built fine roads and erected splendid buildings. They possessed a well-developed art and literature. Although portions of their writings remain, no one has thus far mastered the language in which they were recorded. When authentic records begin, these people had already passed their zenith and the Latins knew them as a self-indulgent race, fond of feasting and carousing, given to sports of a cruel nature. Rome later took over their gladiatorial contests, and superstitions connected with their gloomy religion penetrated to other lands. The soothsayers of Rome probably had Etruscan origin.

At length the Etruscans were driven back into Etruria by the Italians, to whose race the other important tribes in Italy at this time belonged. Of these, the Umbrians are supposed to have been most ancient. They, however, were soon crowded into the country which bears their name—between the Tiber and the Apennines. The Sabellines, second of Italian tribes, were mountaineers, who lived in little hamlets and tilled the soil. When Rome came into prominence, these people were divided into little clans in their mountain home, and were held together by a loose confederacy of cantons. In the south of Italy lived the Oscans, to which general division belonged the Samnites, Luscanians and Bruttians. The Samnites were strongest, and, highland freebooters as they were, fought long to maintain their liberty. Their raids may be likened to those of the Scottish clans, restless and chafing under a restraining hand.

Finally, on the western plain were the Latins. They covered the Campania, now a desolate lowland, but once well populated. Latium means plain, and the Latins originally were plain-men. They peopled not only the country which bore their name, but spread over the undulating plain of the Campania as well.

The only remaining people of consequence at this time in Italy were the Greeks, who as early as the eighth century before Christ settled in the southeastern part of the peninsula. Tarentum was one of their earliest settlements. Colonies were also established by them in Sicily, chief of which was Syracuse, a proud and wealthy city in the days of Athenian supremacy.

Were we able to trace the many stages through which these various peoples passed, from their exodus from Asia to their establishment in Italy, such accounts would avail us little. It is important, however, that we see what contributions each made to future Rome.

"From Etruria came the division into tribes, curies, and centuries, the array of battle, the ornaments of magistracy, the lictors, the triumphs, and public games, the sacred character of property, the political religion of the state. From Latium were derived the names of praetor, consul, the dictator, the habits of husbandry, together with national respect for it, and finally the Latin league itself. From Sabellia, the region of the Sabines, were deduced the names of military weapons.

This mixed formation of Roman society may be mythically represented to us by the legends which describe the first and third kings as Latins, the second and fourth as Sabines, while the last three of the seven are Etruscans."

## ROME—ITS POSITION AND ADVANTAGES.

The name Rome is now believed to have been derived from a Latin word which means stream;[1] Ruma or Rome was the stream city, and thus the importance of the Tiber was from the first apparent. This river takes its rise in the mountains of Etruria, more than 250 miles north of Rome. Taking a course almost parallel with the Apennines, it makes two bends through the present city, and fifteen miles below, reaches the sea. Geologists tell us that while the river was eroding its channel, it entirely surrounded three of the Roman hills, leaving them exposed on all sides to its action. This accounts for the complete isolation of those nearest the present river-bed. While no official statement has apparently been made concerning its depth, it has been estimated to be twelve to eighteen feet deep. Narrowest in Rome, its current is there swiftest.

The hills of Rome are proverbial. "Old as the hills"—the eternal hills of Rome. The river alone would never have enabled the little settlement of shepherds to develop into a great metropolis. Primitive people needed the protection of hill-tops. It was necessary to have defense against neighboring hostile tribes. On this account, some steep hill was chosen, since it could easily be fortified and commanded a wide outlook over the adjacent country. Perhaps the early settlers of Rome were conscious of another reason for occupying the heights. Latium is low and has always been infested with malaria. The hill-tops were freer from mists and fever-breeding vapours, and hence were desirable for habitation.

At a very early time, prehistoric tribes appear to have lived in the vicinity of the Palatine and used this hill for their cemetery. However, the Romans made their first settlement upon the hill itself. For several reasons the Palatine offered advantages; in the first place, it was large, comprising about twenty-five acres. It was nearly level, and being steep save upon one side, was easily defended. Moreover, two neighboring springs enabled the settlers to get water easily. The hill was near the river and thus gave access to the sea. Another advantage which was later to appear, although it may not have occurred to the earliest Romans, was its proximity to other hills, allowing these to be incorporated within the original city.

[1]The origin of the word Rome is a matter of conjecture. The above theory has excellent support.

Palatine probably comes from a word meaning pasture, and is clearly connected with Pales, god of pastures. This name commemorated the early occupation of the people. They were herders, who drove their cattle off to the northeastern part of the later city during the day and brought them back for safe keeping within the Palatine walls at night. Many of the oldest legends center around the Palatine. Beneath it, by the river, was the Lupercal, the cave whence issued the wolf who cared for the abandoned children. At the top of a flight of stairs leading down to the foot of the hill was the house of Romulus, the first king, according to tradition.

The history of the Roman state and its religion are inseparably interwoven. The family, not the individual, was the unit of the Roman state. Three gods were important in every household: Janus, god of the door, or the doorkeeper; Vesta, goddess of the hearth; Penates, god of the store-closet. These divinities who presided over each hut, presided as well over the collection of huts, or the village; and to the Palatine, Janus and Vesta gave their protection. We shall see that when settlements upon nearby hills united with the hamlet the Palatine, the hearth of Vesta and the temple of Janus had to be moved down into the valley, in the center of the new city.

Capitoline was another hill to be early peopled. This is smallest of the seven. Until the time of Trajan it was not wholly isolated, being connected with a spur to the Quirinal. This ridge was excavated to make room for Trajan's forum.

The Aventine is largest and highest of the Roman hills. The others, Quirinal, Viminal, Caelian and Esquiline, are but outlying spurs of a high tableland that reaches off to the east. In course of time all these heights were settled, and the various tribes occupying them found it of mutual benefit to affiliate rather than make war upon one another. Thus, all the hills were included within the city wall; paths leading from one place to another grew into highways, then into streets. The intervening valleys gradually were appropriated for meeting places, markets, sites for national festivals and games. This came about slowly, and we do not know by just what stages it was accomplished. Rome, like other ancient cities, originated in obscurity, and many stages of progress had been passed before authentic records begin.

Why Rome, rather than a dozen other villages of ancient Italy, should have developed to such vast proportions, has often been asked. Evidently the reason is not to be found in her people, for they were similar to those of neighboring towns. The position of Rome had, beyond doubt, much to do with it. Located midway along the western coast, far enough from the sea to be protected from roving seamen, and near enough to gain access to the ocean, having a river with a swift current as a boundary between the Romans and the Etruscans, and especially possessing several hills whereon tribes might learn to dwell in harmony before attempting to subdue neighboring districts—these were factors important in shaping the future of the embryo world capital.

JANUS.

## CHAPTER II.

### THE KINGDOM—LEGENDARY HISTORY.

Regarding the early chapters of Roman history we are little better off today than were the Romans themselves. They were forced to perpetuate old legends and traditions, and we can merely find flaws in these without ourselves unraveling the true story. For many centuries the Romans were too busy fighting to think of chronicling their deeds, and when the attention of men was drawn to the matter of preserving their history, only legends and folk stories remained to account for the formation of the Roman state. Even these no longer held to their original form, but for generations had been rounded out and filled in, as a more discerning people grew to see inconsistencies. As a result, the composite tales of early Rome have comparatively little value for us as explaining the actual course of events. Yet, on the other hand, they are the tales which the early Romans themselves believed, generally speaking, and they have become embodied in literature, so we must become acquainted with them, even though they have little historic value. Livy, himself a Latin historian, realized this perfectly well in his day, for he wrote: "As to the relations which have been handed down of events prior to the founding of the city, or to the circumstances that gave occasion to its being founded, and which bear the semblance rather of poetic fictions, than of authentic records of history— these, I have no intention either to maintain or refute. Antiquity is always indulged with the privilege of rendering the origin of cities more venerable, by intermixing divine with human agency; and if any nation may claim the privilege of being allowed to consider its origin as sacred, and to attribute it to the operations of the gods, surely the Roman people, who rank so high in military fame, may well expect that, while they choose to represent Mars as their own parent, and that of their founder, the other nations of the world may acquiesce in this, with the same deference with which they acknowledge their sovereignty. But what degree of attention or credit may be given to these and such-like matters I shall not consider as very material. To the following considerations I wish every one seriously and earnestly to attend; by what kind of men, and by what sort of conduct, in peace and war, the empire has been acquired and extended."

Putting aside for the time any but legendary history, let us trace the foundation of Rome as the early Romans themselves recounted it.

Among those to escape from burning Troy were Aeneas, his father Anchises, and his little son, Iulus. Aeneas had invariably declared that Paris should in justice be turned over to the Hellenes and the wearisome siege ended. For this reason, the Greeks were not unwilling that he should escape the wholesale slaughter which followed their entrance into Troy. Setting sail from Ilium with Trojan fugitives for companions, he met with many stirring experiences and underwent many hardships. In course of time his father died. The gods had ordained that Aeneas should found a new state, and he was bidden to journey along until a sign was given him. At last it came in Central Italy. Here he found King Latinus reigning over the Latins. Some accounts say that Aeneas and his band defeated this king in battle and that afterwards the leaders—King Latinus and Aeneas—ruled jointly; other stories relate that King Latinus welcomed Aeneas, seeing in him the fulfillment of a dream. In any event, the two leaders were soon friends, and King Latinus gave Aeneas his daughter Lavinia in marriage. However, this princess had been earlier betrothed to a neighboring chief who resented the idea of a stranger appropriating his intended bride. He waged a battle against the Latins and their allied Trojans, and both he and King Latinus were killed. This left the kingship to Aeneas, who founded a long line of rulers. He built up a new town, naming it Lavinium, in honor of his wife. His son Ascanius succeeded him, and he in turn founded Alba Longa, to relieve other thickly populated settlements. A long line of kings followed, one bearing the name Tiberinus.

He was drowned in the river henceforth called the Tiber. Finally the crown passed to Numitor, but Amulius, a younger brother, wanted it for himself, so he deposed Numitor, killed his sons and caused his daughter Rhea to become a vestal virgin. But the god Mars became enamoured with her charms and in course of time she bore him twin sons—Romulus and Remus. When Amulius heard of this, he ordered the mother to be put to death and the babes to be cast into the Tiber.

"Neither gods nor men screened her or her children from the king's cruelty; the princess was loaded with chains, and cast into prison, and the children were ordered to be thrown into the stream of the river. It happened providentially that the Tiber, overflowing its banks, formed itself into stagnant pools in such a manner, as that the regular channel was everywhere inaccessible, and those who carried the infants supposed that they would be drowned in any water, however still. A story prevails that the retiring flood having left on dry ground the trough, hitherto floating, in which they had been exposed, a thirsty she-wolf from the neighboring mountains directed her course to the children, showing so much kindness that the keeper of the king's herds found her licking the boys with her tongue; and that this shepherd, whose name was Faustulus, carried them home to his wife Laurentia to be cared for."[1]

In course of time the boys grew to manhood. Learning of their noble birth, they re-established their grandfather Numitor on the throne, slaying their wicked uncle. Then the brothers determined to found a city on the site where they had been rescued. An angry quarrel arose between them regarding it and Romulus slew his brother Remus. He reigned over the people in the new settlement for many years. Meantime Rome supplanted Alba Longa as head of the League of Thirty Cities.

After awhile, the senate grew dissatisfied with Romulus and his rule, and strange to say, just about that time he suddenly disappeared. The people murmured openly about his disappearance, but some one stepped forward and affirmed that he had seen Romulus translated to heaven.

"Proculus Julius, a person whose testimony in any case, as we are told, deserved respect, while the public were full of grief for the king, and of displeasure against the senators, came out into an assembly of the people and said: 'Romans,

[1] Livy: History of Rome.

yesterday at the dawn of day, Romulus, the parent of this, our city, descending suddenly from heaven, appeared before me; and when, seized with horror, I stood in a worshiping posture, and addressed him with prayers, that I might be allowed to behold him without being guilty of impiety, Go, said he, tell the Romans that it is the will of the gods that my Rome should be the metropolis of the world. Let them therefore cultivate the arts of war; and be assured, and hand this assurance down to posterity, that no human power is able to withstand the Roman arms. After these words he went up and vanished from my sight.'

"It was wonderful how readily the story was credited on this man's word; and how much the grief of the people, and of the army, was assuaged, by their being satisfied of his immortality."[2]

The story of the Sabine women is connected with the age of Romulus, and reflects a rough, primitive society. It seems that when Romulus established his settlement on Palatine hill, he populated it with rough shepherds, but few had wives. Now it was not easy to persuade women to come to live in this new village, yet only by building up permanent homes would the growth of the village be assured. In this situation Romulus and his companions hit upon a deceit which they successfully carried through. They invited the neighboring Sabines to visit their settlement to celebrate a religious festival. The unsuspecting farmers gathered with their wives and families, whereupon the men of Rome seized each upon some comely daughter of a Sabine, holding them captives. Taken so unawares, the guests could only depart to incite their kinsmen to avenge this outrage. Being well defended on the Palatine, the Latins held also a stronghold on Capitoline; this was guarded by Tarpeius. His daughter Tarpeia betrayed the fortress to the Sabine soldiers, who promised her the bracelets of gold which they wore on their arms. She was crushed to death as the soldiers crowded into the fort, and henceforth the rock was called Tarpeian, and traitors were thrown over it to certain death. Following the surrender of the fort on Capitoline, a battle was waged between the Latins and the Sabines, but at length

[2]Livy: Hist. of Rome. 16.

the daughters who had been stolen from their families were torn by their anguish for their fathers and their husbands, and, rushing between the lines of battle, implored each side to yield. Overcome by their entreaties, the Romans and Sabines entered into a treaty, agreeing to live at peace with one another in the future.

We are told that one year after the death of Romulus, Numa Pompilius, a Sabine, was chosen to rule over the Romans. Tradition says that he divided among the people lands thus far conquered and instituted the worship of Terminus, god of boundaries. He established a state religion and organized a priesthood. Whereas Romulus had brought into use a calendar of ten months, Numa added two more, January, named for the god Janus, and February, from *februa,* purification. Both had to do with religious ceremony and worship.

Numa's reign was long and prosperous. The people of the rude hamlet learned to be law-abiding and to cultivate the arts of peace. Obedience to order, industry, care in religious observation—these were developed and stimulated by Numa.

The second king was succeeded by Tullus Hostilius, a Latin noble. He was war-like, plunging immediately into difficulty with the inhabitants of Alba Longa. This city he destroyed and brought its people to Rome, where they were given homes on the Aventine. How long he reigned is not known, but under his administration the arts of peace were supplanted by vicissitudes of war.

Ancus Martius, grandson of Numa, became the traditional fourth king. He turned attention once more to law, order and religion. However, he was not destined to revive the peace of his illustrious ancestor. Latin tribes thought the opportunity favorable for an attack upon Rome, whereupon the king proved himself as able in war as in peace. Not only did he defeat his aggressors, but took many of them captive, compelling them henceforth to make their homes in the city. The fortifications of Janiculum, the large hill across the river together with the bridge which connected it to the city are attributed to Ancus. Moreover, the laws of the city were inscribed on tablets and hung in the market place.

During the reign of Ancus, a Greek exile, originally from

Corinth, migrated to Rome from Tarquinii in Etruria, to mend his fortunes. He soon gained the confidence of the people and the king, who left him guardian of his sons. It was a comparatively simple matter to persuade the populace that Tarquinius, as he was called, would prove a more efficient ruler than the boyish heirs, and the people proclaimed him king. He carried on successful campaigns with the Etrurians and having established peace abroad, turned to local improvements.

The sons of Ancus, who had been set aside by the usurping Tarquinius, fearing that the throne would pass to the king's adopted son Servius Tullius upon his death, now formed a plot to kill both Tarquinius and Servius. The murder of the king was accomplished, but Servius was clever enough to defend himself and appropriate the crown for himself. He was the first king to hold his place without the consent of the people. He espoused the cause of the common people and this gave opportunity for the patricians to unite against him, calling attention to his irregular succession. Finally they were able to substitute a noble, known as Tarquinius the Proud, in his place.

The haughty bearing of the seventh king incited the people. He compelled men to labor on public works at scanty pay, thus arousing the indignation of the masses. Only a spark was needed to occasion an outbreak. This was supplied when one of the Tarquinians insulted Lucretia, wife of Brutus. Making common cause, the citizens of Rome rose up and drove the family out of their city, ending for all time the kingship in Rome. By popular consent, they declared that one who might in the future express himself as in favor of a king should be put to death as a public enemy.

These are the happenings which tradition has handed down from time immemorial in Rome. In later years historians have seen in the stories certain elements of truth. For example, it has been suggested that each king as a matter of fact, represents an indefinite period, characterized by general tendencies which in the legend are treated as personal attributes of one ruler. "Romulus is to Alban Rome what the name Pharaoh is to ancient Egypt—a gathering up into one name of the kings or captains who, through a whole period, exercised government there."

While the Romans flattered their vanity by relating that their ancestors elected Numa, a Sabine, to rule over them, it is probable that the reign of a Sabine in Rome proves conclusively that the Sabines at this particular period became stronger than the Romans. The Sabines were very religious, and Numa strongly impressed religion upon the town. So firmly were certain religious customs associated with his name that future generations regarded him as the founder of Roman religion—quite as the ancient Hebrews attributed to Moses the origin of laws which in reality came into existence long centuries after his death. How long the Sabines ruled we have no idea. Being an agricultural people, caring little for war, they left an imprint of this disposition upon Rome. However, the tide turned again. The Latins rose up and made one of their own number king. With restoration of Roman rule, we find an abandonment of peace for the ways of war.

Ancus Martius, the fourth king, was once again a Sabine, bringing in the habits of his tribe. Whether or not the Pons Sublicius was actually built during his reign cannot be ascertained, but tradition ascribed it so. Sublicius—from *sublica*, a pile—was made entirely of wood, no metal whatever being used in its construction. Because of some religious significance, this bridge was never allowed to fall into decay, but was rebuilt again and again.

The last three kings were Etruscans, and we find at once a change with their incoming civilization. Tarquinius introduced at once those elements which were conspicuous in Etruscan culture.

"His first war was with the Latins, and having brought thence a greater quantity of booty than had been expected, he *exhibited games* in a more expensive and splendid manner than any of the former kings. On that occasion the ground was marked out for the circus, which is now called 'maximus' (the principal), in which certain divisions set apart for the senators and knights, where each were to build seats for themselves, which were called Fori. The games consisted of horse races and the performances of wrestlers, collected mostly from Etruria; and from that time continued to be celebrated annually, being termed the Roman, and sometimes the great, games. By the same king, lots for building were assigned to private persons, round the forum, where porticoes and shops were erected.

"The Sabine war being concluded, he then applied himself to works of peace, with a degree of spirit which even exceeded the efforts he had made in war; so that the people enjoyed little more rest at home than they had during the campaigns; for he set about surrounding with a wall of stone those parts of the city which he had not already fortified; which work had been interrupted at the beginning by the war with the Sabines. The lower parts of the city about the Forum, and the other hollows that lay between the hills, from whence it was difficult to discharge the water, by reason of their situation, he drained by means of sewers drawn on a slope down to the Tiber. He also marked out and laid the foundations for inclosing a court round the temple of Jupiter which he had vowed during the Sabine war, his mind already presaging the future magnificence of the place."[3]

Very recently doubt has been thrown upon the question of Servius' wall, archaeologists suggesting that this wall may not have been constructed until after the invasion of the Gauls. Be that as it may, the public games instituted by the Etruscan kings, and the construction of drains, sewers, public buildings, and the like, were exactly what we would expect from an Etruscan conquest of Rome. The Etruscans stood for absolute monarchy; the Romans possessed a strong spirit of liberty even in earliest days, and the overthrow of kings probably signified at the same time the re-establishment of Latin supremacy.

[3]Livy: Hist. of Rome, I., 38.

OLD ROMAN PLOW.

## CHAPTER III.

### INHERITANCES FROM REGAL ROME.

We have found the legendary kings of Rome to have been half-mythical rulers—seven, according to old stories, but in reality probably more. However, just as succeeding generations ascribed to these kings various qualities and characteristics, so they attributed to the age of the monarchy certain general conceptions of government, society and religion. Systems of government, social customs and religious ceremonies proved more lasting than a line of kings, and these lived on after the republic was established, with little change or modification.

As in Greece, so in Rome, the earliest government was vested in a king, a council or senate, and a general assembly. The king's power was limited only by the strong influence of custom. He was chosen by the senate, and proclaimed king by the general assembly. He was high priest and supreme judge, as well as chief executive, possessing authority of life and death over his subjects.

The senate was composed of the heads of the old families. They advised with the king at his request, were the guardians of law and custom, but had little power save upon the death of a king, when they themselves governed until a successor to the throne should be agreed upon.

The general assembly was made up of all the fighting men, of whatever rank. They gave expression of their approval or dissent by shouts or brandishing of arms, taking no part in deliberations.

After the establishment of the republic we shall find a similar system of government. In place of the king, two magistrates, known as consuls, exercised executive control. The power of the senate was increased, and while at different times considerable authority rested with the general assembly, this body possessed great power only in the later republic.

Rome had once embraced three tribes: Ramnes, upon the

Palatine; a body of Sabines, called Tities, which settled upon Quirinal Hill, and a third division, whether Latins or Etruscans we do not know, that made their homes on the Caelian, and were known as Luceres. The very word *tribe* had its beginning under these circumstances—tribus, one-third. Members of these three tribes enjoyed equal privileges and their descendants made up the patrician class. The tribes, however, were soon lost sight of, and the patrician remained bound to his clan, or gens.

The clan—gens—was made up of all men and unmarried women descended from a common ancestor. The oldest male relative—whether father or eldest son—ruled over the family with absolute power. The *pater familias* might sell the others into slavery or put them to death. He was high priest, judge and king so far as family affairs were concerned and the state in no wise interfered or limited his control. Notwithstanding, the powerful influence of custom restricted his actions, and in spite of possessing unusual control, we hear little or nothing of its abuse. The family, not the individual, was the unit of state. Family affairs and state affairs, family religion and state religion—these were the two divisions into which early Roman interests fell.

The political division next higher than the family was the clan—a number of families, related by ties of blood. The several families composing the clan dwelt near one another and held part of their territory in common. Higher still was the curia—a number of clans or gentes, uniting originally for protection and gradually acknowledging a chief in times of peace as well as war. The tribe included several curiae.

The patricians, already mentioned, alone possessed full rights of citizenship in early Rome. Second were the clients— foreigners and freed slaves, who attached themselves to patricians because they could not hold property in their own names. In turn for protection they gave service and fealty. In court, the client could obtain a hearing through the voice of his patron.

Finally the plebeians made up the rest of the population. save for the slaves, who possessed absolutely no rights whatever. The plebeians could hold property. buy and sell, but

they had no active part in the government. In the beginning,
the population of a conquered village was often brought into
Rome, and these people were known as 'clients of the king.'
They took the name plebeian, or it may have been forced upon
them; and their number was gradually swelled by small farmers who came into Roman territory for protection. Later,
when they began to obtain political power, they were joined
by the clients. The situation might be stated in this way: In
early Rome there were two classes—citizens and non-citizens.
Whatever privileges there were belonged to the first class,
while those shut out from citizenship were quite at the mercy
of the nobles. They had no rights recognized by law and no
way to seek redress save through some patrician who gave
protection in turn for some consideration.

Generally speaking, these social and political conditions
lived on in Rome and upon them the future organization of the
state was built. To what extent they had been developed during the kingdom we do not know, but it is plain that they were
of long standing.

Concerning early Roman religion, comparatively little is
known. Suffice it to say that the popular idea that the religions of Greece and Rome were identical, or that Rome simply
took over the religion of her Hellenic neighbors, is mistaken
and misleading. Before the Latins came in contact with the
Greeks they worshipped the forces of nature, and long after
they had assimilated the beliefs of the Greeks, their own early
religious conceptions influenced the worship of adopted deities.
Roman religion was observed by the family and state, and the
worship of family gods remained closer to the hearts of the
Romans than the ceremonies connected with the gods of state.

Originally the *Lares* were the gods that guarded the farms.
Each farm had its own Lares, but these were worshipped
where four farms met. Here in remotest times among the
Latins, families gathered for religious festivals. Later the
Lares became gods of the house as well, and each household
had images of them set up by the hearth. In towns the same
deities were taken over, and at the intersection of four streets,
shrines would be raised to the Lares. Cakes, flowers, and
sacrifices of a like nature were offered and blessings asked of

the divinities. Besides the Lares and Penates—god of the store-house—ancestors were worshipped by the Romans in the privacy of the family. Each person was thought to have his double or *genius,* and it was an act of piety to worship the genius of a departed relative.

Aside from these domestic gods, the elements of nature were worshipped. The sun, the rain, the wind—all these were forces to be appeased and propitiated. However, the Romans did not possess sufficient imaginations to develop such a world of stories around these deified forces as did their neighbors, the Hellenes.

"The gods of early Rome were neither married nor given in marriage, they had no children or grandchildren and there were no divine genealogies. Instead they were thought of occasionally as more or less individual powers, but usually as masses of potentialities, grouped together for convenience as the 'gods of the country,' the 'gods of the store-room' and the 'gods of the dead,' etc. Even when they were conceived of as somewhat individual, they were usually very closely associated with the corresponding object; for example, Vesta was not so much the goddess of the hearth as the goddess 'Hearth' itself, Janus not the god of doors so much as the god 'Door.'"[1]

Saturnus was probably the most ancient Italian deity. As the tribes of Italy emerged from a pastoral to a settled life, they grew anxious to propitiate the god who taught men to sow and reap. Long afterwards, men looked back upon the simple life of their fathers as a happy time, and Saturn's reign was called the Golden Age. The feast of Saturnalia was commemorated throughout the republic.

Janus, already mentioned, was also an ancient god. One story related that he had once been a king, who after death was deified. He was regarded as the god of origins, "the introduction of the system of years, the changes of the seasons, the ups and downs of fortune, and of the human race by means of agriculture, industry, arts, and religion.
It is easy to explain the great honor paid to Janus by a people like the Romans, who, as a rule, had this peculiarity of pon-

[1] Carter: The Religion of Numa, 17.

dering well the prospects of an undertaking before entering upon it. The beginning of everything was a matter of great importance to them, and Janus was the god of a good beginning. Janus opened and closed all things. He sat not only on the confines of the earth, but also at the gates of heaven. Air, sea, and land were in the hollow of his hands. The world moved on its hinges at his command." [2]

Terminus, god of boundaries, was another Italian god. He was honored by stones placed along the boundaries of men's holdings. Numa is supposed to have given importance to his worship.

Flora, goddess of flowers, Pomona, goddess of fruits, Ceres, goddess of harvest, Liber, god of wine—these were deities native to Italy. The people of the Italian peninsula lacked the imaginative skill for weaving stories about them. They were more practical than their Greek neighbors. Yet with an inborn sense of divinity, they feared the forces of nature and wished to appease and propitiate them. Later, when they added Greek divinities to their own, they still thought of them in their own way—a way unlike the Greek. One notable difference is always apparent: whereas the Greek thought of his gods as possessing the same passions, desires, needs and aspirations as he himself experienced, the Roman never personified his deities to any such extent. They still remained forces of nature—everywhere existing, everywhere to be worshipped, but with a total absence of the human element or the intrigues common to the gods of Hellas. The religion of early Italy was therefore much more completely a worship of nature.

[2] Murray: Hist. of Mythology.

## CHAPTER IV.

### STRUGGLE FOR POLITICAL EQUALITY IN ROME.
#### 509-367 B. C.

The date assigned by tradition as the year in which Rome was founded is 753 B. C. As a matter of fact, the settlement was probably made considerably earlier. With equal lack of authenticity, 509 B. C. was the year believed by later Romans to have seen an end of the Roman monarchy. While both dates may be subject to question, they are commonly accepted and so should be remembered.

The patricians and plebeians had united to abolish the kingship, but it was soon forced upon the minds of the common people that only the upper class was benefited by the change of government. The republic established upon the expulsion of the Tarquins was not the kind of republic with which we are today familiar, but was, rather, an aristocratic republic. Only members of a certain social class were allowed to participate in the affairs of the state, and this class governed all the rest of the population according to its own will. For this reason one hundred and fifty years were consumed by the Romans in struggling among themselves, the common people striving to obtain, first, some voice in the government, and finally, equality with the aristocrats. This struggle was peculiar in that it was fought out for the most part without bloodshed. Whereas in Hellas political revolutions were usually accompanied by civil war, the Romans possessed a different temperament. They could contend very vigorously for their rights, but in early days they did not quickly resort to arms; during the kingdom they had learned the lesson of obedience to law, and this stood them in good stead. Moreover, when internal excitement was at high pitch, and the common people were even threatening to depart to found a city for themselves, if foreign foes appeared, all city strife was for the moment laid aside and, shoulder to shoulder,

common people and patricians went forth to defend their little
state.

Upon the expulsion of the kings, the government was
vested (1) in two consuls; (2) the senate; (3) the popular
assembly.   The consuls were elected by the popular assembly
from the patrician class and served one year, whereas the king
had ruled for life.   Moreover, the king was absolute, but in
the case of two consuls, the will of one frequently restrained
the other.   The pomp of office was diminished.   In place of
the purple robe, the consuls had merely a purple border in their
togas, and while the king had ridden in a chariot, the consuls,
like other Roman citizens, walked about the city.   The priestly
power which had belonged to the king was taken away from
the executives, and left to one called "the king of the sacrifice," and finances were managed by two quaestors, chosen by
the people.   Thus we see that the power of the executives
was greatly curtailed.

The Romans were from the first distinctly a military
nation, and they saw at once that special needs might require
supreme control to be temporarily vested in one officer alone.
Should the enemy threaten, for example, the two consuls
might be divided upon the policy it were best to follow, and
while they delayed, much might be lost.   On this account it
was provided that in such an emergency a dictator should be
appointed, and while he controlled, his will was to be supreme.
From his decision there was to be no appeal, and he was to be
implicitly obeyed.   However, his term was invariably limited
to six months, after which time he might be called upon to
answer for any act committed during his rule.   We shall find
that several times in the course of Roman history it was deemed
necessary to appoint a dictator, although in later years his absolute control was generally limited to the campaign he was
waging, while within Rome itself the senate ruled.

The two consuls were to act in conjunction with the advice
of the senate, which had existed during the monarchy, but
had fallen in dignity under the proud Tarquin.   The first consuls immediately restored its membership to 300, which number was retained until the time of Julius Caesar.   Only patricians were eligible to places in the senate.

The popular assembly was made up of all citizens capable of serving in the army. The plebeians, with the clients who had become identified with them, belonged to it. This body elected the consuls, but could vote merely upon the names presented by the senate. Its acquiescence was supposed to be necessary for the passage of any important measure, but as it worked out, the patricians controlled the government.

The lot of the plebeian soon became a sorry one. He could hold no public office nor defend his rights. In fact, he had no rights. When war broke out, he took his sword and went forth to serve the state. During his absence his little farm often sank into decay—his house was a mere hut, his implements the most primitive, and his cattle few. When he returned, in order to get started again he must borrow, and only the patrician was able to lend. If poor crops followed for a season or two, he was unable to pay back what he had borrowed, and the patrician seized him as a slave. Sometimes he imprisoned him and his family. There was no redress, and the common people were sinking into a hopeless state of despondency. The public land which they had helped to win from outside tribes they saw appropriated by the upper class, which exercised the power it possessed to do as it would.

At length, in 494 B. C. the plebeians to a considerable number went out of the city and took up their position upon Mons Sacer, a hill beyond the Anio. Here, they declared, they would establish a city of their own. In consternation the patricians roused to the situation. Here was the main strength of their army gone, and what would they do if word of this dissension should reach the ears of their enemies, who would at once march against the divided city? In any event, they must induce the common people to return. So they sent thither a man who was known to be friendly to the people, and who was also trusted by the patricians. He told them a fable of how the various parts of the body had once cried out against the stomach, which apparently did nothing, although the hands gave food to the mouth, the teeth masticated it, etc. These parts of the body decided to starve out the stomach, but they soon found that each portion was growing weak as the stomach weakened, and at length realized that all parts must work in

III—26

harmony.   The lesson was not hard to draw, and the plebeians
were probably anxious to return if any tolerable conditions
should be offered.   They held out bravely, though, and asked
that all existing debts be canceled and all persons held for debt
be released.   Further, they insisted upon having two officers
of their own whose persons were to be sacred during their
term of office.   These men, chosen by themselves, were to
cry out—to *veto,* to forbid, any law or action which should in
their judgment be injurious to the common people.   Moreover, two aediles, or policemen, were to be chosen from the
lower class.

The patricians felt constrained to grant these requirements,
although they hoped to keep authority in their own hands.
The quarrel was settled in this way, and the plebeians returned
to Rome.

In 486 B. C. Spurius Cassius, a consul, tried to lessen the
injustice connected with the public lands, and brought forward
an agrarian—or land—law.   This was designed merely to
give the commoners some part of the lands taken in war, but
the patricians managed to defeat it and killed the consul as a
traitor.

Thus far Rome had possessed no written laws.   In tribal
days the father had ruled absolutely in the family, and the
chief had settled difficulties and punished crimes within the
tribe.   These judgments, handed down from father to son,
grew into the laws of Rome, which were, however, not always
uniform, and were variously interpreted.   Only the patricians
knew what they were, each son of the aristocratic class being
instructed in them as part of his education.   Although a knowledge of these laws was confined to the patricians, the plebeians
were nevertheless judged by them, and finally a tribune, Gaius
Terentilius Harsa, asked that they be collected and published
where all might read them.   Reasonable as this request seems
the patricians declared that the laws were too sacred to be
given to the low-born plebeians, and for ten years the two
classes struggled and strove, one to secure the publication of
the common law, the other to hold it secret.   At last the plebeians tired out the others and it was agreed that ten men,
the decemvirs, be appointed to collect and publish the laws.

While they were occupied in so doing, all other officers of the
city were to be suspended, and these ten men were to rule
absolute.  At the close of a year they were to make their
report.

The decemvirs started upon their task in 450 B. C. and
inscribed upon ten brass tablets the laws they collected.  The
next year, 449 B. C., ten more were appointed to complete the
task.  They published two more tablets of laws, and then,
strange to say, refused to resign, inferring that they wished
to make themselves absolute.  The plebeians saw in this some
design to withdraw their privileges, and thereupon threatened
to secede once more, whereupon the decemvirs were forced to
lay down their power.  Two consuls who were friendly to the
plebs were now elected, Lucius Valerius and Marcus Horatius.
The common people also compelled a general recognition of the
right of appeal in criminal cases, both for patricians and plebeians, of the sanctity of the tribunes, and that laws passed
by the popular assembly were binding upon all citizens alike.
This legally established the popular assembly as the legislative
body of Rome.

In 445 B. C. a marriage law was passed which was directed
toward the gradual removal of social distinctions.  Heretofore marriage had been only possible within one's own social
class; patrician married patrician, and pleb married pleb.  Now,
however, intermarriage was made legal.  This law alone tended
to break down the old barriers of class distinction and to
create a united social body.

Although the plebeians had won several important conces-
sions, they were not satisfied.  Until political equality might
be established in the city, the strife between patrician and
plebeian would not end.  In 444 B. C. the lower class made a
stand for admission to the higher offices of the city.  The
patricians were ready to grant anything rather than admit
plebeians to consulship, and they now offered to create new
officers with powers equal to the consuls but having less honor
than these.  The new officers were to be called consular
tribunes, and it was to be each year determined whether they
or the consuls be made executives for the following term.
Although this temporarily appeased the plebeians, it never
aided them much in gaining additional control.

The next year, 443 B. C., fearful lest too great power come into the hands of the commoners, the patricians created a new office: the censorship. Two censors were to be chosen, and to them part of the consular duties were given. They were to make up the census—a statement of each man's property, and they were to decide who was eligible to sit in the senate.

Meantime, wars had been going on and the plebeians had again become very much impoverished. The situation was alarming, and two consuls were elected who were known to sympathize with the poor people. These men, Licinius Stolo and Lucius Sextus, secured the passage of the following laws:

1. Interest already paid by the plebs should be deducted from the principal of their debt, and the remainder might be paid within three years.

2. Public lands were to be open to all, no man being allowed to take possession of more than 300 acres.

3. The number of slaves employed upon any one farm was limited in order to give opportunity for free labor.

4. The college of priests having charge of the Sibylline Books, supposed to contain prophecies concerning Rome, was to be open to the plebeians.

5. The consular tribunes were abolished. Two consuls were to be chosen as before, but hereafter one was to be a plebeian.

The people, in gratitude for his efforts in their behalf, chose Lucius Sextus for their first consul.

Some few difficulties remained to cause dissension, but it is generally agreed that the passage of these laws in 367 B. C. threw all offices open to all classes, and brought about political equality in Rome.

### Selections from the Twelve Tables of Laws.

*Table I. Proceedings Preliminary to Trial.*

1. If the complainant summon the defendant before the magistrate, he shall go; if he do not go, the plaintiff may call a bystander to witness, and take him by force.

2. If the defendant attempt evasion or flight, the complainant may lay hands upon him.

6. If the parties do not agree, the plaintiff shall state his

case in the comitium or in the forum before midday. Let both parties appear, and argue out the matter together.

### Table II.  The Trial.

1.   The amount of the stake to be deposited by each litigant shall be either 500 ases or 50 ases; 500 when the subject of dispute is valued at 1,000 or upwards, 50 when at less than 1,000.  But when the subject of dispute be the freedom of a man, then, however valuable the man may be, the deposit shall be only 50 ases.[1]

3.   A party that is in want of a witness shall go and cry aloud at the door of his house, thus summoning him to attend on the third market day following.

4.   Theft may be the subject of compromise.

### Table III.  Execution.

1.   In the case of an admitted debt or of awards made by judgment, 30 days shall be allowed for payment.

2.   In default of payment, after these thirty days of grace have elapsed, the debtor may be arrested and brought before the magistrate.

3.   Unless the debtor discharge the debt, or some one come forward in court to guarantee payment, the creditor may take the debtor away with him, and bind him with thongs or with fetters, the weight of which shall not be more (but, if the creditors choose, may be less) than 15 pounds.

4.   The debtor may, if he choose, live on his own means, otherwise the creditor that has him in bonds shall give him a pound of bread a day; or, if he choose, more.

5.   In default of settlement of the claim, the debtor may be kept in bonds for 60 days.  In the course of this period he shall be brought before the praetor in the comitium on three successive market days, and the amount of the debt shall be publicly declared.  After the third market day the debtor may be punished with death or sold beyond the Tiber.

### Table IV.  Patria Potestas.

1.   Monstrous or deformed offspring may be put to death.

2.   The father shall, during his whole life, have absolute

---

[1] An *as* was a bronze coin—(copper, tin, and lead)—weighing one pound.

power over his legitimate children. He may imprison the son, or scourge him, or keep him working in the fields in fetters, or put him to death, even if the son hold highest offices of state, and were celebrated for his public services. He may also sell the son.

3. But if the father sell a son a third time, the son shall be free from his father.

### Table V. Inheritance and Tutelage.

1. All women shall be under the authority of a guardian; but the vestal virgins are free from tutelage.

3. The provisions of the will of a paterfamilias concerning his property and the tutelage of his family shall be law.

9. Debts due to or by a deceased person are divided among his co-successors, by mere operation of law, in proportion to their shares in the inheritance.

### Table VI. Ownership and Possession.

1. The legal effect of every contract and of every conveyance (made with the money and the scales) shall rest upon the declaration made in the transaction.

7. If a man finds that his timber has been used by another in building a house, or for the support of vines, he shall not remove it.

8. But he shall have a right of action against the other for double its value.

### Table VII. Real Property Law.

1. A clear space of two and a half feet shall be left around every house.

5. For the settlement of disputes as to boundaries, three arbiters shall be appointed.

7. The neighboring proprietors shall make the road passable; but if it be impassable, one may drive one's beast or vehicle across the land wherever one chooses.

9. The branches of trees that overshadow adjoining land shall be lopped to a height of 25 feet from the ground.

10. Fruit that falls from one's trees upon a neighbor's land may be collected by the owner of the tree.

### Table VIII. Torts.

2.   If a man breaks another's limb, and does not compromise the injury, he shall be liable to retaliation.

3.   For breaking a bone of a freeman, the penalty shall be 300 ases; of a slave, 150 ases.

6.   A quadruped that has done damage on a neighbor's land shall be given up to the aggrieved party, unless the owner of it make compensation.

7.   He that pastures his animals on a neighbor's land is liable to an action.

8.   A man shall not remove his neighbor's crops to another field by incantations, nor conjure his corn.

11.   If a man wrongfully fell his neighbor's trees, he shall pay a penalty of 25 ases in respect of each tree.

12.   A person committing theft in the night may lawfully be killed.

18.   A usurer exacting higher interest than the legal rate of 10 per cent per annum is liable to fourfold damages.

23.   False witnesses shall be hurled from Tarpeian rock.

24.   If one kill another accidentally, he shall atone for the deed by providing a ram to be sacrificed in place of him.

### Table IX. Public Law.

1.   No laws shall be proposed affecting individuals only.

3.   A judge or arbiter, appointed by the magistrate to decide a case, if guilty of accepting a bribe, shall be punished with death.

5.   Whoever stirs up an enemy against the state, or betrays a citizen to an enemy, shall be punished capitally.

6.   No one shall be put to death except after formal trial and sentence.

### Table X. Sacred Law.

1.   A dead body shall not be buried or burned within the city.

9.   Gold shall not be buried or burned with the dead, except such gold as the teeth have been fastened with.

### Table XI. Supplementary.

1.   Patricians shall not intermarry with plebeians.

*Table XII.   Supplementary.*

2.   If a slave commit a theft, or do any other injury, the master may, as an alternative to paying the damages assessed, surrender the delinquent.

5.   The most recent law repeals all previous laws that are inconsistent with it.

—(*Collected from fragments in Latin writings, codified and printed in Hunter's Roman Law.*)

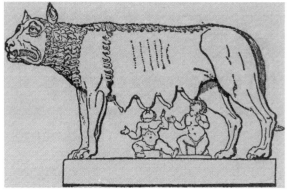

ROMULUS AND REMUS.

## CHAPTER V.

" Thine, Roman, is the pilum:
    Roman, the sword is thine,
The even trench, the bristling mound,
    The legion's ordered line;
And thine the wheels of triumph,
    Which with their laurelled train
Move slowly up the shouting streets
    To Jove's eternal fame.

Beneath thy yoke the Volscian
    Shall veil his lofty brow:
Soft Capua's curled revellers
    Before thy chairs shall bow:
The Lucumoes of Arnus
    Shall quake thy rods to see;
And the proud Samnite's heart of steel
    Shall yield to only thee.

The Gaul shall come against thee
    From the land of snow and night:
Thou shalt give his fair-haired armies
    To the raven and the kite.
The Greek shall come against thee,
    The conqueror of the East.
Beside him stalks to battle
    The huge earth-shaking beast,
The beast on whom the castle
    With all its guards doth stand,
The beast who hath between his eyes
    The serpent for a hand.

Where soft Orontes murmurs
    Beneath the laurel shades;
Where Nile reflects the endless length
    Of dark red colonnades;
Where fur-clad hunters wander
    Amid the northern ice;
Where through the sand of morning land
    The camel bears the spice;
Where Atlas flings his shadow
    Far o'er the western foam,
Shall be great fear on all who hear
    The mighty name of Rome."
        —*The Prophecy of Capys.*

### Rome's Conquest of Her Neighbors.

During the period of the monarchy, Rome had done something toward subduing her immediate neighbors. Among the Latins she had gained temporary ascendency. However, stories of wars fought under the kings, and, indeed, prior to the invasion of the Gauls, are largely mythical. We may not wholly ignore them, for they include some of the stirring tales in which the later Romans delighted; while partly legendary, they are partly true. They give us the ideals of those early years; the heroes of these battles prevailed because of their bravery and undaunted courage; because they put state first; because they spoke the truth and remained faithful to their agreements. Such qualities actually raised Rome to leadership in Italy and then raised her still higher—to be supreme in the ancient world. So if we would rightly understand the ancient Romans we must follow the course of their first wars as they themselves transmitted the accounts, from one generation to another by word of mouth, for long centuries. From this standpoint, their value is by no means diminished because recent archaeological investigations have thrown doubt upon the actual site of battles, or have brought into question the period during which some particular wall or fortification was constructed.

As we would naturally expect, the deposed Tarquin did not see his kingdom taken from him, and his family banished, without making great effort to recover his realm. He hurried to his own kinspeople, the Etrurians, and besought them to restore him to power. Lars Porsena, king of Clusium and head of the Etrurian league, raised an army and marched upon Rome. He succeeded in taking the fortress on the Janiculum and forced the Roman army, sent to repulse him, back across their wooden bridge. So long as the bridge held, it gave the Etruscans access into Rome itself, but, if destroyed, the swift current of the Tiber at this point supplied a well-nigh impassable barrier. Horatius, with two companions, faced the whole army of the Etruscans, to prevent the bridge from falling into their possession. When the Romans were about to cut it free, the two companions crossed safely, while

Horatius, committing himself to the god of the river, sank with it. But the gods preserved him and enabled him to swim to shore. It is probable that at this period the bridge was merely a series of floats.

Horatius was declared the saviour of his country. "For this deed," we are told, "the Romans set up his statue in the Comitium, and gave him as much of the common land as he could plough in a day."

The Romans were able to defend their city, but they soon realized that they would be starved into submission, for famine began to stare them in the face. Then Caius Mucius stole into the Etruscan camp, intending to slay the king, Lars Porsena— for without their valiant leader it was thought the army would make a retreat. But by some mistake, Caius Mucius slew the scribe instead, and was haled before the king. Threatened with torture unless he laid bare the situation at Rome, Caius voluntarily thrust his hand in a flame of fire, saying that glory was sufficient reward for pain. Puzzled by such a demonstration, the king bade him go, whereupon Caius then explained that three hundred Romans, of which number he was one, had pledged themselves to make attempts upon the king's life, in turn, until they were successful. Lars Porsena thereupon made peace with Rome, taking back from the Romans the territory around Veii, which they had previously conquered, and asking ten youths and ten maidens as hostages.

Cloelia, one of the maidens delivered by the Romans as pledges of good faith, wearied of her exile and roused her companions to mount horses and swim across the Tiber. The Romans welcomed their children back, but when they found that they had escaped, they immediately returned them to the king. Lars Porsena was so impressed with their fidelity that he thereupon gave the hostages free permission to go back to their parents, and departed with his army for his own land.

Disappointed in not gaining back his kingdom by Etrurian help, Tarquin stirred up the Latin cities. It was not difficult to rouse them to strike for their earlier independence. In consternation, the Romans appointed their first Dictator, Titus Lartius, and then, when the Thirty Latin Cities delayed, Aulus Postumius was chosen as second dictator. After a year or two had been spent in preparation, the army of the Latin League, under command of Octavius Manilius, together with Tarquin and his followers, marched against Rome. A battle was fought at Lake Regillus, in Tusculum; and now one side, and now the other, gave way. At length Aulus, the Roman dictator, vowed a temple to Castor and Pollux were he victorious. And shortly after, the story goes, two soldiers appeared amid the Roman ranks. They fought for Rome, and the Thirty Cities gave way before their fury. When the battle ended, with plenty of spoils for the Romans, these two strangers turned toward Rome, watered their steeds in the Forum, and disappeared as mysteriously as they had come. Such evidence was sufficient to satisfy the Romans that the twin gods, Castor and Pollux, had actually taken part in the battle in their behalf. A temple was erected to their honor in the Forum, and some of its pillars remain to the present time.

This ended any attempt of the proud Tarquin to regain his kingdom, but it did not end Rome's struggle. It was supposed, and rightly, that political change in the city would tend to weaken the state, and envious neighbors even planned to entirely subdue the vigorous Roman settlement. For half a century Rome fought for her very existence. To be sure, in later years, stories of great conquest and glorious triumphs were told of these years, but when one tries to find out what was actually conquered, the records fall short.

To this half-legendary age belongs the story of Coriolanus. This Roman, it would appear, received this name in this way: When the Romans were besieging Corioli and were repulsed, he rallied the men and forced a way into the town. His companions called him Coriolanus, since he had "fluttered the Volscians in Corioli."

Coriolanus was a patrician, however, and when corn was finally received in Rome during a famine, he proposed that it be withheld from the plebeians until they agreed to give up their tribunes and aediles, which officers they had recently won. Indignant, the tribune summoned him before the popular assembly, but Coriolanus could hope for little mercy at the hands of this body, and fled. He took refuge among the Volscians, enemies of his people, and incited them to march

Claudian Aqueduct.

against Rome. Attius Tullius, their chief, was quite ready to do so, but the people had been given sufficient evidence of Rome's skill in war and would not fight merely to satisfy a stranger. Shortly after, the great games drew many visitors to Rome, and Attius Tullius, unknown to the consuls, cautioned them about leaving the Volscians within their city after nightfall. Fearing trouble, the consuls issued a proclamation to the effect that Volscians must depart from Rome before sundown. Naturally, these people felt that some slight was offered them and were thereupon ready to comply with Coriolanus' request, and offer battle.

Coriolanus led them first against the Latin cities, which gave way before them. When it was known that the victorious army was on its way to Rome, the city was prostrated by the news, for so many wars had exhausted the Roman army. Accordingly, an embassy was sent to intercede for Rome, but Coriolanus would not confer with it. Then the priests were dispatched to plead for mercy. These were not more successful. At last it occurred to the city fathers to send the matrons of Rome, led by the wife and the mother of the rebellious Roman. The sight was too much for Coriolanus; he exclaimed: "Mother, thine is the victory; thou hast saved Rome, but destroyed thy son." Some stories say that the repentant Roman died in grief, an exile. Others hold that the Volscians put him to death for deceiving them. In gratitude, however, for their delivery, the Romans raised a temple to Woman's Fortune in the Forum.

The story of Cincinnatus is more important for the light it throws upon the sterling worth of the early Roman than for any recital of actual happening. It was said that Cincinnatus, a retired soldier, was ploughing his fields, when officers of Rome appeared before him and begged him to head an attack against enemies who were threatening the city. Leaving his team standing in the field, he went at once, won a victory, was given a splendid triumph by the people, and then went quietly back to his farm to resume the work where he had left it.

We come upon an historic event in 493 B. C. when Spurius Cassius formed a great league with the Latin cities, for the purpose of quelling the Aequians and Volscians. The Hernici

joined the aggressive league in 486 B. C.   For fifty years this
alliance prevented any attack upon Rome from the south, and
the Etruscans were not free to wage wars of aggression
because the Gauls were harassing them upon the north.
Indeed, several factors worked for the advantage of Rome in
these years.   Not only were the Etruscans occupied in defend-
ing their northern territory, but their proud fleet had shortly
before suffered total defeat at the hands of Hiero of Syracuse.
At the same time, the Samnites were prevented from making
raids upon lands belonging to Rome.   Southern Etruria was
assailed by the Romans, who besieged Veii for ten years.   During this war Rome's army for the first time was forced to
keep the field both summer and winter.   When the town was
carried, it was sacked and laid waste.

390 B. C. is the date usually assigned for the invasion of
the Gauls.   They had spread over the Po valley, and, while
appropriating this fertile region, did not give up their nomadic
ways, but continued to make occasional raids.   Upon this
occasion they drew within twelve miles of Rome before an
army was prepared to meet them.   At Allia a battle was
fought, and the impression of this Gallic attack was never forgotten by the Romans and their descendants.   These Gauls
were big men, carrying huge shields.   Their hair was long and
they made a furious onset.   Only a few Romans escaped from
the field of disaster to carry news of a defeat to the anxious ones
at home.   When their report was heard, many fled from the
town.   Even the Vestal Virgins hid the sacred utensils used
in their services and hurried away.

The patricians determined to guard the citadel, on Capitoline Hill.   The rest of Rome was left practically deserted,
and when the Gauls approached the walls and found them
unguarded, and the gates unlocked, they thought some ambush
awaited them and quietly remained outside.   After a day or
two they ventured in and could scarcely believe themselves
free to pillage and burn as they would.   The fort upon Capitoline held out for some time.   At length, the story goes, when
sentinels slept, some Gaul found a by-path up the hill and
would have overtaken the camp had not the sacred geese of
Juno been frightened into loud cackling, which awoke the
guards and saved the day.

Presently rumor came that the territory of the Gauls had been attacked upon the north, and they left as speedily as they had come. This contact with them made a tremendous impression upon the Romans, and many years after, when war was to be waged with the Gauls, it required a brave man to inspire the Romans with hope of victory.

Now the task of rebuilding the city fell upon those who survived the invasion. When danger was passed, the exiles returned home, and ere long the buildings were restored and Rome breathed the breath of freedom once again.

THE PALLADIUM.

## HORATIUS.

Lars Porsena of Clusium
    By the Nine Gods he swore
That the great house of Tarquin
    Should suffer wrong no more.
By the Nine Gods he swore it,
    And named a trysting day,
And bade his messengers ride forth,
East and west and south and north,
    To summon his array.

East and west and south and north
    The messengers ride fast,
And tower and town and cottage
    Have heard the trumpet's blast.
Shame on the false Etruscan
    Who lingers in his home,
When Porsena of Clusium
    Is on the march for Rome.

There be thirty chosen prophets,
    The wisest of the land,
Who alway by Lars Porsena
    Both morning and evening stand:
Evening and morn the Thirty
    Have turned the verses o'er,
Traced from the right on linen white
    By mighty seers of yore.

And with one voice the Thirty
    Have their glad answer given:
" Go forth, go forth, Lars Porsena;
    Go forth, beloved of Heaven;
Go, and return in glory
    To Clusium's royal dome;
And hang round Nurscia's altars
    The golden shields of Rome. "

And now hath every city
    Sent up her tale of men;
The foot are fourscore thousand,
    The horse are thousands ten.
Before the gates of Sutrium
    Is met the great array.
A proud man was Lars Porsena
    Upon the trysting day.

But by the yellow Tiber
    Was tumult and affright:
From all the spacious champaign
    To Rome men took their flight.
A mile around the city,
    The throng stopped up the ways;
A fearful sight it was to see
    Through two long nights and days.

Now, from the rock Tarpeian,
    Could the wan burghers spy
The line of blazing villages
    Red in the midnight sky.
The Fathers of the City,
    They sat all night and day,
For every hour some horseman came
    With tidings of dismay.

They held a council standing
    Before the River-Gate;
Short time was there, ye well may guess,
    For musing or debate.
Out spake the Consul roundly:
    "The bridge must straight go down;
For, since Janiculum is lost,
    Nought else can save the town."

Just then a scout came flying,
    All wild with haste and fear:
"To arms; To arms! Sir Consul:
    Lars Porsena is here."

On the low hills to westward
    The Consul fixed his eye,
And saw the swarthy storm of dust
    Rise fast along the sky.

But the Consul's speech was sad,
    And the Consul's speech was low,
And darkly looked he at the wall,
    And darkly at the foe.
"Their van will be upon us
    Before the bridge goes down;
And if they once may win the bridge,
    What hope to save the town?"

Then out spake brave Horatius,
    The Captain of the Gate:
"To every man upon this earth
    Death cometh soon or late.
And how can man die better
    Than facing fearful odds,
For the ashes of his fathers,
    And the temples of his Gods?

"Hew down the bridge, Sir Consul,
    With all the speed ye may;
I, with two more to help me,
    Will hold the foe in play.
In yon straight path a thousand
    May well be stopped by three.
Now who will stand on either hand,
    And keep the bridge with me?"

Then out spake Spurius Lartius;
    A Ramnian proud was he:
"Lo, I will stand at thy right hand,
    And keep the bridge with thee."
And out spake strong Herminius;
    Of Titian blood was he:
"I will abide on thy left side,
    And keep the bridge with thee."

" Horatius," quoth the Consul,
    " As thou sayest, so let it be."
And straight against that great array
    Forth went the dauntless Three.
For Romans in Rome's quarrel
    Spared neither land nor gold,
Nor son nor wife, nor limb nor life,
    In the brave days of old.

Then none was for a party;
    Then all were for the state;
Then the great man helped the poor,
    And the poor man loved the great:
Then lands were fairly portioned;
    Then spoils were fairly sold:
The Romans were like brothers
    In the brave days of old.

Now while the Three were tightening
    Their harness on their backs,
The Consul was the foremost man
    To take in hand an axe:
And Fathers mixed with Commons
    Seized hatchet, bar and crow,
And smote upon the planks above,
    And loosed the props below.

The Three stood calm and silent,
    And looked upon the foes,
And a great shout of laughter
    From all the vanguard rose:
And forth three chiefs came spurring
    Before that deep array;
To earth they sprang, their swords they drew,
And lifted high their shields, and flew
    To win the narrow way.

But now no sound of laughter
    Was heard among the foes.
A wild and wrathful clamour
    From all the vanguard rose.

Six spears' lengths from the entrance
　　Halted that deep array,
And for a space no man came forth
　　To win the narrow way.

Yet one man for one moment
　　Strode out before the crowd;
Well known was he to all the Three,
　　And they gave him a greeting loud.
" Now welcome, welcome, Sextus!
　　Now welcome to thy home!
Why dost thou stay, and turn away?
　　Here lies the road to Rome."

Thrice looked he at the city;
　　Thrice looked he at the dead;
And thrice came on in fury,
　　And thrice turned back in dread:
And, white with fear and hatred,
　　Scowled at the narrow way
Where, wallowing in a pool of blood,
　　The bravest Tuscans lay.

But meanwhile axe and lever
　　Have manfully been plied;
And now the bridge hangs tottering
　　Above the boiling tide.
" Come back, come back, Horatius ! "
　　Loud cried the Fathers all.
" Back, Lartius, back, Herminius !
　　Back ere the ruin fall ! "

Back darted Spurius Lartius;
　　Herminius darted back ;
And, as they passed beneath their feet
　　They felt the timbers crack.
But when they turned their faces,
　　And on the farther shore
Saw brave Horatius stand alone
　　They would have crossed once more,

But with a crash like thunder
  Fell every loosened beam,
And, like a dam, the mighty wreck
  Lay right athwart the stream:
And a long shout of triumph
  Rose from the walls of Rome,
As to the highest turret-tops
  Was splashed the yellow foam.


" Oh, Tiber! father Tiber!
  To whom the Romans pray,
A Roman's life, a Roman's arms,
  Take thou in charge this day ! "
So he spake, and speaking sheathed
  The good sword by his side,
And with his harness on his back,
  Plunged headlong in the tide.

No sound of joy or sorrow
  Was heard from either bank;
But friends and foes in dumb surprise,
With parted lips and straining eyes,
  Stood gazing where he sank;
And when above the surges
  They saw his crest appear,
All Rome sent forth a rapturous cry,
And even the ranks of Tuscany
  Could scarce forbear to cheer.


"Curse on him !" quoth false Sextus;
  "Will not the villain drown?
But for this stay, ere close of day
  We should have sacked the town !"
"Heaven help him !" quoth Lars Porsena,
  "And bring him safe to shore;
For such a gallant feat of arms
  Was never seen before."

And now he feels the bottom;
   Now on dry earth he stands;
Now 'round him throng the Fathers
   To press his gory hands;
And, now with shouts and clapping,
   And noise of weeping loud,
He enters through the River-Gate,
   Borne by the joyous crowd.

They gave him of the corn-land,
   Which was of public right,
As much as two strong oxen
   Could plough from morn till night;
And they made a molten image,
   And set it up on high,
And there it stands until this day
   To witness if I lie.


And still his name sounds stirring
   Unto the men of Rome,
As the trumpet-blast that cries to them
   To charge the Volscian home;
And wives still pray to Juno
   For boys with hearts as bold
As his who kept the bridge so well
   In the brave days of old.

—*Macaulay.*

### BATTLE OF LAKE REGILLUS.

"Hear, Senators and people,
   Of the good town of Rome,
The Thirty Cities charge you
   To bring the Tarquins home:
And if ye still be stubborn,
   To work the Tarquins wrong,
The Thirty Cities warn you
   Look that your walls be strong."

The Herald of the Latins
  Hath hied him back in state:
The Fathers of the City
  Are met in high debate.
Then spake the elder Consul,
  An ancient man and wise:
"Now hearken, Conscript Fathers,
  To that which I advise.
In seasons of great peril
  'Tis good that one bear sway;
Then choose we a Dictator,
  Whom all men shall obey.
Comerium knows how deeply
  The sword of Aulus bites,
And all our city calls him
  The man of seventy fights.
Then let him be Dictator
  For six months and no more,
And have a Master of the Knights,
  And axes twenty-four."
So Aulus was Dictator,
  The man of seventy fights;
He made Aebutius Elva
  His Master of the Knight.
On the third morn thereafter,
  At dawning of the day,
Did Aulus and Aebutius
  Set forth with their array.
Sempronius Atratinus
  Was left in charge at home
With boys, and with grey-headed men,
  To keep the walls of Rome.
Hard by the Lake Regillus
  Our camp was pitched at night:
Eastward a mile the Latins lay,
  Under the Portian height.
Far over hill and valley
  Their mighty host was spread;
And with their thousand watch-fires
  The midnight sky was red.

(The battle next day gives victory now to the Latins, now
to Rome. Manilius and Herminius, two leaders, go down
together dead, while Aulus the Dictator mounts Auster, Herminius' steed, to avenge his death.)

So spake he; and was buckling
  Tighter black Auster's band,
When he was aware of a princely pair
  That rode at his right hand.
So like they were, no mortal
  Might one from other know:
White as snow their armour was:
  Their steeds were white as snow.
Never on earthly anvil
  Did such rare armour gleam;
And never did such gallant steeds
  Drink of an earthly stream.

And all who saw them trembled,
  And pale grew every cheek;
And Aulus, the Dictator,
  Scarce gathered voice to speak.
"Say by what name men call you?
  What city is your home?
And wherefore ride ye in such guise
  Before the ranks of Rome?"

"By many names men call us;
  In many lands we dwell:
Well Samothracia knows us;
  Cyrene knows us well.
Our house in gay Tarentum
  Is hung each morn with flowers:
High o'er the masts of Syracuse
  Our marble portal towers;
But by the proud Eurotas
  Is our dear native home;
And for the right we come to fight
  Before the ranks of Rome."

So answered those strange horsemen,
  And each couched low his spear;
And forthwith all the ranks of Rome
  Were bold and of good cheer:
And on the thirty armies
  Came wonder and affright,
And Ardea wavered on the left
  And Cora on the right.
"Rome to the charge!" cried Aulus;
  "The foe begins to yield!
Charge for the hearth of Vesta!
  Charge for the Golden Shield!
Let no man stop to plunder,
  But slay, and slay, and slay;
The Gods who live forever
  Are on our side today."

"Hail to the great Asylum!
  Hail to the hill-tops seven!
Hail to the fire that burns for aye,
  And the shield that fell from heaven!
This day, by Lake Regillus,
  Under the Portian height,
All in the land of Tusculum
  Was fought a glorious fight.
Tomorrow your Dictator
  Shall bring in triumph home
The spoils of thirty cities
  To deck the shrines of Rome!"

Then burst from that great concourse
  A shout that shook the towers,
And some ran north, and some ran south,
  Crying, "The day is ours!"
But on rode those strange horsemen,
  With slow and lordly pace;
And none who saw their bearing
  Durst ask their name or race.
When they drew nigh to Vesta,
  They vaulted down amain,
And washed their horses in the well
  That springs by Vesta's fane.
And straight again they mounted,
  And rode to Vesta's door;
Then, like a blast, away they passed,
  And no man saw them more.

               —*Macaulay.*

## CHAPTER VI.

### The Subjection of Italy. 367-272 b. c.

By 367 b. c. the question of political equality within the city of Rome had been settled. Upon the abolition of the monarchy wars of defense had followed, lasting over fifty years. During these years Rome had held her own against a various foe, and was even now as strong as any power south of the Apennines. In the next century she was destined to win, step by step, the Italian peninsula, and more than this, to organize the state thus won into a firm nation. Nations before had proven themselves efficient conquerors; it was left for Rome to excel all others in the matter of unification and government.

The wars upon which the Roman army now launched differed from those previously fought in several particulars. In the first place, heretofore, Rome's battles had been fought within two or three days' march of the city. For the ensuing century, armies were called away from Rome, among peoples of different languages and traditions. Again, so far Roman soldiers had been confident that they possessed military skill equal to that of their hostile neighbors. Yet before the next period was to close, they were fated to cross swords with Greek soldiers, and to face the Macedonian phalanx.

Relations with the Latins should be kept in mind. Rome thus far was but the leader of the Latin league, whose various cities possessed perfect equality with her. Terms of a treaty concluded between Rome and the Latins after the battle of Lake Regillus have come down to us:

"Let there be peace between the Romans and all the Latin cities as long as heaven and earth shall remain in their present position.

"Let them neither make war upon one another themselves, nor bring in foreign enemies, nor grant a safe passage to those who shall make war upon either.

"Let them all with their forces assist one another when attacked by enemies, and let both have equal shares of the spoils and booty taken in their common wars.

"Let suits relating to private contracts be determined in ten days among that people among whom the contract was made.

"Let nothing be added to, or taken from, these treaties except by the joint consent of the Romans and all the Latins."

However, this equality was not destined to stand. In the first place, Rome was obliged to bear the brunt of wars directed against herself and the Latin League, and naturally appropriated the lion's share of the spoils. It came about as an inevitable result, that Rome made peace and declared war, settled colonists where she would, without consulting her ally in the least. Thus it happened that the political rights of the Latins were ignored, while their civil rights remained untouched.

Hostilities arose first with the Samnites, a vigorous race of mountaineers, who realized the danger threatening the various Italian tribes as Rome grew in power. A loose confederacy bound the different branches of the Samnites together, although there was no strong bond of union among them. They herded their flocks upon the mountains and made occasional raids into the adjacent valleys, where plunder was certain, and in 343 B. C. some of their number attacked a settlement of Samnites who had taken up lands in the Campania and broken loose from their mountaineer kinsmen. The settlement at Capua appealed to Rome for aid, which was refused until the people agreed to come under Roman protection if assistance were given them. Thereupon the Roman army was sent out to their relief, and within three years Rome had taken possession of the surrounding districts.

Now a new danger to the growing state arose, this time from among her own kinsmen. The Latins wearied of Rome's attempt to lessen their privileges and demanded complete union. One of the consuls, they insisted, and half the senate, should be chosen from their midst. This request was instantly refused, whereupon war broke out between Rome and the Latin League. We know very little about the struggle, but in the end Latium fell to the share of Rome. The Latin League was abolished, save for its religious functions, and its various cities were bound to Rome by individual treaties.

Meantime the Samnites had not been idle. They saw with clear vision the fate of their nation and all others who yielded not to Rome, and were not averse to bringing on fresh hostilities. In 327 B. C. the Samnites stationed a garrison in Neapolis—later Naples. Rome asked that it be withdrawn, and the Samnites refused unless Rome would remove a colony she had planted upon their borders. Allying herself with tribes in southern Italy, Rome sent an army against Neapolis. Within a year the city surrendered. Little is known about the movements of the two armies until 321 B. C., when suddenly the Samnite chief achieved a triumph by entrapping the whole Roman army in a mountain fast. Unable to retreat and feeling that it was hopeless to fight, the generals surrendered. Pontius, the Samnite leader, did not wish to take advantage of the enemy's plight, but stipulated for a permanent peace, with the acknowledged independence of his nation. To these conditions the entrapped generals were powerless to object, and the whole Roman army was sent under the yoke, their arms taken from them. Six hundred hostages were retained, while the rest were allowed to return home, all officers having pledged themselves to get sanction of this treaty from the senate.

When the report of this inglorious defeat reached Rome, the city was cast into mourning. The senate stoutly refused to recognize the treaty made by the defeated generals, in spite of the fact that this was shown to be the only honorable course to take. All who had consented to it were returned to Pontius, who refused to retaliate upon them for Rome's dishonorable policy. "Put your army back in the mountains," insisted the Samnite chief; this naturally was not done, and the war went on. In course of a few months the Samnites lost what they had previously won, and in 304 B. C. a treaty ended this second war. By it Rome gained little more than she had in the beginning and both sides felt that it was merely a truce.

Trouble with the Etruscans on the north caused the consul, Fabius Maximus, to proceed upon a new policy of carrying the war at once into the land of the enemy. Roman leadership was already recognized as far north as the Ciminian Forest, in southern Etruria. Beyond this a chain of Etruscan cities now made war against Rome. With a series of brilliant victories, Fabius extended Roman sway to the Apennines.

In 298 B. C. complaints reached Rome that the Samnites were once more infringing upon lands subject to her, and the army was dispatched thither. However, it occurred to the Samnite chief to lead his soldiers north to join the Gauls and Etruscans, who might be depended upon to oppose Roman advance. Consternation filled the mind of the Roman general when this union of opposed forces became known. The Etruscans failed to stand by the allied armies, and at the battle of Sentinum Rome won with heavy losses. The Samnites continued to carry on desultory fighting, but peace was made in 290 B. C. The leadership of Rome was acknowledged, and the Samnites agreed to furnish help in time of war. To make the conquest sure, Rome at once planted colonies in their midst. With the conclusion of this treaty, Rome was left supreme in Italy from the Apennines to the Greek cities in the south.

We have seen that before the sixth century the Greeks established colonies in the Italian peninsula. These grew to such proportions that the southern part of Italy received the name Magna Graecia. These Greek cities carried on extensive commerce and became wealthy and indolent. As they weakened, some fell to the share of the tyrant of Syracuse, while others simply sank into decay. Tarentum still remained important and maintained a fair trade. The Romans had entered into an agreement to send no ships into their waters, but in 282 B. C. a few Roman vessels put into the Tarentum harbor. Feeling sure that this boded ill for them, the Tarentines fell upon the ships, sank five of them, killed the admiral, and either killed the sailors or sold them into slavery. Rome demanded satisfaction, and Tarentum delayed until she found a willing ally in Pyrrhus, king of Epirus. This Grecian king wished to build up a great empire, and he imagined that opportunity awaited him in the west.

In 280 B. C. Pyrrhus landed in Italy with 25,000 soldiers

and many elephants. Now for the first time Rome was called upon to meet troops presumably better trained in military tactics than her own. The Roman legion had never encountered the Macedonian phalanx, and the result could not be foreseen. In a battle fought at Heraclea the elephant proved too much for the Roman cavalry, and while the Roman army stood its ground, the victory belonged to Pyrrhus. However, the Greek king had sustained such heavy losses that he sued for peace, but the Romans refused to treat with him unless he withdrew his army from their peninsula. The following year, another battle was fought with similar results; the Romans were defeated, but their opponents were badly crippled.

Pyrrhus now went into Sicily, where he remained until 275 B. C., when the third battle was fought with Rome. This time the Romans knew how to meet the onset of the elephants, and they won the day. Pyrrhus in disappointment went home, and without his support Tarentum could not long hold out against a Roman siege. In 272 the city fell to the share of Rome, leaving the whole Italian peninsula south of the Apennines undisputed.

It was one thing to win this territory, and quite a different thing to keep it. This last was the part in which Rome excelled. She never passed on to new territory while the old was yet unsettled. As far as she went, the country was bound to her with lasting bonds. Two particular means were taken to make conquests secure; the planting of colonies, and the maintenance of good roads. These facilitated a consolidation such as the world has never seen before or since.

Roman subjects were classified as citizens and allies. The citizens were of two classes, those who possessed full rights, and those who possessed passive rights. To the first division belonged the men of Rome and the early colonists who went forth from Rome to make their homes in new lands taken in conquest. This land was public domain and was given to those who wished to benefit themselves by taking a share in it. Again, many towns in Latium and the Campania were merged in the state; moreover, in coast towns, it was not deemed prudent to leave the original inhabitants in control, but rather, a garrison was stationed in the maritime cities, this garrison being composed of Roman citizens. The political advantages conferred by full citizenship—voting, eligibility for office, and share in making the laws—could be realized only in the city of Rome. If one lived elsewhere, these advantages could be enjoyed only when he returned to Rome.

The passive rights of citizens allowed them to intermarry with the Romans and to carry on commerce with one another. Cities possessing these rights generally managed their own local affairs, to their own satisfaction. The full Roman citizenship was a hardship rather than a privilege in early times, when people preferred their own local administration to any other. Hardest was the condition of the maritime cities, where a garrison was stationed to administer municipal affairs.

Finally, all conquered tribes, aside from those given full or passive citizenship, were known as allies. They furnished soldiers in time of war, and were subservient to Rome in questions of peace, war, and the coining of money.

With their colonies scattered all over the peninsula and their roads radiating in various directions, the Romans had already secured a firm hold upon Italy. The old saying: "All roads lead to Rome" was literally true. Cross roads were discouraged. To make the whole country dependent upon the one great city was an aim soon realized.

## CHAPTER VII.

### POLITICAL ORGANIZATIONS AND GOVERNMENT.

In earliest times in Rome, the position of the king in the state was similar to that occupied by the father in the family. The family was the unit of the state, and the father's power was absolute over the various members. He offered sacrifices at the family hearth and it was the duty of his wife and daughters to see that the fire upon this hearth was kept burning. Naturally, it was a serious matter in antiquity to allow fire to become extinguished; either coals must be brought from some distance, or fire must be ignited by a laborious process. Thus fire was considered sacred and had to be watched with constant care. The government of the family was the only government with which the early Romans were familiar, so when different tribes united under a king, to him was accorded rights similar to those of the father in the family. As the father performed sacrifices for his household, the king offered them for the state. As the fire upon the family hearth was guarded, so the vestal virgins, daughters of the state, were chosen to tend its sacred fire. As the father had power of life and death over his household, so the king exercised absolute authority over his subjects. From his decision there was no appeal. He commanded the troops in time of war and divided the booty among his fighting men.

While there was no apparent check upon the command of the father or the king, nevertheless, both were actually influenced by custom and by the religious law. The religion of the Romans declared a man who sold his son into slavery to be accursed. This largely prevented such action on the part of any father. The king likewise might act freely so long as he acted in accordance with custom, but when he chose to depart from the customs of his fathers, he must needs consult with the elders of his tribe and win support to his plan.

The king ruled so long as he lived and before his death it

was customary for him to name a successor. After his demise the elders of the tribe met, either to approve or disapprove of his choice. They themselves governed until a successor was decided upon.

Rome was originally made up of settlers upon the Palatine; in course of time, however, three tribes united to form the city. Any member of any clan composing these three tribes enjoyed all rights of citizenship. These early Romans called themselves *patricians*—"children of their fathers," to distinguish themselves from illegitimate sons, or from those who had no blood connection.

Families united to form clans; clans joined together into tribes but between the clan and the tribe came another division—the curia. There was an old tradition that at one time, ten families formed a clan, ten clans composed a curia, and ten curia, a tribe. This did not long obtain, if, indeed, it was ever true. Like the family, clan, and tribe, the curia had its own center of worship. In early times the meeting of the curia, or the Comitia Curiata, was important. In it each curia had one vote, determined by the majority of its members. Questions regarding offensive wars, involving frequently the violation of a treaty, were here voted upon.

During the period of the monarchy, another class of people arose—the plebeians. Apart from the patricians just described, outside the membership of clan and tribe, *plebeians,* or "the crowd" grew up. The population of conquered villages, freed slaves, and foreigners who came in for purposes of trade made up this class. They possessed the right of holding property and engaging in trade, or the *jus commerci.* The right of intermarriage and of participation in the affairs of state they did not have.

"No plebeian could be king, sit in the senate, or vote in the *comitia curiata.* The reason for this was in no small degree religious. . . . The plebeian woman could not marry into a Roman family, because this would admit her to the worship of gods in whose favor she had no share. So the Romans resisted the admission of foreigners to political privileges, because they were not willing to intrust the sacrifices to the city's ancestors to men who had no kinship with them. This was a state of affairs which was long maintained, because there is nothing more powerful in its influence over men's minds than religious superstition, but in the end it had to yield to a more just and equal system."[1]

At first, only the patricians had duties in the state. They had to fight for the cause of Rome, and tilled the king's land in time of peace. Servius Tullius, however, made it obligatory for all who held land to fight for the state. Having no political rights, the plebeians were now subject to political duties.

This same king is accredited with having divided the fighting population into hundreds, or *centuries*, for military purposes. In these hundreds, patricians and plebeians assembled on the Campus Martius at the call of the king. Soon this military organization assumed political powers. Especially the question of war was shortly taken from the Comitia Curiata and decided by the Comitia Centuriata. It was quite reasonable that the ones who were to do the fighting should decide whether or not a war be undertaken. As time went on, the Comitia Curiata was left with little else than religious matters for deliberation.

The abolition of the kingship was the work of the patricians, who wished to gain greater power for themselves. The religious duties of the king were given to a king of the sacrifice, or the *rex sacrorum;* the civil functions of the king were bestowed upon two consuls, elected for one year. One would serve as a check upon the other, and measures agreed upon by both were alone to be carried out. Since the needs of war might require speedy action, it was arranged that a dictator might be chosen by one of the consuls, he to receive the obedience of all during his term, which might never exceed six months. That he might be free to use his best judgment and not be hampered by the opinions of others, he was not held answerable when his term expired for any action as were other officers. Care of the public treasury was given two quaestors, who also had judicial power.

The organization of the senate claims attention. In earliest times, as clans united to form a tribe, the chieftains of each clan became elders of the new community. Tradition held

[1] See Laws previously quoted from Twelve Tables.

that there were 300 senators in Rome because there had once been 300 clans. The duty of this council of elders, or senate, as it was later called, was clearly defined. The senate was expected to choose a new king upon the death of a ruler. Until one was chosen, this council itself reigned. The king was supposed to consult with the council, which was primarily an advisory body. In 435 B. C. a censor was created to fill vacancies in the senate. His authority was limited by the fact that any ex-curule officer was entitled to a senatorial seat. Although constitutionally the senate was an advisory body, it nevertheless exercised a powerful influence in the affairs of the republic.

The history of Rome's land system is intimately connected with her constitutional development. As a pastoral people, the Romans attached no definite claim to land. Even when they began to raise crops each year, it was the *crop*, not the land, that was claimed. Waste land was held in common, for purposes of pasturage. Land was for the use, not the property, of families.

When authentic history begins in Rome, the early stages of land ownership had been passed. Each father owned a small area of land which contained his garden; here his house stood and here were the tombs of his ancestors. This small portion was not to be sold. It had been granted by the state and was sacred to the family and the family altar. It was not, however, sufficient to support the family, and the public land was still depended upon for maintenance. The public domain ever increased in Rome. When nearby territory was conquered, it was simply annexed to the original extent; when villages somewhat distant were conquered, Rome took the public lands in these as her own, regranted part of them back to the village, and used the rest for her own citizens.

Under the monarchy, the plebeians as well as the patricians had shared in the public lands. When the patricians drove out their kings, they desired to retain the public domain for their own purpose and convenience, and the plebeians found themselves shut out. In 494 B. C. the plebeians left Rome and took their position on the Sacred Mount, where the patricians were obliged to visit them and entreat them with promises to return. Their particular gain on this occasion was the tribunes-officers chosen by themselves to offer protection to individuals against the greed of the wealthy patricians. A tribune could rescue a plebeian from a military levy, or release him from seizure for debt. As time went on, the duties were more than two officers could dispatch and ten tribunes were created. Gradually, too, the tribune came to veto general actions of legislation, and no longer restricted his protection merely to individuals.

It was understood that there was some danger, some contradiction, in having officers within a state who could veto whole measures in favor of some particular class and in 451 B. C. ten men were appointed to draw up the laws of Rome and publish them, the hope being that when they were well known, the tribune might be no longer necessary. These ten men were to govern freely during their term, while consuls and tribunes were temporarily suspended. This body might be compared to a constitutional convention, except that civil and criminal law was considered, as well as political law. In 449 B. C. the men were discharged. The laws they had formulated were nevertheless accepted. The powers of the consul were more closely defined; the tribunate was restored. Henceforth the tribune came into the senate and heard the deliberations of that body. Vetoes were given at once to measures deemed unwise, and less time was lost.

In 367 B. C. the consulship was open to the plebeians. One of the two consuls might be chosen from the common people—or, indeed, were they sufficiently strong, both might be taken from their class. At once the patricians tried to lessen the power of the consuls. In 435 B. C., as has already been noted, the censorship was created. Every five years the censor made a list of all citizens, together with their property possessions. On the basis of this list the position of each was determined and his eligibility to a seat in the various assemblies and the senate.

Among the Greeks and more especially the Romans, it was impossible to separate religion from state affairs. The later Greeks grew away from their early gods, and the Romans did also; nevertheless, when religion fell away from affairs of state in Rome, Rome herself was fast declining. Besides the king of the sacrifice, and the pontifex maximus, there were several colleges of Roman priests. The college of pontiffs was the repository of the sacred law of the country. At the head of this college was the pontifex maximus. He selected the vestal virgins and appointed priests for the cults of different deities. The interpretation of religious law was his special function. He might prevent any state action by showing it to be contrary to the religious law or custom. The college of augurs announced whether or not actions were agreeable to the gods, reading their wills in the flight of birds or in the entrails of the animals offered upon the altar. They also studied the position of the constellations, and by observation of the heavens foretold disaster or success. So long as the membership of these colleges was confined to the upper class alone, any policy dictated by the common people might be successfully baffled. On this account, the plebeians struggled to obtain membership in these colleges and eventually secured it.

There are not lacking instances in Roman history when the assemblies of the people administered the government, setting aside the authority of the senate. Generally speaking, however, during the republic the senate was the great governing body, conservative and stable.

"The government of the senate, in the last years of its power, has received the just censure of those who are capable of criticising it. But the rule of the tribunes, who voiced the caprice of the city rabble, was but little better than anarchy. The ultimate outcome was the establishment of the empire. Rome thus accomplished the circle through which, in theory, all governments tend to pass—monarchy, aristocracy, democracy, anarchy—and began the round again."[2]

[2] Development of the Roman Constitution: Tighe, 131.

# CHAPTER VIII.

### Conflict with Carthage.

Carthage was originally a Phoenician trading post, founded at an early time by exiles from Tyre.[1]  For centuries the Carthaginians served as carriers for the ancient world and by this means became very wealthy.  Bent wholly upon trade, they never developed a strong political state, although their settlement expanded into a great city, and many towns and wide districts became their dependencies.  Having no political aspirations, and desiring simply to maintain an uninterrupted commerce, Carthage merely crippled the commerce of her dependencies and imposed heavy tributes upon them.

It was natural to expect that the growing city of Rome would be watched by the Carthaginians.  Probably as early as 509 B. C. the following treaty was made between the two cities:

"There shall be friendship between the Romans and their allies, and the Carthaginians and their allies, on these conditions:

"Neither the Romans nor their allies are to sail beyond the Fair Promontory, unless driven by stress of weather or the fear of enemies.  If any one of them be driven ashore, he shall not buy nor take aught for himself save what is needful for the repair of his ship and the service of the gods, and he shall depart within five days.

"Men landing for traffic shall strike no bargain save in the presence of a herald or town clerk. . Whatever is sold in the presence of these, let the price be secured to the seller on the credit of the state—that is to say, if such sale be in Libya or Sardinia.

"If any Roman comes to the Carthaginian province in Sicily, he shall enjoy all rights enjoyed by others.  The Carthaginians shall do no injury to the people of Ardea, Antium,

[1]See Carthage as described in the Story of Phoenicia.

Laurentium, Circeii, Tarracina, nor any other people of the Latins that are subject to Rome.

"From those townships even which are not subject to Rome they shall hold their hands; and if they take one, shall deliver it unharmed to the Romans. They shall build no fort in Latium; and if they enter the district in arms, they shall not stay a night therein."[2]

This agreement was renewed from time to time, and during Pyrrhus' invasion of Italy and Sicily, a defensive treaty was made between the two peoples—the Romans and Carthaginians.

Carthage possessed the greatest navy of her time and had already made the Mediterranean Sea her own. Rome, with her extensive coast line, needed outlets for her commerce, and especially needed to be able to defend her shores. Unless complete control of the Mediterranean was to be accorded the Carthaginians, sooner or later the two states must measure swords. An indefinite delay of the struggle might have obtained, but for unexpected events which brought matters to a climax.

Sicily had long been a bone of contention between the Greeks and Carthaginians. As the power of the Greeks lessened, Carthage gained a foothold. Her territory grew until she held the entire western portion of the island.

Upon the death of a tyrant of Syracuse ruling the southeastern portion of Sicily, a band of Campanian mercenaries, who had fought for him, were disbanded. On their way north, these soldiers seized the city of Messana, killed the citizens and took captive their wives and children. Here they established themselves and divided the property with one another, taking the name Mamertines, or Sons of Mars. Quite naturally, the Carthaginians and Hiero, the new tyrant of Syracuse, felt it necessary to drive out these daring outlaws, and the latter, realizing their inability to hold out alone, hesitated as to whether they would best seek Roman or Carthaginian protection.

When an embassy from Messana came before the Roman senate and asked for protection, this body scarce knew what

[2]Trans. in Source Book of Roman History: Munro, 80.

course to take. There was not the slightest justification for the conduct of these mercenaries, yet if Rome held aloof, Carthage would certainly make the most of the opportunity to increase her Sicilian territory. Unwilling to take the responsibility for such a course as now was offered them, the senate summoned the people and left the decision to them. It is plain that a strong element in the senate desired to check the power of Carthage, and the people clamoured for war. It would be difficult to find another occasion in Roman history when so critical a question hung in the balance. It meant, in reality, whether Rome was to be a continental or a world power.

" 'It was a moment of the deepest significance in the history of the world, when the envoys of the Mamertines appeared in the Roman senate.' If the Romans acceded to their request, they would not only do violence to their own feelings of right and wrong, by receiving into alliance a band of adventurers stained with the worst crimes, whose very kinsmen in Rhegium they had just punished for the same offense, but they would throw aside their views of establishing a mere sovereignty in Italy for the wider and more dangerous policy of interference with the outside world—a policy which could not fail to bring them into complicated relations with powers strictly outside their own land."[3]

It was determined to aid the Mamertines, and the first Punic[4] war was begun. Before tracing the main events of this struggle, let us compare the resources of the belligerents upon the eve of their hostilities.

Carthage, as we have seen, was a wealthy commercial power. Riches flowed into the private treasuries of her citizens from their trade; vast wealth accrued to the state treasury each year from the mines of Spain and from tributes imposed upon the dependencies. Instead of expending such wealth upon mercenaries who might enlarge the borders of the state, it had been harbored within the city of Carthage itself. Thus upon the eve of war, the treasuries were overflowing. Again, as we have noticed, Carthage possessed the one

[3] Mommsen's Student's History of Rome, 128.
[4] Punicus, the Latin word for Carthaginian.

great fleet in the third century before Christ, and her many trading outposts were of undoubted advantage to her. In her citizens she was both fortunate and unfortunate. They were ready to defend their state, to be sure, but they were very jealous of each other. This even interfered with leadership being left long in the hands of the ablest generals. In leaders, Carthage was fortunate, but even her two greatest generals, Hamilcar and Hannibal, suffered greatly because the state would not give adequate support, and hampered them in the most annoying way by withholding the pay of the soldiers. Besides this weakness, the tributary tribes hated Carthage because of her high-handed oppression. Tribute to one-half the yearly production was required of some, and all were bitterly oppressed. While possessing a splendid fleet, the land forces were altogether mercenaries, and these were not accustomed to such rigorous discipline as were the Romans.

Rome, on the other hand, had no great treasury to draw upon. For three hundred years she had been fighting, first for existence, and latterly, for territory. Her commerce was in its infancy, while her people were largely farmers, who by thrift and industry had prospered. Lacking the opulent burghers of Carthage, however, Rome was fortunate in her substantial citizen body, accustomed to the hardships of war, and not yet given over to the indulgencies of peace. All Romans stood for Rome—the humblest as well as the aristocrat. Rome was the city in which the fortunes of all were involved. Having but a small fleet, and that indifferently maintained, Rome had an army which had come forth victorious from a war with Greek mercenaries. This army and her strong political government that had followed close upon the heel of conquest, were the two important sources of Roman strength.

Any comparison of Roman and Carthaginian resources must take into account the character of the two races. The Carthaginian was greatly elated by victory and deeply depressed by defeat. The Roman possessed a fortitude which neither success nor failure could shake, and never does the Roman character shine forth more courageously than during the dark years of reverses met during the Punic wars.

When it was decided to dispatch help to the Mamertines,

an army was sent into Sicily. Meantime, those among the Mamertines who favored Carthage had given the city into her charge, and the Romans found a garrison in possession of Messana. Nevertheless, by deceit the garrison was dislodged and in turn, the Roman army occupied. Quite as might have been expected, Carthage declared war. During the first two years of the struggle—from 264-262 B. C.—Rome gained control of the eastern portion of Sicily, and Hiero, the new tyrant of Syracuse, transferred his alliance from Carthage to Rome.

Agrigentum, a most important point, was fortified by Carthage, but after a seven months' siege it fell to the share of Rome. Elated by the victory, the Romans now determined to drive Carthage out of the island altogether. This, however, could not be accomplished without a fleet. Such ships as Rome possessed were old and out of date, and a wrecked Carthaginian galley was taken as a model for the new fleet. Within two years 100 ships were ready. Realizing their superiority over their enemies in hand-to-hand conflicts, the Romans provided their ships with drawbridges, which could be thrown down upon Carthaginian decks, holding firmly by means of iron clamps. Thus the regular land forces could be brought into service.

In 260 B. C. the first naval engagement occurred, off Mylae on the northeastern coast of Sicily. The Carthaginians were so sure of themselves that they did not take ordinary precautions, and they were consequently defeated by Duilius, the Roman admiral. For this, their first naval victory, the Romans gave Duilius a splendid triumph and erected a pillar in his honor.

In 256 B. C. it was thought best to carry the war into Africa, and a fleet of 330 ships set out under the Roman commanders, Regulus and Vulso. They encountered the Carthaginian fleet off southern Sicily and defeated it. Then they proceeded to Africa and landed near Carthage. It is difficult to understand how such stupid blunders could have been made by competent leaders as were committed on both sides in this war. Had Carthage been aggressive throughout, she might easily have crippled Rome. Now the Romans made a fatal

mistake: Vulso was recalled to Rome with the greater part
of the army and fleet, it being deemed unnecessary to keep so
many soldiers in Africa. The winter was wasted by both
Romans and Carthaginians, and in the spring, Regulus was
defeated, while the fleet sent to bring home the remnant of
his army was wrecked on its return.

The war reverted to Sicily and for eight years nothing
decisive occurred on either side. In 247 B. C. Hamilcar took
control of the Carthaginian army, and decided to tire out the
Romans. For six years the latter suffered constant defeat,
and it seemed as though the island must be abandoned. The
treasury was empty, and there had been fearful loss of men.
Now the private citizens of Rome supplied the means for
equipping a new fleet, and before the enemy was aware of
any change, this fleet was upon them. The Carthaginians had
lost their fleets, and now could only command such vessels as
they could quickly muster to meet the new Roman navy. After
two battles in which Rome was victor, the Carthaginian general felt it was useless to longer hold out, and he sued for
peace. The terms required by Rome were difficult but were
not deeply humiliating. The following terms were stipulated:

"The Carthaginians shall evacuate Sicily and all islands
lying between Italy and Sicily.

"The allies of neither of the parties to the treaty shall be
attacked by the other.

"Neither party shall impose any contribution, nor erect any
public building, nor enlist soldiers in the dominions of the
other, nor make any compact of friendship with the allies of
the other.

"The Carthaginians shall within ten years pay to the
Romans two thousand two hundred talents (about $4,000,-
000), and a thousand on the spot, and shall restore all prisoners without ransom to the Romans."[5]

Carthage was shortly beset by her mercenaries, whom she
could not pay, and Rome took advantage of the situation to
appropriate Sardinia and Corsica. When Carthage strenuous-
ly opposed such robbery, Rome threatened war. It was this

[5] Munro's Source Book, 91.

unwarranted deed which caused Hamilcar to hate Rome with undying hatred.

For the next twenty years Rome was busily occupied in organizing her new territory. The tyrant of Syracuse was left independent in Sicily, which otherwise became a Roman province. Sardinia and Corsica together constituted the second province. Over both these provinces a governor was placed, he having control of the army, acting as executive and judge. From his acts there was no appeal. While heretofore Rome had never imposed tribute, but had allowed her conquered people in Italy to contribute soldiers in time of war, tribute was now imposed upon the provinces.

Rome's provincial administration was destined to become an important factor, and it is interesting to watch its development from this point.

Two wars occurred during the twenty years following the peace with Carthage in 241 B. C., the first being a naval engagement to clear the Adriatic Sea of infesting pirates, and the second a war with Gaul. After the Punic war, the Romans settled colonists in lands claimed by the Gauls, who saw in this action the beginning of an effort to drive them out of their territory. In the war which followed in consequence of their revolt, Rome extended her boundaries to the Alps, annexing into her own state Cisalpine Gaul. She was occupied in colonizing this region when suddenly her attention was averted from enemies upon the north to a greater danger from the south.

ROMAN GALLEY.

SCHOOL OF GLADIATORS.

## CHAPTER IX.

### The Second Punic War. 219-202 b. c.

The Romans undoubtedly well understood that the peace of 241 b. c. would not be lasting. Certainly all Carthaginians regarded it as temporary. The unpardonable greed of Rome in seizing Sardinia and Corsica at a time when Carthage was endangered by the Mercenary War, and their demand for $1,-500,000 indemnity when the Phoenicians expostulated, kindled undying hatred for Rome in the breast of Hamilcar Barca. He vowed deep revenge for the unwarranted robbery, and devoted his life and the lives of his sons to the cause of vindicating his country.

It is impossible to understand the attitude of Carthage during the second Punic war without considering political conditions within the city itself. Two political parties existed, the peace party, and the war party. The peace party included the wealthy, indolent, leisure-loving aristocrats, whose aspirations were merely commercial. Like the traders found in Tyre and Sidon by early Assyrian conquerors, they desired peace on almost any terms, for peace alone rendered their merchant-ship safe upon the sea. The question of maintaining honor and integrity was one which concerned them not at all. The war party, on the other hand, included the progressive, generous-hearted, patriotic element of the population, who were not content to barter for peace today and leave their children without a country tomorrow. First one and then the other party would gain popular support, but the peace party had the advantage of being able to buy supporters for its cause. No position was too untenable, no argument too absurd to find favor with its adherents. When Hamilcar returned home, after conducting the first Punic war, the peace party called him to answer for the Mercenary War, which, it was said he had caused by promising to pay the mercenaries, when in reality he was unable to do so. This preposterous attempt failed because of its apparent absurdity. Nevertheless, it was plain to Hamilcar that upon him devolved not alone the task of vindicating his country, but he must himself provide the money and soldiers for such a purpose. Carthage could not be depended upon to provide either the one or the other.

Accordingly, in 237 B. C. Hamilcar collected such soldiers as remained to him and crossed into Spain. With clear vision, he saw that the gold and silver of Hispania could be made to yield treasure for equipping a soldiery, and that the bar-barians, when conquered, would make sturdy fighters. So far Carthage had maintained only commercial relations with Spain, and hence that hatred so invariably found in her dependencies was altogether lacking here.

Hamilcar was successful from the start. Within a few years he had penetrated to the river Ebro and had collected a large army. Upon his death—and it was not left for him to carry out his plan—his son-in-law Hasdrubal assumed command of the army. He organized the empire which Hamilcar had brought so quickly into being, and founded New Carthage for its capital. The natives had discovered that it was to their advantage to serve generals who treated them fairly and paid them well for their work; consequently many flocked to the Carthaginian standards.

In 221 B. C. Hasdrubal was assassinated by one who held a personal grudge, and Hannibal, son of Hamilcar, succeeded to the command of the army and was recognized by the government at home. Before taking up the career of this great general of antiquity—greatest perhaps of all military leaders—let us give brief attention to the character of the man himself.

It is significant to note that we know Hannibal only through his enemies. The Carthaginians left no records; yet in spite of the hostile channels through which our knowledge comes, the character of this military genius stands forth with marvelous brilliancy. Late in life, when his mighty plans had failed, Hannibal told for the first time of his early consecration to the service of Carthage. While his father was offering the usual sacrifices to the gods, before starting out upon his campaigns in Spain, he kept his son with him. Asking the lad if he would like to accompany his father upon the cam-

paign, Hannibal eagerly replied that he would.   Thereupon
Hamilcar bade him place his hand upon the consecrated sacrifices and swear eternal enmity to Rome.   This naturally
made a deep impression upon the boy's mind.   He believed
that the vindication of Carthage was his mission and he gave
himself to it with unwavering fidelity.

"Nature had bestowed upon him gifts both mental and
physical, which were no mean qualifications for his mighty
task; education and association had completed nature's work.
Brought up from his infancy to cherish thoughts of vengeance
on Rome, trained as a soldier in early youth under his father's
eye, already highly distinguished, as the commander of the
Spanish cavalry, alike for personal bravery and for the higher
qualities of a leader, Hannibal was especially fitted to carry
out the great projects of his father.   Anger, envy, and meanness have written his history, but have not been able to mar
the pure and noble image which it presents. . . . 'Every page
of the history of the period attests his genius as a general;
and his gifts as a statesman were, after the peace with Rome,
no less conspicuously displayed in the reform of the Carthaginian constitution, and in the unparalleled influence which, as
a foreign exile, he exercised in the cabinets of the eastern
potentates.   The power which he wielded over men is shown
by his incomparable control over an army of various nations
and many tongues—an army which never, in the worst times,
mutinied against him.   He was a great man; wherever he
went, he riveted the eyes of all.' "[1]

In 226 B. C. two settlements, Saguntum and Emporium, on
the east coast of Spain, realized that Phoenician power was
drawing near them, and sought the protection of Rome.   Accordingly, Rome made a treaty with Carthage whereby these
towns should be left unmolested and stipulated that the Ebro
should be the northern boundary of Carthaginian Spain. Seven
years later, however, Hannibal felt ready to begin his march
into Italy, and believing that the Romans were but biding
their time to make war upon his people, he precipitated the
struggle by taking Saguntum.   Immediately Rome sent her
ambassadors to the Carthaginian senate, asking that Hanni-

[1] Mommsen, 144.

bal's act be repudiated and an indemnity paid. But Spanish gold had been sent too freely into Carthage to allow the senate to recall Hannibal at this juncture, whereupon Rome declared war.

It is significant again to note the situation of each country upon the eve of renewed hostilities. The ultimate object of the Spanish campaign had not been generally understood in Carthage itself at the beginning, although the Barca family had fondly cherished the secret hope of revenge upon Rome. The Phoenicians could feel reasonably well prepared for war now, while if a longer delay was made, Rome too would be prepared, as at this time she was not. A strong infantry, splendid Numidian cavalry, and a well-organized empire in Spain as headquarters, gave Hannibal fair prospect of success.

Rome, on the other hand, had intended to further discomfit her rival, but had expected to do so at her pleasure and advantage. She had been fighting the Gauls and subsequently organizing their territory, and she had utterly failed to understand the advantage of Spanish operations in strengthening the Carthaginians. When the gauntlet was thrown down she would not fail to accept the challenge, but her delay in getting started proved how slightly the real situation was understood by the Roman senate.

Hannibal chose to prosecute the war by land rather than sea for two reasons: in the first place, he believed that the Gauls of both Trans and Cis-Alpine Gaul would come to his support, and that the old enemies of Rome would gradually fall away and join his standards, and secondly, to have employed a fleet to any great extent would have meant that he must fall back upon Carthage for support, and Carthage had proved before a "bruised reed." Leaving Spain guarded by 15,000 Libyans, and Libya protected by the same number of Spaniards, Hannibal set out upon his famous campaign to Italy, taking 90,000 infantry, 12,000 cavalry, and 58 elephants. Crossing the Ebro, he subdued hostile tribes between the river and the Pyrenees. This district had been regarded by the Romans as a sort of buffer territory, and they had rested secure in its protection. Leaving plenty of soldiers to hold the land just conquered, and sending home 10,000 soldiers drawn

from tribes in Spain whom he soon perceived to be disheart-
ened at the journey ahead of them, Hannibal crossed the
Pyrenees and reached the Rhone with 50,000 foot soldiers and
9,000 cavalry.

In 218 B. C. Sempronius Longus and Cornelius Scipio were
elected consuls. In view of the coming war, Sempronius was
sent to Sicily with a good sized army, while Scipio was sent
into Gaul, thence to proceed to Spain. Because of negotiations
between Hannibal and the Cis-Alpine Gauls, these tribes had
broken out in revolt, driving out the Roman colonists recently
planted in their midst at Placentia and Cremona, and seizing
the commanders of the fortresses. Putting down this revolt,
Scipio proceeded leisurely on his way to Massilia, when he
suddenly heard that Hannibal had reached the Rhone.

Upon reaching the Rhone, Hannibal found his progress
checked by Gauls somewhat north of Massilia. Sending a de-
tachment north to a comparatively easy crossing, he waited until
these troops had attacked the rear of the Gauls, whereupon he fell
upon their front ranks. They were utterly routed and in comparative ease the remainder of the Carthaginian army crossed
the Rhone. From the Allobroges, who occupied the angle
between the Rhone and the Isere rivers, the Carthaginian soldiers received necessary food and clothing.

It is not known by what route Hannibal crossed the Alps.
Each path has in turn been suggested as the one through which
his army came into Italy. Certain it is that greatest hardships
attended the march over the mountains. It was late autumn
before Hannibal reached the Alps, although he had expected
to make an earlier crossing. Avalanches fell upon the army
in the defiles, ice and snow made well-nigh impassable its
progress; horses lost their footing and rolled down to vast
depths with their riders. After days of marching under such
conditions, there were no suitable places for making camp at
night, and food was scarce indeed. Hostile tribes from above
threw stones down upon the army. No less a genius than
Hannibal would have been equal to the task of inspiring soldiers to continue under such dreadful circumstances, but it is
worthy of note that at no time were there murmurings on the
part of Hannibal's followers; his great personality won men to

II₁—29

him and held them by strong bonds. It has been estimated
that 20,000 soldiers were lost in the passage of the Alps, by
which number alone we may gather some conception of its
attendant difficulties.

With 20,000 infantry and 6,000 horses, Hannibal came
into the smiling valley of the Po. His army was emaciated
by cold and hunger. Fortunately for them, Scipio, who had
been evaded by Hannibal, did not approach at once, and opportunity was given for rest. When a battle was fought at
Ticinus, the Numidian cavalry proved too much for the
Romans, who suffered a defeat. Scipio retreated across the
Po, to await Sempronius, who had been summoned from
Sicily. By an ambush Hannibal defeated the consolidated
Roman army at Trebia, and the Gauls flocked to his standards.
In the spring the great Phoenician general evaded the two
armies that awaited his approach, and crossed the Apennines,
far to the west where he was not expected, coming into the
valley of the Arno. Hannibal now posed as the liberator of
the Italians, making war only on the Romans. He hoped that
the Italian confederacy would gradually break up. This year
the great battle of Lake Trasimene was fought, wherein the
Roman infantry was completely annihilated, while the cavalry
to the number of 10,000 fell next day into Hannibal's hands.

Under circumstances so urgent, the Romans made Fabius
Maximus dictator. He inaugurated a waiting policy, which
won him the name "the delayer." Instead of waging battles,
he simply followed Hannibal around, hoping in this way to
gradually wear out the Carthaginian army, to cut off supplies,
and possibly surprise Hannibal in some disadvantageous spot
where he might be worsted. As a matter of fact, instead of
saving Rome, this policy allowed all Italy to be plundered
by the invading army and failed completely in driving it out.

In 216 B. C. the Romans blundered in electing Varro, the
people's choice for one consul, Paulus for the other. Varro
had little to commend him, but the people were tired of war
in their very midst and ascribed its continuance to the senate.
Varro was known to be opposed to the senate and this alone
commended him to the populace. Through his ignorance and
misguided zeal, the battle of Cannae was fought. Hannibal

commanded 30,000 troops; the Roman consuls commanded 80,000—nearly three times as many, yet 50,000 Romans were left upon the battle field and 20,000 were taken prisoners. The Roman army was destroyed; one-fifth of the population had been exterminated in this dreadful war, and now there was mourning in every house. We are told that the wailing of the women outside the Senate House was so deafening that the senators could hardly be heard in their deliberations. Surely Hannibal had made Rome pay well for her mistaken greed of earlier years.

"Four times over he had now measured his sword with the future conquerors of the world, and each time he had been victorious in an ever ascending series of successes. At the Ticinus he first met the Roman cavalry, and it was their hasty retreat from the field of battle which alone saved them from a rout. At the Trebia, however the consul might try to disguise it, it was no retreat at all, it was a total rout. At the Trasimene it was neither retreat nor rout, it was the extermination of an army. At Cannae it was the extermination, not of one but of two armies, and each of them twice its usual size. This was the pinnacle of Hannibal's success, and a pinnacle indeed it was."[2]

Through these dark days for the Romans, the composure of the senate was indeed commendable. When the people were swayed by one motive or another, when everything seemed discouraging and no one could foresee the end, day after day the Roman fathers conferred in the senate for the common good. They remained calm when all else was in turmoil; they held fast to their belief in the ultimate triumph of Rome when others weakened. Nor should we lose sight of the fact that the Italian confederacy did not, as Hannibal had hoped, fall apart in consequence of these astonishing victories. The Gauls, to be sure, joined with Hannibal, but they had never been entirely subdued. Certain of the Greek cities which had been oppressed by Roman rule went over to the Phoenicians, but the great mass of communities and peoples remained true to Rome, which fact alone speaks well for that city's government.

After the battle of Cannae a change came over the war.

[2] Rome and Carthage: Smith, p. 167.

The Romans never fought better than when in extremity, and their four successive defeats merely spurred them on to greater efforts. It was determined to risk no more battles with a general who could win with such chances against him. Certain events still portended well for Hannibal. Capua voluntarily came into his hands, and he took Magna Graecia. All this time, it must be remembered, no aid had come to him from Carthage. The aristocracy of that city said the war had been made by Hannibal, who must now fight it out. The empire in Spain could send no aid, for a Roman army guarded any communication thence, and Philip V. of Macedon, from whom Hannibal had expected to get help, was himself involved in a war with the Greek states. Without recruits other than those who in Italy had voluntarily joined him, without aid of any sort from Carthage, this greatest general of antiquity had maintained his army in the land of the enemy for three years, and had been successful in every engagement.

In 212 B. C. Marcellus continued the war in Sicily and two years later, Syracuse was taken and entirely destroyed. In Italy, Fabius took Capua during a temporary absence of Hannibal, and meted out dire punishment to those who had deserted the cause of Rome. Gradually Hannibal was losing ground, and in 209 B. C. he retired into southern Italy to await reinforcements which he felt must reach him from Carthage or from his brother Hasdrubal in Spain.

Late in 211 B. C. Publius Cornelius Scipio was elected to take command of the army which guarded Spain. He was a brilliant young man, of commanding presence and wide influence. In 209 B. C. he captured New Carthage, the capital of the Spanish empire, thus falling heir to the Carthaginian stores. Hasdrubal evaded him and moved toward Italy, only to be met and defeated by Gaius Claudius Nero, one of the consuls for the year. With characteristic Roman brutality, Nero sent the severed head of Hasdrubal to Hannibal's camp, and the great general, hitherto ignorant of his brother's movements, realized that help would not be forthcoming and that his cause had failed.

Yet Rome was not through with her terror. After the siege of Capua Hannibal had moved into Latium—the only portion of Italy yet unvisited by him, and blazing villages at night announced his arrival in the very neighborhood of the capital. His camp for some days was but three miles from the city walls.

"Unmolested by the Romans and almost within their view, he ravaged the whole country round, destroying the gardens and the villages, and carrying off into his camp with stern delight, the crops and cattle, and the booty of every kind on which he could lay his hand. Then with a body of two thousand horsemen he rode right up to the Colline gate, and passed leisurely along the walls to the temple of Hercules, gazing wistfully at the cruel stones which alone saved the inhabitants, Roman though they were, from his avenging sword. The fates were against him, but he must have felt that he had nobly kept his vow."

The strain through these years had been fearful upon Rome and her allies. In 209 B. C. several of the old Latin colonies gave notice to the Roman senate that they need not ask further assistance of them, since they had no more men or money to contribute. This announcement brought consternation to Rome, for if the example were followed by others, after all that had been endured, failure might yet overtake Rome.

Successful in Spain, Cornelius Scipio returned to Rome in 206 B. C. and was made consul. Two years later he invaded Africa and Hannibal was recalled home. "Hannibal hath been conquered," that general is said to have exclaimed, "not by the Roman people, who have been so often slain and routed, but by the Carthaginian Senate, through envy and distraction." He had been worsted and in the battle of Zama the Carthaginian army was destroyed. Scipio offered terms of peace and Hannibal urged his people to accept them, heavy though they were. Carthage was to cede Spain to Rome; all ships with the exception of twenty were to be given up; for fifty years an annual tribute of $240,000 was to be paid. Carthage was not to wage war with any one without permission of Rome. It was greatly to Scipio's credit that he made no insulting requirements of the defeated country. Rome, not less than Carthage, needed peace, for she had lost 300,000 of her vigorous men, all her money, her agriculture had sunk into decay, and the terrors of war had brutalized her people. Surely the refining influences of peace were sorely needed in the Italian peninsula.

As for the Carthaginians, they suffered no pain keener than that of witnessing their fleet, their particular pride, towed out of the harbor and burned before their very eyes.

# CHAPTER X.

## Conquests in the East.

During the Second Punic War, Philip V. of Macedon had shown a disposition to aid Hannibal. To prevent him from so doing, Rome sent a small force into Greece and stirred up troubles nearer home for the ambitious king. These hostilities are known as the First Macedonian War, but their only object and result was the prevention of Greek support being rendered to Carthage.

Rome was not likely to forget such demonstrations on the part of the Macedonian king, and the close of the Second Punic War gave opportunity for Roman interference in the East.

Upon the death of Alexander the Great, his vast empire fell into three large kingdoms—Macedonia, Syria, and Egypt; and into several smaller kingdoms—Rhodes and Pontus among them. Two Greek leagues survived—the Aetolian and the Achaean. Egypt had become an ally of Rome, and desired a peace policy. Syria and Macedon were ruled by ambitious kings who wished most of all to extend their territories. In 200 B. C. hostilities broke out between Rome and Macedon, because Philip had made an alliance with Antiochus to divide Egyptian possessions between them. Egypt being an ally of Rome, especially valued since she supplied large quantities of grain to the Italian peninsula, found protection in the Romans, who made war on Philip. In 197 B. C. the Roman legions defeated the Greek phalanx for the second time in history. This is known as the Second Macedonian War.

Because the populace at home was not disposed to carry on extensive wars in the east at this time, Rome desired only to cripple Philip V. and did not now appropriate territory in Greece. Rather, on the occasion of the national games, the victorious Roman general proclaimed Greece free, to the tumultuous joy of the people. Nevertheless the protectorate soon established by the Romans showed that in this matter they had not been actuated wholly by generous motives

The Aetolian League was not satisfied with Roman interference in Greece, however, and appealed to Antiochus III. of Syria to drive the Romans out of the peninsula. With 10,-000 troops, Antiochus landed in Greece, only to be defeated. Not content, the Roman army pursued him in his flight to Asia, and in 190 B. C. fought a decisive battle at Magnesia The misguided king was killed by his own people.

The Third Macedonian War broke out in 171 B. C., lasting until 168 B. C. It came about in this way: Upon the death of Philip V. of Macedon, his son, Perseus, succeeded to the throne, and regarded the time as favorable for throwing off Roman protection. He was defeated after some lesser victories, and Macedonia was divided into four districts, each to be self-governing, but separated from the rest.

In the Peloponnesus, Corinth, as head of the Achaean League, tried to extend her sway over the various Peloponnesian states. In spite of their long centuries of strife, the Greeks had not learned that in union they could alone maintain themselves against outside powers. Immediately, Sparta, jealous of the commercial city, asked the Roman senate to prevent such aggressions on the part of Corinth. The Romans themselves were establishing a commerce and looked with envy upon the extensive trade which centered in this Greek port. However, ambassadors were sent from Rome to investigate the situation and report to Rome, but Corinth was rash enough to insult them when they arrived before the convened delegates of the league. Rome had won too many victories during the last fifty years to brook such treatment in patience. It was determined thereupon to break up the league and to destroy Corinth. We cannot read today of the wanton destruction of this ancient city without deep feeling of regret that so much Hellenic beauty was thus heedlessly ruined. Being a wealthy port, the seat of a wide commerce, Corinth had accumulated rare works of art; her own artists had produced more, and her buildings were many of them splendid. Passing over the blind fury which impelled men to blot out of existence ancient cities, thereby killing or selling into slavery their sands of helpless people, we realize the tremendous loss of Greek remains attendant upon the destruction of Corinth in 146 B. C.

In 1909, divers in the Mediterranean Sea came upon the remains of a Roman galley. Loaded too heavily with plunder from the stricken Corinth, the vessel had been overpowered by a storm and had gone down with all her passengers and freight. Not only have hopes run high that fragments of Corinthian art may be recovered from this wreck, but it has appeared not unlikely that similar finds in the vicinity may add still more to our knowledge of Greek statuary.

Nor was Corinth the only ancient seat of civilization to be wiped out in this memorable year. From Europe and Asia the scene reverted to Africa and Carthage. After the peace of 201 B. C., Hannibal showed himself to be skillful in peace as well as war. He compelled the Carthaginians to revise their constitution, to remove the Hundred Judges, or senators, whose selfish, self-centered, commercial spirit had led to the disaster of the war. In their places, public-spirited men were chosen. No longer was the public treasury subject to the dishonesty of the aristocrats, and we may infer how great a benefit this proved when Carthage was able to wipe out the complete war indemnity in thirteen years.

There were Romans, however, who looked with suspicion upon the stricken city which was so valiantly coming again into a more prosperous condition. Especially strong was the influence of Cato, a conservative and short-sighted senator, who is said to have concluded every speech in the senate by the ominous sentence: "Carthage must be destroyed." This attitude was so persistently held by a certain element of the Roman population that gradually it became more general. Various steps were taken which led up to the crowning disaster. In the first place, Rome demanded the surrender of Hannibal, who alike in peace and war had proven himself the great defender of his country. To spare his countrymen the humiliation of replying, Hannibal went into voluntary exile. He took refuge for a time at the court of Antiochus, offering to command the Syrian forces against Rome in the conflict already mentioned. It is quite certain that, had this offer been accepted, the war would have assumed an altogether different aspect, but Antiochus was too jealous of the great Carthaginian to allow him to win laurels in this way. Later, Hannibal became a wanderer, and ended his life by taking poison when he was about to fall into Roman hands.

When the great leader was out of the way, Rome still found means of harassing Carthage. She had helped to establish the king of Numidia upon his throne, and now, when his people continually encroached upon Carthaginian territory, Rome secretly gave him assurance that such a course was not objectionable to her, while to the Carthaginian ambassadors who repeatedly came to seek redress, empty promises were given. At length the citizens of Carthage lost all patience. They would no longer sit by and see their fields plundered by the Numidians and make no effort to protect them. Among the conditions stipulated by Rome in the peace treaty of 201 B. C. was one which prevented Carthage from making war with any people without first asking Roman permission. It was useless to ask it in this case, so on their own responsibility hostilities broke out between the people of Carthage and Numidia. This gave Rome a pretext which she had long wanted. At once she sought redress. The Carthaginians realized how useless was any attempt at force, and yielded to her in her demands. Three hundred children were demanded as hostages; these the people reluctantly voted to give, and at last they were torn from their agonized mothers. Next Rome demanded that the city walls be leveled. This was conceded. Soon she bethought her of another requirement: that the arms of the Carthaginian citizens be collected and yielded up. This was complied with. Finally, heaping insult upon insult, she commanded the Carthaginians to tear down their city and build another where they liked, providing it be ten miles from the sea! This proved the last straw. Asking a month for consideration, Rome haughtily gave it in scorn. Driven to extremities, the people made their last heroic effort; they constructed new walls and made new weapons. Every man, woman and child helped to prepare for the last struggle. So well did they succeed that when the Romans appeared to hear their decision they were amazed by the defense of the city.

An army was sent to destroy the town, but it was unable to make an entrance. After several efforts, the assailing force was greatly increased. Finally, in 146 B. C., the fortifications gave way. Nor was the struggle over yet. The Roman soldiers were compelled to fight their way in every house, and to take the town step by step. We are told that at the beginning of the siege the population numbered 700,000. At the close, 50,000 were sold into slavery. The remainder had fallen in defense of their city. At last the Roman army was satiated with blood and plunder, but the Roman senate was inexorable in its demand that every stone be razed and the site of the city ploughed.

Thus ended the last Phoenician city, so long the seat of Asiatic civilization. Yet Hannibal was right; it fell because of its own inherent weaknesses rather than Roman greed. While we sympathize with the mighty Hannibal and follow his defeats with regret, we must recognize how greatly he surpassed his fellow townsmen, generally speaking, and must see that if the ancient world had to bow at the feet of either Rome or Carthage, the latter would have been far the greater evil of the two.

## CHAPTER XI.

### RESULTS OF CONQUEST.

It was inevitable that two hundred years of conquest would bring great changes in the Roman republic. Particularly the fifty years that preceded the fall of Carthage, bringing the Italians into immediate contact with eastern culture, wrought many changes in social as well as political life. The ideas and ideals of the people became different; modifications and growth of the political system attended the acquisition of wide territory; and the civilization of Italy was greatly affected by the influx of foreign influences, made possible by the eastern wars.

The early Romans had been austere and pious, loyal to the state above all things, and unselfish in its service. Abundant stories remain of fathers who sacrificed their sons without a murmur when the misdoings of these endangered the state. While the particular instances recounted may perhaps be mere traditions, they nevertheless indicate plainly the ideals of the times. By 146 B. C. the Roman of this type was fast disappearing. In his place the ambitious, power-loving, self-seeking citizen was to be found. Inestimable plunder resulted from the wars in the east, and consequently war was found to be a short road to wealth. The fair-dealing of earlier times disappeared and avarice took its place. Moreover, the simplicity of living gave way before riches and luxury. Indeed, it may be said that many of the ideals of the people were no longer Roman, so far as social life was concerned. Greek thought and Greek culture permeated the peninsula, and, unfortunately for Rome, Greek civilization had sunk now to its lowest ebb.

These disadvantages were offset by certain striking advantages. The Greeks possessed a broader view of life than their Roman neighbors, and it was unquestionably this new feature that enabled the Romans to blend the Mediterranean countries into one great empire. With all its faults, Roman government was the best the world had seen. Peace came at last to many little states hitherto exposed to frequent invasions and unrest. The laws of Rome were vastly superior to those they now displaced. Before taking up provincial administration, let us turn to conditions within the city of Rome itself.

During the period of conquest, the old distinctions between patrician and plebeian had disappeared. A new nobility had arisen which included the wealthiest and most influential of both classes. While it is frequently said that this nobility was based upon office holding, it would be truer to say that it was based upon wealth and influence, for these two qualifications were essential to an aspirant for magistracy. The higher offices in Rome were known as the *curule* offices, because those holding them were entitled to sit in curule chairs. In monarchical days, the king sat upon an ivory chair—a curule chair—when administering affairs of state. Those who later assumed kingly duties—the consuls, praetors, censors, dictators appointed in times of imminent danger, and the higher aediles—were themselves entitled to curule chairs. Any one, whose ancestors had held such office, belonged to the noble or senatorial class. The visible sign of nobility was the ancestorial image set up in the home. Constitutionally, any full Roman citizen was eligible to the curule offices, but as a matter of fact, only the wealthy could command them. In addition to these, there were inferior magistrates, inferior aediles, eight quaestors, with certain judicial duties and care of the treasury, and ten tribunes.

The great political body of Rome was the senate, whose members were chosen by the censors from those who had held curule offices—ex-consuls, ex-praetors, etc. Others might from time to time be appointed, but if so, they had but the right to vote, and were not called·upon to speak, as were the rest who had earlier been curule magistrates. Constitutionally, this body had but advisory powers, and existed to confer with the consuls. Nevertheless, the senate became the one staple governing body of the early republic. Its members, once elected, served for life, and the three hundred senators thus chosen formed the conservative element of the Roman state.

Polybius, a Greek taken captive in the war between Rome and Macedon, spent his later years in compiling a history of the Romans. In this is to be found a treatise upon the constitution. Regarding the duties of the senate, consuls and people, he wrote:

"The senate has first of all the control of the treasury, and regulates the receipts and disbursements alike. For the quaestors cannot issue any public money for the various departments of the state without a decree of the senate, except for the service of the consuls. The senate controls also what is by far the largest and most important expenditure, that, namely, which is made by the censors every lustrum for the repair or construction of public buildings; this money cannot be obtained by the censors except by the grant of the senate. Similarly all crimes committed in Italy requiring a public investigation, such as treason, conspiracy, poisoning, or wilful murder, are in the hands of the senate. Besides, if any individual or state among the Italian allies requires a controversy to be settled, a penalty to be assessed, help or protection to be afforded,—all this is the province of the senate. Or again, outside of Italy, if it is necessary to send an embassy to reconcile warring communities, or to remind them of their duty, or sometimes to impose requisition upon them,—this, too, is the business of the senate." [1]

Constitutionally, the management of finances, control of public works, the direction of the foreign policy, and the administration of the provinces, belonged to the senate; yet, as a matter of fact, its duties were greater. It largely determined the nature of the legislation, and was, in reality, the real sovereign of the Roman state.

As the senate's power increased, the importance of the assemblies declined. Nor was the expansion of senatorial power the only reason for diminishment of democratic authority. The citizenship had been conferred upon many who did not live in Rome, yet citizens dwelling elsewhere might at any time come to the city and take part in the legislation of the people. The assemblies became such large bodies that discussion was impossible; measures to be brought before them were usually referred from the senate and a negative or affirmative vote was given. An opportunity was offered for

[1] Polybius' Hist. Rome.

demagogues to gain the upper hand in molding the public mind, and this they were quick to appreciate.

"After this one would naturally be inclined to ask what part is left for the people in the constitution, when the senate had these various functions, especially the control of the receipts and expenditures of the exchequer; and when the consuls again have absolute power over the details of military preparation, and an absolute authority in the field? There is, however, a part left the people, and it is a most important one. For the people is the sole fountain of honor and of punishment; and it is by these two things, and these alone, that dynasties and constitutions, and, in a word, human society, are held together.        The people then are the only courts to decide matters of life and death; and even in cases where the penalty is money, if the sum to be assessed is sufficiently serious, and especially when the accused have held the high magistracies.

"Again, it is the people who bestow offices on the deserving, which are the most honorable rewards of virtue. It has also the absolute power of passing and repealing laws; and most important of all, it is the people who deliberate on the question of peace or war. And when provisional terms are made for alliance, suspension of hostilities, or treaties, it is the people who ratify them or the reverse." [2]

A tribune presided over the assembly of the people; a consul over the senate. Here it is also convenient to consider the function of the consuls:

"The consuls, before leading out the legions, remain in Rome and are supreme masters of the administration. All other magistrates, except the tribunes, are under them and take their orders. They introduce foreign ambassadors to the senate; bring matters requiring deliberation before it; and see to the execution of its decree. If, again, there are any matters of state which require the authorization of the people, it is their business to see to them, to summon the popular meetings, to bring proposals before them and to carry out the decrees of the majority. In the preparations for war also, and, in a word, in the entire administration of a campaign,

Polybius' Hist. Rome.

they have all but absolute power. They have authority to expend as much of the public money as they choose.

"As for the people, the consuls are pre-eminently obliged to court their favor, however distant from home may be the field of their operations; for it is the people, as I have said before, that ratifies, or refuses to ratify, terms of peace and treaties; but most of all because when laying down their office they have to give an account of their administration before it."

The point to be especially noted is that, as a result of the foreign conquests, the power of the senate increased and the power of the people decreased. Had Rome confined her interests to the peninsula, the same result would have been sure to come as the population increased. The ancients knew nothing of our modern system of representation, and it is evident that a great, unwieldy mass of people could not administer affairs of state nor deliberate upon questions of general concern in any adequate degree.

With great acquisitions of territory, provincial administration had to be provided by Rome. By 146 B. C. Rome possessed eight provinces: Sicily, Sardinia and Corsica, Hither Spain, Further Spain, Illyricum, Macedonia, Africa, and Pergamum—a kingdom of Asia bequeathed to Rome by its dying king This last was known as *Asia*. As she had isolated the Italian cities, so now Rome sought to destroy any relations between her provinces. If they were allowed to maintain inter-provincial relationships, they might combine in some effort to free themselves from their dependency upon Rome, and such opportunity was not to be given. While the Italian cities had been merely required to contribute soldiers and military supplies in time of war, the provinces were required to pay tribute—money and grain, and in addition, to pay a land tax.

Over each province a governor was placed. He had no salary, and only a slight allowance was made for his expenses. This in the very outset gave opportunity for provincial oppression. The governor was in the beginning a praetor, elected by the people; later it became customary to send an ex-consul, or an ex-praetor (pro-consul; pro-praetor) to the provinces.

These men had to make a living and support a family, and if they had political aspirations, they must accumulate money to win over the Roman populace, so it was evident from the beginning that corruption was sure to arise.

During the governor's term of office, which lasted one year, he was the chief military and civil magistrate of the province. He commanded the provincial army, maintained peace and repelled any invader; he controlled the collection of taxes, being aided by the financial agent—a quaestor. The governor had judicial power, and upon his return to Rome was responsible alone to the senate, composed of men of his own social standing. These were disposed to look with indulgence upon his misdeeds and to sanction his accumulation of riches at the expense of his subjects. In their turn, others expected to have an opportunity to do likewise.

In local matters, citizens retained their own magistrates, so far as was practicable, and hold the province under the rule of Rome. In judicial matters, the local judges decided disputes between townsmen, but when disputes arose between citizens of different towns, the governor heard and decided them. When entering upon his term of office, the governor issued an edict, setting forth the basis for adjusting such matters. The following governor usually re-issued the same, adding many changes he expected to make. In time, this embodied the code of law for the province.

Provincial cities were not all treated alike. Some were taken as ally towns; others were free from tribute. The great majority were, however, tributary.

There were certain advantages for the dependencies, in that peace was now maintained and invaders were quickly repulsed. Local government usually prevailed, and those provinces which had previously been dependencies of other countries, such as the earlier provinces of Carthage, paid no more tribute—often not so much—than they had previously done. The law now administered was invariably better than that earlier in force. The disadvantages were nevertheless strongly marked: the officers sent to represent Rome were not given a fixed salary, but were allowed to make whatever they could during their administrations, and even worse, taxes

III—30

were farmed out. Rome required a given amount yearly from each dependency. Men would assure this amount to the state and then would collect as much in excess as they were able. Naturally the provincials suffered greatly by this injustice, and had little or no redress. As a result, industries declined and the people sank into hopeless poverty in wide districts. Commerce between cities was discouraged, and general prosperity often disappeared.

"From the end of the Second Punic War down to the time of the Gracchi, Roman history is very monotonous and uninteresting to the reader. It is little more than the record of the haphazard building up of an empire, by the unintentional and unsystematic conquest of various disconnected districts round the Mediterranean. The wars are uninteresting, because they are waged by men who are little more than names to us; the commander, be he a Flaminius or a Mummius, disappears from the historical stage when his consulship is over, and is lost to view once more in the ranks of an impersonal senate. Even the younger Scipio Africanus, who has to serve as a hero in these times for want of a better, soon palls upon us; he stays in our mind only as a vague impersonation of civic virtue and somewhat cold-blooded moderation.

"After 133 B. C. all is different; at last we have living, interesting, individual men to deal with; the names of Tiberius Gracchus, or Sulla, or Caesar, are not remembered merely as connected with files of laws or lists of battles. At the same time both the internal and the external history of Rome becomes of absorbing interest. Externally the question arises whether the sporadic and ill-compacted empire built up in the last hundred years shall endure, or whether it shall be swept away by the brute force of the Cimbri and Teutons, or carved in two by Mithradates. Looking at the growing imbecility of Roman generals in that day, and the growing deterioration of Roman armies, it is not too much to say that, but for the intervention of two great personalities, the Roman empire might have been swept away. If Marius had not appeared, a few more generals like Mallius and Caepio, would have let the Cimbri and Teutons into Central Italy, and the exploits of Alaric in 410 A. D. might have been perpetrated by his remote ancestors. Similarly, but for Sulla the Nearer East might perchance have passed back, seven hundred years before the appointed time, into the hands of oriental rulers, and have shared the fate which overtook Hellenistic Babylon and Bactria, by losing its touch with Western civilization under a dynasty almost as thinly veneered with Greek culture as the Parthian Arsacidae or the Bactrian Scyths."

—*Oman: Seven Roman Statesmen.*

ROMAN AQUEDUCT.

## CHAPTER XII.

### THE GRACCHI; MARIUS AND SULLA.

In order to understand the beginning of that civil strife which tore Rome asunder and ended only upon the establishment of the principate, it is necessary to dwell upon the conditions, social, political, and economic, in the year 133 B. C.

There were four classes of society: the aristocratic, composed of senators and equestrians or knights; the poor citizens, made up of the city rabble and the country farmers; the non-citizens—Latins, Italians, and provincials; and fourth, the slaves. The senators, discussed in a general way in a preceding chapter, were in power and ruled only for themselves. The knights or equestrians had been originally Roman cavalrymen, but in later years the horde of allies had taken their places. This allowed the equestrians to become the great merchants, money changers and financiers of Rome. They were not included in the senate and had no particular place in the political system. The poor citizens had not prospered with the influx of wealth during the last fifty years of conquests. Leaving their small farms for places in the ranks, they returned to find them greatly reduced and often sold them for small sums to some great landed proprietor, who converted the holdings into sheep and cattle pastures. Having naught else to turn to, the farmer would take his family into Rome, hoping there to find work, and to share in the free distribution of grain which followed a triumph or was bestowed by men seeking popular favor. Some of these small farmers still remained on Roman public land, scattered over the peninsula. These men were uniformly discontented because the economic conditions were such that agriculture was fast declining in Italy.

The non-citizen class comprised all grades of men, ranging from the Latins, who possessed the private and commercial rights of citizenship to the provincials, who, as a rule, had no privileges of citizenship whatever.

The slaves deserve greater explanation. In early times there were no slaves in Italy; with early conquests, captives taken in war were reduced to slavery, yet for many years there was abundant demand for free labor. However, with the conquests of two hundred years, slaves had become very numerous. Vast numbers of them were thrown upon the market after every victory. 150,000 captives were sold after the Macedonian wars; 50,000 captives were offered for sale upon the destruction of Carthage; Sicily and Sardinia supplied unceasing quantities of them. Nor was war the only means of acquiring servile help. Some of Roman dependencies paid tribute in these human chattels; others were procured by pirates who made slave-hunting their business. No chapter in negro slavery offers such disheartening reports as those which have survived in references of Roman writers to the condition of these slaves. In the cities, slaves were wholly at the mercy of fickle owners, but they generally led a possible existence; in the country, where large companies of these unfortunates were employed in tilling the soil and performing various labors, they were worked in chains, under cruel drivers, and herded in dreadful dungeons at night. So wretched did their condition become in Sicily that Eunus, one of their number, collected a force and overcame the Romans. Large numbers of slaves escaped and rallied to his standard, for three years defying the Romans and defeating four armies sent against them. This slave revolt was finally put down in 132 B. C. with terrible severity, but it had shown plainly that danger to Rome lurked in this outraged class, so numerous throughout the realm.

It is evident that throwing the many small farms of earlier Italy into wide estates of landed proprietors, together with the employment almost exclusively of slave labor, forced free men out of work. A great unemployed class gathered in the city of Rome and supplied the rabble—the mob—of the later republic. This was the condition that Tiberius Gracchus found when in 133 B. C. he was elected tribune.

Tiberius and Gaius Gracchus belonged to a well known family in Rome. Their father, Tiberius Gracchus, had wedded Cornelia, daughter of Scipio. The Gracchus family had always sympathized with the common people and to the promising young tribune the democracy looked for succor against the greed of the aristocracy. It was once the custom to see in the Gracchi champions of the oppressed, who fell because of their disinterested aid in espousing the popular cause. Serious investigation of recent years has confirmed the unselfish ambitions of the elder brother at least, in his efforts to benefit the oppressed, but it has condemned his methods, while in the case of Gaius, his methods and aims were perhaps both questionable.

It appeared to Tiberius Gracchus that the remedy for the poor, the salvation of the unemployed of Rome, lay in a new distribution of the public lands. The old Licinian laws—providing that not more than 300 acres of the public domain should be left in the possession of one man—had fallen into disuse. For generations the large land proprietors had leased great quantities of this land, used for the most part for pasturage. When now Tiberius brought forward the plan of reclaiming this territory for the poor and distributing it among them in small portions for nominal rents, consternation was felt by the wealthy who held possession of it. Immediately Tiberius found himself confronted by angry men who exclaimed that he was working their ruin. Proprietors from all parts of Italy hurried to Rome to work against the *agrarian* or *land law*. To appease them, Tiberius conceded that sons of a family might be allowed to retain certain amounts of the estates in the possession of the family, allowing not more than 1,000 acres to be held in any one family; also he planned to compensate the present proprietors for whatever improvements they had made. The agrarian law called forth bitter opposition, however, and when it was read before the people, Octavius, the other tribune, vetoed it in the interest of the wealthy. In vain did Tiberius plead with him excitedly to aid the people; at last, when two or three attempts to pass the law had been frustrated, Tiberius proposed to the people that they depose Octavius from his position as tribune, since he was not proving their friend. This suggestion was promptly taken and Octavius was dragged down from the rostrum. The law was quickly passed when no opposition remained.

This was a new way of enacting legislation in Rome. It

was unconstitutional and brought on no end of trouble later. Having found that violence could be substituted for legal procedure, both sides continued to resort to it. Many felt that this was a reprehensible measure, and Tiberius knew that when his term ended he would be called upon to account for his illegal conduct. To protect himself, he determined to become a candidate for immediate re-election. This was illegal again, for the Roman constitution required a succession of tribunes, and none had been allowed to succeed themselves. On the day of the election, while the supporters of Tiberius surged around their leader, a riot took place in the forum and Tiberius, with some of his followers, was killed by the senatorial faction.

For ten years no leader appeared for the common people. The re-division of land had gone into effect after the passage of the agrarian law, and many farms had been apportioned among the people. However, farming no longer continued to be a paying business in Italy, and discontent prevailed among these newly created farmers.

In 123 B. C. Gaius Gracchus espoused the cause of the popular party. His first measure was most ill-advised, and its deadly effect should have been plain to any thoughtful statesman of the times. It was to the effect that the poor of Rome should be allowed to procure grain from the state store-houses for about one-half its value, or selling price. This reform was hailed with joy by the idle of the city. It meant that henceforth, if they so chose to do, they might live and support their families at the cost of the state, paying but one-half the prevailing price for bread. Not only did it make confirmed paupers of them, but it dealt the death blow to the farmers who still cultivated their fields. There was little hope of market for their grain if the state itself was supplying grain at one-half its value. Worse still, a time was coming when this would not suffice; free *bread* would be the cry ere long.

Best of Gaius' reforms was his plan of colonization, settling the poor of Rome and Italy in new towns which he planted on the sea coast. One such settlement was organized upon the site of Carthage; one at Capua, and another at Tarentum. These prospered at first, but no particular interest was manifested in them by the Romans.

In addition to these measures, Gaius Gracchus also revived the agrarian law of his brother, and weakened the senate by allowing knights to serve upon juries. Hitherto this had been the function of the senators, whose training in a large measure fitted them for this office. They had become quite corrupt, and this was the reason offered by the reformer for putting the equestrians in their places. Some one has suggested that the result was similar to that which might be expected to come about if only the members of the Stock Exchange should today be allowed to serve in this capacity. It was not long before the corruption of the knights so far surpassed anything previously known that people looked back with regret to the period when senators alone had acted as jurymen.

Gaius' final measure, to give the citizenship to the Italians generally, was defeated. It brought a storm of outcry from all citizens, who objected to their privileges being shared with others. Gracchus' followers deserted him and he, too, was killed.

Having seen Rome depart from the safe path of legal procedure, we now find another innovation. in that Marius, a new leader of the popular party, and himself a general. enrolled the idle of Rome into his army. and used the army as means of procuring his political ends. He was a gruff, untutored man of the common people, successful in the war against Jugurtha,—a usurper of the Numidian kingship. His service to Rome was far greater in his defeat of the Cimbri and Teutons who invaded Italy from the north in 113 B. C. The first generals sent against these dreaded invaders were wholly incompetent, and allowed the war to drag along. Under their mismanagement 60.000 soldiers were destroyed. Thereupon the people cried that the failure of the army was due to the ineffectual government of the aristocrats. and elected Marius consul. He conducted the war against the Germans and destroyed them in 101 B. C. On his return to Rome he was given a great triumph, which was well deserved. for without vigorous attack, other invaders would soon have followed the tribes which entered Italy in 113 B. C.

Marius was hailed as the saviour of the people, and thus far all was well. Moreover, he shortly became associated with

Saturninus, who brought forward measures which enraged the aristocratic party; he proposed to reduce the price of corn still further, to open Gaul to the poor Italians, and to give territory in the provinces to Marius' veterans. In the face of strong opposition these laws were passed, but when Saturninus tried to secure his own re-election to the tribuneship, riots followed and the senate asked Marius, as consul, to put them down. He did so, and then, feeling that he had misused his opportunity for power in Rome, retired. This incident is important, for it was the first time the army was used in Rome for the purpose of attaining political results. Unfortunately, it was not to be the last.

Troubles within the city of Rome were thrown in the background in 90 B. C. by the breaking out of the so-called Social War. This was the struggle of the Italians to secure Roman citizenship. Those Italians who lived in remote parts of Italy naturally had little desire to take part in the legislation of Rome, but there were certain advantages which citizenship would bring which they did want badly. In time of war, if a consul drafted soldiers in the army, the tribune could protect such of the people as were unfitted for service. He also protected them against needlessly harsh treatment while in service. Whenever a Roman citizen felt himself wronged, he could appeal to the tribune, who existed for the protection of the common people. Such recourse as this the Italians did not have, and this they deeply desired. The question had been agitated some time. Gaius Gracchus had failed to secure its passage, as had others who brought it forward. Now the Italians determined to secure citizenship for themselves by forcing Rome to confer it. At least, if it were not to be obtained they were firm in their intention to found a new state, Italica, which might in time absorb all Italy.

It was not to be thought of that Romans would allow their state to be thus divided, and Marius returned to Rome. However, the command of the army was given to Sulla, who had distinguished himself in the war against Jugurtha. After 300,000 men had lost their lives, Rome offered citizenship to all who had remained loyal to her and to all who should enroll themselves within two months. Thus the war closed, and

Italians and Romans together shared alike the privileges of political equality.

The advent of Sulla into public life is important. He belonged to the aristocratic party, and now gave the senators a military leader to offset Marius. The presence of the Roman army was needed in western Asia, where Mithridates, king of Pontus, was trying to drive out the Romans and establish his own power. To understand the full significance of this war it is necessary to recall the deplorable condition in the Asiatic province, where taxes were farmed out and the people were so oppressed that they had rapidly sank from a prosperous to a poor people. Because of their misrule, the Romans were so hated that the moment this Asiatic king sought to claim this territory, the people flocked to him as to a deliverer, and in a single day put to death the 80,000 Romans who were settled there. It was to check this king that Sulla was dispatched in 88 B. C.

Marius could not look with any tolerance upon Sulla's succession to general favor, thus setting him wholly aside. Immediately, then, upon Sulla's departure for the East, he began to win over to himself a band of followers. Full of revenge, Marius gathered his earlier friends about him and these elected Sulpicius tribune. Soon several laws, known as the Sulpician laws, were passed by noisy mobs in the forum, and most significant among them was one which gave Marius, instead of Sulla, command of the army. Upon the passage of this questionable legislation, messengers were sent to notify Sulla that he must deliver the command to Marius. Sulla had little intention of being thus set aside for a leader of the Roman mobs. He called upon his soldiers to stand by him, and with the fidelity that soldiers feel for the one who has led them to victory, they proclaimed their willingness to do so. Thereupon Sulla marched to Rome. Marius and some of his adherents fled from the city. Sulla convened the senate and asked this body to declare the followers of Marius outlaws. The recent laws were repealed, and the senate was restored to power. This being accomplished, Sulla set out again for the East and in 84 B. C. compelled the king of Pontus to sign a treaty of peace.

During Sulla's absence the popular party struggled for power and civil war ruled in Rome. Men fought each other in the streets, and now one side, now the other, wielded authority. It has been estimated that 10,000 citizens fell in these riots. Marius secured a company of Numidian cavalrymen and charged upon the people in Rome. When others gave way before him, he shut up the city gates and for five days satiated himself with slaughter. At last he died, the terror of Rome.

This period of democratic triumph was to be dearly paid for. In 83 B. C. Sulla returned from his triumph over Mithridates, and once more civil war raged in Rome. He had himself declared dictator, and outlawed all who had taken part against him. Lists of the proscribed were posted and rewards were offered for their heads. The most degraded, brutal aids carried out his orders. Probably 5,000 men were put to death, without trial or opportunity to be heard. When he considered his enemies removed, Sulla set about reconstructing the constitution, and it must be said to his credit that he evolved a constitution that was at least practical and might have proved sufficient had the senate of the later republic been the stable body that it had earlier been. An aristocrat himself, Sulla had no patience with popular rule, which he had seen the cause of so much tumult in Rome. To the senate, then, he gave fullest authority.

To eliminate the difference between senators and equestrians, he appointed many equestrians to the senate. This united the aristocratic and wealthy into one body, with common interests. The people were no longer allowed to pass upon laws which had not gained the sanction of the senate. The tribune was deprived of all power save that originally his, to intervene in behalf of the people. Sulla prevented magistrates from re-election, and made the consul merely a civil officer, instead of as before, commander of the army. Senators alone were allowed to serve on juries. Such were the important features of his new constitution.

Having organized the government upon the old, aristocratic basis, Sulla returned to private life and died in retirement.

## CHAPTER XIII.

### TO THE DEATH OF CAESAR.

For many years, as we have seen, a political struggle had been waging in Rome, the question being: where was authority to be invested, in the senate or in the people? Both the aristocracy and the populace had ruled alternately, or rather, actual power had been lodged in the senate save when, through the aid of efficient leaders, the popular party gained ascendency, and the government of either element had been poor. Indeed, Rome was not destined to see sustained peace until the republic merged into the principate.

During the period of Pompey's leadership—78 to 59 B. C.— the strife continued. While the people were still to be satisfied, the tendency was in the direction of the one-man rule, even as it had been in the days of Marius and Sulla. Unrest and reaction followed upon the death of Sulla, and under incompetent leaders, the masses attempted to check the power of the senate. First of these leaders was Lepidus, formerly a supporter of the aristocratic party, which he abandoned because investigation revealed gross irregularities in his provincial administration, and fearing the disapproval of his own party, he sought the favor of the people.

Lepidus now tried to set aside the constitution which Sulla had forced upon Rome. Many disliked this new legal code, but Rome had suffered so greatly from evil strife that the most discerning ones were opposed to any sudden change which might bring riots and mob-rule in its wake. Failing in his purpose, Lepidus raised an armed force and tried to accomplish his plan by the use of the sword. At this juncture the senate sent Pompey, distinguished as a lieutenant in Sulla's army, to put down the rebellion, and in 77 B. C. Lepidus was overcome.

This bungling effort to increase the power of the people was shortly followed by an attempt on the part of Sertorius, an adherent of the democracy. He went to Spain and there

THE APPIAN WAY

tried to establish an independent republic. After three Roman armies had been repulsed, Pompey was sent thither and ended the trouble in 72 B. C.

Far more formidable than either of these revolts was a third, led by Spartacus, a gladiator. Turning against those for whose amusement men had fought wild beasts or each other in the arena, a band of gladiators fortified themselves in Italy and were soon joined by slaves and outlaws who flocked to them from all parts of the peninsula. Army after army was sent against them, but proved unable to check their ravages. Few situations show better the depths to which Rome had sunk than this, wherein a comparatively small number of abandoned men held out against four Roman armies sent to subdue them. Crassus, an aristocrat who had served under Sulla, was finally delegated to end the insurrection, and defeated the outlaw band in 71 B. C. Those who survived fled into Spain, where Pompey overtook them and, having destroyed the remnant, took greater credit to himself than he really deserved.

Three attempts to exalt the popular party by armed forces had failed, and the senate took pride in having thus overcome the masses and enhanced its own rule. Now the victorious generals, Pompey and Crassus, returned to Rome and desired to be elected consuls. Fearing their strength, the senate refused its support. Failing here, the two men turned to the people, who welcomed any opportunity to strike a blow to aristocratic government. In 70 B. C., accordingly, the generals were elected to the consulship. This office had been conferred upon them in accordance with their promise to overthrow the constitution of Sulla, and upon their entrance to consular duties the old government was re-established. Law making reverted to the people, the tribune received his earlier power; no longer could senators alone serve upon juries: the censors were restored, and the senate was purged of sixty-four members. The rights of the people were thus vindicated, and this, too, with no attendant bloodshed.

Serious conditions in the East required attention. While the Romans had been putting down civil revolts in their very midst, pirates had established themselves to a degree unknown before or since upon the Mediterranean. Commerce was nowhere safe from their bold robberies. Even the proconsuls, setting forth from their provinces, were not safe from their clutches. With strongholds at Crete, these daring sea robbers preyed upon vessels, little and great, and Roman commerce was at a standstill. Furthermore, Mithridates, king of Pontus, was once more making his power felt in Asia, and if Rome was to hold her provinces she must measure swords with this eastern potentate.

The tribune of the people came forward with a bold plan, which was to the effect that Pompey be given supreme command over the sea for three years, and that his authority be extended around the sea for fifty miles inland. Armies and fleets were to be organized at his direction and piracy upon the Mediterranean ended. In vain the senate protested that delegating such wide authority to any one was unconstitutional. The people declared that senatorial rule had allowed existing conditions to arise, and they would demonstrate the ability of the people to change them. Accordingly, Pompey was dispatched to the great sea of antiquity, and within three months he had taken or destroyed one thousand pirate ships. Strongholds erected by these sea bandits were leveled, and commerce was once again able to follow its way.

After this great victory all felt that Pompey was needed in the East to check the progress of Mithridates, and thither the general was sent. His success was quite as remarkable there. Mithridates was defeated; Syria was taken and organized as a Roman province.

"The achievements of Pompey were enough to dazzle even the flagging minds of the all-conquering people. All the nations on this side the Euphrates had submitted absolutely to his dictation. After expending 3,900,000 pounds in gifts upon his officers and men, he was still bringing home to the state treasury more than 2,000,000 pounds. The conqueror of unheard-of nations, the founder of nine and thirty cities, what opposition could be made to any claims he might choose to advance?"

Meanwhile the government of Rome had sunk so low that Catiline, a depraved noble, planned to make himself ruler of the city. His famous conspiracy was discovered and frustrated by Cicero, and his allies were put to death. Elections were ordinarily accompanied by riots and armed forces paraded the streets and domineered over the helpless people.

In 61 B. C. Pompey returned to Rome. He quite naturally expected expressions of appreciation for his splendid victories, but these were not forthcoming. The nobles hated Pompey and the people were afraid of one so powerful. His soldiers, however, remained faithful. The great general made his wishes known to the senate. He wanted to be consul for the coming year, wanted to have his acts in the East confirmed, and lastly, desired that his veterans be given homes. To his amazement, these reasonable demands were unheeded, and once again he was obliged to turn to the people. For mutual advantage, the three strongest men in Rome at this time— Pompey, Crassus and Julius Caesar—formed a league, known as the First Triumvirate. Pompey brought the support of the army; Crassus was the wealthiest man in Rome, and Julius Caesar gave promise of a successful career. Rome was now a plaything in the hands of three men who could exercise their political influence for maintaining their places. According to the agreement at this time, Caesar was to be consul for 59 B. C., and after that was to go as proconsul to Gaul. Pompey's veterans were to be given farms, and his acts in the East were confirmed; Crassus was to be given opportunity to increase his wealth. In 56 B. C. Caesar, who had already spent two years repulsing the Germans, who threatened an invasion, discerned discontent in his colleagues and summoned them to a meeting. The result of this conference was to extend Caesar's term in Gaul five years, to give Pompey and Crassus the consulship for 55 B. C., and then give Pompey Spain and Crassus, Syria.

Crassus died shortly after his arrival in the East, fighting tribes where the hope of plunder was strong. Julia, daughter of Caesar and wife of Pompey, died, severing a bond of feeling between the two men. Henceforth they were to be rivals for supreme power in Rome. Pompey stayed in Italy and sent representatives to his province in Spain, but although a successful general, he was not a good political leader, and allowed several opportunities for gaining strength to slip by. Riots continued in the city, and finally, when he was made sole consul, a formal break came with his earlier colleague.

In 49 B. C. Caesar had completed his Gallic campaign. The senate feared one who had made his name such a terror in the North, and asked him to disband his soldiers before returning to Rome. However, Caesar desired the consulship for the next year, and felt that without his army he would be no better off than any private Roman citizen. However, he agreed to disband his soldiers if Pompey would do likewise. This Pompey refused to do. Thereupon the senate unwisely notified Caesar that he must dismiss his army by a certain date or be declared a public enemy. Caesar was satisfied that without his army he would be helpless in Rome, and, marching rapidly, crossed the Rubicon, the stream north of Rome, over which no army had been allowed to come. Upon learning of his approach, Pompey gathered together what forces he could and moved south. Contrary to the fears of the Romans, Caesar brought order instead of turmoil to the city. No massacres, proscriptions or riots marked his entrance to the capital. Having established himself there, he moved to meet Pompey, for there was now civil war in Italy and one of two leaders had to prove himself master of the situation. Caesar brought a well trained body of soldiers, whereas Pompey had hurriedly gathered his forces together. As might have been foreseen, Pompey was defeated. Fleeing to Egypt, he was treacherously slain. This left Julius Caesar in control of the Roman world.

Having re-established the Ptolemies upon the throne of the Pharaohs, Caesar returned to Rome. There he proclaimed a holiday of fifteen days. He celebrated four triumphs: one for Gaul, one for Egypt, one for Pontus, and one for Africa. His rule in Rome was brief. He gathered into his own hands the important offices of the government, and instituted reforms that lived long after his time. First of all, he believed that Rome should be the capital of a great empire, not simply the recipient of advantages conferred by this wide area. Accordingly, the rights of citizenship were extended to the Gauls, Spaniards, and other provincials. Again, districts in the provinces were open to settlers from Italy. Instead of leaving provincial taxes to be longer farmed out, each town was made responsible for its share.

The senate lost its aristocratic nature when Caesar increased its membership from 600 to 900 and brought into it men from various parts of Italy and the provinces. Economic conditions were bettered by the requirement of free laborers as well as slaves on estates, and many idle men of Rome were given employment on public works now undertaken. Moreover, imprisonment for debt was abolished.

Caesar made the fatal mistake, however, of setting aside the prejudices of men regarding the *forms* of government. There were those who failed to see that the days of the republic were in reality passed, and they resented Caesar's indifference to republican forms and appearances. These men found in Brutus a worthy although perhaps a misguided leader, who vainly hoped to restore the old republic by removing the great statesman of the age. A conspiracy was formed and in 44 B. C. the mighty Caesar fell in the senate house, a victim to the mistaken conceptions of eighty senators. Time was to show their attempt a failure, and to demonstrate that the sacrifice of Caesar could not stem the tide of natural forces.

Many characterizations have been made of Julius Caesar. Some have seen in him the "entire and perfect man," in the words of a German historian. Others have believed him a tyrant and destroyer of republican government. Democratic, Caesar certainly was not; his ideas were not entirely different from those of Alexander the Great. He undoubtedly desired to make himself absolute, and yet, he would probably have administered a wise government. The age had passed when the average Roman citizen was capable of taking a loyal, disinterested attitude in the government of his country, and the vast extent of the empire demanded a strong centralized government. The one-man rule was bound to come, and Caesar's death could not restore the wholesome conditions of early Rome.

"Caesar died the greatest man that Rome ever produced. His life has left an indelible impress upon the world's history in every direction. Equally great as a general, as a statesman, and as a law-giver, he combined in his one person gifts such as but two or three men in the world's history have possessed. Had he lived to perfect his work, the whole history of the Roman empire might have been different; in his death Rome lost a man such as the ancient world was never to see again."

III—31

## CHAPTER XIV.

### THE END OF THE OLD REPUBLIC.

The conspirators had planned no farther than the death of Caesar. Having persuaded themselves that the fall of this mighty statesman was essential to the welfare of the Roman world, they lost sight of the fact that the people generally had not been following their growing conspiracy. Instead of being hailed as the liberators of the land, their first announcement of the death of "the tyrant" was received by the crowd gathered in the Forum with a significant silence. Not feeling too confident themselves, in all probability, they hastened to fortify a stronghold upon Capitoline hill. On the following day Brutus again came down among the people to justify Caesar's death. He was heard with respect, but the other conspirators were hissed and hastily returned to the Capitoline.

Caesar's Master of the Horse had been Lepidus, who commanded a legion just outside the walls of Rome. Antony, Caesar's fellow-consul, managed to get from Calpurnia, Caesar's wife, the great dictator's will. Moreover, with the aid of his brothers, one a praetor, one a tribune, Antony opened the public treasury and secured enough money to carry out his immediate plans. He made overtures to Lepidus, whose support was most important, inasmuch as he commanded the troops. Caesar's veterans had loved him dearly and were ready to serve one who would avenge his untimely death.

Two days after the death of Caesar, Antony summoned the senate. The question upon which this body had to rule was whether Caesar had been a tyrant, and what should be the attitude of the state toward the assassins. Many of the senators had been directly or indirectly implicated in the plot, or were at least in close relations with the conspirators, and the disposition of the majority at first was in favor of declaring Caesar a tyrant, thus justifying his death. Antony reminded them, however, that this would mean the annulment of all Caesar's acts and all his appointments, some of which had but were laid of many of the institutions that still exist. Thus feudalism not only affected us through chivalry, wherein its ideas reached their highest expression, but it impressed on men a new view of government. The feudal lord no longer looked upon his sovereign as a Roman had regarded the emperor, as a divine and sacred personage whose will was law. Rather, the king was looked on as subject to the law equally with his subjects. The vassal was bound to his lord only so long as the lord observed the terms of the contract. If the vassal failed to perform his duties the lord could deprive him of his land, but on the other hand, if the lord failed of *his* duties, the vassal might rebel against him.

Moreover, it was during the Middle Ages that representative government was first devised. The Ancient World knew little or nothing of the principle of representation. It was during the Middle Ages that this new device was first seriously applied to government. It came to be an accepted maxim that one of the duties of the vassal was to give to his lord advice and counsel, and that it was the duty of the lord, on his side, to seek such advice. It is on the basis of such principles that, in all the feudal monarchies of the Middle Ages, some form of *National Assembly* arose. As illustrations of these, we need only note the parliament in England, the states-general in France, and the cortes in Spain. However much they might differ in their forms and powers, yet these assemblies, by their existence, testified to the principle that the people must be to some extent consulted by the government, and that some things required their consent. It is true that the people were not viewed in any democratic sense, but rather signified the various *classes* which had made themselves sufficiently powerful to count in politics; that is to say, the nobles, the clergy, and the people of the towns. Still, when all reservations are made, it is none the less true that the foundations, of modern representative government were laid in the Middle Ages—that the very idea first conceived during that period.

There was indeed much war and barbarism in the Middle Ages, but they have played a decisive part in the making of the Modern World. During this long period, it was not all confusion or ignorance. It was a time when important work was done. In the turmoil of this period, three great elements of our modern civilization were welded together. The classic culture, taken up and preserved in the vast organization of the Mediæval Church, Christianity, itself, and the Germanic ideas and customs all met and were, at length, more or less perfectly harmonized. Then, after a long period of feudal anarchy, built up out of feudalism itself, and using it as in part a means, arose the modern nations. The Europe of the Roman Empire is a Europe welded into one vast centralized despotism, having a single civilization. The Europe that emerged from the Middle Ages was a Europe divided into separate nations, each having its own culture, life and institutions.

# DESCRIPTION OF ILLUSTRATIONS
## IN PART IV

### The Coliseum.

This great building was also known as the Flavian Amphitheater. The Flavian house was of humble origin and by gigantic building enterprises sought to win popular favor. This vast amphitheater covered nearly six acres, the walls rising to the height of 160 feet. Eighty entrances led to various parts of the building, which had a seating capacity of 80,000 and afforded standing room for 20,000 more. Underneath were subterranean chambers for gladiators, beasts, all kinds of apparatus, particularly water equipment adequate for the immediate conversion of the whole into a lake or to quickly carry off the water. Every day for months at a time scenes of murder and slaughter went on for the amusement of Rome's idle upper scum, as well as for pleasure seekers of all classes.

### Baths of Caracalla.

These were the largest and most magnificent of all the Roman baths. Caracalla was one of the later emperors and never saw his gigantic building completed. With its pleasure grounds, these baths covered thirty-three acres, and combined all the advantages of a modern club house with a gymnasium, lectures, discussions and social enjoyments. There were many halls, courts, galleries, etc., under one roof, the great hall or Tepidarium being 170 feet long, 82 feet wide, and 108 feet high. Adjacent were cold rooms and hot rooms, warm rooms and sun rooms, swimming pools, visitors' galleries, and many retiring rooms, for what particular purposes none at present can tell. Sixteen hundred bathers could be accommodated at once, while others waited their turn, attendants gave assistance, directors of the gymnasia instructed, philosophers lectured, and crowds disported themselves in the spacious parks. For beauty of finish and elegance of decoration these baths had no equal.

### Arch of Titus.

Triumphal arches were distinctively Roman. At least thirty-eight of them were erected in the course of Roman history. The Arch of Titus was raised in honor of Titus' victory over the Jews and his destruction of Jerusalem. In course of time much of this arch was destroyed and in 1823 Pope Pius VII. caused it to be restored. Two extensive reliefs have deep interest for the student: the portrayal of Titus' triumph, and the spoils of war that graced it. In the first the emperor is shown in his triumphal car, while above Victory holds the crown on his head. The golden table for the shew-bread, the silver trumpets and the seven-branched candle stick were carried along in the procession and are believed to have been faithfully represented in the relief.

### Temple of Vesta.

The worship of Vesta was probably brought into Rome by the Sabines, and the first temple was erected in her honor by the early kings. During the greater portion of Roman history, the temple of Vesta stood on its early site—the extreme eastern end of the Forum. When destroyed by the Gauls and again by the great fire of Nero's time, it was always immediately rebuilt.

Within this temple the sacred fire was always kept burning. The custom originated in a remote age when it was most difficult to rekindle an extinguished flame. Six Vestal Virgins were entrusted with the care of Vesta's fire and they were severely punished if it was allowed to go out. The House of the Vestal Virgins was discovered in 1883 by those carrying on excavations in behalf of the Italian government.

## PANORAMA OF ROME FROM ST. PETER'S.

We often think of the ancient city of Rome, forgetting that Rome is again a great throbbing city of today. This view is taken from the top of St. Peter's, overlooking a considerable portion of the capital. One great difficulty confronting the modern explorer is the fact that the modern buildings stand on the site of those long since fallen into decay and life of the present prevents extensive examination into life of the past.

## DEATH AND THE PLOWMAN.

This is one of a long series of illustrations popular in the Middle Ages and known collectively as the Dance of Death. Poets sang the story and artists painted it. By either poem or picture Death was represented as coming unexpectedly to king, cardinal, peasant, bridegroom—to men of every station. (Refer to the Dance of Death, Part VI., page 178.)

> "Lo! I am Death! With aim as sure as steady,
>   All things that are and shall be I draw near me.
> I call thee,—I require thee, man, be ready!
>   Why build upon this fragile life? Now hear me!"

## MOSAIC—WORSHIP OF THE MAGI.

It is scarcely possible to give an adequate conception of mosaic pictures by reproductions of this kind. This is a copy of a wall picture made in mosaic in a church of Ravenna. The three wise men, guided by the star are clearly shown; Christ and His mother are fashioned after the Byzantine School—elongated, expressionless figures. While this belongs to the sixth century, in the uppermost tier may be seen the ship, which symbolized the Church. However, the use of symbols was not so great as in centuries earlier.

## PLOWING IN LUZON—AS IN MIDDLE AGES.

Here we see the farmer scratching the ground, preparatory to planting the seed. This is a daily sight in the Philippines, in many oriental lands and in the Middle Ages might have been seen in Europe. Methods of farming have advanced rapidly in progressive countries during the past hundred years, but even yet in Mohammedan lands and wherever the strong hand of custom prevents rapid innovations, early methods still continue to be used.

## MINIATURE—QUEEN OF SHEBA BEFORE SOLOMON.

This is one of a collection of miniatures treasured today in the Library of St. Mark, Venice, and adorning the Grimani Breviary. This particular

# DESCRIPTION OF ILLUSTRATIONS

## IN PART III.

### THEATER OF DIONYSUS.

Dionysus, god of wine, was worshipped by songs and dances at an early period. From these celebrations, frequently boisterous in nature, developed the first Greek drama. The Greater and the Lesser Dionysia were observed during the later period of Greek ascendency, these being occasions when competitive plays were presented before large audiences—still in honor of Dionysus.

The celebrated theatre in which these plays were performed in Athens was hewn out of the living rock, the seats having the form of steps rising tier upon tier. The entire structure was open to the sky.

### THE ERECHTHEUM WITH PORCH OF THE CARYATIDES.

Erechtheus was a mythical king of Athens. Later he was revered much as a god, and the temple known as the Erechtheum was the very center of Athenian worship. This building was irregular in shape, and adhered to the Ionic style. The Porch of Caryatides, or Maidens, is very famous. Six female figures in stone support the roof in the place of columns. Modern architects have occasionally adopted the idea in certain buildings.

### THE PARTHENON.

This was a temple erected in honor of Athena, protecting deity of that city. Begun by Cimon, the temple was completed under the direction of Phidias, greatest of Greek sculptors. It followed the style of Doric architecture, being a noted example of Greek simplicity. The pediments at the east and west ends set forth stories connected with the great goddess. One pictured Athena springing forth in full armor from the head of Zeus; the other recorded her contest with Poseidon for the naming of Athens.

Some of Phidias' finest work was done upon this temple.

### METOPE FROM THE PARTHENON.

The two friezes of the Parthenon are sometimes confused. One surrounded the cella and its vestibules, commemorating the Panathenean festival; the exterior frieze consisted of metopes and triglyphs. The best preserved metopes today were originally along the south side of the temple and picture scenes from the fabled contest between the Lapiths and Centaurs—a favorite subject with the Greeks. Some of these ninety-two metopes are today in their original position; some in the British Museum; some in the Acropolis Museum.

### TEMPLE OF WINGLESS VICTORY.

After their defeat of the Persians, the Greeks erected a temple to Victory-Nike. However, lest she should take flight and leave them, they represented her without her accustomed wings, hence *Wingless* Victory.

## ROMAN FORUM.

The Forum held the same relative position in Roman life that the Agora did in Greek life. Here the Senate held its deliberations, here men met daily for interchange of ideas, here until a later period the business of the Romans was transacted. Even after the various markets were relegated to other sections of Rome, still the courts were in the Forum and vital interest for a great nation centered here.

Of the many buildings which occupied this district, only a few pillars remain at the present time. A new city has grown up where an old one once stood, and the imagination must reconstruct the Forum of the past as best it may.

## CLAUDIAN AQUEDUCT.

Rome's water supply came from a distance. It was possible to obtain pure mountain water by going from thirty to sixty miles outside of Rome. To convey it for such distances, huge aqueducts were constructed, nine supplying enough for the city's use. Ruins of these aqueducts today add picturesqueness to the landscape and constitute one of the few connecting links with antiquity.

## SCHOOL OF GLADIATORS.

The ruins of a gladiatorial school has been laid bare by the spade of the excavator in Pompeii. Gladiatorial contests became so popular in Rome that criminals and captives taken in war were allowed to receive training and in this way escape immediate death. The training given was severe indeed and men thus inured to hardship and cruelty became a dangerous element in society—as the Gladiatorial War demonstrated.

## THE APPIAN WAY.

This was one of the early thoroughfares of Rome. Built in an early day, it extended from the Servian wall to the city of Capua, some hundred and thirty miles southeast of the capital. Their early laws forbade the Romans to inter their dead within the city walls; consequently the space along roadsides was regarded as desirable for burial and the Appian Way became lined with tombs and monuments.

Travel out of Rome kept this road open in the vicinity of the city, but the south end lay covered by vegetation for hundreds of years. Finally in 1850, Pope Pius IX. put into action a plan for uncovering a portion of this old highway. Twelve miles of it were laid bare at an approximate cost of $15,000, and involving about three years' labor.

"A wise man will select his books, for he would not wish to call them all under the sacred name of friends. Some can be accepted only as acquaintances. The best books of all kinds are taken to the heart, and cherished as his most precious possessions. Others to be chatted with, and laid aside, but not forgotten." –Langford

## THE DRAMA

"There is in human nature a tendency to reproduce and communicate to others the impressions received from the surrounding world; indeed, the manifestation of such impressions is the basis of every kind of art . . . . In every human being there is a primitive capacity for artistic production; everybody is capable to a certain degree of receiving and reproducing impressions, and it is this universal innate gift that lends art its greatest importance." –Karl Mantzius: History of Theatrical Art

## ORIGIN OF THE DRAMA

The dramatic instinct is inherent in man and has found similar expression among primitive peoples widely separated in point of time and locality. For example, we find that the dramatic attempts of the early Greeks, the American Indians, and the present

South Sea Islanders present striking characteristics in common.    Of the four mediums of dramatic expression–dancing, music, acting and recitation–dancing is first developed by the savage. This appears to be a natural and spontaneous manifestation of joy, employed first for religious worship.    Indeed, dancing has been lacking only among such peoples as have not yet developed a religion.  Gradually there comes an impulse to imitate well-known birds and animals, and soon that is followed by attempts to imitate the appearance of such creatures. Feathers are assumed for these dances or the heads of animals worn.   It will readily be seen that these meager efforts are but stepping stones to a final dramatic art.

Having learned to reproduce the movements and noises of familiar animals, in time, man, growing out of the early stages of savagery, tries to portray some of his daily occupations in the dance.  Fishing dances are evolved wherein movements of the body call to mind a boat rocking on the water or a net cast out by the fisherman.  War dances come quickly into being, and among our Indians, in a certain scalp dance, motion ceased now and then to allow someone to recount the exploits of a recent battle.

Various semi-savage nations attained this stage in dramatic development but progressed no further. It remained for the Greeks to exceed the limits held by earlier peoples and to originate a drama which is still wonderful to us today. However, it should be borne in mine that in many particulars the beginnings of their art were in some respects identical with those of their predecessors, with our Indians and with semi-barbarous tribes today–the same human sacrifice, changed afterwards for the offering of a goat; the same secret societies with mystery surrounding them; similar dances and music and the same association with religious worship.

## I. THE GREEK DRAMA

### a. Greek Tragedy

1. In what celebrations did the Greek drama originate? 3:1

2. What two important festivals were celebrated in Athens each year? 3:1

3. What was the attitude of the Athenians toward amusement? 3:2

4. From what does our word 'tragedy' come, and what was its early significance?  3:4

5. Mention one particular in which Greek audiences differed from those of today.  3:4

6. How did Aeschylus treat the familiar story of Prometheus?  3:5

7. How many plays is Sophocles believed to have written?  3:29

8. Antigone is one of the most charming productions in all literature.  It is sometimes presented today by student bodies.  Some knowledge of it will prove gratifying to all readers.  3:30

9. Babes exposed by parents for different reasons in Greece were often rescued and brought up under the care of the temples.  Ion had been so brought up from infancy.  Note how beautiful is the song he sings as the play bearing his name opens.  3:41

10. Compare Euripides with other Greek dramatists. 3:43

11. What men were known as the Three Tragic Poets? 3:84

12. What precaution did the Athenians take to insure accurate renderings of their plays? 3:84

13. After the decline of Athens, what city became the center of culture? 3:85

b. Greek Comedy

1. Where do we find the beginnings of Greek comedy? 3:62

2. What wholesome influence did comedy often exercise in Athens? 3:62

3. Who was the greatest writer of comedy? 3:62

4. One would do well to become familiar with one of Aristophanes' comedies. 3:38

5. The Clouds and The Birds have both been occasionally reproduced. What did each ridicule? 3:63
6. Who were writers of the later Greek comedy? 3:63

BOOKS FOR FURTHER READING:

Aeschylus, trans. Plumptre
Aristophanes, trans. Frere
Euripides, trans. Coleridge
Sophocles, trans. Coleridge
The Ancient Classical Drama, by Moulton

## I. DEVELOPMENT OF GREEK LITERATURE

1. What is offered as a possible explanation of the rise of the Fable?  3:45

2. Why have Aesop's Fables remained popular so long?  Are they still widely read?

3. Who were noted among Greek historians/ 3:149-158

4. The Anabasis is read today in schools where Greek is taught.  Who wrote the Anabasis and of what does it treat?  3:159

## II. MASTERPIECES OF GREEK POETRY

1. Tyrtaeus' spirited songs spurred men on to victory. We today can feel something of the courage they

inspired. Read Courage and Patriotism, 3:219, also To Spartan Youths, 3:221

2. Simonides of Amorgos wished to marry a widow of his acquaintance. When she spurned his suit he was so chagrined that he wrote such a vindictive satire against woman-kind as has never been exceeded. This is given in 3:228

3. The Greeks generally regarded life upon earth as infinitely more desirable than existence after death. Pindar, however, expressed other sentiments. 3:233

4. Note how cleverly Pindar interwove the story of Hercules and the serpents into his Nemean Ode, 3: 235.

5. Theocritus wrote many idyls. Read The Syracusan Women, 3:254.

6. What is an Anthology? 3:300

7. Lucian write a series of Dialogues of the Dead. One is given in 3:311

8. See how delicately Cupid as a Guest is written, 3:245; also The Grasshopper, 3:249

9. In his Is Life Worth Living? who does Menander consider fortunate?  3:83

10. Greek tragedy is considered in connection with The Drama.  However, some of the most powerful passages of poetry are to be found in them. 3:84

NOTE: All poetry loses much by translation into another tongue; especially is this true of Greek poetry, for the Greek language admitted of far greater subtleties of meaning than does ours today. However, it is possible to acquire a fair understanding of Greek thought and literature through English versions, and it is recommended that the general reader wander at will through the writings of various authors until a taste for them may be cultivated or increased.  A wide selection is offered here for this purpose.

III. MASTERPIECES OF GREEK PROSE

1.  Herodotus' story of Pythius the Lydian is well known. 3:149

2.  Xenophan tells of the joy of the Ten Thousand Greeks when at last they beheld the sea after their long march through Asia.  Thenceforth the route was easily followed.  3:174

3. Aesop's Fables are always entertaining. Read those given in 3:146

4. Some of them have been rendered into verse.

5. The death of Socrates impressed men as his teachings never could have done. Read The Farewell of Socrates, 3:134

6. For some time Demosthenes tried to stir up the Athenians to check the gradual approach of Philip of Macedon. Read the first of the Philippics, 3:211

7. Read Aeschines' Attack on Demosthenes, 3:203 and the latter's reply, 3:214

8. No pastoral is prettier than the one from which Dephnis and Chloe is here quoted. 3:333

IV. GREEK ARCHITECTURE AND ART

1. By what stages was the Greek temple evolved? 3:341

2. What building materials were available in Greece? 3:342

3. What are known of the three Orders of Greek

architecture? 3:342

4. Look at the picture of the Temple of Wingless Victory for a perfect speciman of Ionic style. 3:321

5. What festival was commemorated by its magnificent frieze? 3:350

6. What significance had the pediments? 3:349

7. What has been the fate of the Parthenon? 3:349

8. Where are the Elgin marbles, and why are they so called? 3:349

NOTE: These specimens of Greek masterpieces in marble have had a marked effect upon those who never travelled in Greece. For example, see Keats' sonnet to them, and find out how deeply they influenced him.

9. What are our sources for a study of Greek art, today? 3:346

10. What are votives? 3:346

11. Of what materials did the Greeks make their

statues? 3:347

14.  How did these differ in appearance from those seen today?  3:347

15.  What Greek city was a noted art center in antiquity?  3:348

16.  What additions to the remains of Greek art resulted from the excavations made at Olympia?  3:356

NOTE: It is generally conceded that one gaines a more comprehensive idea of Greek art from a single specimen actually seen than from years of study upon the subject. Nevertheless, some familiarity with the subject is most essential for those who expect to enjoy the advantage of foreign travel.

BOOKS FOR FURTHER READING:

Greek Literature

History of Greek Literature, Fowler
Ancient Greek Literature, Murray
Masterpieces of Greek Literature, ed. Wright
Studies in Greek poets, Symonds
History of Greek Literature, Mahaffy

Greek Anthology, R.C. Jebbs
Greek Literature, R.C. Jebbs

Greek Art

Grammar of Greek Art, Percy Gardner
History of Greek Art, F.B. Tarbell
Handbook of Greek Sculpture, E.A. Gardner
Art of the Greeks, Walter

## EDUCATION

1. Read Aristotle's treatise on Education, 3:112

## GREEK PHILOSOPHY

1. How did Thales answer the question: What is the ultimate reality of the world? 3:92

2. What other answers were made by materialistic philosophers?

3. Contrast the theories of Heracleitus and Parmenides. 3:92-3

4. What did Empedocles substitute for one world-material? 3:93

5. How did Anaxagoras abuse the patience of his countrymen? 3: 93

6. Can you explain why it was that the Sophists fell into disrepute? 3:94

7. Was Socrates one of their number? 3:95

8. How did Socrates treat the problem of a world-material? 3:95

9. Is it true that Socrates' influence was increased and his power enhanced because he was put to death? Would you expect this to be the case?

10. What is meant by Platonic idea? 3:106

11. What was Neo-Platonism? 3:108

12. Compare the three greatest philosophers of Greece–Socrates, Plato and Aristotle–in their lives and inheritances. 3:106

13. What schools of philosophy were based upon some aspect of Socratic teaching? 3:106

14. Are people still asking: In what lies the greatest

good?

15. Where did the Stoics get their name? What was their attitude toward life? 3:140

16. The Epicureans held pleasure to be the chief end and aim. Are there people today who cling to the same idea? 3:141

NOTE: Philosophy is the profoundest study with which the human mind occupies itself. It attempts to formulate the universe–to find the explanation of universal laws and truths. It is customary to begin any investigation of the subject with the philosophy of the Greeks, for from them we have received in the main our general structure of thought and ideas and then, too, by approaching the matter from their standpoint, we can the more easily grow into it.

When the old myths no longer satisfied, earliest Greek philosophers attempted to answer the inquiry: What was the origin of the world? This question was paramount until the time of Socrates, who said that men could not hope to satisfactorily answer it–that the study for mankind was man, his relations to the world in which he lived the aims and purposes of life, and above all, to determine what for him constituted the highest good.

Philosophy has expanded to meet the new conditions of each generation, and for convenience sake we divide it into distinct periods, as the Philosophy of the Middle Ages, Modern Philosophy, etc. It is far beyond the scope of the present course to give any adequate consideration to this branch of human interest, but something has been done to arouse the attention of the reader to the introductory portion of the story–Greek philosophy. Abundant material is available on every hand for as comprehensive investigation as one may desire.

BOOKS FOR FURTHER READING:

History of Philosophy

History of Philosophy, Weber
The Greek Philosophers, Benn
Outlines of Greek Philosophy, Zeller
Short History of Greek Philosophy, Marshall

"It is a well known fact that in many cases when a man engaged in some business all his life suddenly gives up his work and retires to enjoy his old age, the change kills him. He has nothing to fall back on, no resources within himself. He has ceased to make money, to buy and sell; he has no interest in life, and dies from sheer ennui. But the man whose mind is enriched with knowledge, who loves books, who delights in collecting rare editions or choice prints may have no fear of such a fate; he may retire from active business at any time, and still in his retirement be as happy and busy as ever." -Bits from an Old Bookshop

## POLITICAL AND SOCIAL LIFE OF ROME

Modern civilizations have for the most part descended directly from Rome. Our code of laws, and those obtaining in all enlightened lands, are based on Roman laws; many of our ideas of government and social organization come from Rome. During the Middle Ages Roman conceptions lived on. The Germanic peoples who conquered Italy were themselves conquered by Italian civilization. They adopted Roman customs and spoke the Roman tongue. When out of the Middle Ages modern nationalities had their birth, they in turn were largely founded upon principles inculcated by the Romans.

While it is often forgotten, it is nevertheless true that our daily life at present has been largely shaped and modeled after that of Rome. Upon the firm basis she built, modern peoples have continued to build. Roman vices are frequently spoken of with the scorn they deserve; Roman virtues are seldom mentioned at all. While in later Rome there was an upper scum that was utterly degenerate and which tended to corrupt the whole, we should remember that in our land there is also an upper scum whose doings are comparable in many particulars with that of classic fame. In ancient Rome there was a substantial middle class whose life was wholesome throughout; this was to be found away from the capital. Today there is a great social body whose life is pure and wholesome. In Rome it happened that the administration of government passed wholly into the hands of the demoralized element; it remains to be seen whether or not our government is to be saved from the unprincipled class which strives constantly by subtle means to control it.

## I. PREHISTORIC ROME

1. Consult the map of Italy and note its position relative to other Mediterranean lands. Study it freely in connection with 3:378

2. What is the probable meaning of the word Rome? 3:383

3. Whence comes the expression 'od as the hills,' and what hills are meant? 3:383

4. How did it happen that Rome, rather than some other settlement, became the great city of Italy? 3:385

5. What value have old Roman legends for us? 3:386

6. What were the Lares? 3:396

7.  Who were some of the deities native with early Italians. 3:397

8.  Under what circumstances were the Roman laws written down?  3:402

9.  Compare the laws quoted from the Twelve Tables, 3:404 with the Code of Hammurabi, Book 1

10.  On what occasion did the Romans erect a temple to Woman's Fortune in the Forum?  3:413

11.  It was the sterling worth of men like Cincinnatus that permitted Rome to become supreme. 3:413

12.  Macaulay's Horatius sets forth admirably an old Roman legend.  3:416

13.  On what occasion was a temple erected to Castor and Pollux in the Forum?  3:412

14.  This is also related in Macaulay's Battle of Lake Regillus 3:422

II. POLITICAL LIFE AND GROWTH

1.  What three classes made up the social body of

Rome?  3:395

2. What was the political status of each?

3. By what steps did the plebeians win political equality?  3:399-404

4. How did Rome acquire her wide empire–by conquering near or remote peoples?  3:410-426

5. How did she bind new territories to her own?  3:430

6. In early times, what was the form of government in Rome?  3:432

7. What powers had the Senate?  Of how many members was it composed?  3:435

8. Were political or industrial reasons at the basis of the conflict between Rome and Carthage?  3:438

9. What were the comparative resources of each country on the eve of hosilities?  3:441

10. Hannibal was one of the greatest military leaders the world has ever known.  Follow his course in the Second Punic war.  3:448

11. Upon what occasion was the wailing of Roman women so deafening that the Senate could scarcely proceed with state affairs? 3:451

12. What really caused Hannibal's defeat? 3:453

13. What was the final outcome of this protracted struggle? 3:457-459

14. Was it fortunate or unfortunate that Rome won? With which side are our sympthies?

15. What part was played by the Gracchi in the latter republic? 3: 468-72

16. What were the curule offices, and why were they so called? 3:461

17. What four classes of society do we find in Rome in the later republic? 3:468

18. For what object was the Social War waged? What was its result?3:473

19. Was the death of Caesar advantageous or not to the welfare of the people? 3:481

20. Did it result as the conspirators had expected?

BOOKS FOR FURTHER READING:

Histories

Greatness and Decline of Rome, Ferrero
History of Rome, Mommsen, 5 volumes
History of Rome, How and Leigh
For Children: Story of the Romans, Guerber

## RELIGION AMONG THE ROMANS

1. Is much known today concerning the early religion of the Romans? 3:396

2.   What were the Lares and where were they worshipped?

3. Compare the gods of the early Romans and the Greeks. 3:397

4. Who was Janus? Terminus? Saturnus?

Made in the USA
Columbia, SC
21 February 2018